AF412289

Alan Read
THEATRE, INTIMACY & ENGAGEMENT
The Last Human Venue

Shannon Steen
RACIAL GEOMETRIES OF THE BLACK ATLANTIC, ASIAN PACIFIC AND AMERICAN
THEATRE

Joanne Tompkins
UNSETTLING SPACE
Contestations in Contemporary Australian Theatre

S. E. Wilmer
NATIONAL THEATRES IN A CHANGING EUROPE

Evan Darwin Winet
INDONESIAN POSTCOLONIAL THEATRE
Spectral Genealogies and Absent Faces

Forthcoming titles:
Adrian Kear
THEATRE AND EVENT

Studies in International Performance
Series Standing Order ISBN 978–1–4039–4456–6 (hardback)
978–1–4039–4457–3 (paperback)
(*outside North America only*)

You can receive future titles in this series as they are published by placing a standing
order. Please contact your bookseller or, in case of difficulty, write to us at the address
below with your name and address, the title of the series and the ISBN quoted above.

Customer Services Department, Macmillan Distribution Ltd, Houndmills, Basingstoke,
Hampshire RG21 6XS, England

Indonesian Postcolonial Theatre

Spectral Genealogies and Absent Faces

Evan Darwin Winet

First published 2010 by
PALGRAVE MACMILLAN

Palgrave Macmillan in the UK is an imprint of Macmillan Publishers Limited, registered in England, company number 785998, of Houndmills, Basingstoke, Hampshire RG21 6XS.

Palgrave Macmillan in the US is a division of St Martin's Press LLC, 175 Fifth Avenue, New York, NY 10010.

Palgrave Macmillan is the global academic imprint of the above companies and has companies and representatives throughout the world.

Palgrave® and Macmillan® are registered trademarks in the United States, the United Kingdom, Europe and other countries.

ISBN-13: 978–0–230–54688–2   hardback

This book is printed on paper suitable for recycling and made from fully managed and sustained forest sources. Logging, pulping and manufacturing processes are expected to conform to the environmental regulations of the country of origin.

A catalogue record for this book is available from the British Library.

Library of Congress Cataloging-in-Publication Data

Winet, Evan Darwin, 1971–
  Indonesian postcolonial theatre : spectral genealogies and absent faces / Evan Darwin Winet.
     p. cm. — (Studies in international performance)
  Summary: "Drawing examples from as early as a 1619 production of Hamlet and as recent as 2007 performances by Indonesia's most famous presidential impersonator, this book considers how theatre functions as a uniquely effective medium for representing the contradictions of Indonesian identity in the urban colonial/postcolonial metropole"—Provided by publisher.
  Includes bibliographical references and index.
  ISBN 978-0-230-54688-2 (hardback)
  1. Theater and society—Indonesia. 2. Theater—Indonesia—History—20th century. I. Title.
  PN2904.W56 2010
  306.4'84809598—dc22   2009048533

10 9 8 7 6 5 4 3 2 1
19 18 17 16 15 14 13 12 11 10

Printed and bound in Great Britain by
CPI Antony Rowe, Chippenham and Eastbourne

For Anne,
yang menabahkan kemauanku terus dan terus

and for W. S. Rendra (1935–2009),
flights of angels sing thee to thy rest

Frontispiece A promotional packet of Djarum cigarettes depicting W. S. Rendra as Hamlet, 1994 (Author's collection)

Contents

List of Illustrations

Series Editors' Preface

In 2003, the current International Federation for Theatre Research President, Janelle Reinelt, pledged the organization to expand the outlets for scholarly publication available to the membership, and to make scholarly achievement one of the main goals and activities of the Federation under her leadership. In 2004, joined by Vice President for Research and Publications Brian Singleton, they signed a contract with Palgrave Macmillan for a new book series, 'Studies in International Performance.'

Since the inauguration of the series, it has become increasingly urgent for performance scholars to expand their disciplinary horizons to include the comparative study of performances across national, cultural, social and political borders. This is necessary not only in order to avoid the homogenizing tendency to limit performance paradigms to those familiar in our home countries, but also in order to be engaged in creating new performance scholarship that takes account of and embraces the complexities of transnational cultural production, the new media, and the economic and social consequences of increasingly international forms of artistic expression. Comparative studies can value both the specifically local and the broadly conceived global forms of performance practices, histories, and social formations. Comparative aesthetics can challenge the limitations of perception and current artistic knowledges. In formalizing the work of the Federation's members through rigorous and innovative scholarship, we hope to contribute to an ever-changing project of knowledge creation.

Preface

This book culminates over a decade of research, beginning with my first trip to Indonesia in 1996 on a 'clown exchange' to Bali with the Dell' Arte Players of California. On this trip, I was privileged to study *topeng* (masked dance) with the late I Ketut Kantor, *wayang kulit* (leather shadow puppetry) with the late Agus Partha and *kecak* (monkey chorus) with I Wayan Dibya. I had just completed a master's degree in the Asian/Experimental Theatre Program at the University of Wisconsin-Madison, under the direction of Phillip Zarrilli, and approached Balinese theatre with an orientation shaped by intercultural actor training and avant-garde *mise-en-scène*. Like many outsiders who come to Indonesia by way of Bali, I lived there in a cultural bubble, highly insulated from consciousness of being in a vast nation with complex political and economic ties to Southeast Asia, the Islamic World and Australia. As Bali possesses a unique religious culture shaped through the admixture of ancient animist practices with Hindu-Buddhist traditions brought by survivors of the Majapahit dynasty as they fled east from Java in the fourteenth century, visitors find little evidence there that Indonesia has the largest Muslim population of any contemporary nation. Since the Dutch only completed their conquest of Bali in the early twentieth century, at which point an 'ethical' policy influenced a more 'humane' colonialism than they had practiced in Java, the legacy of European colonization appears relatively minor and benign there. I felt my vision limited by this bubble, and by the over-determined maintenance of a culture whose function in the Indonesian economy depends precisely on its isolation from the rest of the nation (negatively demonstrated by the 2002 Legian bombings). Much as I admired *topeng* and *wayang*, I felt confined by a narrative perennially scripted as an encounter between modern Western artists and a-historical, a-political Asian practitioners.

On subsequent trips, I have spent the majority of my time in Jakarta, Indonesia's capital. Of course, like any administrative metropole, Jakarta is its own kind of bubble. As I discuss in later chapters, Indonesians themselves have typically found the city disorienting, alienating and stressful. However, the city is a primary site of convergence for colonial and postcolonial histories and for the negotiation of an Indonesian national identity and culture. Declared 'Batavia' in 1619 after an ancient Germanic tribe of the Low Countries by officers of the Dutch East Indies Company (VOC), the city had served as the Asian administrative center of the Dutch colonial empire for over three centuries. In renaming the city 'Jakarta' upon Indonesian Independence in 1949, a significant act of forgetting had taken place. Three centuries of European presence were erased to revive

'Jayakerta' (glorious victory), the Sundanese town that had been razed to build Batavia. Whereas Indonesian nationalists commonly use the term 'Indonesia' to project a primordial cohesion on all the constitutive regions of the modern nation throughout their histories, the difference between colonial Batavia and postcolonial Jakarta is more commonly maintained. In this book, I will switch names as context dictates, and utilize Batavia/Jakarta to refer trans-historically to the city.

The performance practices, textual traditions and institutions I began to study at this time may be differentiated from *wayang, topeng* and other so-called 'traditional' Indonesian theatres in a variety of ways. Over the course of its history, Indonesians have called it *tonil* (Dutch), *sandiwara* (Sanskritic) or, more recently, *teater* (Anglophone). Each of these terms denotes a theatre informed by Western practices that developed in the urban centers of Java (Batavia/Jakarta, Surabaya, Yogyakarta, Bandung) and, to a lesser extent, other islands of the Indonesian archipelago. Typically, it relies on written scripts (whereas many traditional forms give substantial scope to improvisation); spoken (rather than sung) text with limited scope for music; is performed in theatre buildings with prosceniums or other Western stage configurations (whereas most traditional forms are performed outdoors or in makeshift spaces); and makes use of Western performance conventions, such as realistic acting (whereas most traditional forms rely on more precisely codified conventions). Although *teater* is not synonymous with 'modern theatre' in Indonesia, it differs from other modern genres such as Javanese *ketoprak* and *ludruk* or Betawi *lenong* in that it is produced expressly within national and transnational contexts. Whereas these other modern genres are typically performed in local ethnic languages, *teater* is performed in the national language, Bahasa Indonesia. Whereas other genres make extensive use of local references and performance techniques to reach specific local audiences, *teater* paradoxically claims a greater universality insofar as its Western roots are equally foreign to all (as Jakarta itself is equally foreign to all). The singular expediency of *teater* performed in Jakarta to the production of a national Indonesian theatre is offset by the challenges it poses to Indonesian artists ambitious to address a national audience. Much of the development of the genre has been driven by desires to indigenize it (which, paradoxically, almost always involves elements of one of Indonesia's dozens of local ethnic cultures that lack meaning for others) and thus to popularize it. However, as Goenawan Mohamad pointed out early in the Suharto administration, there is no 'general public' for performance in Indonesia, but rather groups who attend events because of specific affiliations. The project of developing a national Indonesian theatre has always been limited by the irreducible multiplicity of sub-national identities, as well as by the lingering trace of colonization in the form and content of *teater*.

In *Indonesian Postcolonial Theatre*, I trace continuities in practices of modern theatre in Batavia/Jakarta across colonial and postcolonial histories. Three generations of nationalist cultural polemics have claimed Independence as a moment of rupture, after which foreigners were disenfranchised and all who remained were accepted as Indonesians. However, Jakarta's theatre buildings, acting pedagogies and dramatic repertoires are still haunted by the colonial experience. European theatre in Dutch Batavia, likewise, had been continually haunted by comparison to theatre in Amsterdam and to the 'superior' European theatres of France and England. A discourse of peripheral amateurism has pervaded both colonial and postcolonial theatre histories. Theatre is a uniquely effective medium for representing the contradictions of Indonesian identity in the urban colonial/postcolonial metropole. As a form that operates through the embodiment of ghosts, theatre in Batavia/Jakarta has represented faces rendered absent by the persistent all-encompassing presence of paternalistic leaders.

The first four chapters survey genealogical developments in relation to different aspects of the art. Chapter 1, the Introduction, reviews colonial and postcolonial theatre histories to trace the canonization of certain narratives and exclusions. It also contrasts readings of two incommensurable 'first practices', neither of which are entirely reconcilable to the narratives that claim them either: Roestam Effendi's 1926 play and an apparent performance of *Hamlet* in the Dutch *kasteel* in 1619. Chapter 2, 'Unimagined Communities', turns to the theatrical legacies of two crucial ethnic groups difficult to reconcile to Dutch or Indonesian narratives: the *Indisch* (Eurasian mestizos) and the ethnic Chinese (*tionghoa*). Chapter 3, 'Sites of Disappearance', and Chapter 4, 'Despite their Failings', trace developments across the watershed of Independence in the areas of theatrical space and acting pedagogy respectively. 'Sites' includes genealogies of Batavia/Jakarta's two most significant theatrical venues as well as considerations of alternative spaces in the metropole, Soekarno's theatrical activities in the prison camp at Bengkulu, and the spatial significance of the beach at Parangtritis as invoked by several Javanese theatre artists. 'Despite Their Failings' considers the amateur/professional binary as a rubric whereby a continuity can be glimpsed from the abjective stance of Dutch language colonial theatre vis-à-vis professional French troupes to postcolonial struggles to develop an Indonesian theatre of the caliber of European and American examples.

The final three chapters deal more exclusively with Indonesian theatre from the revolutionary struggle onward. Chapter 5, '*Hamlet* and *Caligula*', compares colonial and postcolonial productions of 'the world's greatest play', which has always been a foreign play in Batavia/Jakarta. The remainder of this chapter describes the production history of Camus' *Caligula*, which served very different functions around the 1966 transition from the Soekarno to the Suharto regimes and in the mid-1990s as Suharto's own regime declined. Chapter 6, '*Umat* as *Rakyat*', considers the significance of Islam to the modern national theatre of the world's most populous Muslim nation, and why most Indonesian theatre artists have disavowed religious identification even as it informs their aesthetics and values. Finally, Chapter 7, *'Teater Reformasi'*, depicts selected practices in modern theatre since the resignation of Suharto in May, 1998, and considers why the ex-president, and more broadly the presidency itself, continues to haunt the stage.

In approaching these histories, I touch on some highly canonical figures and others who are less so. In some cases, I emphasize elements and relationships that may strike some Indonesianists as peculiar or even perverse. My choice to emphasize continuities between colonial and postcolonial practices and to devote substantial space to the former should in no way be taken as an apology for colonialism. On the contrary, I hope that by showing the persistence of certain discursive formations across commonly presumed historical ruptures that I might contribute to a framework for understanding why modern Indonesian theatre has never stepped beyond the shadow of coloniality. It is my stance that certain oft-repeated pieties regarding the authenticity of native rather than colonial sources serve ideological needs at odds with good historical method. This should not be taken as a definitive or in any way comprehensive study. I have elected mostly to limit my investigation to Batavia/Jakarta as the 'mainstage' of colonial and subsequently national culture. Histories that take Bandung, Yogyakarta, Surabaya or other urban centers as their foci will inevitably encounter other forces, such as the regional ethnic cultures which dominate in most parts of the nation outside the capital. The broad historical scope of this work is intended to contribute a new approach vis-à-vis the prevailing frames of inquiry at the acknowledged cost of historical depth. It is my hope that this work will not be the end of a historiographic genealogy, but will inspire further studies of greater depth and divergent perspectives.

Over the course of ten years working on this research, I have been supported by a variety of colleagues and institutions. My dissertation research, which provided the earliest foundation for this book, was supported by the graduate school of Stanford University and a 1999 Henry Luce Foundation pre-dissertation grant in affiliation with Australian National University. A 2004 research trip was supported by the Cornell University Council for the Humanities, and in 2007, I completed the fieldwork for this book under a Fulbright Senior Scholar research award. I would like to extend special gratitude to Ellen Rafferty, Craig Latrell, William Peterson, Amin Sweeney, Sylvia Tiwon, Kenneth George, John Emigh, Kathy Foley, Barbara Hatley, Virginia Hooker, Amrih Widodo, Marshall Clark, Michael Bodden, Matthew Isaac Cohen and Cobina Gillitt for deepening my understanding of Indonesia and its arts over a wide variety of conversations. Harry Elam, Alice Rayner, Carl Weber, Jean-Marie Apostolides, Shannon Steen and Irma Mayorga were all crucial partners from within Theatre, but outside Southeast Asian studies as I found my interdisciplinary voice. Mary Karen Dahl and J. Ellen Gainor believed in my work and mentored me from within institutional homes as I struggled to balance the claims of a scholar and a teacher. As I reach further back in my professional genealogy, I must reserve special places for Judith Hamera who first inspired me to pursue a life of performance scholarship and Phillip Zarrilli who invited me to the University of Wisconsin where this particular journey began.

I am indebted to a great many artists and intellectuals in Indonesia who shared generously of their time, hospitality and often their homes. I cannot possibly name them all here, but I must acknowledge a few. Over the years, none have been more indispensable to me than Jose Rizal Manua who facilitated nearly every contact I made in Jakarta in 1999, hosted many wonderful discussions in his bookshop at TIM, and then invited me to act in his production of *Abang Thamrin*. This book could not have been written without Ratna Sarumpaet, Nano and Ratna Riantiarno, W. S. Rendra, Ken Zuraida, Putu Wijaya, Afrizal Malna, Yudi Ahmad Tajudin, Benny Johannes, Yoyo Durachman, Emha Ainun Nadjib, Butet Kartaredjasa, Arahmaiani, Remy Sylado, Rahmann Sabur, Mbak Sugiyanto, Amin Setiamin and Mutiara Sani. I hope that I have done justice to your perspectives even as I have interpreted them from my own.

For the unswerving love of my sister Wendy Boyd, my parents Howard and Carol Winet, and my parents-in-law Dominic and Betsy Campisi, I am humbly grateful. Your belief in me and unquestioning support for my pursuit of this strange profession have been an astounding solace. To Anne, I cannot begin to tell you how much your love has meant to me over the long years as we each work on our epic book projects. Now it's your turn! And a special thanks to my dear friend, Zachary Baquet, who tracked down a copy of *Jan van Schaffelaar* in the rare collections of the University of Amsterdam and recorded the entire text for me on his digital camera.

Versions of some of the research and arguments contained in this book have appeared previously in *The Journal of Dramatic Theory and Criticism* and *Theatre Journal* as well as in chapters in *Writing and Rewriting Theatre Histories* (Iowa, 2004) and *Shakespeare in Hollywood, Asia, and Cyberspace* (Purdue, 2008). Some of this research has been presented at academic conferences. In this regard, I would like to thank Steve Wilmer, Natalya Baldyga and the members of the *National Identities/National Cultures* research group of the *American Society for Theatre Research*. Lastly, let me thank Janelle Reinelt who believed in this project and gave me every support a first time author could hope for.

1
Introduction: Colonial Foundations and Precessions of Postcoloniality

Spectral genealogies

Contrary to nationalist histories, Indonesia did not exist prior to European colonization. Thus, in at least a chronological sense, all articulations of an Indonesian history and culture are inherently postcolonial projects. To privilege an 'Indonesian' identity over all others, one must view the not-yet-president Soekarno's declaration of independence from Dutch rule in 1945 as a watershed whose past may either be recuperated towards a history of the present or discarded as belonging to other peoples. As Goenawan Mohamad notes, nearly each generation of Indonesians has been asked to imagine their time as a clean break from tainted immediate and more distant pasts. This heuristic of repeated amnesia is manifest throughout national culture, including the modern theatre. Practitioners in the 1950s ignored European colonial theatre and the modern urban theatres of the ethnic Chinese (*tionghoa*) and mestizo (*Indisch*) populations in order to set the origins of their genre in the 1920s alongside the birth of the nationalist movement. In the 1970s, artists claimed to 'Indonesianize' modern theatre. Since the 1990s, many artists have used the national stage to assert their links to global cultures. Despite such narratives of indigenization and elective globalization, modern Indonesian theatre remains in a state of cultural debt in its dramaturgy, repertoire, pedagogy, patronage, spatial discourse and imbrication in global neoliberal economies. Between idigeneity and alterity, a spectral duality plays over the faces of modern Indonesian actors. However, this 'failure' may constitute the singular relevance of the genre in a contemporary nation whose democracy and sovereignty from Western economic and political power remain dubious at best.

Since at least the fifth century, when rulers in Java and Kalimantan styled themselves 'rajas' and appended '-varman' to their names to do business with Indian Brahmins, Indonesian history has been haunted by 'spectres of comparison' with powerful external others. The oft-remarked Javanese penchant for cultural synthesis is connected to the extraordinary absence of cultural homogeneity within communities at the maritime crossroads of Asia. Javanese, as well as many of the other peoples who would become Indonesians, frequently adopted new faces into their genealogical imaginations. At the same time, as in all societies, Indonesians (including Javanese) have responded to historical trauma through imaginative incorporations, symbolically remembering diverse faces but only through forgetting the distinctive features of those faces that connect them to other irreducible identities. As Joseph Roach writes in *Cities of the Dead*, the process of 'surrogation' whereby successive generations take up the spectral roles of their ancestors is frequently haunted by the complexity thereby forgotten:

> The process of surrogation continues, but it does so in a climate of heightened anxiety that outsiders will somehow succeed in replacing the original peoples, or autochthons. This process is unstoppable because candidates for surrogation must be tested at the margins of a culture to bolster the fiction that it has a core. That is why the surrogated double so often appears as alien to the culture that reproduces it and that it reproduces. That is why the relentless search for the purity of origins is a voyage not of discovery but of erasure.
>
> (6)

When the Dutch christened their castle 'Batavia' in 1619, they anxiously affirmed the Dutchness of an enterprise staffed by employees of disparate European nationalities, not to mention Chinese middlemen and native slaves. As the Dutch United East India Company (*Vereenigde Oost-Indische Compagnie*, VOC) consolidated its influence from Batavia, it defended the racial purity of power against the threat of ethnic Chinese (resulting, most seriously, in the massacre of 1740), and then proceeded to 'purify' colonial society. This erasure of hybridity (and invention of the categories of Europeans and Natives) progressed through the nineteenth and early twentieth centuries, and set the groundwork for an Indonesian national culture defined ecumenically across hundreds of localities in distinction from Europe. In the late eighteenth century, when the Javanese Sultans felt compelled to acknowledge the VOC as a political power on Java, they composed new narratives to incorporate the foreigners into their own genealogies.

In *Spectral Nationality*, Pheng Cheah looks to Northern European nationalism to understand the disappointments of postcolonial nationalisms in the twentieth century. He notes that Hans Kohn's description of 'bad' cultural nationalism as 'an overcompensation for political backwardness in the modern world by claims to "spiritual" superiority based upon the legendary glories of pre-modern traditions' is equally applicable to nineteenth century German idealism and subsequent postcolonial nationalisms (32). Both proceed from an 'organismic logic' based on a disjuncture perceived between the existing state and the ideal image of the nation (for example, between a besieged castle and 'Batavia', or between the alienating metropolis of Jakarta and 'Indonesia'). According to this logic, the national spirit must be 'resurrected' in order to 'inspirit' the degraded present reality of the state (11). Cheah expands here on the observations of post-structuralist historians and artists that the nation forgets where it has come from (that is, colonization preceded by feudalism) to imagine a bright new future, yet animates itself paradoxically through the resurrected spirits of the past:

> The postcolonial nation lives on, in, and through a certain kind of death that also renews life [...] There is a persistent flickering between death and life, ideology and the people's spontaneous will. The state is an uncontrollable spectre that the national organism must welcome within itself, and direct, at once *for itself and against itself,* because the state can also possess the nation-people and bend it towards global capitalist interests.
>
> (391)

Perceiving the inability of national life to free itself from these hauntings not only in history, but even within works of postcolonial literature, Cheah concludes that the 'ghost' rather than the 'organism' is the most fitting trope for postcolonial freedom. Furthermore, Cheah's foundation of this discourse in European nationalism suggests the precession of 'postcolonial' discourse deep in coloniality itself. In 1619, colonial Batavia was already haunted, animated and threatened by global capitalism, flickering between life and death, inviting ancient and foreign ghosts to revive a degraded state.

This spectrality that Cheah sees imbricated in the life of postcolonial nations is elaborated by Alice Rayner as a fundamental aspect of theatrical performance. She considers ghosts in general as tropes that, like metaphors, join 'two unlike entities,' but 'a ghostly double involves secrets and a return':

> Ghosts hover where secrets are held in time: the secrets of what has been unspoken, unacknowledged; the secrets of the past, the secrets of the dead. Ghosts wait for the secrets to be released into time [...] The figure of the ghost accounts for a specific force in repetition and the double that cannot be identified simply as an imitation or a representation.
>
> (2006: x)

Like Cheah's paradoxical national culture inspirited by forgotten pasts, theatrical representation is haunted in performance by something entombed in a culture. The spectrality of the actor, in Rayner's description, resembles Cheah's 'organismic metaphor':

> They are unforgetting the presence of something absent, whether that be called a text or a character, history or the past. The living energy of the actors measures an absence, in work that is specifically not trying to

imitate life but to engage with life in its fullest aspect, which requires contact with death.

(2006: xvi)

Through acts of 'unforgotting,' theatre negotiates with the experience of history in a manner distinct both from writing and memorialization. Citing Michel de Certeau's statement that 'in the sepulcher which the historian inhabits only emptiness remains,' Rayner counters that the 'cryptic' space of theatre foregrounds the uncanny presence of absent pasts. Whereas historical remembrance regards the past across 'the syncopation of the gap' generated by the irremediable passage of time, theatrical ghosts 'whisper to the living through repetition' making of the past not an 'other' but a paradoxical singularity:

> In theatrical space, performance [...] raises the dead from within the paradoxical space of sameness and repetition, sameness and difference. It must be haunted if it is to be effective. It must take the ghosts from the tombs of written memorialization and return to an audience the affective sorrow of experience rather than the sealed tomb of memorialization that leads not only to forgetfulness but also to the further violence of congealed nationalism.

(Rayner, 2006: 61)

Theatre thus might be said to acknowledge Cheah's dilemma of the impossibility of having done with national spectrality even as the uncanniness of the ghostly theatrical double problematizes the notion of an organismic singularity.

Rayner turns often to *Hamlet* in her study, invoking Lacan's statement that 'Hamlet is always at the hour of the Other':

> I take it to mean that Hamlet's deferred action has something to do with being caught in the temporality of an impossible demand, a paternal demand, that holds his attention and suspends him in time like 'John a-dreames.' When his time becomes his own, which is to say when his consciousness turns from the demand to his own 'readiness,' he begins to live his own life.

(2006: xxx)

Hamlet exists in the syncopation between the past moment of paternal death and an eternally deferred future act of revenge. Like postcolonial Indonesian artists speaking between various past authoritarian patriarchies and the eternally deferred apotheosis of revolution. Like colonial Batavians speaking between European pasts and futures to which they would always remain categorically peripheral.

Aparna Dharwadker, in her thoughtful history of postcolonial Indian theatre, *Theatres of Independence*, raises dissatisfactions with historical and critical frameworks offered by postcolonial and performance studies. She faults the NYU school (following from Richard Schechner) for lending respectability to the Orientalism of the Western avant-garde. By epitomizing such Asian traditions as the Sanskrit theatre in terms of the formal alternatives they suggest to Euro-American literary realism, performance studies encourages a specific blindness towards India's 'principally *urban* literary drama and experimental performance, associated with dramatic authorship, publication, and translation at one level, and with institutionalized amateur, professional, and state-supported productions at another.'[1] When performance studies does attend to modern drama, it places a disproportional emphasis on 'the range of classical, traditional, religious, folk, intermediary, and popular genres of performance that have ancient and premodern historical origins but exist synchronously in the present' (Dharwadker, 2005: 17).

At the same time, Dharwadker laments that postcolonial studies, despite its avowed trajectory as a corrective to Orientalism, has three biases that work against the needs of theatre scholarship: an emphasis towards the discursive/textual rather than the performative; a valorization of migrancy rather than the locality of any performance event; and a predilection towards Westernized modernity and Europhone writing rather than indigenous languages and precolonial performance traditions. She faults the modest introductory attempts by Helen Gilbert and Joanne Tompkins (1996) and Brian Crow and Chris Banfield (1996) to articulate general theories of postcolonial performance for reducing all practices to acts of resistance to cultural subordination:

> Since independence, theatre practitioners in India have both embraced and rejected the colonial inheritance in terms of form, language, ideology, and conventions of representation. Despite the emphasis on anticolonial critique, their work remains deeply connected to modern and postmodern Western practices, especially to specific forms of social-realist, existentialist, absurdist and Brechtian political theatre. Through translation, adaptation, and intercultural appropriation, contemporary Indian theatre also maintains an extensive intertextuality with classical and modern European and Anglo-American drama. This multi-faceted engagement with the West coexists with a complicated relation to the classical, post-classical, and colonial Indian past, both as a cultural possession and an object of knowledge.
>
> (Dharwadker, 2005: 11)

However, even as she calls for greater nuance in studying how Indian theatre addresses colonial legacies and Western influences, Dharwadker insists on retaining Independence as a watershed marking 'the beginning of a highly self-conscious, self-reflexive period in Indian theatre during which most practitioners are engaged in creating a "new" theatre for the new nation' (13). In short, she seeks to redeploy the category of the postcolonial to engage with practices defined not by any single narrowly conceived ideology, but by the ambiguous, multi-faceted experience of life in the wake of colonialism.

In Indonesia, Keith Foulcher's 1995 article, 'In Search of the Postcolonial in Indonesian Literature' provoked a brief outpouring of writings on the *pascakolonial*.[2] However, his own mapping of the terrain evinces many of the limitations that Dharwadker looks to transcend. He argues that the modern literature of Indonesia does not fit the profile advanced by postcolonial theorists in relation to Africa and India. He claims that Indonesian literature is unconcerned with the condition of 'inauthenticity' described by Homi Bhabha (in a 1991 interview) as a fundamental aspect of 'postcolonialist consciousness.' Instead, Foulcher finds that Indonesian literature and post-Independence criticism primarily concerns itself with 'universal humanism' and an 'internationalist' bourgeois nationalism that are 'never linked politically with an anticolonialist stance' (1995: 161). He finds in Indonesian post-war literature an extraordinary disinterest in Dutch political, social and cultural legacies, which he attributes to the multi-faceted translation of the colony into a new entity with its own new problems. Whereas most postcolonial nations struggled to articulate their new identities in a European language, postcolonial Indonesians articulated their struggles in their own new language. Whereas most postcolonial nations articulated 'nativist' projects in relation to 'pre-colonial' traditions, Indonesia's lack of a common history necessitated an emphasis on new traditions. The legitimacy of this singularly unlikely new nation (politically, culturally *and* linguistically) in relation to all its constituent identities has remained the defining issue of Indonesian postcolonial discourse. Foulcher concludes, 'the overriding legitimacy of the nationalist project never opened up a space for a linking of nationalist ideology to the interests of a post-colonial elite or a questioning of the Self-Other binary on which nationalism depends' (164). Although colonial inequalities have persisted in post-Independence Indonesia as much as in other post-colonies, the issue of national unity, perceived as an interminable 'crisis' by officials and intellectuals alike, has muted the usual postcolonial investigations.

Foulcher makes several crucial points. The transformation of the colonial world of the Dutch East Indies into a sovereign Indonesian nation brought with it a grand imaginative 'forgetting of the past' as Mohamad has put it, following Ernest Renan (see Mohamad, 2002; and Renan, 1990). In their modern drama, as in their other literature, there is remarkably little representation of the Dutch, and Indonesian dramatic criticism also concerns itself primarily with issues of humanism and nationalism. However, there is much concern in modern Indonesian theatre with the neo-colonialism of the

Indonesian nation-state, as well as with the capacity for nationalism itself to transcend colonial frameworks. Humanism, existentialism, social engagement, postmodernism, nativism and internationalism are all vehicles for an overriding concern with continuing the anti-colonial revolution in the soul of every Indonesian. These 'other' concerns *are* postcolonial concerns. As Foulcher rightly points out, post-Independence Indonesia is not so much a post-colony as a neo-colony, which maintains colonial mechanisms of control from an expressed logic of existential threat, a continuous 'state of emergency.' State discourses have typically silenced questions regarding the legitimacy of Indonesian identity. Nevertheless, many theatre artists have defined their practices from a concern with 'inauthenticity.' The great 'Indonesianizing' movement of 1970s theatre was articulated as an effort to transcend the inauthenticity of borrowed Western dramaturgy and performance training. Many other theatre artists have embraced the contradictions of this consciousness, asserting the complexity of their unique modern identities. As Putu Wijaya writes in sorting out his own unique mixture of identities:

> if I work in a continuous and consistent manner, I alone will create my own tradition that will exhibit its own unique features. One that will distinguish me from other Balinese/Indonesians/Asians. Such that ultimately there will be two traditions co-existent within me. A Balinese ethnic identity with entirely Balinese aspects. And a personal tradition as one who is contaminated by various influences, with all the shortcomings and advantages that have created something resembling my personal identity.
>
> (1997: 94)

Nevertheless, Wijaya asserts an individualism here with which most Indonesian artists (including, at times, Wijaya himself) remain uncomfortable. Narratives and arts whose genealogies claim origins in the distant past of pre-colonial dynasties have commanded a special legitimacy in cultural discourse, especially under Suharto's New Order regime. The post-1965 impulse to view modern theatre as a 'new tradition' (*tradisi baru*) (see Wijaya, 2000; and Gillitt, 1995) or a 'trans-ethnic theatre' (see Saini, 2000) arises from an anxiety regarding the succession from native tradition to a potentially foreign modernity. In this way, modern Indonesian theatre is fundamentally haunted by colonialism. Whether performing Western plays as Indonesians, Indonesianizing a foreign repertoire, or performing entirely original local works on a proscenium stage, modern Indonesian actors appear as uncanny doubles inspiriting the national culture even as the hybridity of what they present confounds the myth of pure native origins and core culture.

Here Cheah's claim that postcolonial freedom is a ghost rather than an organism comes into play. The special utility of the modern theatre for Indonesian national culture as a 'trans-ethnic' genre cannot easily be separated from its reliance on Western theatre.

Western theatre architecture, stagecraft, dramaturgy, acting technique and (most flagrantly) dramatic repertoires continue to be important to Indonesian practitioners, partly because of a preference for the foreign that may imply a denigration of the local. However, they are also important because they enable Indonesian practitioners to participate in both national and transnational economies. The significance of this is perhaps most clear if we consider contemporary groups such as Teater Gapit, which have chosen to assert locality by performing in the Javanese language rather than Indonesian (see Feinstein, 1994; and Weix, 1995). By doing so, they have escaped the bureaucratic staleness that many Indonesians find in the national language, and attracted enthusiastic Javanese audiences. However, they have done so at the cost of attracting audiences of Indonesians who do not understand Javanese or share specifically Javanese cultural knowledge (approximately 60 percent of the population). Most Indonesian artists working in modern theatre choose to accept the conventions of a national theatre deeply informed by Western practices. Consequently, as early as 1948 with Abu Hanifah's admonition at the first cultural conference articulating national arts policy for the not-yet-postcolony (see T. Sumardjo, 1950: 107–8), critics have urged theatre artists to bring their work closer to the *rakyat* (the people).

Between Batavia and Indonesia

European history reached the Indies with the arrival of the Portuguese in 1511, but it was the Arab narrative mode of *sejarah* (genealogy) that had a more profound impact on Javanese temporal perspectives.[3] Portuguese merchants, looking to circumvent Muslim control of the spice trade, captured the port of Melaka in 1511 and established a base at Ambon a year later. Thus began the European struggle for trade dominance in the region, which would be joined by the English in 1591 and the Dutch in 1595. While English and Dutch companies made rapid advances against Portuguese claims in the early seventeenth century, the native sultans of Java consolidated their inland empires. Jan Pieterszoon Coen broke the siege of the Sultan Ranamanggala of Banten against the VOC castle (a fortification of their warehouses), and established Batavia in 1619. A decade later, Batavia withstood a campaign by Sultan Agung of Mataram. These victories were integral to the establishment of a Dutch presence on Java. However, from the perspectives of Banten and Mataram, Batavia remained a mere nuisance on the periphery of their empires. The Dutch abetted their indifference for the subsequent two centuries by restraining themselves to diplomatic interventions in Javanese politics. While the Europeans busied themselves with establishing port garrisons and negotiating commercial treaties, the interior civilizations of Sumatra, Java and Sulawesi rapidly acculturated to Islamic influences that had been circulating in the region for hundreds of years.

The Central Javanese Demak Dynasty adopted Islam as state religion in 1480 and the West Javanese Sultan of Banten did the same in 1525. In 1527, the Demak Dynasty conquered the Hindu Majapahit Dynasty (the remnants of which fled east, bringing Indic traditions to Bali), and Fatahillah, a vassal of Banten, defeated a Portuguese party attempting to set up camp at the port of Sunda Kelapa. For his 'glorious victory' over the infidel, Fatahillah established the town of Jayakerta (which would be razed in the founding of Batavia 90 years later).[4] Thus, less than two decades after the arrival of Europeans in the region, most of Java came to be governed for the first time by two Islamic states. In 1581, the Mataram dynasty eclipsed the power of Demak, and its famous second ruler, Senopati Ingalaga, established the syncretic practice whereby the Muslim sultans legitimized their power through symbolic marriage at the beach of Parangtritis to the animistic power of Nyai Loro Kidul, Queen of the South Seas. Early modern Javanese narratives, recorded in court annals (*babad*) and in the narrative traditions of such performance genres as *wayang* shadow puppetry, intricately interweave the stories of local pre-Islamic civilizations with that of the *wali sangga* (the nine saints credited with bringing Islam to the region). For example, *wayang*, which chirological evidence places as early as the year 930, is claimed in the *Babad Tanah Jawi* as an invention of the *wali*, Sunan Kalijaga, who lived in the fifteenth or sixteenth century. Historical verifiability is of little importance in this context, of course. Through genealogies linking contemporary leaders to these foundational saints, Javanese princes claimed a part of their legitimacy in relation to the advancement of Islam.

Against Court intrigue and later colonization, such narratives could take on a distinctly counter-discursive character. Thus, Prince Diponegoro, disenfranchised from the Court of Yogyakarta by Dutch interventions in the 1810s, studied with rural holy men and mounted a guerrilla war against the colonial government that lasted five years (1825–30). Indonesians would later claim Diponegoro as a national hero on account of the unprecedented grassroots support his rebellion inspired. However, his popular legitimacy derived not from nascent ethnic nationalism, but from the perception that he led a *jihad* against the infidels. As much as the nationalists, beginning with Soekarno in the 1920s, would struggle to assimilate Islamic anti-colonialism to the task of nation-building, Indonesian Muslim organizations have not always accepted an ecumenical 'Indonesia' as a legitimate object of struggle. Late colonial Muslim socio-political organizations such as Sarekat Islam (founded in 1912) is remembered as a 'transitional' stage in anti-colonial nationalism. However, when the Darul Islam group moved to establish an 'Indonesian Islamic State' in West Java and South Sulawesi in the midst of the revolutionary war, the nationalists understandably treated it as a terrorist organization. The strong showing of Muslim parties in the 1955 general election contributed to governmental anxiety over the consequences of democracy, leading to Soekarno's imposition of 'guided democracy' in 1957.

When President Suharto took power in 1966, he enjoyed the support of many conservative Muslim groups glad to see the elimination of the 'atheistic' communists. However, the proliferation of Islamic politics at local and national levels since 1998 shows how much Suharto's New Order (*Orde Baru*) regime had contained their aspirations for over three decades. One of the most significant recent manifestations of this power in relation to theatre is the passage in 2008 of a broad anti-pornography bill, whose language may allow prosecution of various non-Islamic forms of cultural performance. Many Javanese have expressed dismay that such initiatives do not reflect their own syncretic cultural perspectives. Some have seen this conflict as evidence of the persistence of an Islamic imperial discourse from the Middle East that reached Java at nearly the same moment as European imperialism.

Javanese accounts of the European presence, initially quite sparse, proliferated sometime after the 1755 Treaty of Giyanti in which the VOC brokered the split of the Mataram dynasty between the courts of Surakarta and Yogyakarta.[5] Several of the babad composed over the following 70 years interpolate the VOC into the local genealogies and patterns of power. One set of stories repeated in the *Babad Tanah Jawi* (the seminal 'babad of Javanese lands'), begins with a princess of the West Javanese Pajajaran Dynasty (emphatically distinct from Mataram, yet legitimately autochthonous nonetheless). This princess is possessed of a dangerously potent sexuality, and so is banished to the island of Onrust (a major site of the Dutch shipping operation off the coast of Batavia). A Dutch captain finds her there, marries her and they sire all the subsequent generations of Europeans on Java. The Sultans of Mataram themselves claimed a similar marital legitimacy dating from a tryst between Senapati Ingalaga (who ascended the throne in 1587) and Nyai Loro Kidul, Queen of the South Seas, also a banished Pajajaran princess. Thus, the Dutch in Java could be understood as local kin to Mataram.

An even more astonishing story follows Baron Sakendher, a name which historian Anthony Reid sees as a combination of the title of Governor-General Baron von Imhoff (r.1743–50) with the Javanese variant of Alexander the Great (a figure who had passed through numerous Malay stories). This story represents the Netherlands itself as the dynasty of Nakhoda ('shipbuilder' or 'supercargo') who sires Sakendher and Baron Sukmul. In this story, it is Sukmul who marries the Pajajaran princess and they give birth to Jangkung (Jan Pieterszoon Coen). Jangkung founds Batavia in the course of avenging the insult to his Javanese mother. Baron Sakendher, for his part, has a series of miraculous exploits (in the tradition of Malay stories of Alexander such as the *Hikayat Iskandar*), which includes founding the VOC. However, when Sakendher actually arrives in Java, he encounters magical forces beyond his power, and so enters the service of Senapati Ingalaga, thus lending some of the magical power of Nakhoda to the Mataram dynasty (Ried, 1994). In these stories, both written during a time when the Javanese Courts had begun to recognize the VOC as a significant political power rather than simply a merchant organization, the European colonial empire is seen as continuous and harmonious with the noble lineage of the Javanese Courts. In the nineteenth century, as Dutch colonial power intruded into increasingly intimate aspects of Javanese life, such narratives provided frameworks for mediating the subjugation of the Javanese aristocracy to European hegemony.

In the early twentieth century, nationalists would engage in new feats of synthesis, building from the work of European archaeologists and anthropologists a nativist genealogy for a sovereign Indonesia. Prior to the late colonial period, there was little on which to base the concept of a single cultural identity encompassing all the subject peoples of the Dutch East Indies. A British anthropologist, J. R. Logan, coined the name 'Indonesia' in 1850 from the Greek components *indos* (India) and *nesos* (island) to connote an ethnographic analogy with 'Polynesia'. The name was popularized in an 1884 book, *Indonesien*, by German anthropologist, Adolf Bastian, employed in a political sense by the 'Indonesian Students Association' in Amsterdam in 1917, and subsequently claimed by the nationalist movement in the colony in the 1920s. Dutch authorities resisted the term for its implication of ethnic unity through 'Indian' cultural influence. A steady stream of significant European discoveries over the course of the nineteenth century provided material to justify nationalist claims that Indonesia not only existed, but possessed an impressive history preceding the arrival of Europeans. Thomas Stamford Raffles, who governed Java during a British interregnum while the Netherlands were allied with Napoleonic France (1811–16), had first called the world's attention to such Javanese cultural riches as the ninth century Borobudur temple. In 1891, Eugène Dubois discovered the fossil remains of 'Java Man', one of the first known specimens of *homo erectus*, on the banks of the Bengawan Solo river (demonstrating to the nationalists the antiquity of *homo Indonesius*).

In the 1920s, archaeologists identified two seminal pre-colonial Javanese manuscripts: the *Negarakrtagama* and the *Pararaton*. Like the *Babad Tanah Jawi*, these texts related the genealogies of kings, and the founding and early conquests of major dynasties. The *Negarakrtagama* (1365) depicts the rise of the Hindu Majapahit dynasty from its founding in 1292. According to this text, Majapahit's influence extended at its height from Sumatra to New Guinea, a territory usefully similar to the Dutch colonial empire that the nationalists hoped to liberate. The *Pararaton* (fifteenth–sixteenth century) chronicles the kings of the East Javanese kingdoms that preceded Majapahit. Nationalist dramatists such as Muhammed Yamin and Sanoesi Pane would find in the *Pararaton*'s tales of Ken Arok and Kertajaya suggestive parables of dynastic unification and nation-building. Also at this time, a French scholar named George Coedès discovered evidence of the forgotten Sriwijaya empire, a Buddhist state whose rulers had governed areas of southeast Sumatra and northwest Java and conducted trade with China in the seventh century. Whereas the courtly *babad* had established genealogical syntheses of disparate local narratives, this string of scientific discoveries enabled the Indonesian nationalists to elaborate their political vision within the sort of diachronic framework used by Europeans to project their national origins into antiquity.

Despite its narrow economic rationale, the VOC nevertheless aligned its activities with the mythic imagination of a Dutch homeland only just emerging into nationhood. When the Portuguese arrived in the Indies in 1511, the Dutch 'Low Countries' were still possessions of the Hapsburg Empire. The Dutch began to rebel against Spanish rule and religious persecution in 1568, and the 'Seven United Netherlands' declared independence from Spain in 1581. Fourteen years later, the first Dutch ships reached the Indies. The speed with which the Netherlands turned from object to subject of conquest was dictated by the need to match Spain's coffers of American gold with their own imperial source of revenue. To this end, in 1602, the major Dutch overseas trading companies combined to form the United East India Company (VOC). The Company's board of 17 gentlemen in Amsterdam took full control of the Dutch effort to monopolize the spice trade. It was not until Spain acknowledged Dutch sovereignty at the Treaty of Münster in 1648 that the existential dimension of the VOC's mandate subsided. In other words, the VOC began building the Dutch colonial empire while the Netherlands were not yet quite sovereign. In 1605, VOC forces seized Ambon from the Portuguese, and in 1610 built their first warehouses at the port of Sunda Kelapa, where Fatahillah had repelled the Portuguese a century previously. Now, however, Ranamanggala entertained rival commercial treaties from the Dutch and from the English, who built their own warehouses at Sunda Kelapa soon after.

In 1618, the Dutch governor-general, Jan Pieterszoon Coen, fortified the 'Nassau' and 'Mauritz' warehouses at Sunda Kelapa into a castle. A series of military reprisals between the Dutch and English ensued. An English fleet of 14 ships arrived in the harbor and Coen fled to Ambon with his precious merchant fleet, leaving the castle to its own defenses (Figure 1.1). Forces of the English and the local Prince Wijayakrama, chose not to press their advantage. In January, Ranamanggala sent his own forces to resume the siege. Disinclined to surrender to a native potentate without the British involved, the VOC personnel remained behind their walls and waited. The stalemate persisted into the Spring. According to a VOC journal, a Dutch yacht called the Tyger attempted to approach on 4 March, having taken on high water, but was compelled by the English fleet to sail on to Ambon. On the 23rd, they received word from Banten that four Dutch ships had narrowly escaped a fleet of seven English vessels in the Sunda Strait (between Java and Sumatra) (De Jonge 1862: 152–3) There was no relief in sight, and England appeared dominant in the larger conflict. Reduced to piling up their precious stores of silk and cotton to buttress the barricades, it is little wonder that the VOC personnel spent their time in drunken debauchery and prayer. (See Valentijn, 1724; De Haan, 1935; and Abeyasekere, 1987.)

Figure 1.1   The *kasteel* of the VOC under siege by the British East India Company and Wijayakrama's forces in January 1619 (Author's collection)

Nevertheless, on the morning of 12 March 1619, the head merchant, Captain van der Broeck, gathered the population of the castle together to deliver a message:

> that our government had given the fort with all four points a name, like all other forts in India, and the fort was named Batavia, as Holland had been called in the old days, and the head portal was named Westvrieslandt, and the northwestern point by the river was named Hollandia for Holland, and the sea point was named Seelandia for Zeeland, and the eastern land-point was named Geldria for Gelderland and at each of these points there was a new flag set and a shot fired and Raey [sic] permitted all the officers to have their dinner in the midday and they drank with each other to the fort Batavia.
>
> (de Jonge, 1862: 153)

In their darkest hour, the employees found solace by remapping their confined space through a spectral comparison to the Dutch homeland.

Not only did they name each of their points of defense for one of the contemporary provinces thereof, but in taking the Latin name for the tribe inhabiting the low countries, they summoned a potent spirit of European myth to haunt a faraway land. The rediscovery of Tacitus's *Germania* in the mid-fifteenth century had done much to fuel nascent Northern European nationalisms. A brief mention of the *'batavi'* as brave warriors in Chapter 39 of this work provided the imprimatur of the ancients to a new Dutch nationalism as early as 1517 in Cornelius Aurelius's *Cronyke van Hollandt, Zeelandt ende Vriesland*. Hugo Grotius had recently revived the same origin myth in his *Liber de Antiquitate Republicae Batavicorum* (1610) (see Schöffer, 1981). Though there were in fact numerous 'founding' tribes in the ancient Rhine delta region, the idea of Batavia had become a rallying point against Dutch vassalage. To a Dutch Union emerging from the shadow of European empires, the valor of the ancient Batavians (blessed by Roman imprimatur) inspirited a postcolonial nationalist pride. Another, unique concern was answered by summoning the ghosts of Batavia to haunt the Dutch castle at Jayakerta. It amalgamated a multi-ethnic polyglot community into a uniform historical nationality. When this multi-ethnic community emerged from their castle victorious two and a half months later, they did so as Batavians, founders of a new Dutch colony even as their spectral ancestors had founded the Netherlands.

Though nationalists would later speak of '350 years of Dutch colonialism,' the first two centuries after the founding of Batavia saw only modest, strategic territorial expansion. By the end of the century, the English had relinquished their claims on most of the islands (including the trade of the nutmeg-rich island of Run for Manhattan at the Treaty of Breda in 1667). With their defeat of the last major rival fort at Makassar in 1669, the VOC consolidated their control of the spice trade. In 1682, Ranamanggala granted the VOC exclusive trading rights through Banten, effectively expelling the English East India Company from operation in Java.[6] The soaring profits of the Company turned Amsterdam into the financial capitol of Europe, and little could have been gained through territorial expansion beyond the port garrisons. By the mid-eighteenth century, however, the Company's fortunes turned permanently for the worse (and London began to supplant Amsterdam's financial pre-eminence). The spice trade stagnated, epidemics decimated the colonial population and corruption sapped the Company's profits. In 1796, the Netherlands, newly reconstituted as a Napoleonic 'Batavian Republic,' nationalized the Company. On 1 January 1800, the Company charter expired and was not renewed. For the first time, Dutch holdings in the Indies officially became colonies of the Netherlands, albeit a Netherlands that was itself once again somewhat less than sovereign in relation to Napoleonic France.

The 'truly colonial period of Javanese history' (Ricklefs, 2001: 155) lasted barely over a century and was preceded and followed by brief, but consequential interregnums of other empires. In 1811, British forces took control of Java in the course of engaging France in the colonial maritime theatre, and returned the colony to the Dutch in 1816. In 1940, the Dutch abandoned their colonies in the face of the advancing Japanese military, returning in 1945 to fight bitterly (and unsuccessfully) to reconquer a people freshly mobilized for resistance. During the first interregnum, the British introduced elements of their own administrative and military model that would be retained by the returning Dutch regime. They promoted the cultivation of a protected sphere of European culture within Batavia. They began to publish a government newspaper and founded the longest-lived European theatre venture in the colony thus far. As already mentioned, Raffles took an active interest in approaching Java as an object of Orientalist knowledge, advancing the perspective that Java's true cultural riches belonged to its Indic rather than its Arabo-Islamic past. From his example, later colonial administrations would adopt a curatorial attitude towards native cultures that would persist in such postcolonial institutions as President Suharto's *Taman Mini* amusement park, whose pavilions memorialize each of Indonesia's official ethnic cultures.[7] In 1812, when the Court of Yogyakarta defied the authority of Batavia, British forces shelled the palace with artillery, plundered the treasury and library, exiled the Sultan to Penang and installed his son, Hamengkubuwono II to the throne. This was the first time in history that a Javanese Court had been conquered by a European military.

The reverberations of this action were still playing out in 1825 when Diponegoro launched his rebellion against the colonial regime. At the conclusion of Diponegoro's war in 1830, the Dutch began to administer the interior of Java as regencies of the colonial bureaucracy. They instituted the 'cultivation system' (*cultuurstelsel*), which replaced a looser taxation system with a colonial plantation economy in which each village was compelled to provide export crops to Batavia. This combination of measures effectively dismantled the revenue structure of the Javanese aristocracy. From this point, later reforms responded to shifts in political sentiment in the Netherlands, but avoided undermining the colonial system. The 'liberal policy' (1870) introduced economic liberalism to the plantation system, allowing European entrepreneurs to own Javanese land. The 'ethical policy' (1900) acknowledged a 'debt of honor' to the native population whereby opportunities for education, employment and even political representation would be made available. A small elite thereby received access to Western education in the Indies and in Europe, and in 1918 a *volksraad* provided a political voice for native representatives. These initiatives proved crucial in nurturing the revolutionary leadership, but were never designed to develop towards actual Indonesian sovereignty. An Organic Law, passed in 1854, had explicitly defined a separate legal and judicial system for natives and indigenous non-native Muslims and Chinese. No policy pursued by the Dutch between 1830 and 1940 undermined this fundamental racial system.

However, the authoritarian regimes of postcolonial presidents Soekarno and Suharto would learn valuable lessons from the intentionally ineffectual gestures of the late colonial government towards the fulfillment of democratic aspirations.

As the British interregnum modeled the 'truly colonial' phase of Javanese history, the Japanese interregnum transformed the disenfranchised nationalist movement into a broad-based revolution. Like the VOC in the seventeenth century, the Japanese arrived in the Indies with an urgent existential mandate to provide resources for war. The brutality of the *romusha* (forced labor) squads employed to this end left many Indonesians with worse memories of the Japanese than of the Dutch. Though the Japanese occupation did little to deliver on their promise of a 'Greater East Asia Co-Prosperity Sphere,' they nevertheless found it expedient to promote local anti-European nationalisms. As Japanese fortunes in the war deteriorated, the occupation government prepared the Indonesian people for revolution. The Japanese immediately removed all Europeans from positions of authority, banned the use of European languages, changed the name of Batavia back to Jakarta and the Dutch East Indies to Indonesia. From early in the occupation, nationalist leaders such as Soekarno and Mohammed Hatta were given access to national media. In 1942, a Javanese arts administration was established, followed by various other organizations to promote the arts. Although there was considerable oversight to ensure that these organizations served the needs of Japanese propaganda, artists enjoyed a far greater freedom to explore nationalist sentiments than they had in the final decade of Dutch rule. Indeed, the dramatic output during this period has hardly been matched since. In 1943, the Japanese established 'Protectors of the Homeland' (PETA), a native militia which became the nucleus of the Republican revolutionary army. On the eve of Japanese surrender in 1945, Soekarno made a public declaration of independence, an action that would have seemed desperately premature six years earlier.

From the emergence of the Indonesian nationalist movement in 1926 to the dawn of the 'reformasi' era in 1998, there was exactly one transfer of executive leadership, and a continuity of authoritarianism rationalized by the need to defend the nation against external threats. From 1926 to 1965, Soekarno defined Indonesian nationalism against the persistent threat of colonial imperialism. From 1966 to 1998, Suharto promised development and modernization against the spectre of latent communism. Ironically, it was an early failed communist rebellion (against the Dutch in 1927) that cleared a space for Soekarno's Indonesian Nationalist Association to emerge as the leading anti-colonial movement. Emboldened by a series of youth congresses at which representatives of regional ethnic organizations swore to struggle for 'one language, one people, one nation that is Indonesia,' the 'Association' was declared a 'Party' in 1929, inciting the colonial regime to remove this overly radical strain from the carefully managed 'civil society' of their 'ethical policy.' Soekarno and other nationalist leaders spent most of the 1930s under Dutch arrest outside Java (where Soekarno channeled his silenced political talents into theatre). The Japanese instrumentalized Soekarno as a mouthpiece for the Asian awakening in Indonesia, which strengthened the grassroots legitimacy that he carried through the revolution and into his presidency. As president, Soekarno rationalized all his policies in terms of decolonization, from nationalizing Dutch businesses to telling the West to 'go to Hell' with its economic aid, to pursuing territorial 'integrity' through the annexation of Dutch West Papua in 1963 and *konfrontasi* (confrontation) with British Malaya. He presided, in 1955, over the Bandung Conference of Asian and African nations, declaring solidarity with a 'third world' refusing to be instrumentalized in the Cold War. Even his implementation of 'guided democracy' in 1957 and his increasing support for Leftist political factions were rationalized in the context of securing the revolution against the persistent spectre of *nekolim* (neo-colonial imperialism).

President Suharto, then, built his 'New Order' (*Orde Baru*) on a mandate to forget a traumatic memory ascribed to Soekarno's 'Old Order' (*Orde Lama*). On the night of 30 September, 1965, a group of communists abducted and murdered six top-ranking generals in an apparent *coup* attempt. The little-known Lieutenant-General Suharto assumed command of the military, rapidly suppressed the small band of perpetrators, and over the following half-year presided (overtly and tacitly) over the arrest and genocide of hundreds of thousands of 'communists.' A movement that had been a foundational strain of Indonesian anti-colonial politics since the 1910s was dismantled and criminalized in a matter of weeks. With the support of the military, students, Muslim groups and other constituencies antagonistic to the communists, Suharto carefully consolidated his control of the government, and in March of 1966 maneuvered Soekarno into officially relinquishing the presidency. In 1971, the Suharto government finally acquiesced to a general election, whose implausibly overwhelming affirmation of the president demonstrated the neutralization of Indonesian civil society. Subsequent elections, called 'festivals of democracy' by the government, confirmed the efficiency of the New Order at undermining all non-governmental politics. In his persona as 'Father of Development,' Suharto reversed Soekarno's defiant stance by opening Indonesia to global capital investment. There was no more mention of 'nekolim,' but rather a new yoking of national dignity to GDP. The new coalition of an emerging Indonesian middle class with Western business interests had silenced any uncomfortable digging into history, and abetted a convenient domestic and international indifference when Indonesia invaded and annexed East Timor in 1975 (the first Indonesian territorial expansion with no basis in Dutch colonial claims). Suppression of civil society, including a seven-year ban imposed on W. S. Rendra, the foremost theatre artist of the 1970s, was accepted at home and abroad as a sacrifice for economic growth. By the end of the 1980s (and the fall of the Soviet Union), however, an increasingly globalized Indonesian middle class began to lose patience with the suppression of civil liberties. In the 1990s, criticisms of the government in the media and arts multiplied. When the Asian monetary crisis struck in 1997, and more than half of all Indonesians fell below the government's own official poverty lines, the economic rationale for authoritarianism collapsed. Protests escalated into confrontations with police and riots in the spring of 1998. In response to mounting pressures on the streets and within his own government, Suharto relinquished power to his vice-president, B. J. Habibie.

It did not take long for the euphoria of 'Era Reformasi' to give way to a sense that the nation remained in a state of crisis beyond Soekarno's promise of postcolonial dignity or Suharto's promise of economic prosperity. When Indonesia relinquished East Timor in 1999, disgracefully inciting sponsored local militia to murder thousands and pillage the fragile new nation in the process, many wondered if Irian Jaya (West Papua) and Aceh would soon follow. There were causes for guarded optimism. Increasingly legitimate national elections in 1999 and 2004 bringing in three subsequent presidents, the relatively unfettered establishment of dozens of oppositional political parties, a new proliferation of non-governmental organizations, loosening of press and media restrictions, the release of political prisoners (including Pramoedya Ananta Toer), and the release of restrictions on Leftist and Chinese publications and cultural expressions all suggested the clearing of a space for civil society absent since the early 1950s. However, such promising developments were offset by persistent corruption and unwillingness on the part of the government to address the crimes of the Suharto regime. Religious tensions (generated and exacerbated during the New Order by mass transmigration programs between Java and the outer islands) re-emerged in open conflict between Muslims and Christians. Militant Islamist groups, though appealing to an extremely small portion of Indonesian Muslims, nevertheless took advantage of the new freedoms to expand their operations. The bombing at Kuta by *Jemaah Islamiyah* in 2002 devastated the Balinese tourist economy (a significant portion of Indonesia's overall industry). In combination with the devastation to Aceh caused by the Indian Ocean earthquake and tsunami in 2004, there was no clear sense that the effects of the 1997 monetary crisis ever came to an end. A decade into the new millennium, as some Indonesians eagerly look beyond the old framework of the nation to negotiate regional and transnational affiliations, an old anxiety persists that strong leadership may be required to prevent latent social divisions from erupting into innumerable local conflicts. By 2009, the optimistic epithet of 'Era Reformasi' is no longer in common use – it has been replaced by the term 'post-Suharto.' This 'post,' like the same prefix in 'postcolonialism,' implies an ambivalent lingering, a 'moving towards' that cannot quite free itself from the spectre of that which it would transcend.

In this new moment of crisis, as the relevance of the postcolonial nation-state comes under increased scrutiny in the face of neoliberal globalization, there is a renewed significance to 'unforgetting' the anti-colonial and decolonizing legacies of numerous groups besides the nationalists. Of course, this includes Islamic groups who may trace their anti-colonial genealogies through Sarekat Islam all the way back to Fatahillah and the wali sangga, although many progressive Muslims have avoided aligning their politics to their faith. Although few Indonesians are so bold as to align themselves with Marxism in any direct way, worker's groups and artists such as Indonesia's celebrated novelist, Pramoedya Ananta Toer, have made some effort to exonerate Indonesia's twentieth-century Leftist political legacy. Brutal anti-Chinese riots in the midst of the overthrow of Suharto awakened many Indonesians to the hypocrisy of the nationalist 'acceptance' of ethnic Chinese as full citizens in 1949.

There had been ethnic Chinese communities in Indonesia since the first millennium, and throughout the history of Batavia/Jakarta. Indeed, poet-playwright Remy Sylado, in a 2006 play titled *9 Oktober 1740*, noted the ominous parallel between the 1998 riots and an incident in which the VOC had suppressed an uprising of ethnic Chinese who believed their country-men were being murdered at sea. In that 1740 massacre, 10,000 ethnic Chinese had been killed, and historians often connect the rapid decline of the Company for the remainder of the century to the ensuing paucity of Chinese middlemen. In 1949, resident ethnic Chinese had been granted full Indonesian citizenship, but in 1967 Suharto banned Chinese schools and other organizations, outlawed the use of Chinese characters in public signage and printed materials, and banned Chinese cultural performances. Ethnic Chinese were suspected of communist sympathies, and many, such as director-filmmaker Teguh Karya (Steve Lim), adopted native-sounding names. Since 1998, these restrictions have gradually been repealed, some outward display of Chinese ethnicity has resumed, and various scholars and artists (such as Sylado) have begun to recall the contributions of ethnic Chinese to the articulation of an Indonesian culture distinct from that of Europe.

There has been less progress in the recovery of Indonesia's Eurasian mestizo legacy, which is not surprising given that this group had effectively disappeared from the country through emigration and assimilation by the late 1950s. Nevertheless, it was these mestizos who set the first examples of organization towards democratic representation in colonial Java. Inspired by the European socialist revolutions of 1848, they formed a 'People's Assembly' in Batavia in the same year. The *Indische Bond* (Indisch Association, 1898) inspired the similarly proto-nationalist native *Java Bond* and *Sumatranen Bond*, and the *Indische Partij* (Indisch Party, 1912) established a precedent for the Indonesian Nationalist Party. As Matthew Isaac Cohen argues in his book, *Komedie Stamboel*, mestizo syncretic culture modeled a heterogeneous Indonesian culture decades before the nationalist movement attempted to imagine 'unity in diversity' (the national motto). However, Indonesians have avoided grappling with the deep complicity of mestizo culture with colonial European society. In a nationalist ideology built on a division between native and European, the Eurasian mestizo remains all but unthinkable.

The first Indonesian play

Throughout the colonial era, the European community appeared distinctly impoverished in its theatrical culture compared to an enormous variety of performance practiced amongst the peoples of the Malay archipelago. Many of these forms might trace fascinating lineages attesting to long histories of regional and global commerce. The *wayang* puppet theatre, in its myriad two- and three-dimensional manifestations practiced in Java and Bali, had probably arrived from India (though possibly with Chinese influence) and retained narrative elements from Indic and Arabic sources. Balinese forms such as *topeng* and *gambuh* mixed local animist elements with Hindu elements brought with the fleeing Majapahit dynasty in the early sixteenth century. Throughout the Islamicized regions of the archipelago, Quranic recitation constituted a form of performance in its own right as well as influencing the aesthetics and techniques of other forms of performance. Ethnic Chinese communities practiced 'lion dances' and other traditional theatrical forms brought from mainland China. The intense heterogeneity of negotiations between local devotional practices and layers of Indic, Islamic, Chinese and Christian influences produced styles of performance that might differ even in adjacent villages, a diversity that would eventually provide ongoing sustenance to the fields of anthropology and ethnomusicology. In response to Western theatre, drama and scenography transmitted through direct example (as well as in hybrid forms such as the 'Malay opera' troupes that reached Sumatra via British Malaya and India in the 1880s), a variety of 'modern' theatres emerged in the late colonial era. Mestizo and ethnic Chinese impresarios promoted the development of urban commercial theatres that toured through the leading cities of Java and Sumatra and sometimes beyond. These modern urban theatres on Western models would provide much of the basis for what would become the Indonesian national theatre. However, there were also other more local modern theatres that for linguistic and more subtle cultural reasons remained confined to specific ethnic groups, such as East Javanese *ludruk*, central Javanese *kethoprak* and Betawi (native Batavian) *lenong*. Ironically, despite the phenomenal richness of this native theatrical heritage, the Indonesian national theatre has at least as much to do with the obscure thread of the European theatre in colonial Batavia.

The history of European theatre in the Indies begins in the fortified castle of the VOC at Jayakerta in 1619, when assorted Company employees apparently mounted the first production of William Shakespeare's *Hamlet* in Asia.

After being trapped for over four months by a succession of forces loyal to the British East India Company, Prince Wijayakrama, and finally Sultan Ranamanggala of Banten, the assorted soldiers, merchants and slaves in the fortified compound of *godowns* (storehouses) turned at last to amateur theatrics. The sole surviving evidence of this piece of 'warehouse theatre' (on which all subsequent historical accounts are based) is a brief mention in the more detailed of two surviving Dutch journals. Though leaving room for doubt on the exact identity of the play, this anecdote paints a vivid picture of its context:

> On an Easter Monday's midafternoon, there was in the hall a play performed *of the King of Denmark and of the King of Sweden* and in the evening then Ray [one of the officers] let these players up to fetch dinner and the women with their men, that had been married to them by Speranty [another officer], who also had to be there and [they] were merry until about midnight, then were the blacks with their women also brought up, and the blacks were allowed to play the bomba, the flutes, and shawms [a double-reed precursor to the modern oboe], as if we were at a country fair, but we were just in a besieged fort, and the men became drunk and domineering with the women, but so it went, that we wondered at ourselves, Godless and plagued with adultery, that our government was thereby finished, they were so overcome with arak [palm liquor], that they must thereafter endure all the same and see no rations of arak; but where the herder wanders, so roam the sheep!
>
> (De Jonge, 1862: 153–4)

Nothing further is recorded of this extraordinary event, but some details may be surmised from the documented conditions within the castle. There is little doubt that the players were amateurs drawn from amongst approximately 350 company employees. Only half of those present were ethnically Dutch. About a fifth were slaves. There were slave owners and native concubines; free and enslaved Asians; European merchants, settlers, soldiers, shipwrights, carpenters, sailmakers and other artisans. Besides Dutch, there were Germans, French, Scots, English, Danes, Flemings and Walloons.[8] As the journal entry suggests, it was a rowdy lot. A court established in 1617 had regularly heard cases of insubordination, blasphemy, brawling and drunkenness. This same Dutch journal reports 'nightly orgies within the Dutch compound, and marriages rowdily celebrated between Company servants and "black women".' M. C. Ricklefs describes the colonists as 'spending their time in a mixture of debauchery and prayer' (1993: 30). From the perspective of mainstream Dutch Calvinism, this colonial outpost must have seemed 'an unweeded garden that grew to seed things rank and gross in nature.' Never mind the fact that it had been christened 'Batavia' 20 days earlier.

Although N. P. van den Berg, whose description of the event in an 1881 history of Batavian theatre is clearly the source for all subsequent citations, is circumspect in suggesting that 'The King of Denmark and the King of Sweden' was actually Shakespeare's masterpiece, a variety of vectors support and add interest to the claim.[9] It seems unlikely that a motley group of Europeans would have chanced to improvise on so specific a topic. Further, a variety of plausible scenarios may have connected one or more of them to this most famous of European plays over the 15 years since Shakespeare had written it. Van den Berg reasons that one might have witnessed a production by one of the traveling English troupes that had begun to perform *Hamlet* on the European continent as early as 1603 (Van den Berg, 1904: 102). For that matter, perhaps a spectator who attended the play's premiere at the Globe in 1600–1 survived to attend its Javan revival two decades later. No doubt, numerous theories could account for a memory if not a text of the play reaching Jayakerta over the course of two decades. However, there is another alternative that surpasses all such speculations. William Keeling is well known to Shakespeare scholars as the eccentric captain of the *Dragon* who conducted performances of *Hamlet* and *Richard III* off the coast of Sierra Leone in September 1607. Loomba chronicles the critical history of these first 'colonial' performances, noting presumptions regarding 'company men' similar to that of van den Berg. British Shakespeare scholars questioned the ability of mere sailors to grasp the great tragedies and proposed that these performances were instead improvisations based on common knowledge. Loomba sees such critical narratives establishing a fundamental rhetoric for Shakespeare vis-à-vis British colonization: 'Shakespeare is simultaneously both popular and aristocratic – he embodies "national" culture' (1997: 109–14).

What goes unremarked in the account of Loomba (and most other British Shakespeare scholars) is that Keeling's performances took place while en route to the English East India Company's spice trade headquarters in West Java. The *Dragon* put in at Banten in 1609. From there, the most famous of all Western plays needed merely to traverse the seventy kilometers to Jayakerta at some point in the ensuing decade. Members of Keeling's crew might have performed again in Banten or in the English camp at Jayakerta and been seen by a later inhabitant of the castle. Perhaps a member of Keeling's crew switched employers. Perhaps a later Batavian acquired a manuscript through one of Keeling's men. Keeling's *Hamlet*, whether as text, oral tradition or fragmented memory may well have found its way to this new Elsinore.

If the VOC *Hamlet* was indeed the first 'colonial' production of Shakespeare in the womb of what would become the Dutch East Indies, it hardly seems to fit within Loomba's discussion of British colonial education. Neither does it fit the 'canonical discourse' that Gilbert and Tompkins describe various commonwealth Shakespeares as 'countering.' Indeed, there are many aspects of this first colonial performance that are arguably already postcolonial.

An already heterogeneous, diasporic and transnational population sits under existential threat, first by a coalition of a greater European imperial power (England) with a local prince, and then by a greater monarch (Sultan Ranamanggala) suppressing the maneuvers of his subordinate. Three weeks earlier, the defenders had summoned a ghost from their primordial past (Batavia) through which to imagine a more robust present nation than their current abjection would suggest. Now, they took a play by Shakespeare, which for them in this context was precisely *not* a canonical work from Dutch national literature, but rather a text appropriated from their rivals and current oppressors, the English. This text they undoubtedly localized in various ways. As in Keeling's shipboard productions, the Batavian performance would likely have been multilingual, including use of Portuguese (still the language of global trade) and, presumably, Dutch. Perhaps 'black' women recently betrothed to some Company men played Gertrude (assuaging Hamlet in Portuguese) or Ophelia (wandering mad in Balinese). The ghost of the elder Hamlet might have been played by one of the garrison soldiers (already dressed for the part), calling out as the ghosts of Batavia had called three weeks earlier: 'Remember!'

The themes of *Hamlet* – burdens of inheritance, duty to kin and nation, search for identity in a time 'out of joint' – could all have taken local resonance within the specific context of a (trans)national fortress awaiting conquest. Perhaps the players saw their own castle as the embattled Elsinore, or more charitably considered the over-reaching Wijayakrama, whose treachery to his relative and liege (as that of Claudius to the elder Hamlet) had brought his small state to ruin. However the topicality of the play may have been parsed, this foreign play fitted the moment: a castle caught in a tide of war, spurred on by ghosts and racked by doubt; a fortified metonymy of a distant fatherland christened, like the Netherlands itself, while still under existential threat. That Coen would arrive shortly to reverse the hierarchy decisively does not alter the fact that at this precise moment, a cosmopolitan utopia (or, more properly, a 'heterotopia' in Michel Foucault's sense) of besieged Europeans used Shakespeare from a position of resistance, speaking back to a conquering power.

On 30 May 1619, Hamlet (or Fortinbras, perhaps, if one sees Wijayakrama as the Dane) returned to liberate Elsinore. Jan Pieterszoon Coen returned from Ambon with 17 ships, routed the English fleet, broke the sultan's siege, and burned Fatahillah's city of 'glorious victory' to ashes. The Dutch microcosm of Batavia expanded into a newly emptied-out municipality to which it extended its military protection and nationalist mythos. As Fatahillah had renamed a town cleansed of infidels, so Coen renamed a town cleansed of natives, then so too Soekarno would rename Jakarta's streets from the old invocations of the Dutch homeland to the new registry of Indonesian national heroes and erect monuments to the glorious victory of the people. Thus too Suharto would dwarf Soekarno's revolutionary monuments with glittering glass and steel monuments to global capitalism. The transformations of Batavia/Jakarta as exemplary center for successive Dutch and Indonesian regimes has followed a familiar modernist revolutionary impulse: the desire to wipe the slate clean; to exorcise the old ghosts and to summon new ones.

Although the revelry described in the chronicle of the 1619 *Hamlet* attests to a 'contamination' of Batavian society from the very start, the distinction between European and Native became increasingly stringent over the following centuries. Dutch colonial authorities under the VOC, and even more so the civilian administration that succeeded the Company's collapse, segregated European and Native spheres of culture and arts. A neoclassical proscenium theatre, erected in Batavia's Weltewreden district in 1821 for a Dutch amateur theatrical society with a Latin motto, also served as an exclusive venue for European performing arts. During the same period, many regional native theatrical genres passed into new patronage structures that valued conservatism over dynamism. Thus, as in many other colonized societies, a stark distinction between European and Native increasingly slipped into a distinction between modernity and tradition. When new popular urban theatres began to appear in the late nineteenth century, their impresarios struggled for legitimacy against an ideology of segregation that could not cognize a modern native theatre. Although the Soekarno regime (1950–66) saw a valorization of modern native theatre as a vehicle of national culture, its practitioners and critics continued to privilege European dramaturgy and theatrical technique. Under the Suharto regime (1966–98), artists increasingly explored intracultural approaches to modern theatre, but the government encouraged rigidly programmatic definitions of native and modern traditions. Despite constant debate and experimentation, Indonesian modern theatre (and its historiography) remains to a large extent under the shadow of the Organic Law of 1854, which strictly segregated the social and cultural life of the colony into European and Native spheres.

From an Indonesian nationalist perspective, the first production of *Hamlet* in Asia might be acknowledged (as theatre historian, Jakob Sumardjo, does) as the beginning of European theatre *in* Indonesia. However, it would be unimaginable to consider it the beginning of *Indonesian* theatre. *Wayang* and *gambuh* might be nationalized from their Javanese and Balinese contexts as ancient progenitors of 'Indonesian' theatre, but European theatre categorically cannot be Indonesian. This seemingly commonsensical distinction has, however, generated some historiographical difficulties in describing the emergence of the national theatre. The Chinese and mestizo urban commercial theatres that I will discuss in Chapter 2 are Western-influenced and not yet Indonesian. They tend to be discussed by nationalist historians as 'transitional,' implying a presentist orientation towards a national theatre as the object of transition. In order to assign a 'beginning' to Indonesian theatre, nationalist historians have chosen to ignore the fact that Teater Dardanella was a commercial enterprise in order to emphasize its nationalist credentials. These credentials are not obvious from Dardanella's repertoire or aesthetic. However, they were significantly promoted by troupe member, Andjar Asmara, who wrote numerous brief surveys of Indonesian theatre history starting in the 1930s, and continued to play an influential role in the Indonesian arts scene (especially through film) into the 1950s.

In order to assign a 'beginning' to Indonesian drama, nationalist historians find what seems a less controversial watershed in Roestam Effendi's 1926 play, 'Sweet Liberty' (*Bebasari*). However, various aspects of *Bebasari* must be forgotten in order to view it purely as a nationalist work. Though one might insist that previous works use the Indonesian language in gestures towards nationalism, there is no question that *Bebasari* promotes an anti-colonial nationalist agenda with groundbreaking directness. It employs an intracultural dramaturgy, appropriating narrative elements from (regional Malay-Javanese) *wayang* versions of the Hindu *Ramayana* and (ethnic Sumatran) *pantun* poetic meter to the imagination of an Indonesian national culture. The protagonist is a noble poet/prince who fights not for his own sake as in the old folklore, but rather to free the *bangsa*, the Indonesian people (or nation). The play opens with a prologue in which a shackled woman (evidently, though not explicitly, Princess Bebasari herself) laments the darkness of her oppression and yearns for a liberator. As the action progresses, Bebasari, whose name synthesizes '*bebas*' (free) and '*sari*' (essence), is overtly identified with the colonized nation, and her rescue with decolonization. This takes place through a transparent reworking of the familiar *Ramayana* narrative in which Lord Rama must rescue his wife, Sita from the demon, Rawana.[10] It invokes the meditation and battle narratives common in *wayang* performance scenarios, in which a noble knight meditates in order to accumulate power before going into battle against the ogres from across the seas (construed in the Hindu tradition as the denizens of Lanka or Ceylon). The young hero, Bujangga, is both *pemuda* (radicalized youth) and *pujangga* (noble poet), the champion of the new age bearing timeless wisdom and faith. He spends the first half of the play struggling against the fears of his elders: his father, Takutar (from *takut*, 'timorous'), and his uncle, Sabari (from *sabar*, 'patient'). These men are the elite of the previous generation who had consented to accept modest social and political liberalization without actual sovereignty. Bujangga is encouraged in his rebellion by a succession of prophetic ascetics. These true elders raise his consciousness and bolster his confidence, revealing to him that Princess Bebasari is his destined bride and that he can defeat the ogres through greater spiritual fortitude. In the final act, which follows the dramaturgical pattern of the culminating flower battles (*perang kembang*) of *wayang* performances, Bujangga faces and defeats Rawana and his demons, evicting them from the land of his birthright, thereby liberating Bebasari.

Effendi first wrote the play while working as a schoolteacher in Padang, Sumatra, and rehearsed it to be performed by his students. However, local authorities prevented this premiere. He refers to this censorship in the introduction to a 1953 edition of his poetry collection, 'Scattering of Thoughts' (*Pertjikan Permenungan*), explaining that he was compelled subsequently to mask his politics in safer themes:

> In the characterization of my play, *Bebasari*, the clamoring of freedom was to be heard clearly and strongly, with all its powerful impetus. Its style was basically heroic. But the colonial authorities were in no hurry to see it performed. *Bebasari* met with obstacles and also with threats. *Pertjikan Permenungan* thus had to undergo certain verbal changes. Because of the threat of committing some 'crime' or other, the poems dealing with love were emphasized, the patriotic poems being regularly altered in that direction. The voice of freedom was dressed in lover's clothing: what had been 'heroism' in *Bebasari* now became 'eroticism' and 'romanticism.'
>
> (Effendi, 1967: 204; 1953b, 6)

Indeed, many of Effendi's poems in this collection, such as 'I'm tied in by these stinking days' (*Bukan Beta Bidjak Berperi*) speak to precisely such a stifling of his voice (1953b, 28; 1967, 52). In retrospect, historians (beginning with H. B. Jassin in 1953) recall a first play written in a year of the emergence of Soekarno and the nationalist movement, but which was too radical to pass the Dutch censors.[11] Curiously, it appears that Jassin and subsequent critics have canonized the date of composition, whereas Effendi himself emphasizes its publication two years later.[12] In his Introduction to a second printing of the play in 1953, Effendi aligns his project to the Second Youth Congress (where the famous pledge for one nation, people and language was taken) rather than the founding of the nationalist movement:

> 'Bebasari' was published for the first time in 1928, at a time when our national aspiration had just begun to inflame the hearts of our youth, who were at that moment being lulled to sleep by the ideology of the colonizer.
>
> (1953a, 10)

The one significant ideological advantage to 1926 over 1928 is that it places *Bebasari* clearly before Mohammed Yamin's *Ken Arok dan Ken Dedes*, which was written for the Second Youth Congress and performed, apparently, without incident.

In either case, the play was composed at a unique moment in nationalist discourse. By the time the *Poedjangga Baroe* writers had begun to compose Indonesian plays in the early 1930s, the colonial government had begun to restrict anti-colonial free expression much more aggressively. (See Kahin, 1952: 61–2; Foulcher, 1980: 14–15; and Bodden, 1997a: 36–7.) Soekarno and other nationalist leaders had already been arrested, and the movement quieted to a cautious ebb for the remainder of the 1930s. *Bebasari* was neither truly representative nor widely imitated by the *Poedjangga Baroe* playwrights, but was the only play to represent nationalist struggle explicitly before worse times compelled the modernists to dress their aspirations less provocatively.

Nevertheless, Effendi was not exclusively aligned to the nationalist cause. Like many subsequent Indonesian dramatists, he adopted a nationalist perspective in resistance to colonial systems and legacies. However, he was also a communist, a Muslim, a Minangkabau and a liberal individualist who channeled these distinct ideologies and identities through his nationalism. The point here is not to question the sincerity of his nationalism, nor to propose any alternative hierarchy of identities. Rather, it is to insist upon the ideological complexity of an artist operating at the confluence of numerous traditions and interests who chose to channel his inspirations through anti-colonial nationalism. The institutionalization of nationalism beginning with the Japanese Occupation secured Effendi's legacy. However, the narrowing of its scope to marginalize Islam and (after 1965) communism, have greatly minimized our understanding of Effendi's art. This origin myth of Indonesian theatre covers up the disparities of numerous competing interests to mainstream nationalism.

He was born in Padang, West Sumatra, in 1903, and raised in a climate of anti-colonial politics. His father, Soeleiman Effendi, was active with the Indische Partij, a radical socialist forerunner of the Indonesian nationalist party whose mestizo leaders were exiled in 1913. (See Van der Veur, 2006.) Roestam himself received a Dutch education in Bukittinggi and then studied in Bandung, Java, where he mingled with Soekarno and the young Indonesian nationalists. He was active in the proto-nationalist youth organization, *Jong Sumatranen Bond* in Minangkabau from 1924 to 1927, and also affiliated with the Indonesian Communist Party. He participated in the communist uprising in West Sumatra in 1927, and when it was suppressed was sent into exile in the Netherlands for the following 20 years. A quintessential *pemuda* (radical youth), he had written the two works that secured his place in Indonesian literary history by the age of 24.

As a student in the Netherlands, Effendi joined the Indonesian Association (PI) under the leadership of Mohammed Hatta. The PI advocated Indonesian independence, and allied itself with the Dutch Communist Party (CPN). In the early 1930s, Effendi assumed the pseudonym Alfaroes, and studied in Berlin and Moscow. On his return to the Netherlands, he began to publish political treatises on Indonesian freedom, and quickly rose within the ranks of the CPN. In 1935, he was named a Dutch delegate to the Seventh Comintern Congress in Moscow. As a Dutch Communist politician, Effendi wrote and lectured in support of the anti-colonial uprisings in the East Indies. Finally, in 1938, he was imprisoned in Blaricum for his radical views, and remained there throughout the Second World War. Upon his release in 1946, he returned to Indonesia, and helped form the short-lived Proletarian Party (1948–50).[13] After two decades defining his politics at the intersection of nationalism and communism, Effendi declined to join the Indonesian Communist Party (PKI) in the 1950s, turning instead to Muslim politics. He joined Masyumi, the prominent Muslim party, and during this time made his pilgrimage to Mecca. This shift from association with communism surely stood him in good stead in 1965. He weathered the purge, and lived out his days in Jakarta. He and his works are remembered as nationalist, not communist. However, in his youthful works, the diversity of his views is still apparent.

Subtleties of language in *Bebasari* suggest Effendi's grounding in socialist and communist thought. The land that Bujangga will emancipate is never called 'Indonesia,' but rather *bangsa*, one of several Indonesian words often translated as 'nation,' but which more specifically connotes 'the people.' That is to say, its use to mean 'nation' in a political sense implies the liberalist notion of a nation constituted in its nationalized populace. The moaning subjugation of the 'people' in *Bebasari* recalls the imagery of the suffering proletariat 'behind the mask of Karl Marx' in Soekarno's seminal 1926 pamphlet, *Nationalism, Communism, Islam* (Soekarno and McVey, 1970: 53). In fact, one might see a communist perspective as most productive in reading the defeat of the ogres at the end of Effendi's play. They are not killed, but rather sent to the Hindu heavens. Given a communist edge, they might be seen as returning to a bourgeois sphere, leaving the proletariat to their earthly paradise. The postcolonial struggle thereby gains connotations of class.

One might argue, though, that from a communist perspective, the aristocratic *wayang* framework of the play (that is, depicting revolution as love between a prince and a princess who speak in pantun meter) is problematic. In this play (as in the early historical plays of Yamin and Pane), a feudal system is paradoxically accepted as the framework for imagining Indonesia. Nevertheless, *Bebasari* does use suggestively communist approaches to resist several other Indonesian problems that nationalism has done little to address. Foremost, *Bebasari* resists dynastic *'bapakisme'* (the political primacy of father figures) by placing revolution in the hands of a youth who must reject the teachings of his fathers. When Bujangga has passed through meditation and emerges in the third act as the emancipator of Bebasari, the text marks the protagonist's full emergence by referring to him in the stage directions and in later dialogue as *Bangsawan* or *Bangsawan Negeri* ('noble' or 'patriot' 'of the people'). Bujangga has become noble, not through heredity, but as a result of his struggle to bring justice to the people. In contrast, the ogres are described as having worn nobility falsely in order to deprive the people of their wealth:

> Rawana seemed a proper noble, sweet his words, refined betrayal
> Prisoners' property, he seized all, precious human rights' refusal,
> Like beasts, the people he did shackle, sign that they were merely chattel.
> Outer trappings used to swindle [...]

(Bodden, 2009: 9)

In short, the young man rejects the compromises of his elders to fight an ennobling revolution to liberate the people from the shackles of an economically oppressive regime. Bujangga is generally legible as a traditional 'noble warrior' (*ksatriya*), but he is inspirited by the spectre of communism.

Other elements in the play evoke specifically Islamic anti-colonial rhetoric. The ascetics who encourage Bujangga in the first act are recognizable as *kyai*, religious leaders who train disciples in their boarding schools (*pesantren*), often towards political ends. Bujangga and his kyai advisers openly acknowledge throughout the play that effective anti-colonial resistance is rooted in mystical piety. As the last in a series of advising ascetics, Sabaineratju, tells Bujangga, 'Faith in God will be your weapon' (Bodden, 2009: 20). When Bujangga worries that he stands no chance against the superior technological knowledge of his foes, he is advised that he will wield a superior spiritual knowledge. Even Rawana acknowledges upon his own defeat that 'this is the will of almighty God' (30). Though this is certainly legible as the sort of 'organismic metaphor' discussed by Cheah in relation to nationalism (and, within an Indonesian context, further suggestive of Pane's position in the cultural polemic), it would also be legible to Indonesians as an Islamic perspective regarding Western technological supremacy. It is not merely the Indonesian *bangsa*, but the entire global Islamic community (*umat*) who will prevail against Western machines through spiritual power.

Bebasari invokes an Islamic framework in more subtle ways as well. Bujangga often identifies himself as an orphan raised by foster parents, recalling the prophet Muhammed himself, who was raised by his uncle. In contrast, the Dutch ogres are strongly associated with the more ambivalent context of the *Ramayana* narrative. The demon Rawana is the only character in the play whose name is adopted directly from the *Ramayana*; he dwells in the *Ramayana*'s 'land beyond the seas'; and when he is defeated, he is not killed, but rather evicted to the abode of the Hindu gods. Through such coding, the anti-colonial struggle appears not only as the spiritual path of a pesantren student (*santri*) under the tutelage of *kyai*, but also as an expulsion of exogenous Hindu elements from the *bangsa* (articulated, ironically, via a Hindu narrative tradition!). The struggle is nationalistic, to be sure, but the post-colonial nation is legitimate insofar as it is Allah's will. The agent of change is a revolutionary nationalist, but his revolutionary consciousness is achieved through a mystical reckoning that carries orthodox (anti-syncretic) Islamic overtones.

Although *Bebasari* takes pride of place within the 'archive' of the nationalist dramatic canon, the play has not found much interest in the 'repertoire' of nationalist theatre troupes. Other than the curtailed performance amongst Sumatran schoolchildren in 1926, I have discovered no records of subsequent productions prior to the *Teater Kami* revival in 2001 (Figure 1.2). Other plays of the era that are no less literary or didactic have been revived regularly from the pre-war youth congresses on (Yamin claimed 39 productions of *Ken Arok*

Figure 1.2   Teater Kami's production of Roestam Effendi's *Bebasari*, 2001 (© Teater Kami)

dan Ken Dedes between 1934 and 1948 [1951: 5]). This specific lack of interest in the first Indonesian play may reflect the general disinterest of Indonesian artists in representing coloniality noted by Foulcher. *Bebasari* displays an unusual attempt (reflective of a brief window in pre-war anti-colonial discourse) to inspirit an Indonesian nation from a wide range of foreign and local spectres through the person of an amalgamating youth figure. Cheah writes of the hero of the typical first generation postcolonial *Bildungsroman*:

> These protagonists must undertake a cognitive mapping of the boundaries, strata, and contents of the entire social world to qualify as model proto-national subjects, and the novels seem to invite their implied addressees to do the same through specular identification with the protagonists.
>
> (2003: 244)

Bujangga, insofar as he organicizes nationalism, communism, Islam, and even the legacy of the colonial ogres, appears as a model for this sort of identification in keeping with the contemporaneous nationalism of Soekarno. Nevertheless, there is something unsettling in his quest for Bebasari that suggests an impossibility of fulfillment. She appears to him in his meditations as a vision of a radiant promised face, 'even in my mind's impression' (Bodden, 2009: 10). However, the freedom he offers her is saturated with feudal and paternalistic elements of autochthonous tradition. As Cheah writes, the nation is haunted even in the process of *bildung*, consigning the future life of the nation to an indeterminacy between life and death. 'It makes the homeland *unheimlich* (uncanny)' (2003: 247). The nationalist hero appears in the playtext and onstage as a ghostly double, unsettling to say the least as the standard bearer of an organicist ideal. The very process of *bildung* ironically 'renders us vulnerable to an other, an image by means of which we transform ourselves,' a disparity in the moment of rupture from colonial time, which demonstrates 'that the possibility of alienation is always already inscribed within freedom' (384).

With nationalism as an organizing perspective and *Bebasari* as a starting point, the subsequent history of Indonesian postcolonial theatre can be interpreted as progressing according to a tension between Western inspiration and indigenization. In the 1930s, a core group of writers aligning themselves with the nationalist movement began publishing a literary journal called *Poedjangga Baroe* ('Modern/new poet'), which emerged as the primary literary venue for articulating an Indonesian nationalist discourse. Within the pages of this journal, Sutan Takdir Alisjahbana advocated that Indonesian national culture be yoked to Western modernity and modernism. In his famous phrase, the pre-colonial past was *'mati se-mati-mati-nya'* ('dead as dead can be'). Against this perspective, Sanoesi Pane advocated a more 'nativist' approach recovering the ancient legacies chronicled in such texts as the *Pararaton* and celebrating the spiritual 'Arjuna model' of the East over the materialist 'Faust model' of the West. This argument, remembered as the *polemik kebudayaan* (cultural polemic) came to epitomize (though somewhat reductively) the major 'choice' for postcolonial Indonesian aesthetics, which subsequent generations would refine without substantially refuting.[14] Although theatre artists and critics in the Soekarno era worried about a 'crisis' in Indonesian creativity, and some playwrights (especially on the political Left) experimented with ways to indigenize the national theatre in form and content, Alisjahbana's perspective generally prevailed. Indonesian dramaturgy during the first 15 years of independence is mainly derivative of Western realism and existentialism. In keeping with Suharto's official policy of amnesia regarding the achievements of the previous generation, the modern theatre of the New Order proceeded as if it had given birth to itself. W. S. Rendra, who returned in 1967 from four years in New York City to found *Teater Bengkel* ('Workshop theatre'), became the prophet of a (mostly) new generation of practitioners.[15] These artists and critics expressed what they felt to be a new concern with legitimizing modern practices in relation to traditional genres, an emphasis epitomized by the term *'tradisi baru'* ('new tradition') coined by Umar Kayam in 1980 (Kayam, 1981). From this tradisi baru perspective, Indonesian modern theatre must close the distance that separates it from the legitimacy and popularity of ethnic theatre traditions. By borrowing technique, form and content from local ethnic traditions, practitioners who came to prominence in the 1970s claimed an authenticity for their works that had been lacking in the previous generation. Since, in 2009, much of the national theatre remains dominated by the surviving members of this generation, it would appear that Indonesian theatre remains within the tradisi baru paradigm. However, from the late 1980s onward, there have been younger practitioners who make strategic use of global aesthetics such as postmodernism, performance art and multimedia to articulate aesthetics that appear to privilege identities no longer contained by ethnic affiliation or national culture. As some of these practitioners explicitly address topics and histories suppressed under the New Order, it seems likely that strains and potentials within the tradition of Indonesian modern theatre that predate 1966 will also be rediscovered.

In her 1967 history of the development of Indonesian drama, the most influential Indonesian study on the subject to date, Boen Sri Oemarjati devotes considerable space to establishing *Bebasari* as the first work of modern Indonesian drama. To this end she argues that neither Dutch colonial drama nor any of the plays written or adapted for urban popular theatres should be considered 'Indonesian' for the reason that they belong more properly to different literary traditions (for example, Dutch and Chinese Malay). There is considerable circularity to this argument. The Indonesian language was not overtly identified as the medium of nationalism until the second nationalist youth congress of 1928. Thus, although dozens of modern plays in Malay precede it, *Bebasari* was among the first to be associated specifically with Indonesian.[16] Ultimately, though, it is the fact that the play espouses nationalism that secures Oemarjati's claim. She asserts that the exigencies of postcolonial nationalism give critics the 'right' to elide historical niceties in the interests of imagining more cogently an Indonesian canon:

> Though the 'status' of the two aforementioned genres – those in Dutch and those in Malay-Chinese – cannot be considered national, nevertheless, as discussed, their contributions to the history of the development of a national literature are not minor, and cannot be described in separation from the body of works developing an Indonesian people. But precisely in describing the history of the Indonesian national movement, we nevertheless have the right (*berhak*) to speak of the development of the Indonesian language.
>
> (Oemarjati, 1971: 85)

Essentially, *Bebasari* is the first Indonesian play because it is the first nationalist play, and it is the first nationalist play because it is the first anti-colonial play associated with the Indonesian language. Contrary to Oemarjati, I would suggest that *Bebasari* deserves a distinctive space in the canon of Indonesian postcolonial theatre precisely because it presents a struggle against colonialism that has not yet been incorporated into a nationalist singularity. The face of Bebasari is the face of liberty, a face that claims justice across numerous anti-colonial ideologies.

Absent faces

In *Bebasari*, the apotheosis of anti-colonial struggle appears as a feminine face that is a sublime metonym of the people, an 'essence of freedom.' This is a complicated and unsettling strategy that might be interpreted in contradictory directions. Christopher Balme reminds us of recent critiques of the deployment of metonymy in ethnography, whereby performance or fragments thereof represent an entire culture:

> As a figure of speech, metonymy is suspended in an interesting paradox between connotations of authenticity on the one hand and incompleteness on the other. Viewed in this context, metonymy as a trope of cultural discourse carries with it more than just the signature of abbreviation typical of most figures of speech. It has inscribed in it already a discursive strategy symptomatic of colonial discourse: the penchant to circumscribe and contain.
>
> (2007: 97)

Balme's caution regarding this sort of metonymy may apply also to the specific metonymy of faciality.

In the seventh chapter of *Mille Plateaux*, Gilles Deleuze and Félix Guattari argue that the face is a projection of internalized totalitarianism that has been with us at least since the normative model of Christ's divine countenance.[17] As Deleuze and Guattari see it, the logic of white European racism proceeds directly from the Christ-face; from the Christian faciality machine's computation of normality. This racism does not begin with exclusion or the designation of otherness. Otherness is a 'primitive' concept. Modern European racism proceeds from a concern with deviance from 'your average ordinary White Man':

> From the viewpoint of racism, there is no exterior, there are no people on the outside. There are only people who should be like us and whose crime it is not to be. The dividing line is not between inside and outside but rather is internal to simultaneous signifying chains and successive subjective choices. Racism never detects the particles of the other; it propagates waves of sameness until those who resist identification have been wiped out.
>
> (Deleuze and Guattari, 1987: 178)

Racism cannot, in its inciting gestures, be about otherness or difference because racist faciality only admits sameness. It only operates through deterritorializing corporeal spaces in order to recode them as white wall/black hole systems. Faciality cannot, of course, succeed in homogenizing human identity, and it copes by negotiating truces with difference. However, it never actually acknowledges *difference*; only *divergence*. There is no 'other,' but only distance from the same, a *lack* of sameness. There is, consequently, no truly foreign land, or at least no other land possessed of sovereignty. There is no territory that cannot be understood as a proper object of colonization. It is only a matter of closing the distance.

The deterritorialization of faciality dehumanizes, mechanizes, and thus objectifies us. That is, it turns our bodies into objects and instruments of fascism. As Deleuze and Guattari emphasize, the faciality machine precedes other organizing heuristics, including psychoanalysis and phenomenology, whose discourses of presence and interiority are always already alienated. If we are always already deterritorialized by faciality, our being-in-the-world (the Heideggerean *dasein*) is always already 'uncanny' or 'unhomely' (*unheimlich*) in Sigmund Freud's sense of the unsettling quality of the animated inanimate, the automaton, the object that paradoxically lives (Freud, McLintock and Haughton, 2003) Is it possible, then, from within this vicious hermeneutic to resist such totalitarianisms as racism?

Frantz Fanon wrestles with a related question in *Black Skin, White Masks* (1952 [1967a]). The metonymic juxtaposition of the work's title seems to encapsulate a compelling psychological narrative of colonial racism. Following the politics of *negritude* and other black nationalisms, one might assume that it privileges the first element of the binary as an inner truth dissembled by the self-hating will to assimilate to hegemonic whiteness. Conversely, following Bhabha's influential readings of Fanon in the 1980s and early 1990s,[18] the binary might be imagined as a slippery, undecidable negotiation of postcolonial hybridity. Between these interpretations, much of critical race studies and postcolonial theory over the past half-century have found Fanon to their liking. However, there has been little consideration, even amongst scholars of theatre and performance, that Fanon chooses an explicitly theatrical trope (the mask) to describe the psychology of the colonized. To the extent that one finds potential for resistance in white masks, it is an explicitly performative agency. To the extent that one yearns for the true skin beneath the mask (and Fanon does, curiously, speak of skin (*peau*) rather than faces (*visages*)), it is an anti-theatrical, anti-performative logic. To Fanon, black skin is, in no sense, the true face dissembled by false masks. Black skin is not, as Charles Markmann's translation suggests, a 'fact.' Rather, it is closer to Deleuze and Guattari's description of faciality as a deterritorializing system. Insofar as the white masks of assimilation to European civilization are less real than black skin, the realization of this artifice does not facilitate self-realization. Fanon insists that the psychoanalytic telos of self-realization is not available to the colonized black man. Indeed, racist interpellation strips the white mask from the black body. Revelation of the 'natural' blackness underneath is an epistemic violence committed through the objectifying Look. Internalized negrophobia makes identification with black skin and corporeality impossible for the Antillean (that is, the Europeanized black man).

However, in his 1959 essay, 'Algeria Unveiled,' Fanon suggests a certain possible reversal of this insidious logic. Here, Fanon reads the veil in the revolutionary context essentially as a racial superficial schema that may be used strategically (Fanon, 1967b: 35–63) If, as Kaja Silverman suggests in relation to the 'screen of Blackness,' the distance between veil and face is intentionally maintained, it may be used to disrupt the totalizing system itself (Silverman, 1996: 27–30). Suzanne Gauch analyzes Fanon's reasoning:

> As the colonizer comes to comprehend the revolutionary use of the veil, his former characterization of it as a sign of oppression suffers, and he too perceives a distance between the veil and the Algerian woman who wears it, a distance that reveals a glimmer of subjectivity where formerly there was only objecthood. Fanon's essay implies that as the revolution progresses, the colonizer can no longer be certain what he sees when he looks at a veiled woman, for he knows nothing of her.
>
> (2002: 121)

In this gesture, Fanon moves in a similar direction to Cheah. He had already rejected the organicist metaphor for postcolonial freedom in *Black Skin, White Masks*, when he asserted the impossibility for postcolonial subjects to transcend colonial epidermalization. In 'Algeria Unveiled,' Fanon claims colonial uncanniness through the doubled face. By denying the face of the colonized to the colonial gaze through a metonym of culture that is itself colonially constructed, the veiled woman resists colonialism from within. There is an obvious irony, of course, in that the exchange of gazes between free, decolonized individuals is acknowledged as not yet possible.

The Jewish Lithuanian philosopher, Emmanuel Levinas, rigorously differentiates the phenomenal countenance from what he calls the transcendent face of the other. There are significant differences between the positions of Deleuze and Guattari and Levinas in this regard. Nevertheless, Levinas agrees with Deleuze and Guatarri and Fanon in connecting the phenomenal face to totalitarianism and racism, insofar as we only cognize divergence from the same in our perception of physiognomy. Where Levinas carves out a distinct category is in claiming that in our perception of the phenomenal face of the other, there is a trace (and this is the source of Derrida's 'trace') of the infinite. Levinas calls for a philosophy that begins, not from ontology, nor even from metaphysics, but from the ethics of that experience of the trace of the infinite in the face of the other. To say that this face is infinite, Levinas means that it rejects our will to totality, to seeing the world through the image of the same. This transcendent face is, of course, considerably more elusive than the phenomenal face, and its 'appearance,' uncannily combining proximity and distance, is a kind of apparition with strong affinities to spectrality:

> In the end, Levinas' reflections on the proximity and remoteness of the other's face are focused on the crucial motif of trace. The trace 'shines (*luit*) as face of the other.' Being present only as remnant of somebody who has passed, thus referring to an immemorial past, the trace of the other marks and even constitutes the other's face. The high presence of the face-to-face yields to the *ritardando* of a mere after-face. The other enters through a back-door.
>
> (Waldenfels, 2002: 77; Levinas, 1981: 12)

The face of the other demands to be privileged, to be spared the epistemic violence of one's totalizing self-epistemology. This is not a duty that one can ever fulfill, but an ethical life and a just world are only possible insofar as we struggle to do so. From Levinas's perspective, we might say that we don't encounter real faces in the world. All our lived experience is of masks, but in these masks we may experience fleeting epiphanies of difference, of an escape from fascism. Through Levinas, the *vis-à-vis* (the 'face to face') becomes a trope for encountering the other as irreducibly different rather than merely divergent.

Foucault follows a similar course, invoking metonymies of masks and faces in describing the 'critical genealogy' on which Roach bases his model. In explaining Friedrich Nietzsche's quarrel with the search for origins, he speaks of how uncritical historiography denies discrepancy:

> This search is directed to 'that which was already there,' the 'very same' of an image of a primordial truth fully adequate to its nature, and it necessitates the removal of every mask to ultimately disclose an original identity. However, if the genealogist refuses to extend his faith in metaphysics, if he listens to history, he finds that there is 'something altogether different' behind things: not a timeless and essential secret but the secret that they have no essence, or that their essence was fabricated in a piecemeal fashion from alien forms.
>
> (Foucault, 1998: 371)

Critical genealogy takes a different attitude towards these 'masks' (Roach's succession of surrogates), attending to the discrepancies and 'petty malice' of the will to historical purity. Foucault writes that 'the good historian, the genealogist, will know what to make of this masquerade' (385). Rather than Deleuze and Guattari's Christ-face or Fanon's *peau noire*, the genealogist addressing the episodes of history 'will await their emergence, once unmasked as the face of the other' (373).

The pivotal event of postcolonial reckoning in Indonesian modern theatre is not, ultimately, about the defeat of foreign ogres with superior technology by spiritualized agents of nation-building. Rather, we see it in the opening scenes of *Bebasari*, when the radical poet-hero gazes through prophetic vision at the ghostly face of freedom's essence. The hero looks to this uncanny countenance of the past and future to inspirit a state enfeebled by compromise to global capitalism in the form of a colonial state. The play concludes with the betrothal of hero and people and the eviction of the colonizers. But herein lies its irony. In Effendi's parable, it is only by expelling the modern West that the Indonesian people can become one with the nation and the organicist metaphor reach fulfillment. However, denial of the colonial legacy merely consigns the hero to a past 'as dead as dead can be.' Much as the assertion of Batavian purity in the castle in 1619 could only be maintained by forgetting the subsequent multi-ethnic Shakespearean improvisation with jam session and orgy. This desire to see only sameness and divergence in the face of the nation has informed understandings of theatre in Batavia/Jakarta on both sides of 1945.

2
Unimagined Communities: Theatres of Eurasian and Chinese Batavia

Neighborhoods and buildings

In a 1978 article on *lenong* (a modern Betawi theatre inspired by bangsawan and Stamboel), Umar Kayam divides Indonesian theatre into two categories defined spatially: *kampongan* and *gedongan*. *Kampongan* theatre comprises all theatre performed in traditional community spaces. These are typically open pavilions or courtyards that are accessible to all people regardless of class and usually free of admission (costs being covered by wealthy patrons or communal funds). It is theatre conceived both as inclusive of all sectors of society and community-based. In contrast, *gedongan* theatre relies on fixed structures with regimented boundaries. Indoor theatres inherently limit admittance and generate greater costs than outdoor theatres, and so a class element enters into *gedongan* theatre. The audience is composed of those able and disposed to buy tickets. From this basic distinction, Kayam outlines a neat binary of practice: *gedongan* theatre is urban, elite and dependent on Western economics and aesthetics, whereas *kampongan* theatre is rural, popular and close to the traditions of ordinary Indonesians (Kayam, 1981b) The model has considerable explanatory force, and assigns a clear positive value to the theatres of W. S. Rendra and his various 'Indonesianizing' descendents on the grounds that they have attempted to infuse their urban *gedongan* theatres with some of the authenticity of the rural *kampongan* (see Thomas, 1994).

However, Indonesians, and especially those located within urban communities, frequently view this 'authentic' *kampongan* culture with ambivalence. Goenawan Mohamad wryly notes that as much as big cities have 'urbanized' throngs of Indonesians arriving from the hinterlands, so these rural immigrants have 'ruralized' the cities:

> there is a constant flow of people with their rural lifestyle entering the city, and in the process making the city more like a village – in the number of infant births and deaths, in superstition and in lack of freedom.
>
> (Mohamad and Lindsay, 1994: 29)

The urban *kampongan* are constantly evoked in modern Jakarta as sites of failed development; sources for poverty and suffering that seem embarrassingly and alarmingly resistant to national progress. James Siegel, in a preliminary reflection on the anti-Chinese riots of May 1998, discusses the difference between *rakyat* (people) and *massa* (the masses, the mob) in this regard. Nationalists frequently invoke the underclass of the *kampongan* as the rakyat, in whose daily struggles and aspirations the spirit of the revolution lives on, ideally informing all national policy. When these inner souls of the city become sites of unrest, however, then their *rakyat* are discussed as *massa*, suggesting an underdeveloped, uncivilized *biadab* (brutality) lurking beneath the surface of the *kampongan* and released in the May riots:

> The *massa*, a transformation or perhaps a remnant of the *rakyat*, are the product of the imagination of the middle class; they are the menace left once the body of the nation has divided in two and identity in both its forms, national and kinship, is thought uncertain [...] The result was rapid swerves in the sympathies and identifications of the middle class: with the looters and against them, sometimes against 'Chinese' but now with 'Chinese' women and against rapists, once with the government and now against it. All these motions are predicated on a fear of the revolutionary tendencies of the underclass, a fear cultivated by the government in different forms during the New Order: fear of Communism, fear of criminality, and fear of the *massa*.
>
> (Siegel, 1998a: 104–5)

Abidin Kusno likewise discusses *kampongan* as the 'internal other' haunting Jakarta's elite urban development. The stark class divide in the city's contemporary spatiality, between glittering high-rises and squalid slums followed, according to Kusno, a distinct logic of postcolonial Indonesian nationalism: remembering a 'place of origin,' negotiating it, and then negating it: 'This leads to a second remarkable "consensual" articulation: there is a "standard" conception that the city is transformative, fascinatingly alienating, but equally unpleasant' (2000: 104). Similarly, Richard O'Connor describes Jakartan consciousness as 'supra-local and supra-ethnic,' with the resulting paradox that Jakarta is seen as conspicuously 'foreign' (1995: 30–45). Ironically, this very foreignness, linked to the transnational character, that enables the capital to act as a 'distribution center' (see Hatta, 1952) connecting Indonesian to global economics and politics, also provides the discursive grounds for an Indonesian nationalist discourse. In a nation as culturally and historically incoherent as Indonesia, such a condition of transnationality and exile positions Jakartans on a threshold of layered (and sometimes competing) narratives (see Kusno, 2000: 150–2). They work in and amidst *gedongan*, but don't like Jakarta. They seek authenticity in the *kampongan*, but fear the *massa*.

The foreign metropole

Postcolonial national discourse presumes as its subject a single *rakyat* (people) or *bangsa* (national people) that creates the future within such spaces of exile, but divides into specific recognized and spatialized indigenous *suku-bangsa* (ethnicities) such as Javanese, Balinese, Acehnese or Betawi (an ethnicity of relatively recent articulation attributed to natives of the Batavia/Jakarta region). This understanding of the racial landscape of the nation and its capital may invert the values of late-colonial race policies, but does not repudiate its overall framework. From its founding, Batavia had served as a transnational port with a cosmopolitan and racially complex population, the 'European' portion of which was initially predominantly mestizo and only marginally Dutch. However, beginning with the administration of Governor General van Imhoff (r.1743–50), this colonial culture increasingly came to be understood as European and Dutch. In the wake of the 1740 massacres that decimated Batavia's Chinese population (see Kemasang, 1985), van Imhoff attempted to instigate a series of Europeanizing reforms in order to supplant the mestizo urban culture. He encouraged the immigration of Dutch families and founded 'civilizing' institutions from schools to a newspaper. Most of these initiatives proved premature, partly because the European population remained small, partly because the Company administration stifled rival enterprises (Taylor, 1983: 79–83). For example, the first Dutch Batavian theatre was established in 1757, but closed a few years later (see Chapter 3). In the nineteenth century, however, following French and British interregna, Imhoff's vision took hold with increasing strictness. The watershed legal initiative in this regard was the Organic Law of 1854, whereby the obvious ethnic complexity of the Dutch East Indies was codified into two categories: 'Europeans' and 'Natives.' A leading historian of the Eurasian mestizo population, van der Veur, argues that some liberal social intentions may have informed this law, but even he acknowledges that the resulting segregation was 'primarily a racial one between (white) "rulers" and (brown) "ruled".' (1968: 200) When possible, persons of mixed heritage tended to claim European status with its attendant privileges, so that racial identity increasingly followed from class identity. As Paul van der Veur writes, 'the colonial status hierarchy granted such high prestige to being a "European" that most Eurasians tried to approximate the model as closely as possible' (201). Batavia's mestizo and multi-ethnic legacy was rapidly supplanted by a highly unforgiving binarism.

Meanwhile, European anthropologists explored and taxonomized the ethnic cultures of the archipelago, contributing to a double vision of Indonesian race: singular (insofar as universally Native vis-à-vis the Europeans) and yet multiple (insofar as defined through the categories of culture and ethnicity). As Cohen points out in *Komedie Stamboel*, this nineteenth-century ethnographic gaze produced a new appreciation of many local cultural traditions, yet, by fixing them in ethnic categories produced ironic blindnesses to some of the most dynamic cultural processes.[1] This discourse informed postcolonial cultural policy as profoundly as the colonial state-apparatus informed postcolonial government. In declaring Europeans foreigners and all who remained, Indonesians *bhinneka tunggal ika* ('made one out of many', the national motto), it might be said that the postcolonial nation-state that came into existence in 1949 merely took colonial race theory to one possible logical conclusion. As in the Dutch East Indies, culture and progress were matters of territory. Through the hinterlands, each culture was seen as cohering within its proper historical space, whereas the proper business of nationalism with its attendant universal humanist culture would take place primarily in the metropole.

Nevertheless, Batavia/Jakarta has also, and at other historical moments, provoked nostalgic or utopian optimism amongst new arrivals. Following the apocalypse of Jayakerta in 1619, Batavia had rapidly grown into one of the foremost port cities in Asia. Company administration and settlement expanded from the *kasteel*, dredging canals and building warehouses, townhouses, administrative halls and roads. Batavia looked increasingly European (and specifically Dutch) in its infrastructure and architecture, although, as Susan Abeyasekere is quick to point out, this outer semblance of European civil society was a thin veneer over a mercantile state whose civilian institutions existed at the leisure of the Company (1987: 19). Jean Gelmen Taylor goes further to say that the society of 'Europeans' in VOC Batavia differed in significant ways from that of the contemporary Netherlands:

> By the mid-eighteenth century [...] Indies society [...] was clearly not Dutch any longer [... It] was exceedingly polyglot in composition, and its 'European' elite secular before agnosticism was a common condition in Europe [...] Economic life was not controlled by guilds of master craftsmen and merchants, but dominated by a monopolistic corporation [...] In contrast to the Calvinist, bourgeois thrift of Holland, there was the Mestizo luxury, the spending on a grand scale, the importance of display. The Indies elite lived in spacious, open villas and alongside Dutch food often ate spiced Indonesian dishes and rice. Many members, especially the women, were not literate; the languages they spoke were Malay and Portuguese, and they sponsored no written literature. In the arts they patronized woodcarvers, assembled slave orchestras, summoned ronggengs [girls hired to dance at parties], and held performances of Indonesian and Chinese puppet plays. That is to say, the entertainments and arts enjoyed by the colonial elite were not yet divorced from the tastes of their Asian retainers.
>
> (1983: 78–9)

Indeed, as the conditions within the warehouses at the birth of Batavia suggest, the colonial capital had never replicated Dutch society, having always consisted of a polyglot of European and Asian inhabitants. The reticence of the 'seventeen gentlemen' who administered the VOC from Holland to allow respectable Dutch women to emigrate there ensured that Company employees primarily married local women. As European Company men were constantly returning home after their tours of duty, it was their native wives who represented the most continuous element of Batavian society. Their mestizo children, though rarely allowed to occupy the highest echelons of government, were nevertheless frequently accorded 'European' status such that they could serve as Company employees and enjoy Company privileges. Before 1816, only a small proportion of Batavians were ever *totok* (pure) Dutch.

Nevertheless, European travelers writing in the decades preceding 1733 (the most prosperous in the Company's history),[2] frequently praised the settlement by comparing it favorably to Amsterdam (Abeyasekere, 1987: 18), especially drawing attention to the very canals that would later be denounced, incorrectly according to Peter van den Berg, as sources of pestilence (P. van den Berg, 2000). One among these admirers was Jan de Marre (1696–1763), a Dutch ship captain, who, in 1728, at the age of 32, had reached Batavia for the first time on a voyage from the Netherlands. This would be one of the last voyages of his 23-year sea-faring career, after which he would return to Amsterdam to become assistant director of the Amsterdamschen Schouwburg. In 1736, he would write a major work of Dutch dramatic literature, *Jacoba van Beieren*, which would later (in 1757) be chosen as the inaugural production of Batavia's first Dutch *schouwburg*. Upon reaching Batavia in 1728, de Marre began writing a six-volume ode to the city, wherein he rhapsodizes:

> O lovely Batavia, that holds me spellbound,
> There your Town Hall with its proudly arching vaults
> Rears its profile! How splendid is your situation!
> Your broad Canals, replenished with fresh water,
>   beautifully planted,
> Need bend before no city in the Netherlands [...]

> (Taylor, 1983: 52; de Marre, 1740)

When it appeared in print in Amsterdam in 1740, this glowing portrait must already have seemed quaint against the increasing reports of contagion and especially against the calamitous escalation of racial tensions, which, that October, resulted in the deaths of 10,000 ethnic Chinese.

Throughout the VOC period, foreign observers from Northern Europe recorded contradictory and ambiguous observations of that part of Batavia that was ostensibly 'European.' They praised its simulation of a prosperous Dutch city, but disapproved of those aspects of its prosperity rooted in locality. The mestizo predilection for displaying prosperity through public performativity, an expected behavior of aristocracy in Javanese and other regional societies, clashed with a Calvinist preference for confining riches to the private sphere. As Taylor discusses, paintings of the period frequently emphasize sumptuary syncretism, especially of mestizo women, who are seen wearing fashionable European dresses and hats, but with native attendants carrying *betel* (a regional tobacco mix) boxes and ornate Javanese parasols (1983: 37–42). Though carriages were, of course, also in common use amongst the gentry of seventeenth and eighteenth century Europe, their extensive use and luxurious outfitting in Batavia provoked frequent disapproval in European accounts. The carriages of VOC Batavia were so famously ornate (and foreign to European sensibilities) that they later became objects of anthropological display in museums and colonial expositions in Europe. Pulled by extravagant teams of horses and accompanied by extensive livery, these carriages served as the VOC equivalent of the black limousines that carry today's economic elite through the streets of Jakarta. They created a private, inner, and often curtained, space of mobility for the urban elite, like a traveling opera box for viewing the city. Further, as with gentry in a lavish opera box, they themselves became a source of spectacle. They were fond of promenading in their carriages with the accompaniment of bands of musicians. J. S. Stavorinus and de Marre both also describe *orembaaien*, boats languidly punted down the canals, whose 'European' passengers were regaled by bands of musicians (see Taylor, 1983: 62–9; N. P. van den Berg, 1904: 100–2).

By the mid-eighteenth century, the (pure Dutch) regents of Batavia took a sufficiently dim view of this widespread opulence that on 30 December 1754, they approved a code drafted by Jacob Mossel, entitled 'Measures for Curbing Pomp and Circumstance.' This was a massive piece of legislation aimed at reinstating clear outer class distinctions between the highest echelons of administration and those below. There were 29 articles restricting the opulence of 'carriages and related matters, horses, etc.,' numerous articles on male and female apparel, and several stipulating limits on retention of servants and slaves (notably restricting all below the governor-general and his councilors from employing European slaves). This code ambiguously acknowledged a mestizo culture of outer display while restricting that culture from obscuring the highest status of the purely European administrators. The code was revoked in 1795, in the waning years of the Company, apparently in response to a new republican spirit of outward egalitarianism (Taylor, 1983: 66–9). The decisive shift came, however, with the British interregnum (1811–16), during which time measures were taken to purify the European society of Batavia into closer conformity with that of Europe, and to restrict membership by race. Over the remainder of the Dutch colonial regime, Eurasian mestizos (known alternately as 'Indisch' or 'Indos') occupied an awkward intermediary position. More privileged than non-European natives, yet barred from full membership in European society, the mestizos were poised to make significant contributions to the emergence of anti-colonial discourses, yet would always be alienated from Indonesian localities. We might say, following Bhabha, that the identities of Eurasians became 'almost the same' as the Europeans, 'but not white,' and almost the same as native Indonesians, but not brown.

This division of Indies society into Europeans and Natives over the course of the nineteenth century pressured the mestizos into affiliations that were generally determined by class. This was by no means a simple process. The colonial government dealt uncomfortably with the mestizo population, which gradually radicalized. For example, the government offered free education to mestizos beginning in 1818, but failed to revise restrictions on employment that prevented them from rising in the civil service. It is hardly surprising that about six hundred mestizos, invoking the example of the contemporaneous socialist revolutions in Europe, met in a 'People's Assembly' in May, 1848, and signed a petition to King William II, requesting liberal reforms. Indeed, one might consider this gathering the first Indonesian anti-colonial congress. The economic conditions of some mestizos improved after 1864, when the Netherlands' government (under William III) relinquished its monopoly on civil service training. In general, however, a sense of disenfranchisement grew amongst the mestizo population over the remainder of the colonial era. A Dutch nationality law in 1892 granted Dutch citizenship to all who already were recognized as 'European' (a privilege expanded considerably after Indonesian independence). However, this left an even larger population of mestizos in an untenable state of in-betweenness. As van der Veur writes, 'The Eurasians, then, were neither economically independent nor rooted in Indonesian soil but merely an appendix to the apparatus of Western production and administration' (1968: 196).

Mestizo nationalism and Komedie Stamboel

In his official account of the 1848 'People's Assembly,' Governor-General Jan Jacob Rochussen warned that the mestizos 'have everything to gain and nothing to lose' (van der Veur, 1968: 194). When the colonial 'liberal policy' began to permit a more free civil society, the mestizos were among the first constituencies to take advantage by forming the first non-governmental political organizations.[3] The first of these was the *Indische Bond*, established in 1898 as a platform for demanding greater political rights and parliamentary representation for *blijvers* (permanent 'European' residents of the Indies who were, in fact, mainly mestizo) than for *trekkers* (expatriate Dutch and other Europeans doing limited 'tours' of the colony). Although the Indische Bond did not advocate freedom for the non-European populations, it did take a nationalist stance regarding its own constituency. As G. J. Andriesse argued, 'the Indies were just as much the possession of the Eurasian as of the indigenous people' because if Java was not the fatherland of the Eurasian, where would his fatherland then be?' (van der Veur, 1955: 82). Andriesse was ousted from the leadership of the Bond for taking too confrontational a stance. Likewise, when Douwes Dekker went a step further in chartering the *Indische Partij* in 1912 as an ecumenical platform for *all* who considered themselves 'native' to prepare an end to colonialism, the government clamped down on the organization. In 1923, A. Th. Schalk headed a small splinter group that proposed a utopian alternative for the *blijvers*: establishment of a new sovereign nation in the territory of Dutch New Guinea. As this last proposal suggests, the political ambitions of the *blijvers* were limited in one direction by a failure to engage effectively with the existing colonial government and on the other by a failure to envision a nationalism encompassing the non-European population. Nevertheless, it is these limited, short-lived *blijver* anti-colonial and nationalist stirrings that constitute the disparate 'origins' of Indonesian nationalism. (van der Veur, 1968: 203–6)

Cohen discusses this mestizo nationalism as part of an 'Indische' aesthetic that gave rise to Komedie Stamboel (Figure 2.1). As he puts it, a valorization of the Indische aesthetic, not as 'culturally degenerate and inauthentic,' but rather as 'a perfect adaptation of the culture of Europe to the tropical clime of the Indies' constituted a crucial move in the development of anti-colonial rhetoric (2006: 296). August Mahieu, Stamboel's leading impresario, brought many aspects of his own mestizo heritage into the troupe (including the *petjo* dialect of Dutch used by Batavian mestizos, syncretic costuming and presentational performance styles). Cohen writes:

> In particular, komedi stambul established the Eurasian appearance as the preferred object of spectatorial pleasure for Indonesian audiences of melodrama; as such, stambul has rightly been called 'a precursor' of the contemporary Indonesian 'Sinetron' or soap operas.
>
> (2006: 344)

In its development of the Malayan *bangsawan* traditions (mediating Arab, Parsi and European theatrical traditions) to fit the tastes of urban mestizo and non-European spectators, Stamboel offered a modern theatre at once more local and differently transnational than the European colonial theatre. At the same time, by deploying names such as 'komedie' and 'opera,' adapting Western plays, techniques and staging conventions, and looking to be produced on European stages and covered in the European press, Mahieu endeavored to cross the boundary of the colonial racial binary.

That said, Mahieu's persistent desire to be accorded respect as 'European' points to a recurrent racial politics in mestizo arts that is not easily reconciled to 'happy hybridity.' For example, the famous *Nyai Dasima* story, an *Indisch roman* (mestizo novel) that was often used as a source for Stamboel and other modern Indonesian theatres, presents a decidedly dubious trajectory for racial crossings. Dasima serves as a concubine of a Dutch administrator.

She gives him a son, and he promises to elevate her. Male members of her community convince her, however, that the European will soon leave her for a white woman. Consequently, she leaves him to accept the protection of a native husband. However, this new husband uses his Muslim piety to justify abusing her; ultimately, he kills her. In the lamentable climax, Dasima's mestizo child and her spurned Dutch husband discover her body floating down the river. As Pauline Milone writes, the story of *Nyai Dasima* suggests something other than racial harmony at work within the 'Indische aesthetic':

> Indische values revolved around a belief in the basic goodness of the European Christian male, an admiration for the Indonesian woman, a view of legal status as an attribute of character, and an identification of light skin with beauty and virtue [...] It identified dark skin with a poor character and a potential for wickedness, and depicted Islamic moral laws as providing a protective cover for nefarious activities, particularly the exploitation of women.
>
> (1967: 425–6)

As Robert Young cautions, the apparent felicity between the image of the 'hybrid' and contemporary poststructuralist formulations of freedom ignores the many ways in which hybridity historically has functioned as a conservative discourse (see Young, 1995: 1–28). Such mestizo narratives as *Nyai Dasima*, in which a white man tragically fails to rescue a black woman from black men, might be taken as a challenge to the most extreme versions of racial segregation (such as what Young terms the 'polgenist species' argument that disavows even the possibility of cross-racial reproduction, 1995: 18). However, they present no fundamental challenge to late colonial racial policies.

Nevertheless, Cohen makes a compelling case for the aesthetic and technical legacy of Stamboel, noting that postcolonial historians have appreciated its genealogical significance to modern Indonesian theatre according to various rubrics. For example, a *Sejarah Seni-Drama* ('History of Dramatic Art') by Tengku Syed Abdulkadir and Zen Rosdy hail Stamboel as a 'transnational root culture,' while K. M. Saini invokes it as a seminal example of what he calls 'trans-ethnic' theatre (Abdulkadir and Rosdy, 1963; Saini, 2000). Indeed, as mentioned in Chapter 1 of this book, all Indonesian theatre histories following from Asmara and Oemarjati have credited Stamboel as an origin. However, Cohen is more iconoclastic in his treatment of Stamboel's legacy than he himself claims. All these post-Independence theatre histories view Stamboel within the tradition of Sanusi Pane's position that a postcolonial aesthetic consists in the admixture of distinct Native and European cultures. From this perspective, the specific 'Indische aesthetic' of Stamboel (as well as the mestizo ethnicity of Mahieu and other innovators of the form) is elided.

Whereas Cohen celebrates Stamboel as a practice that models hybridity, nationalist Indonesian historians have recuperated it either as a European practice moving towards the Native or a Native practice emerging from the European.

Mahieu and many other members of his and rival troupes found a political home with the *Indische Bond*. However, the colonial apartheid of Europeans and Natives had split the Indisch community according to class. In general, Stamboel and similar troupes had attracted to its ranks the poorest and most disenfranchised of mestizos, for whom the hard itinerant life of a player might offer economic advantage. Many members of the Bond were more affluent, and disinclined to form identifications that might risk associating them with Natives rather than Europeans. Mahieu himself was jealous for this kind of legitimacy, and plagued by the fact that European critics generally viewed Stamboel as a low native genre (Cohen, 2006: 350). Its decline in the first decades of the twentieth century was caused in part by mestizo practitioners abandoning it as their fortunes improved. Thus, Mahieu was always something of an outsider to the Bond and to the community of more privileged mestizos. Perhaps his most important acquaintance within the Bond was the celebrated mestizo writer, Hans van de Wall (alias Victor Ido), who was a fan of Stamboel. In addition to newspaper reviews of Stamboel performances, Ido demonstrated his enthusiasm with a novel set amongst a troupe (*De Paupers*, 1912/1922) and a play based on

Figure 2.1 Jali-Jali, a production by Komedie Stamboel, 1906 (Author's collection)

a scandalous theatrical incident (*De Paria van Glodok*, 1916/21). He himself, however, enjoyed European status, and used this privilege to operate directly within the 'high' cultural sphere of Batavia. Despite the obvious advantage of such privilege at those times, it has consigned Ido to a legacy suspended between two worlds. To Dutch critics, he was mestizo; to Indonesian critics, he was Dutch.

Karina Adinda

Despite continuous increases in European immigration to the Dutch East Indies from the early nineteenth century onwards, they and the mestizo sub-group remained a small minority of the total Batavian population in 1942 when European rule came to an abrupt end. The Japanese Occupation admin-istration treated totok Dutch as well as many mestizos as enemy prisoners. If the rise of *pribumi* (native) nationalism in the 1920s and 1930s had already overshadowed the earlier mestizo postcolonial articulations, Japanese policy institutionalized the primacy of native Asian nationalisms vis-à-vis all other anti-colonial ideologies. Within this new Orientalist rhetoric, there would no longer be a space for notions of a hybrid transnational society in which an 'Indische aesthetic' might play a crucial role. Ironically, the mestizo popula-tion received what many had openly desired: full recognition as Europeans, for which they were disinherited from any share in a postcolonial Indonesian future. During the 1945–49 revolution, this rift widened, as the majority of mestizos saw their interests more closely aligned to the returning Dutch. Following the 1949 agreements for transfer of sovereignty, only 20 percent of the mestizo population in Indonesia (approximately 30,000 people) elected Indonesian citizenship. During the tempestuous first decade of the Indonesian republic, as President Soekarno became increasingly strident against the spec-tres of neo-colonialism, the situation for mestizos worsened. Between 1945 and 1958, approximately 100,000 mestizos emigrated from Indonesia to the Netherlands, where many suffered protracted difficulties adjusting to a 'father-land' they had never known. By the beginning of the Suharto regime (1966), they were no longer a legible, recognizable Indonesian community.

In the absence of an active, living community, mestizos have largely disap-peared from Indonesian public memory. More significantly, when they are remembered, they are not distinguished from totok Dutch or trekkers. The amnesty of an Indonesian citizenship granted uniformly across dozens of ethnic identities demanded a leveling of the space in-between Indonesian and foreigner on which mestizo identity had depended. Likewise, the history of the revolutionary struggle (projected back through all colonial and pre-colonial times) would be told, written and remembered as a confrontation between Natives and Europeans. For such Asian minorities as the ethnic Chinese, such thinking conferred a provisional, if recurringly problematic assimilation to native status. The mestizos, however, ceased to be distinguished from the

Dutch, and the substantial mestizo contributions to the emergence of an anti-colonial discourse became 'transitional' phenomena; useful intermediations (or perhaps buffers) between colonial and postcolonial practices whose legibility (to a postcolonial perspective) demanded ephemerality. Any scrutiny beyond the ascription of a limited historical instrumentality would per course reveal inassimilable contradictions within official state histories.

In this regard, the canonization of Stamboel as the origin of modern Indonesian theatre serves as a typical compromise, much as the Indische Bond serves as an acceptable transitional phenomenon towards the *Java* and *Sumatranen* Bonds. Following Asmara's insistence on the legacy of Mahieu, Stamboel has passed into the prevailing historical narrative as a 'transitional' form, implying a teleology from a rigorously distinct pre-modern binary (traditional native theatres vs. imported European theatres) towards the fully emerged modern theatre of the postcolony. In this narrative, Mahieu himself functions as a single exceptional non-native progenitor, shepherding the transmission of various local and regional traditions into modernity, and then stepping aside to allow true Indonesian artists to take over. In order for Mahieu to play this specific role, he had to be separated from such trekker influences as the Dutch actress, Mina Kruseman (see Chapter 5), and such Europhilic mestizo acquaintances as Ido.

Victor Ido was native on his mother's side, though his totok Dutch father bequeathed him a status and upbringing as close to full 'European' as possible in the late colony. He provided Ido a European education in Surabaya in the 1870s, and in 1882 Victor and his brother Constant went to the Netherlands and attended gymnasium at Delft. Upon returning to Java in 1891, his European academic pedigree enabled him to participate in Batavian high society. He quickly established himself as a church organist and music teacher, but soon gained greater recognition as a journalist and writer who, within a milieu nearly exclusive to totok Europeans, could claim privileged insight into mestizo and native culture. Thus, as an art critic for *Bataviaasch Nieuwsblaad*, he played a role in elevating the significance of mestizo arts, such as Stamboel, and later reported on aspects of mestizo life through a weekly radio broadcast (texts of which were published in 1922 as *Indie in den goeden Ouden Tijd)*. Rob Nieuwenhuys comments on Ido's ambivalent position in-between totok and mestizo societies:

> But though he knew the Indo-European milieu better than any other writer, he was never entirely one of them. As a child, he had cause to be distinguished for his appearance (his father was a *totok*), for his speech and his better education. He said of himself that in his neighborhood he was a *'rara avis.'* Therefore, he found himself in a peculiar position: to belong to them, and at the same to stand outside their lives. Perhaps this was really the ideal position from which to write about them.
>
> (Nieuwenhuys, 1973: 298)

As a 'European' artist, Ido was not limited by the economic and social restrictions to which poorer mestizos, such as Mahieu, were subject. Though Ido openly admired Mahieu, he himself participated in a very different theatrical culture, that of European Batavia (see Nieuwenhuys, 1973: 297–301).

Already published as a novelist (*Don Juan*, 1897), Ido established his reputation as Batavia's leading Dutch language playwright with the 1913 premiere of *Karina Adinda* at the *Schouwburg Weltewreden* (Batavia's most prestigious European theatre venue, see Chapter 3). The production was so extraordinarily successful, that it continued to be revived annually for well over a decade and toured to other *schouwburgen* throughout Java. Further, the script (published in 1914 in Batavia) was taken up by other amateur troupes, through whom it received countless additional performances. In 1916, Lauw Giok Lan published a translation in low Malay for the benefit of the Batavian Chinese charity association theatre troupes (known as *opera derma*.) Through all these manifestations, *Karina Adinda* must be regarded as the most popular scripted play in urban Java of the 1910s and 1920s – a work composed initially for a high culture audience of European status, but which spread through other urban communities.

One could certainly argue that Ido drew inspiration and technique from Stamboel. The heightened gestural and oratorical styles recorded in descriptions of Stamboel performances resemble surviving images of actors in performances of Ido's plays. Indeed, various biographers have noted Ido's predilection for romanticism and melodrama, pitting his characters in stark moral confrontations raised to tragic violent climax in which divine mercy and justice are invoked. One might also speak of the relation to source material. Many of Mahieu's works were 'ripped from the headlines.'[4] Others, such as his 1900 dramatization of *Nyai Dasima*, channeled contemporary urban anxieties regarding passion and violence.[5] Ido loosely based his 1916 play, *The Pariah of Glodok*, on a murder that had taken place onstage during a performance of the *Permata Stamboel* company in 1898 (Cohen, 2006: 266–74). Likewise, *Karina Adinda*, as Ido himself wrote in the *Bataviaasch Nieuwsblaad*, took inspiration from three separate contemporary stories: 'the matter of a love affair between a controleur and a regent's daughter in East Java, [and] the matter of the controleur Cohen who risked his own life in a heroic feat to break the sluice to prevent a flood' (Nieuwenhuys, 1973: 301), and the life and tragic early death of Raden Ajeng Kartini. There is no doubt some aesthetic continuity between 1890s Stamboel and Victor Ido's theatre of the 1910s and 1920s. However, such claims are inherently slippery, and both Stamboel and Ido could equally be seen as indebted to the dramaturgy and acting techniques of European melodrama (transmitted through several generations of amateur theatricals in Batavia) and the more recent narrative topicality of Rabindranath Tagore and the European realists (increasingly available in print and valued by the progressive intelligentsia). The case of

Ido's oeuvre highlights the futility of drawing stark distinctions between European and native practices.

The action of *Karina Adinda* takes place within the fictional Javanese regency of Wiriosari.[6] In the opening scene, Boesono, apprentice to the Dutch regional *controleur*, Willem Rennenberg, clandestinely informs the *bupati* (regent) that Willem has discovered, but refused to be corrupted by, a Chinese gambling and counterfeiting operation in which the *bupati* himself is complicit. Boesono reassures the *bupati* that Willem thought so highly of him that he refused to believe his involvement in such criminal activities, carried out at the expense of his own people. Farmers come to plead for money promised them in exchange for use of their lands by the Dutch sugar plantations. The *bupati*'s staff repeatedly stonewall them, whereas Willem encourages them in their suit and even assists them with a cash advance of his own. Thus, from the beginning, Ido contrasts the righteousness of a liberal European *controleur* (who places the development and welfare of the Javanese people foremost) with the corruption and feudal indifference of the native aristocracy.

There is some contradiction, nevertheless, in the *bupati*'s behavior. We soon learn that he has provided not only his son, Koesoemo, but even his daughter, Karina Adinda, with Western educations. However, he becomes increasingly hostile to the egalitarian and revolutionary convictions to which this exposure has brought them. He is troubled by Koesoemo's fascination with the history of revolutions in Europe, from which the young man has begun to draw local conclusions. He is even less willing to allow the intimacy that has developed between Karina and Willem. When the *bupati* introduces his daughter to the *bupati* of Bintarang, with whose son he hopes to arrange a traditional, strategic marriage, she scandalizes both of them by offering a handshake, rather than the submissive *sembah*. Karina then rebukes her father's values:

> Does *Kanjeng* [an honorific address] wish to be respected in this ancient manner? Must a young woman of my position and education grovel at *Kanjeng*'s feet because it is demanded by custom [*adat*]? Is it so? If so, I advance this concern out of compassion for all his women. They are not truly women but only impotent creatures left to ignorance. Wayang puppets are more valued.
>
> (Ido and Lan, 1993: 9)

Karina and Koesoemo both question the *bupati* at various points about why he bothered to provide them with an education if he ultimately intended to limit their horizons according to tradition. Indeed, the two *bupati* agree that nothing good has come of this exposure to the West. Willem, in contrast, deals respectfully with Karina, admiring her European accomplishments (she spends much time painting), and encouraging Koesoemo in his studies.

However, he avoids openly disparaging Javanese custom. As Willem tells Koesoemo, 'You may do as you like. Live in the Javanese or the European manner' (11), Nevertheless, Willem is not glib about where Koesoemo's awakening might lead: to himself, he admits that the boy may prove dangerous.

Increasingly alarmed, the *bupati* decides to murder Willem. First, he attempts to poison him, a scheme that Karina manages to foil. However, a better opportunity soon presents itself. Both Willem and the *bupati* hasten to the river at news that heavy rains threaten to cause severe flooding. Farmers plead for the sluice to be broken so that their fields will not be ruined. Willem confronts Bunkers and van Eelten, Dutch sugar planters, whose interests lie in maintaining the sluices at the expense of the Javanese farmers. A clear mouthpiece of the 'ethical policy,' he insists that the needs of the native farmers must take precedence, and sets off to open the sluice himself. In retaliation, Bunkers and van Eelten stoke the rumors of illicit congress between Willem and Karina to the *bupati*, and pledge their support in eliminating this meddlesome *controleur*. Thus goaded, the *bupati* sends Boesono to betray Willem. Karina's mother, who had previously foretold Karina's love for Willem bringing calamity to the family and kingdom, arrives. She now insists that the son of the *bupati* of Bintarang would be a terrible match for their daughter. She too asks her husband why he bothered to give her an education. He finally answers:

> Before, before! Now I feel it is enough. I feel I have received enough wickedness from the Dutch. They steal our property. Our country, our dignity, our children [...].
>
> (Ido and Lan, 1993: 24)

His wife congratulates his belated insight; too little, too late. News then arrives that the *controleur* has heroically saved the farmers' fields by personally breaking open the floodgate. At the same time, Boesono reports to the *bupati* that at the very moment of this heroism, he had shoved Willem into the flood, and to his martyr's death.

In the final act, the *bupati*'s victory is revealed as bitterly pyrrhic. Koesoemo proclaims that he has no interest in assuming his hereditary role as his father's heir. As he explains to the incredulous *bupati*, he has learned from the study of history the pettiness of his own birthright:

> how narrow life is here. Wiriosari is so small. *Romo* [another honorific] should read the chronicles [*hikayat*] of Europe and America. What life is like in their national capitals. There are many capable people there doing works and becoming important people; more important than a noble or even a King. There is nobility there so-called not because of their lineage or their wealth, *romo* [... But] on account of their actions and ideas.
>
> (28)

The *bupati* realizes now that he has indeed lost his children to the West. When news reaches Karina that Willem is murdered, she is not subdued to her father's marital scheme, but rather elevated to full melodramatic stature (Figure 2.2). Ido gives her a final soliloquy (uninterrupted by stabbing herself in the heart) in which she proclaims to Willem a love that 'might join you in death [...].' She plucks a white flower from the garden, addressing it as her 'blond bridegroom,' taunting her father:

> *Romo*! See, there comes Karina's bridegroom! – Stay here, *Romo*, on this spot. See him well, *Romo* [...[there he comes, the noblest, the finest, the whitest of them all! [...] O, how Karina's heart pounds! (*She seizes her father's kris* [ritual sword] *and plunges it into her heart.*) Karina rushes to meet you [...] o, divine reunion!

The *bupati* is left crying to Allah and cursing Rennenburg. Koesoemo delivers the final line of the play in 'somber irony': 'Thus, the mightiest is revealed!' (Ido, 1913: 125).

It is curious that *Karina Adinda* was Ido's most successful play, and the work chosen by Suyatna Anirun to revive 80 years later for the 1993 *Festival Schouwburg*. Unlike most of the author's works, there are no mestizo characters in this play; the confrontation is entirely between Dutch and Javanese.

Figure 2.2 The debut performance of Victor Ido's *Karina Adinda* at the Schouwburg Weltewreden, 1913 (Author's collection)

That said, the play's two central revolutionaries, Kusumo and Karina, assume a problematic status similar to that of the mestizos. As the *bupati* laments in a soliloquy towards the end: 'What has happened to Karina and Kusumo? They are no longer Javanese nobility now. They have become half European' (Ido and Lan, 1993: 29). The native Javanese in the play are corrupt and ensconced in reactionary feudal customs. The Dutch plantation administrators are simply exploitative, and even the heroic Willem is not entirely sanguine about what might come of mixing European and Javanese ways. He tells Koesoemo that he might choose *either* a European or a Javanese life, conspicuously avoiding the much more dangerous prospect that Koesoemo is actually considering: applying Western lessons to the foment of native revolution. Koesoemo and Karina are unaware of 'native' nationalism, but do espouse revolutionary ideals close to those of mestizo anti-colonialism: they desire to transcend colonialism and feudalism, but only to forge a new European society in Java. What Milone wrote of *Nyai Dasima* applies similarly here. Such blunt eurocentrism would be challenged by native nationalists, yet most Indonesian intellectuals of the revolutionary generation struggled with their own reliance on Dutch education, and preference for European forms. Indeed, the arguments of Sutan Takdir Alisjahbana within the 1930s cultural polemic did not depart radically from the implicit moral of *Karina Adinda*.

From the perspective of New Order cultural politics, however, Ido's absolute preference of European values over Javanese tradition proved unacceptable. Batubara, a critic for *Kompas* (a leading Jakarta newspaper), articulates quite clearly the primary difficulty of the play for an Indonesian audience in 1993:

> [Ido] possessed the concrete perspective of the colonists in articulating-movement for long-term change in the Indies (Indonesia) of the period. From this perspective, the natives tend to be situated in the position of 'losers' who are entrenched and allergic to change – such that the issue must be taken up by their children. Therefore, those who are called the colonists (the Dutch), are of course always presented as 'heroic' figures protecting the interests of the people who are only oppressed at the hands of their own native leaders [...] the Dutch have nothing to learn from the country that they govern.
>
> (Batubara, 1993)

It may thus seem baffling that the staff of the 1993 *Festival Schouwburg* at the *Gedung Kesenian Jakarta* (GKJ, the Jakarta Arthouse) commissioned *Studiklub Teater Bandung* (STB) to revive *Karina Adinda* on its eightieth anniversary. The fact that it was a rare example of a colonial-era Dutch play already translated into Malay undoubtedly played a role. However, Suyatna Anirun also approached Lan's translation of *Karina Adinda* in a manner congruent to the ambivalent identity of GKJ itself as the refurbished Schouwburg Weltewreden (constructed in 1821). STB's production strove to reanimate the building's (colonial) past while maintaining an absolute separation between the colonial and the postcolonial, the Dutch and the Indonesian. Once again, the in-betweenness of mestizo identity could not be admitted.

In general, the tropical climate of Indonesia ensures the rapid deterioration of most buildings, abetting a predominantly oral culture in the oblivion of uncomfortable pasts. In this respect, the Jakarta Arthouse is both peculiarly conservative and counter-cultural. It occupies a point of municipal and national pride as a monumental edifice with a long genealogy of high culture production. However, it is an imposing reminder of the colonial past. In 1993, the *Festival Schouwburg* both acknowledged and distanced itself from this problem by 'inviting' its audience 'to the past,' as to a foreign country. Within this framework, the world of Ido's play could likewise be viewed as a 'foreign country,' relevant to contemporary Indonesia in a universal sense (based on its broad themes) rather than by way of its local specificities. Anirun's widow, Sugiyati (who also designed the costumes), and Eka Gandara (who played the *bupati*) both attest that *Karina Adinda* was, for them, essentially a Dutch play. As such, STB approached it with much the same attitude as any of the other European classics that the company regularly produces (Sugiyati and Gandara, 2007). Anirun and his design staff drew on decades of experience in scenographic realism to place *Karina Adinda* in the past and, more specifically, in an a-historical Dutch culture. Sugiyati's older sister, Ning Darsono, was consulted on use of Dutch language (not because she was a historical linguist with knowledge of *petjo* or Batavian Dutch, but because she had studied Dutch and lived in the contemporary Netherlands). Many Dutch words were retained in the text, and Ning sang 'Dutch' songs during the scene breaks. These musical interludes, which sometimes consisted of Javanese songs as well, featured a *keroncong* orchestra, a hybrid urban style combining such European instruments as ukuleles and fiddles with Javanese musical elements. However, in the 'nativist' performance lexicon of the New Order, *keroncong* has come to stand for the Dutch colonial milieu, a time before national awakening, and thus distinct from Indonesian identity.[7] In choosing these Dutch elements, as well as the setting of the *bupati*'s Court and pavilion, Anirun endeavored to transport the audience to 'a condition different from the present':

> High and solid pillars, antique rocking chairs, marble tables and antique wooden chairs, in addition to live trees customary to regency *pendapa* [pavilions], as well as a golden parasol – all to complete a picture or portrait taken from an old album, which is, of course, distant from the present.
>
> (Anirun and Sugiyati, 1996: 384)

If the original production may have fascinated Batavian European audiences with exotic glimpses of Javanese Court life, this 1993 revival transplanted the play to an antique family album. In keeping with the governing ideology of the Festival, this play set in East Java, written in 1913 by a mestizo son of Surabaya, became legible instead as a work from 'somewhere else.' With a mildly ironic tone, Anirun aligned the production with the Festival theme: 'the point was to be dressed in the past; regardless of whose past, an Indonesian dressing or something from outside the Indonesian nation' (386).

As with most STB adaptations of Western plays, however, Anirun was not entirely satisfied to set the play at a distance. He made substantial revisions in the play's melodramatic ending, which he found 'overly pessimistic.' Rather than allowing Karina to join her murdered 'white flower' of a Dutch lover in death, Anirun introduces a *deus ex machina* reprieve. Karina is interrupted by the arrival of Willem, who, it turns out, was rescued from the threshold of death by sympathetic farmers who nursed him back to health. The *bupati* attempts to murder Boesono to eliminate the witness, but Willem intercedes, demanding both that Boesono answer to a judge and the *bupati* answer to the governor general. Both the divine retribution for the *bupati*'s crime and the melodramatic pathos of Karina's death are thus avoided. Their respective justice and betrothal are left presumptive as the action terminates in a prudent tableaux. Kusumo delivers a very different moral than in Ido's version: 'The true noble is shown by his deeds and ideas [...] O Lord [...] guide us all to the right path' (Ido and Lan, 1993: 33). Rather than a provocative prophecy of the end of feudal backwardness, Kusumo ties the play's democratic sentiment to a broad Islamic moralism.

In one sense, STB's production (Figure 2.3) might be seen as 'reading against the grain' of a colonial play whose trajectory is highly problematic vis-à-vis postcolonial Indonesia. The specific invocation of Allah disaggregates the *bupati*'s conservative feudalism (which is taken as a fair target for criticism) from Islam (which is not). However, rather than grappling with the ambiguous legacy of Ido's 'Indisch' anti-colonialism, the STB production remains comfortably within terrain legible and inoffensive to Indonesian national culture. In *Karina Adinda* (as in other Indisch works such as *Nyai Dasima*) native men are denounced in contrast to a relatively progressive portrayal of native women, a paradoxical feminism with which postcolonial nationalism remains uncomfortable. As Ido had explicitly noted in his article for *Bataviaasch Nieuwsblaad*, the play was inspired by the life story of Raden Ajeng Kartini (1879–1904). Kartini had been the daughter of an actual *bupati,* she had attended a European school in Jepara (a coastal city of Central Java), was given in marriage to another *bupati*, and then died at the age of 25, several days after the birth of her first child. In 1911, a collection of her personal letters (written in Dutch) were published under the title *Door duisternis tot licht* ('From darkness into the light'). In writing, Kartini had advocated equal education for women

Figure 2.3 Studiklub Teater Bandung's revival of *Karina Adinda* at Gedung Kesenian Jakarta, 1993 (© Sugiyati)

and freedom from forced marriage and filial duty. She was soon hailed as a Javanese feminist. In 1913, the year *Karina Adinda* was produced, a Kartini fund was established in the Netherlands to provide education for Javanese women. When one further considers that Ido filled out the original cast with (presumably male) Javanese students from Batavia's *Dokter Djawa* school,[8] the reference to Kartini was sure to be a matter of controversy. However, as Sylvia Tiwon argues, Kartini has remained an ambivalent hero to postcolonial Indonesians as well.

Although Indonesian girls now receive equal access to public education, many aspects of the traditional Javanese patriarchy against which Kartini argued are still strong. Kartini was raised to the status of a *pahlawan nasional* (national hero) in 1964 (at the height, one might note, of communist influence on the Indonesian government). However, Tiwon argues that the true extent of Kartini's radicalism (that is, her call for independence of women from patriarchal control) has been softened in official discourse into a safe, traditional image of *Ibu* [Mother] *Kartini*. (Tiwon, 1996) Though *Karina Adinda* does not go so far as to imagine its heroine forging a life for herself completely free of marriage and childbearing, it does depict a woman willing to break radically from the confines of Javanese tradition. By subverting Karina's final suicide, the 1993 production softens the play's critique of

Javanese patriarchy into a safely universal appeal to divine guidance in order to live a good life. In Ido's text, Karina and Koesoemo, though Javanese themselves, advocate a vision of the future in line with mestizo nationalism, a revolution that will rebuild native society on European values. In 1993, however, Kartini could only be a Javanese woman, and Ido could only be a Dutch playwright.

Chinese Batavian theatre

Taylor points out the extent to which Batavia was never simply a copy of urban Europe, developing, instead, its own distinct mestizo society. However, one might make an even stronger case that the success of the VOC outpost from 1619 to 1740 depended on the co-operation of its Chinese population. The ethnic Chinese were not merely one of the local groups, but crucial partners to the Europeans in building a new global city on the ruins of Jayakerta. It was the presence and influx of significant numbers of Chinese migrant workers that enabled the building and expansion of Batavia. Whereas Peter Nas and C. D. Grijns claim that 'Batavia was a clear cut copy of the Dutch town at that time' (Nas and Grijns, 2000: 5–6), Leonard Blussé counters that the Chinese Batavians had as many skills and inclinations towards the building of a walled city as the Europeans. Before Europeans expanded their own administrative networks much beyond their port towns, Chinese served as invaluable intermediaries between the Company, the Javanese and mainland Asia. For Batavia's first 120 years, the Europeans lived and worked in the *kasteel* while the town of Batavia was dominated by Chinese merchants. Blussé summarizes the economic arrangement as 'a Chinese colonial town under Dutch protection':

> Through an elaborate system of political, social, and economic measures, Batavia castle with its warehouses functioned as the 'keystone' in the system of Dutch trading posts all over Asia, while Batavia town operated as a 'cornerstone' of the Chinese trade network in Southeast Asia.
>
> (1981: 160)

In 1740, however, a series of disputes and reprisals culminated in the European massacre of as many as 10,000 Batavian Chinese, resulting in an exodus from which the VOC never recovered.

As the Chinese were integral to the economy of VOC Batavia, so too did they offer the most skilled theatrical performances. With the original Betawi population driven out after the destruction of Jayakerta and the European society handicapped by immigration restrictions, only the Chinese community was coherent enough to promote the continuity of specialized cultural traditions. As van den Berg laments the failure of

European professional theatre to take root in VOC Batavia, he admits with some chagrin the superiority of Chinese entertainments:

> Thus, during the Company period, the capital of the Netherlands Indies was impoverished in practice of theatrical arts [...] it seemed to people that this domain was not really as familiar to them as the Chinese shadow performances, which at the time, for that matter, were very much in demand by the European population.
>
> (1904: 102)

Indeed, personal journals and other *belles lettres* of the VOC period rarely failed to mention these performances. For example, François Valentijn in the 1720s writes:

> When the Chinese have made a safe voyage by junk or *wangkang*, they are accustomed to give a *wayang* [here referring to Asian theatre in general] [...] The actors are young and impoverished boys and girls who are engaged for that purpose [...]. The performances, whether comedy or tragedy, begin on Mondays at three or four o'clock and last until six; after which they go and eat something and begin performing again from nine in the evening until three or four o'clock in the morning.
>
> (Abeyasekere, 1987: 17)[9]

Such weekly performances lasting upwards of ten hours suggests a rigorous discipline, while the pattern of sponsorship and employment of poor children resemble practices found in mainland China. Reports of devotional performances of *xiqu* (Chinese opera) and shadow puppetry and performances of the *barongsai* (Chinese lion dance) on the occasion of Chinese new year attest to a rich performance culture throughout the eighteenth century.

In his introduction to the first volume of the *Lontar Anthology of Indonesian Drama*, Cohen traces a succession of developments in the performance culture of the Chinese in Batavia, as well as other cities in Java, Sumatra and Kalimantan, which link these eighteenth-century practices to the emergence of Batavia's late colonial urban theatre culture. Besides the continuation of devotional practices as Valentijn mentions, commercial *xiqu* performances also took place. By the nineteenth century, the *peranakan* (locally born Chinese) population was a dominant portion of the Batavian Chinese community. As with immigrant communities elsewhere, a degree of assimilation ensued. Cohen mentions troupes of non-Chinese native women actors trained by Chinese masters, *wayang sinpe* troupes of pre-pubescent youths, and significant Chinese involvement in *wayang cerita* (a west Javanese form developed in the mid-nineteenth century from the admixture of Indian Parsi theatre and *xiqu*).[10] The Chinese performance culture became increasingly syncretic, negotiating with local and recently imported forms, often using the Malay language, which increasingly supplanted Chinese as the primary language of the community. Nevertheless, Chinese Batavian performances of *xiju* to propitiate the Queen of the South Seas in the 1720s are not typically viewed as part of a genealogical thread leading to modern and postcolonial theatre.

In the 1870s, decades before a comparable native modern literature appeared, Chinese Indonesians began writing modern poetry and novels. This began with adaptations of Malay poetry and translations of Chinese classics (such as *Sam Pek Eng Tay*), and by the turn of the century the Sino-Malay novel had emerged as a distinct genre. These works often addressed local issues of the Chinese community, promoting a strain of realism previously lacking from non-European writing. By the 1920s, revolutions in mainland China inspired expressions of cultural nationalism and resistance to the Japanese in some of these works. Serialized in Chinese-owned periodicals and printed separately, the urban Chinese modeled the sort of print nationalism that Benedict Anderson has argued played a crucial role in the rise of Indonesian national culture. (See Allen, 2003; Salmon, 1981; Suryadinata 1996, 2004.)

Chinese artists and entrepreneurs also played a crucial role in the development of urban modern theatres. Though Indonesian critics would associate Stamboel primarily with Mahieu, it was Yap Gwan Thay, a Chinese entrepreneur, who first financed the company to operate out of theatres owned by himself and his associates in Surabaya's Chinatown. As a result, the first audiences of Stamboel were primarily ethnic Chinese, and Chinese stories and traditional performance techniques contributed to the mix of elements from which Stamboel drew. As in most economic sectors not monopolized by the colonial government, it was often Chinese businessmen who had the resources and connections to produce and house urban theatre, and there were many similar arrangements through the remainder of the colonial era, and afterwards.[11]

At the turn of the twentieth century, a Chinese cultural nationalism and emphasis on ethnic communities shaped further developments in the urban theatre. The growth of 'mutual aid' associations (*Tiong Hoa Hwe Koan*) allowed patronage of professional groups inspired by bangsawan and Stamboel, but Chinese in cultural orientation. The most famous of these, *Opera Sui Ban Lian* (founded 1905), 'derived many plays from classical Chinese literature and Chinese dramatic conventions, but also used European musical instruments and theatrical technology, introducing an entire generation of Malay-speaking Chinese to the culture of China' (Cohen, 2009: xi).

Nevertheless, an orientation towards philanthropy rather than profit prompted these associations to promote *opera derma* (charity opera) groups, which consisted largely of amateurs from the local community. Although opera derma retained aesthetic aspects of previous urban theatres, the shift from a professional commercial theatre to an amateur social one encouraged predictable aesthetic changes. The amateur actors being possessed of more limited performance and improvisational skills, more precise scripts were required; a trend further supported by the desire of socially oriented writers to produce more literary works. In short, the model of an amateur nationalist stage featuring literary drama appeared first in Indonesia within these Chinese opera derma troupes. In fact, it was from a desire to provide better scripts for derma troupes that Lan adapted *Karina Adinda* from Dutch into Malay in 1913 (thus producing the translation from which STB began their work eight decades later). It was also opera derma that provided a platform for the first theatrical works of Kwee Tek Hoay, the most famous Sino-Malay author of the early twentieth century. In about a dozen plays beginning with his *Allah yang Palsu* (The False Gods, 1919) for opera derma, Hoay adapted the social realism of Ibsen and Tagore to Batavian Chinese contexts. In 1930, he accepted a commission to write a new play for the leading professional theatre troupe, *Teater Dardanella*.

The Living Corpse

Hoay's *Mait Idup* (*The Living Corpse*, 1930) relates a multi-generational tragedy proceeding from the transmission of syphilis by Yang Bwe, an affluent Chinese Batavian, to his son, Lian Gie. The family doctor, telegraphically named 'Trusty,' urges Yang Bwe to terminate his current marital engagement lest he spread the disease congenitally, enlisting Yang's father, Khik Po, to ensure the welfare of future generations. However, when Yang comes home from a bout of carousing and womanizing with his disreputable friends, Khik Po decides that marriage to Lauw Nio is the lesser danger. The play skips ahead to a future in which Khik Po is deceased, and Yang Bwe still suffers from the disease. As feared, he and Liauw Nio have given birth to a succession of sickly children. The strongest, Lian Gie, is nevertheless sick as well, and is now being treated by Dr Trusty. Of course, Lian Gie is also afflicted with syphilis, and Trusty entreats Yang Bwe to end the cycle and not permit Lian Gie to marry his fiancée, Liesje. Liesje sentimentally confirms her loyalty to her intended, and it appears that nothing will interrupt the repetition of this contaminated genealogy. Lian Gie, however, leaves the city and travels into the countryside, trying to understand the nature of his malaise. He is inspired by the vigor of village life and repudiates the degeneracy of his urban community. He returns home advocating the salvation of poverty only to learn finally the true source of his illness as a dark paternal legacy. Against the pleas of Liesje (and to the lethal shock of his father), Lian Gie kills himself 'for the sake of Liesje's future, the good of society, and the advancement of our people, and the well-being of humanity.' Over the bodies of father and son, Dr Trusty delivers a lecture to the edification of the surviving women and the community:

> This explanation, this final testimony, shows that your fiancé was a young man with a strong and noble heart. He did not hesitate to leave

this world after he found out that he could not contribute to society, after he found out he posed a threat to his descendents. He did not wish for you to remain tied by the binds of betrothal to a living corpse.

(Cohen, 2009: 94)

He resolves to frame Lian Gie's suicide note, and put it on display in his clinic as an example for all.

Living Corpse, like Henrik Ibsen's *Ghosts*, depicts a degenerate national culture in which each generation becomes the new surrogate for a contaminated ancestor. Both Yang Bwe and his son, Lian Gie are described repeatedly as 'living corpses,' uncanny abominations who are 'alive, but also dead!,' as Lian Gie laments upon learning the truth. They are ghostly doubles inspirited by a congenital crime, whatever contribution they might make to society always already sabotaged by this disease that repeats the past within each surrogate. Where Hoay's play departs from Ibsen and assumes a more progressive position in line with postcolonial *bildung*, is in depicting a radical youth choosing to interrupt this contaminated genealogy, thus clearing a possible space for the nation to be re-inspirited. When Lian Gie confronts his father, he inverts the Abrahamic scene, accusing his own father of already having sacrificed his son's aspirations for communal service, leaving him no moral option but to sacrifice himself (and his own genealogical line) to the good of the community.

Although Hoay, writing in 1930, is never so overt in invoking revolution as Effendi had been four years previously, the play is nevertheless easy to interpret as supporting a kind of nationalist vision. In his preface to the book edition of the play, reprinted from an article, 'Intellectuals and the Theater,' Hoay interprets his protagonist's journey to consciousness:

> He is angry and reproaches God for giving him a body that is so weak and sickly, while a poor villager can enjoy a healthy body and live in peace with his family. He contemplates and searches for an explanation of why he has been dealt such a fate. He becomes tangled in fictions for a length of time, but one day he becomes aware of the true causes and grounds of his condition.[12]

(Bodden, 2009: 61)

Though never explicit, this is much like Boedjangga's journey towards an awareness of the degeneracy of his elders. Likewise, Hoay aligns his diagnosis to a clear opposition of Native to European. When, in the second act, we meet the friends in whose company we may assume Yang Bwe contracted the disease in the first place, their society is depicted as parasitic on European tastes. In speech accented with Dutch exclamations, they tempt Yang with reports of a girl who is attractive insofar as she looks Dutch, speaks fluent Dutch and sings *keroncong*, and he agrees to join a party for 'followers of the pleasure principle.' In the fifth act, Lian Gie takes on the role of an ethnographer, questioning the healthy farmers from whom he and his family have become so miserably alienated. He takes the details of their diet and livelihood as a prescription against the depravity of those 'pleasure' devotees. Thus, the alignment of bodily weakness and disease with Westernization is countered by the robustness of traditional village life; a trope that would be repeatedly deployed by anti- and postcolonial writers. For example, in *Kisah Perjuangan Suku Naga* (*History of the Struggles of the Naga Tribe*, 1976), one of the most celebrated plays of the Suharto era, Rendra juxtaposes government officials from Jakarta who suffer from a wide range of embarrassing and exotic ailments against the Naga villagers, whose lack of these afflictions derives from adherence to local tradition (see Winet, 2005). As Cheah points out, however, the attempt to exorcise foreign ghosts never results in an organism free of the past. Lian Gie's impulse to abandon the cities and return to an agrarian life is clearly unworkable for the Batavian Chinese community, for whom integration with the foreign is fundamental to economic survival.

The tainted, syphilitic genealogy is corporealized in Hoay's text through a complex of facial metonyms: pallor, vacant stares and accusing portraits. The Western disease is written, through lack of color, on the face of its Chinese victims. We see the remission of Yang's illness in the second act through a reduction of facial pallor and a return of ruddiness (also ascribed to the villagers). Though mentioned briefly in the text, make-up could easily be used in performance to transform the actors' faces into indices of racial contamination. Hoay establishes a more overt and related dynamic through the relation of 'vacant stares' to various portraits. Like Effendi's unawakened Budjangga, Yang Bwe stares vacantly at nothing in the second act, and describes seeing the face of his love, Siti, in the displaced space-time of dreams. Later, as an old man, Yang Bwe's face is wrinkled, but still vacant. The disease has granted him a long life of tragically veiled consciousness. Meanwhile, an ancestral portrait of Khik Po, 'encircled by other family pictures,' has taken up residence on the wall. Yang prays to Heaven and this portrait to spare his last son. In the emblematic vacancy of his gaze, we read his incapacity to truly see the face of his ancestor and to find in it the rejuvenating spirit he seeks. In performance, this portrait of Khik Po would continue to stare out, its gaze unmet, through the fourth and sixth acts. In Act 5, Lian Gie, in seclusion in the mountains, dreams of his fiancée. Whereas Yang Bwe, in Act 2, recalls the face of his love in dreams, Lian Gie gazes at a portrait of Liesje, kissing and pinching it as if a real face. This is a kind of repetition of a failure to look into the actual, present face of the beloved (a gesture we see again in Teater Sae's 1991 play, *Pertumbuhan di atas Meja Makan*, see Chapter 5). The paternal disease steals from Lian Gie the event of the face even as it stole from his father the faces of beloved and ancestor. His subsequent alienated interrogation of the farmers, perhaps a parody of the European ethnographer, is accompanied by much vacant staring. At the end, Lian Gie demands that his father 'look at the picture of your own father and see how hale and strong he appears,' then carries out his suicide under the approving eye of his grandfather. In his epilogue, Dr Trusty confirms the righteousness of Lian Gie's deed by resolving to turn the suicide note itself into a kind of portrait:

> I will frame the note behind glass and hang it in my reception room, so that anyone who comes to be treated by me will be able to reflect upon and admire this young man whose strength and deeds are not less in honor than most of the world's most famous champions.
>
> (Cohen, 2009: 94)

Although Lian Gie himself was deprived of the faces of his community by the spectrality contaminating his own gaze, his action, facialized as a portrait, may hereby finally do some social good, inspiriting all his countrymen who might look at it.

Hoay's play combines the social morality of an opera derma script, some of the structure and character conventions of European social realism and the big roles and six-act structure (allowing for many interludes) preferred by Dardanella. As Cohen remarks in the introduction to his translation of the play, the influence of Ibsen's *Ghosts* is apparent, but *Living Corpse* is a distinct work with a very different trajectory. In his own preface to the play, the author expresses his hope that it will have a life beyond Dardanella and be taken into the theatrical repertoire.[13] Dardanella performed *Living Corpse* for about a year, in 1931, including a tour to Sumatra and a month in residence in Batavia. In general, Hoay's works were in demand and Dardanella's productions thereof a commercial success. One of the leading actresses, Dewi Dja, recalls the first plays by Hoay being partly responsible for inspiring her to learn to read (so that she could master the literary scripts) (Ramadhan, 1982: 85).

Given Hoay's popularity at the time and the success of works such as *Living Corpse* with the troupe that Oemarjati would canonize as the first nationalist theatre troupe, it is striking that until recently Hoay's works received considerably less attention than those of his nationalist contemporaries. There is much to recommend *Living Corpse* as a nationalist, or at least an anti-colonial work. However, Cohen notes that Andjar Asmara, whose own play, *Dr Samsi*, was introduced to the company the same year, disparaged Hoay's play as mere 'anti-venereal disease propaganda.' Asmara's aggressive self-promotion is largely to blame, but the resulting historiographical emphases have proved consistently unfavorable to Sino-Malay playwrights. *Miss Riboet's Orion*, another professional troupe founded by Chinese writers, Thio Tek Djien and Njoo Cheong Seng, is frequently mentioned as Dardanella's main rival, equally responsible for transforming Stamboel.[14] However, it is clearly Dardanella that dominates the memory of an early nationalist stage, as Effendi, the *Poedjangga Baroe* playwrights and Andjar Asmara have dominated the memory of early nationalist drama.[15]

Jakarta 2039

Both privileged and contained by the Dutch, colonial-era Chinese were regarded with suspicion from all sides. Most popular (and many scholarly) accounts represent the urban Chinese community as 'successful outsiders,' whose closed, transnational economic networks made them both invaluable and inassimilable, empowered and ostracized by their in-betweenness. Colonial-era Javanese denigrated them with the epigram, *Cina wurung, londa durung, Jawa tanggung* ('no longer a Chinese, not yet a Dutchman, a half-baked Javanese') (Allen, 2003: 385). According to nationalist rhetoric, all this changed with Independence, at which point all populations living within the national boundaries (save those of European status) were counted amongst the national citizenry.

In practice, however, the Chinese community has continued to be regarded as 'the same but not quite' throughout the postcolonial era. In tracing previous points of comparison for the 1998 race riots, Heryanto was sobered to find extensive reports of political violence (including sexual violence) committed against Chinese in West Java in 1946, in the early years of the revolution itself (1999: 298). Chinese were also targeted in 1965–66 during the massacres that destroyed the Indonesian Communist Party and put Suharto in power. At this time, they were suspected of latent ties with the PRC, the Suharto administration rationalized measures to erase outward markings of Chinese identity as defusing potential causes of political conflict and violence. Through a 1967 decree, Suharto banned Chinese schools and organizations, Chinese language printed materials, signs and other materials using Chinese characters.[16] Chinese individuals and businesses were compelled to adopt names that sounded more Indonesian. Thus, for example, the director Steve Liem Tjoan Hoak became Teguh Karya. Chinese cultural performances such as those that European travelers had described for centuries were banned. In one sweep, all outward manifestations of Chinese difference were criminalized. Whereas Claudine Salmon and Leo Suryadinata had compiled extensive surveys of previous activities, their narratives end abruptly at 1965. As Pamela Allen writes: 'Despite efforts by a small number of writers to revitalise "low Malay" literature in the early 1960s the category "Chinese-Indonesian literature" for all intents and purposes ceased to exist, (2003: 7–8).

Many ethnic Chinese had assimilated into mainstream Indonesian culture, and claimed that these policies made little difference. Over many generations, Chinese cultural identity in Batavia/Jakarta had lost some of its distinctness from non-Chinese Indonesian culture. Despite supposed physical markers of difference, mainland Chinese visiting Jakarta have claimed that they cannot distinguish Chinese from non-Chinese Indonesians, and many contemporary

Chinese-Indonesians simply consider themselves Indonesians. However, the perception of difference has persisted, demonstrated, for example, by impediments to civil and military service for Chinese Indonesians, and a requirement for Chinese Indonesians to carry a special ethnic identification card (Heryanto, 1999: 160). In the popular imagination, Chinese Indonesians remained affluent foreigners, a perception fueled around 1998 by well-publicized statistics, such as that 'Chinese are 3% of the population, but control 70% of the economy.'[17] Kusno, in describing popular perceptions of Chinese under Suharto's New Order, captures major components of their racialization:

> As Chinese cultural practices have been extruded as mere 'difference,' this social group is susceptible to extra-national signification and being made an unimaginable community of the nation. They are largely visualized through a series of narrowly bounded abstractions by which their cultural signs and identities are fixed to 'money,' their sense of community reduced to 'exclusivity,' and in the optic of the nationalist, their loyalty disappointingly 'transnational.'
>
> (2000: 165)

Though this *masalah Cina* (the Chinese problem) is, of course, an issue specific to the postcolony, this notion of a local prosperity linked to an exclusive transnationality has provoked anxiety towards the Chinese from pre-colonial and colonial rulers as well. Although the Suharto administration's policy of universal assimilation is manifestly opposite to the Dutch colonial policing of difference, the perception of Chinese difference repeatedly resurfaces in times of crisis.

For two days, in May 1998, rioters in Jakarta burned and looted shops belonging (or presumed to belong) to Chinese-Indonesians. Of considerably greater trauma were stories that soon came out of gang rapes of Chinese women. According to the primary investigating NGOs, there were about 150 women, almost all ethnically Chinese, raped during that period. There were stories not only of women being assaulted on the streets, but in their homes, and of them being pulled from cars (which were then set on fire) and raped on the streets in front of cheering crowds. This was in the midst of the overthrow of Suharto, and the generally progressive and optimistic spirit of *reformasi* was dealt a profound blow by this shameful event. There has been a complex progression of attempts to come to terms with it. As after 1740, many ethnic Chinese have left Indonesia. The government has repealed various New Order policies to suppress Chinese identity. Many non-Chinese artists have taken up the 'Chinese problem.'

Seno Gumira Ajidarma, one of the most popular younger Javanese authors, wrote two connected short stories very soon after the riots. *Clara* and *Jakarta 2039* started as related short stories published shortly after the

Figure 2.4   Clara flees 'to the ends of the earth' in a vain attempt to become 'quiet, alone and at peace,' in Asnar Zacky's comic book adaptation of Seno Gumira Ajidarma's *Jakarta 2039*, 2001 (© Asnar Zacky)

riots. Both stories were printed in the collection *Iblis tidak pernah mati* (*The Devil Never Dies*, 1999). A comic book version of *Jakarta 2039* with drawings by Asnar Zacky (Figure 2.4) was published by Galang Press in Yogyakarta in May 2001. The same year, the play version of *Jakarta 2039* was printed by Galang in the collection, *Mengapa Kau Cilik Anak Kami?* (*Why Are You Abducting Our Children?*, 2001). It has received several performances in Yogyakarta and Jakarta.

In the first story, Clara gives the report of her rape to a Jakarta police inspector. The report itself, which forms the main body of the text resembles personal accounts published in Indonesian magazines at the time. Around this, the police inspector narrates his perspective as an agent of the state, duty-bound to afflict a new violence against Clara by forcing her to relate all the particulars of the event. He is skeptical that such a thing could have happened ('is there actually some sinister political purpose she's pursuing by making such accusations?'), but he admits his own dislike of her as another one of those exclusive, wealthy, foreigners ('the 3% of the population who control 70% of the economy'). At one point, he admits that she's cute and he might like to rape her himself.

The second story takes place 40 years and nine months later in 2039. We learn that Clara had a daughter of this rape, but was so ashamed and trauma-tized that she abandoned the child to an orphanage. She wandered the earth, trying to escape the past, but ultimately came back to Jakarta, and now lives alone and lonely. We see the daughter grown to adulthood, alone and lonely in another part of the city, not knowing who her parents were. And finally, we see one of the rapists, now an old man, who on his deathbed confesses to his own grown daughter what he did on that day. This daughter, who loves her father, turns her face away from him, looking out the window into the city as he draws his last breath. Contrary to national myths of progress, Ajidarma imagines a future Indonesia haunted by these racial crimes, these racializing crimes denying the national image of *satu bangsa, yaitu Indonesia* (one people who are Indonesian). Three different isolated rooms spread across Jakarta are the legacy for the national community. In the play version, the figures appeared each in separate acting areas, their faces illuminated in their confessions to the audience, but unavailable to each other.

In boldly taking up 'the Chinese problem' after three decades of enforced oblivion, *Jakarta 2039* and other post-1998 works struggle to rediscover a way to discuss race in Indonesia beyond the comfortable ethnic categories of Indonesian 'diversity.' Ajidarma walks a very fine line between presenting and reinforcing problematic assumptions. In the first story, racism and violence are portrayed as symptomatic of the police and the government, not a wide-spread failing of Indonesian society. The second story, however, challenges this common scapegoating by showing the rapist as an ordinary Indonesian who went on to be a good father and model citizen. More troubling is Clara herself, who fulfills many stereotypes (she is rich, driving a BMW; her father is an affluent businessman; when she is troubled, she expatriates herself easily). Clara, like the common Indonesian perception of ethnic Chinese, is a transnational subject, enabled by affluence to view her Indonesian identity as contingent. Nevertheless, she wanders to the ends of the earth but ultimately returns to her home in Jakarta. In the end, Ajidarma's protagonist is not actu-ally capable of choosing *not* to be Indonesian. Neither can she escape the racism directed against her for being Chinese. She must live in the uncanniness of a home that is the site of her own disappearance.

3
Sites of Disappearance: Expatriate Ghosts on Ephemeral Stages

Jakarta after 1949

Soon after Independence, a community of nationalist artists began gathering in the Senen market district of central Jakarta, near the center of late colonial Batavia, a few miles southeast of the old VOC town. The Napoleonic Governor-General Herman Willem Daendels (r.1808–11) had first relocated Batavia to this new spot at the turn of the nineteenth century to escape the infestation of malarial mosquitoes and to imagine a new capital on republican rather than feudal models. In the 1950s, young Indonesians arrived from throughout the new nation, embracing the postcolonial capital as a site of possibilities unavailable in their various *desa* (villages) and regional homelands. In a series of short vignettes for the literary journal, *Aneka*, collected in 1971 as *Keajaiban di Pasar Senen* (*Miracle at Senen Market*), Misbach Jusa Biran portrays this nascent postcolonial arts culture. Before 1968 when Taman Ismail Marzuki usurped Pasar Senen as a focal point for these gatherings, artists would congregate in transient locales like the Ismail Merapi restaurant. In such places, the *seniman senen* (the Senen artists) drank coffee and debated philosophy and aesthetics. Many of them, according to Misbach, aspired to make 'theatre.' When they used this word, they were never talking about any of the metonymic performance genres studied by ethnographers. Nor were they thinking of Betawi *lenong* or any other local urban genre. 'Theatre' for the *seniman senen* implied a new ideal-driven genre disconnected from village tradition as well as colonial-era commercial entertainment.

Asrul Sani, a leader of the *Gelanggang* (Arena) literary circle and later founder of the Indonesian National Theatre Academy (ATNI, Akademi Teater Nasional Indonesia), did more than any other writer to articulate the aspirations of this new generation. As for the young Fanon, it never sufficed for Sani to attempt to recover or reinvent a mythic ethnic past for the postcolony. Though born, like Effendi, as a Minangkabau (a sub-national ethnic identity that he occasionally foregrounded, as in his popular

1987 film, *Nagabonar*), Sani believed that by embracing Jakarta he had renaturalized himself as a son of the nation. As he put it in an 'intimate interview' in 1968, 'Jakarta is our mother' (Sani, 1997b),[1] the mother of a 'second birth' into a postcolonial culture transcending all sub-national ethnic affiliations. In Sani's view, this frontier of the soul, this *pesantren* (boarding school) city to which he invites the disciplined artist, offers rebirth into freedom from all the feudal and colonial hierarchies, all the 'characters' of old. It is the stage for a new revolution of the soul.

As Mohamad put it, Sani emerged at a time when 'people were speaking with increasing clarity and exuberance about a *"bangsa"* (people) and a *"tanah air"* (homeland) that would no longer take the form of a hope for an unrealized epoch' (Mohamad, 1997: 34). Sani called on his fellow Indonesians to learn to forget the past, abandon old genealogies and journey into the unknown:

> I don't want to talk about East and West anymore, because all the images I know can only be regarded from the perspective of time. Why must we divorce two people who are walking towards each other? One day we will abandon the boundaries that are interfering with our thoughts and actions, and we will regard each other without losing our own selves.
>
> (Mohamad, 1997: 44)

Sani was out of step with many of his contemporaries insofar as he imagined Indonesian identity nurturing the expression of an individualistic selfhood. It would become more common, especially under Suharto's New Order, to speak of the diversity united in one nation as consisting in a stable array of distinct ethnic cultures. This effort to break down boundaries without losing 'the self' generated anxiety for most Indonesians in Jakarta. Arriving from localities in which their social identities tended to be determined by ethnicity, culture and gender, Jakarta struck many as cold and unfamiliar, ironically foreign and alienating. The idea of an Indonesian identity with its promise of a new dignity after colonialism carried all the disruptions of an imposed modernity. Confronted with a metropole in which 'all that is solid melts into air,' communist artists looked to Marx while the *seniman senen* looked to French existentialism.

Indonesian postcolonial culture has lived in the tension between narratives of emancipatory mobility and anxieties to maintain (or re-establish) order. Although some activists and historians remember the early 1950s approvingly as a time of high ideals and real democracy, there is little doubt that deepening perceptions of social chaos abetted President Soekarno in his increasingly authoritarian stance, culminating in his imposition of 'guided democracy' in 1957. By 1953, a debate had begun to rage about a 'crisis' in the arts as well. Though critics never fully agreed on the nature or existence of this supposed crisis, many felt that it had something to do with an incapacity of Indonesians to make use of their new freedoms to create great works. Sani embraced the term 'crisis' with some irony, countering that no meaningful art can be created except in a state of crisis. However, for many artists operating in the new national culture, their separation from the social context in which most Indonesians lived cast suspicion over everything they did. Misbach portrays this situation with wry humor in his story, 'Roby, alias Ibnu Saad & Nandi, Servant to Dramatic Art' (Biran, 1971).

A group of young men have gathered at the Ismail Merapi restaurant to discuss plans to put on a play. The matter of the play is left fairly obscure as serious concerns of funding and advertising and venue are debated. Indeed, these were new problems from the perspective of village performances where social conventions dictated patronage, audience and venue. However, at this little restaurant, these high-minded young men looked only to their own fervor and sincerity with no need to respect the mores of their village cultures. With gleeful abandon, they drew from universal humanism, French existentialism, Italian neo-realism, and so forth. As in the Left Bank or Greenwich Village, these freshly urbanized villagers embraced what Schechner dubiously termed 'a culture of choice.' At the story's climax, Nandi, the 'Servant to Dramatic Art,' presents his play. It turns out, however, that what he has written is not actually a play, but merely a prologue or preamble to future plays:

'All present are lovers of art. In the name of the friends of the producer, above all allow me to pay my respect and my honorable greeting, in the willingness and pure hearts of all present for joining in helping our efforts, whose honest results we will deliver one hundred percent to our children who are not happy, because they have no mothers or fathers any longer. And in the name of all you dramatic artists, once again I give honor and warm greetings for the attention that you have already given us, you lovers of dramatic art who with such pure hearts provide whatever is needed to us for the development of dramatic art in particular and national culture in general. Dramatic art, these days has already had its name defiled by tramps, adventurers who are only responsible to their own stomachs or who are not responsible to anyone or anything. We will ...' And so on, and so forth.

(Biran, 1971: 17–18)

Though Misbach's stories are inflected with nostalgia for these fervent early years of the republic, he recalls here a disillusionment already evident in the life of the postcolony. The ideals of the Revolution had settled into a perpetual 'prologue' to a play that remained unwritten.

Postcolonial Jakarta epitomized the problem itself. Like so many other postcolonial metropoles, it became the focus (and often the only recipient) of development and progress. At the same time, the constant stream of poor villagers arriving to find work turned Jakarta into a center of Indonesian poverty. As Sani eloquently articulated, Jakarta was uniquely suited as the center of postcolonial imagination because, in a spectacularly heterogeneous nation, only such a city could serve as neutral territory. Somewhat like the ideal of the District of Columbia, it was a space equally independent from every region of the nation, which every citizen must cross a border to enter. By the same token, however, Jakarta was equally strange to all, and through its strangeness, the spectre of the foreign has continued to haunt national culture. In a 1952 speech, Vice-President Mohammad Hatta attempted to reconcile the contradiction:

> the Indonesian city was built from without and became a center of foreign power. It is not a place where handicrafts or national economic activities have developed but is primarily a center for the distribution of foreign produced goods. That is why our cities are not capable of filtering the foreign cultures that come here [...] Now that we are consciously building up our culture, the center of this culture-building will be in the cities, too. Let us clean them out and fill them with the national spirit. We must be cautious and selective in the face of foreign cultures. Take the core and throw away the peel!
>
> (Hatta, 1952, translated in Kusno, 2000: 149)

As Hatta's language suggests, Jakarta inspires the sort of organismic ambivalence that Cheah describes in relation to postcolonial nationalism in general. As a foreign legacy, the capital must be animated with the soul of the people. However, its ghosts can never be exorcised, and its contemporary citizens live an uncanny double life. Indeed, as with so many metropoles, the desire to live in Jakarta is typically tempered with profound alienation.

As postcolonial Jakarta has become, by some estimations, the world's fourth largest city, it seems to most a disaster of urban planning.[2] For example, in February, 2007, exceptionally severe annual floods displaced tens of thousands from their homes, and most especially those living in the poorest *kampongan* by the Ciliwang river. In June of that year, Jose Rizal Manua directed a production of Sani's 1987 play, *Abang Thamrin dari Betawi* (*Brother Thamrin of Betawi*) at Taman Ismail Marzuki (TIM). The play is a homage to Mohammed Husni Thamrin, one of the pre-war heroes who had worked for justice within the colonial legislature in the 1920s. In one scene, my character asks Thamrin what he would do if he were elected to the city council. The young patriot (portrayed by *sinetron* actor, Teuku Zacky) replies with incorrupt clarity:

> I want Batavia to be free of flood. Floods bring suffering, and spread disease. I see my friends carried off by flood. I see my companions die from malaria. I feel numb seeing the place where my friend's mother cleans rice with brown water. I see the muddiness of the *kampong*. I want

it all to change. The roads must be paved. Flood eliminated, drinking water should be clean water [...] we must make a canal that cuts into the Ciliwung and carries its overflow into the Krukut.

(Sani, 2007: 18)

This 'campaign promise' elicited the most heartfelt applause of each performance. Many of the spectators had attended as supporters of the production's primary sponsor: Jakarta gubernatorial candidate, Fauzi Bowo.[3] The applause conveyed the implication that a new governor, 80 years later, might finally improve one of the city's most intractable infrastructural failures.

Indeed, this has been one of the recurring themes of the urban discourse from the colonial era on. A terrible epidemic raged through Batavia from 1733 to 1738, claiming 85,000 victims amongst VOC personnel alone, and mortality rates remained staggering (around 50 percent for new arrivals) for the remainder of the century. Peter van den Berg has argued that this new 'unhealthiness' was the result of malaria spread by mosquitoes bred in the coastal fishponds north of the *kasteel*, that the effects were localized to the old city, and that it was mainly new recruits from Europe who succumbed (P. van den Berg, 2000). Nevertheless, the effects and rumor of disease contributed to the economic decline of the company towards its dissolution in 1799. Further, the fact that victims were mainly newcomers helped spread Batavia's global infamy. Captain James Cook, for example, wrote in his diary in 1770 that 'The unwholesome air of Batavia is the death of more Europeans than any other place upon the Globe' (Cook, 1968: 364). As the cyclical crises of postcolonial Jakarta have come to epitomize the stagnation or decline of each subsequent national and municipal regime, so the failure of late eighteenth century Batavia came to epitomize the collapse of the VOC, and of the complex society for which it had stood. The dream of participating in a culture of transnational affluence is haunted by the persistence of poverty. The utopic or heterotopic aspects that allowed Batavia and Jakarta to become cities of imagination for their respective populations never fully escaped the converse experience of alienation from legitimate sources of life, whether in Java or Europe. The postcolonial metropole metonymizes the nation as that space where the organismic metaphor is experienced at its greatest intensity and contradiction.

Cryptic memorials for distant homelands

On 29 March, 1757, nearly a century and a half after the founding of Batavia, the office of the High Regent issued a decree granting permission for Gabriel Besse du Pouget, an old sub-lieutenant of the Dragonder Lijfwacht, to transform his failing gentlemen's boardinghouse into the first permanent Dutch theatre in the city's history.

The decimation of arriving Europeans after the epidemic of 1733, coupled with the general decline of the town following the massacre of 1740, had greatly thinned the arrival of lodgers, and the Regent agreed to allow du Pouget to attempt something more profitable. However, the Council did not view a professional theatre as equivalent to any other honest business, and thus issued along with their permission an additional 19 articles of stipulation. The theatre would be maintained by its managers, inspected regularly, and subjected to the eminent domain of the Council. Each production would require a license from the Regents, along with the extraordinary requirement, laid out in Article 16, for an ambitious calendar, changing with each fortnight:

> For fourteen days, and no more, either a Tragedy or a Comedy will be shown at the Theater, as well as a Farce. And there will in the same fourteen days include a Divertissement, wherein the Acrobats, Vaulters (Voltiseerders) and Dancers show their Arts.
>
> (van den Berg, 1904: 108–9, 184)[4]

Evidently, the Regents greeted du Pouget's proposal not with the generous support one might hope for with such a difficult new venture, but with the same control applied by the Company to all private ventures. It was permitted, to be sure, and given a measure of independence, but with such financial constraints as would severely impair solvency.[5] Further, the imposition of a two-week run for each production prevented even popularity from generating significant profits. Thus, from the very beginning, professional theatre in Batavia was plagued by daunting bureaucratic and financial impediments.

Apart from du Pouget's background as a soldier and landlord, no evidence survives to suggest he knew anything of theatre. Nevertheless, he demonstrated a determination to counter the prevalence of native and Chinese theatre (and the occasional visits by French and Portuguese troupes) with a truly Dutch theatre. Not, that is, a theatre built on works of or about the Batavian colony, but a theatre bringing to the colony works from the Amsterdam stage. Van den Berg records two plays produced under du Pouget's tenure. The *Bataviasche Schouwburg* opened in 1757 with a production of the most famous play by Jan de Marre, that same sailor-poet who had composed an epic ode to Batavia three decades earlier before returning to a successful career with the Amsterdam Schouwburg. The play, *Jacoba van Beieren*, was a historical tragedy in the French neo-classical style about a fifteenth-century leader of Holland who had made of herself a martyr against the imperial expansion of Philip of Burgundy. Du Pouget followed this production with Claes Bruin's five-act tragedy, *De dood van Willem den eersten, Priins van Oranj*, dealing with the heroic sacrifices of the late seventeenth-century Dutch monarch. Both plays had premiered at the Amsterdam Schouwburg in the previous generation (de Marre's in 1738,

Bruin's in 1726). Both treated historical Dutch subjects appropriate to a nascent nationalist literature. It seems likely that du Pouget and the Regents thereby intended to educate Batavians in a heroic version of the history of the Dutch fatherland.

No reports survive attesting to how these productions were received. Regardless, it is unsurprising for the reasons outlined above that in May 1760, du Pouget sold the theatre to a burgher named Jan Adam Keijser. From this point on, the history of the *Bataviasche Schouwburg* is filled more with transactions than performances. Keijser himself disappeared at some point in 1764. A citizen by the name of Joseph Clement came into possession of the estate on 4 December 1764, and petitioned the Indies Council on 21 February 1766 for redress of payment for the upkeep of the building. Clement became the focus of accusations of immorality in regard to the lodging part of the premises, and in 1770 decided to rid himself of the business. He was given permission to transfer ownership of the Lodging and Theatre to Cornelis Domburg, alderman and commissioner of the Currency Bank. Domburg was then quick to put an end to the 'problem' once and for all. On 19 February 1771, he filed a request to tear down the playhouse, ensuring that no more 'Komedie' would be staged there. The council agreed with the reservation that care be taken to ensure that the vacated grounds not come to 'harmful' uses. Their chief concern was that the open through-way might become a makeshift native or Chinese *kampong*. Thus ended Batavia's first playhouse.

A more promising though ultimately disappointing venture emerged a decade later. Jan Bouhon came from an 'acteursfamille,' and had performed at the Amsterdam Schouwburg in 1774. In July 1780, he successfully petitioned the High Regent to 'establish a Theatre (Tooneel) in the south suburbs to present the finest of Dutch drama' (van den Berg, 1904: 119). However, England's declaration of war against the Netherlands in December 1780 rapidly shifted priorities in Batavia. On 21 September 1781, on the decision of Governor-General Willem Arnold Alting, Bouhon's schouwburg shut it's doors 'until further notice.' There would be no further notice nor further attempts at a Dutch schouwburg in Batavia for the remainder of the eighteenth century. Van den Berg conjectures that Bouhon may have built a theatre that was used in the first decade of the next century by *Inschijklikheid voor Lof* (Accommodation for Praise), the colony's first amateur theatrical society (a subscription notice of 1805 features curiously specific references to boxes and seating). Nevertheless, it seems that Batavia was without any European theatre by the arrival of the British in 1811, at which point John Stockdale summarizes the preceding half-century of local theatre history in a single sentence: 'There was a theatre at Batavia, but it was soon given up' (Stockdale, 1911: 116).[6]

If 'colonial theatre' is imagined as a state-supported venture for inculcating 'superior' European literary traditions to the education and civilization of a native population, then the Batavian stage prior to 1814 appears lacking on numerous counts. Like the 1619 *Hamlet*, it suggests a kind of ghostly uncanniness, always already evident in European nationalism, but also already suggestive of postcoloniality. It was a theatre culture in which spectators rented spaces for a season, and these spaces could not possibly all be filled; in which ghosts of ladies and princes who had died for the Netherlands were summoned from the Amsterdam stage to speak through actors who might have the most tenuous of links with any sort of European past; in ephemeral buildings that themselves disappeared. Far from inculcating aspiring or lapsed Europeans into their cultural heritage, these first theatres cleared no spaces, but rather reserved spaces at each performance for the Regents themselves. In short, these theatres performed nothing so much as the ongoing disenfranchisement by trekker Regents on their limited colonial 'tours,' of blijver mestizos, peranakan Chinese, and, of course, the rest of the native population who could not attend these theatres unless as slaves. Like the elite *seniman senen* parodied in Misbach's stories, these high-minded producers of a Dutch theatre never got past the prologue to any kind of civilizing project.

The British, in contrast, took their national theatre seriously. Soon after seizing the Dutch colony from the Napoleonic regime in 1811, British soldiers set about forming an amateur theatrical society. On 6 August 1814, a subscription was announced for the erection of a temporary 'bamboo theatre' accommodating about 250 spectators (Stockdale, 1911: 138). The location was commonly known as 'French Camp,' as it had already been set out as a barracks under Daendels.[7] During its brief run from 1814 to 1816, this 'military bachelors' theatre', on the edge of the English barracks and adjacent to the Chinese market, that would become *Pasar Baroe* presented monthly offerings of Shakespeare and other English plays to English and Batavian audiences. Judging from letters in the *Java Government Gazette*, the Batavian Dutch received these entertainments politely.[8] However, there is also a story that upon news of the return of the Indies to the Netherlands in 1816, a group of Dutch soldiers demolished the theatre during a performance of *Hamlet*. The English reportedly denigrated these vandals as 'mercenaries of Jan Pieterszoon Coen,' spectrally linking their demolished stage with the memory of those British East India Company storehouses destroyed by Coen two centuries previously.[9]

Despite their exceptionalist pretensions, the British ultimately upheld the previous Dutch tradition of short-lived theatrical ventures. The Bachelor's Theatre lasted barely over a year. Nevertheless, its existence clearly inspired the Dutch to build a proper playhouse a few years later. The choice of a British administration to produce Shakespeare certainly parallels the choice of the Dutch colonial administration to produce the works of de Marre and Bruin. At the same time, the expansion of that repertoire to include contemporary comedies suggests a more nuanced view of cultural nationalism, not only through great historical tragedies but also through more popular entertainments. On at least a few occasions, the players adopted the neo-classical convention of appending original prologues, several of which were printed in the *Java Government Gazette*. In this vein, the inaugural production of *The Heir at Law* was preceded by a prologue feigning wonder that beauty and merriment might take root in such a pestilent and unpleasant clime (*Java Government Gazette*, 22 October 1814). Productions of *Henry IV* in the fall of 1815 were preceded by a panegyric to the recent British victory at Waterloo (20 April 1816). Through such gestures, the British soldiers imbued their entertainments with a spirit of timeless English cultural and military superiority. Subsequent Dutch Batavian theatres would never attain the same cultural confidence.

The Schouwburg Weltewreden

In 1818, the restored Dutch colonial government decided to build a 'state theatre,' to be occupied by a new Dutch amateur theatrical society that took its motto from Ovid's *Epistulae ex Ponto*: 'despite their failings, the will may yet be praised' (*Ut desint vires, tamen est laudanda voluntas*, 3/4: 79). This building, which remains the oldest proscenium theatre in Indonesia, was built on the site where the British playhouse had stood. It is in the style of a Dutch neo-classical schouwburg, complete with gallery, wings and an imposing pillared façade. Materials for the construction were cannibalized from the ruins of three buildings of the old city: a prison, a VOC school and a Chinese hospital. The Ovidian motto was inscribed on its gate. In its organization, the new Schouwburg (Figure 3.1) contrasted with du Pouget's venture. Under a new civilian colonial government more encouraging of free enterprise than the VOC had been, the theatre operated as its own private company under a president and a board of directors who oversaw all financial and artistic concerns. Its administration reverted to the Batavian government in 1848, became independent again in 1884 due to financial difficulties (and the dissolution of the Ut Desint company), and at last returned to government administration from 1911 until the end of colonial rule in 1942. Though a modest facility by European standards, the Schouwburg remained the most prestigious theatre building in Batavia/Jakarta, arguably until the construction of the Jakarta Art Center at Taman Ismail Marzuki in 1968. Over the nineteenth century, lighting technologies at the Schouwburg changed more or less in step with European developments. The interior lighting, which began in 1821 with candles and kerosene lamps, turned to gas in 1864 and electricity in 1882. Beginning as a Dutch playhouse with a resident company, there was competition from the start, especially from French performers. After the arrival of a professional troupe in 1835, the French dominated the Batavian stage for the remainder of the century. As the Weltewreden district became increasingly affluent, the Schouwburg supported business at the local Caecilia cafeteria (a theatre café operated by a Frenchman named Servais) and other theatre-themed local businesses (Lombard, 1975; Dorléans, 2002).

Figure 3.1 A view of the Schouwburg Weltewreden from the Chinese 'New Market' around 1900 (Author's collection)

When Komedie Stamboel arrived in Batavia in the 1890s, the schouwburg represented a high culture venue to which Mahieu could not hope to aspire.[10] The fact that mestizo playwrights such as Victor Ido could produce their work there (including the premiere of *Karina Adinda*) attested to a class difference between them and mestizos who did not hold European status. As Taylor argues, the Schouwburg played a vital role in the segregation of 'European' and 'Native' cultural spheres throughout the last century of colonial rule (1983: 130). It allowed trekker Europeans a space wherein they could maintain relatively 'uncontaminated' European lives and *blijver* Europeans and mestizos a space where a proper European life could be imagined. Nevertheless, for Dutch cultural nationalists in Batavia, the Schouwburg presented an ongoing frustration of their aspirations. Dutch geographer, Pieter Veth, comments archly on its repertoire in 1882:

We would be mistaken in assuming that this 'temple of art' (the Schouwburg) is still venerated by devotees of Dutch theater, for in actuality the Dutch of Batavia are consistently intoxicated by whatever smells of France. Supposing that Java had been a colony of Denmark, the playhouse would surely present Danish plays, and the singers would give us Danish songs as well. However, as Java is a Dutch colony, it is, of course, French drama they prefer.

(Veth, Snelleman and Niermeyer, 1896: vol. 3: 53)

Van den Berg openly shares this frustration throughout his history of Batavian theatre, frequently lamenting the failure of local governments and spectators to attract resident artists from the Netherlands. It was apparently a matter of some triumph for this camp when a Dutch troupe under the leadership of Louis Bouwmeester made several tours to Java from 1904–07. However, van den Berg's narrative attests to a preference of Dutch artists and audiences from the days of the *kasteel* onward for English, French or German plays. Remarkably few original plays were written by 'European' Batavian authors prior to the twentieth century. When producers did present Dutch plays, as with du Pouget's productions of de Marre and Bruin, there was inevitably a complex uncanniness generated by the summoning of ghosts from a distant homeland to a colonial stage that could never quite be Dutch. Such was the case with *Ut Desint*'s productions of the plays of Dirk Hendrik ten Kate van Loo. As the apotheosis of Dutch nationalism on the Batavian stage, these productions highlighted the spectrality of colonial life.

In describing various ways in which modern city structures may be haunted, Rayner distinguishes a kind of deadly spatialization of remembrance in the official (state) monument to the kind of spontaneous and ephemeral memorialization that may occur 'after sudden shocks and catastrophic disasters. They appear on roadsides at the site of traffic accidents.' Whereas the formal and permanent monument 'becomes a substitute for grief [that] stands in for the act of mourning' (2006, 67), these ephemeral memorials, by virtue of being performed into existence, and remaining only through repetition of performance, allow a dynamic exchange between the living and the dead. Though permanent edifices, theatre buildings partake of a similar logic to the ephemeral memorial. Unlike 'monumental space,' the 'cryptic space' of a theatre combines locality with the summoning of another past:

> its hollowness both preserves and empties itself through performance, allows remembering and forgetting to be simultaneous instead of sequential, because they are what is 'being done.' In other words, its haunted space reflects the therapeutic space of exchange both between the encrypted past and the present intersubjective space and between living and dead.

(Rayner, 2006: 70–1)

On stage, the 'message' of the dead is summoned into repetition in a space removed from its locality, but which is thereby made present as the site of the performance event. For the duration of the performance, a foreign ghost is expatriated into a new locale, transforming that locale into a surrogate site of its disappearance, and confronting performers and spectators with its potent genealogy. We may see this sort of spectral repatriation in the practices of the premiere amateur Dutch theatre troupe of the 'truly colonial' phase of the Dutch East Indies.

The Death of Jan van Schaffelaar

Like the contemporaneous stage of the European continent, Ut Desint began its career under the sway of August von Kotzebue. In the first year of the Amateur Theatre at Weltewreden (1817), fully half the productions were of works of the popular German playwright, a ratio that changed little over the 20 years of the company's existence. They also produced many works of the French repertoire and a fair amount of Shakespeare. Indeed, the Schouwburg Weltewreden had opened its doors on 21 October 1821 with a production of *Othello*. Shakespeare's tragedy was certainly thematic to the social shift of Batavia from an openly mestizo society to the regimented binarism of Europeans and Natives. The image of Dutch men in gender drag as Desdemona and racial drag as the Moor certainly suggests a more familiar configuration of colonial discourse. At the same time, this Dutch '*vaderland-sch*' theatre opened not with a work of de Marre or Joost van den Vondel or any other Dutch playwright, but an English tragedy, which, furthermore, was actually a Dutch adaptation of Jean-François Ducis's French adaptation of the same. Shakespeare flourished on the Batavian stage in the 1820s, but was generally credited to Ducis and performed in Dutch; a 'Dutch' repertoire appropriated through two layers of precisely those powers who had recently occupied Batavia.

Ut Desint moved furthest from this complexity towards a Dutch nationalist purity a few years later, during the most important war of Indonesia's colonial history. Under the VOC, the Dutch had mainly kept to Batavia and kept their dealings with the sultans and other leaders of Java and the archipelago to trade, diplomacy and subterfuge. In the aftermath of the Napoleonic Wars, as the European powers looked to carve all colonial territories into national protectorates, the Netherlands likewise assumed direct control of Batavia and spread its administrative and economic apparati much deeper into the heart of their colonies. In 1825, Prince Diponegoro of Yogyakarta, enraged by Dutch influence over the Javanese Courts and radicalized by studying in Islamic *pesantren*, launched a *jihad* against the Dutch colonial empire. Rallying substantial popular support to his cause, he harried the Dutch for five years through guerrilla tactics before surrendering in 1830. To Indonesian nationalists, this 'Java War' is recalled as the first battle of the anti-colonial struggle, and Diponegoro as the first national hero. To the contemporaneous Dutch, it was the true beginning of modern colonialism. In the aftermath of the war, a *cuulturstelsel* (cultivation system) was implemented to extract wealth efficiently from Javanese plantations, and the Dutch set themselves (like the British Raj) at the top of an appropriated bureaucracy.[11]

Van Loo was an ideal candidate to lead the cultural nationalist charge. A recent arrival in Batavia, he had been born to an aristocratic family in Amsterdam, and spent his entire childhood under French occupation. As a young man, he had been amongst the 'volunteers' for Emperor Napoleon's *gardes d'honneur*, an experience that he recalls in a set of poems published in 1815. After several more publications of poetry, he turned to drama with a verse adaptation of a 1791 prose play by Pieter t'Hoen about the Dutch hero, Jan van Schaffelaar. Van Loo's version, *De Dood van Jan van Schaffelaar, vaderlandsch treuerspel*, was published in 1820. He had apparently planned a premiere featuring the great Dutch actor, Ward Bingley, who contributes a prologue (dated 1816) to this edition praising the mettle of the Dutch people emerging from the wars, 'Each man a hero as Schaf'laar was, Each youth a Naaldwijk is!' Bingley had died in 1818, however, and I have discovered no clear evidence that the play received a European premiere prior to van Loo's departure. This opens the possibility that the production by Ut Desint at the Schouwburg Weltewreden in April 1826 was both the play's premiere, and the first premiere of an original European play in the Indies.

Jan van Schaffelaar had been a commander in a fourteenth-century war between *Kabeljaauwschen* (Cod) and *Hoekschen* (Hook) factions of the disparate low countries. When his Hook force was besieged by Cod forces in a church tower in the village of Barneveld, Schaffelaar famously flung himself from the tower in exchange for sparing his men. On the basis of this sacrifice for the people, he was retroactively hailed as a Dutch patriot in nationalist histories from the late seventeenth century on.[12] Van Loo's text opens with an epigraph taken from an 1807 poem, 'Jan van Schaffelaar,' by Hendrik Tollens:

> Let him who would Rome's CURTIUS name,
> Give SCHAFFELAAR his due,
> Who was, though lauded less by fame,
> The nobler of the two.
>
> (Tollens, 1845)

Tollens draws comparison here between the Dutch hero and Curtius, a hero who appears in an episode of Titus Livius's *Ad urbe condita*. In the year 362 BCE, according to Livius, an earthquake opened a gap that could not be filled in the midst of the Roman Forum. The oracles declared that only by sacrificing the best of Rome into this gap could the immortality of the Republic be secured. A young warrior, Marcus Curtius, responded. Offering himself to gods and country, he rode in full armor into the chasm, hereafter known as 'the Curtian Gulf' (Livius, VII: 5).

Reaching back to the fourteenth century, with further allusion to Rome, van Loo weaves a long genealogical thread, comparable to the 1619 Company men performing Shakespeare while imagining themselves descendents of Tacitus's *batavi*. In the midst of war with Java, van Loo offers the Batavian populace heroic incidents from Dutch history, treated in the style of French neo-classical tragedy.[13] At a defining moment for the emergence of Batavia as a bureaucratic (beyond merely mercantile) colonial capital, van Loo takes advantage of a swell of Dutch partisanship following restitution of sovereignty to bring viewers to the playhouse. However, he does not celebrate the fortitude of the local community, but rather summons ghosts from the battlefields of Europe.

In Van Loo's *Schaffelaar*, the developments towards the hero's sacrifice provide opportunity for an extended nationalist lesson. The title character (and his heir) model a national community, transcending internecine feudalism through universal humanism. At the end of the first act, when Schaffelaar's brother, Wouter, would charge heatedly into battle, Schaffelaar counsels, 'let us win with honour; Hold humanity still dear as the highest merit' (21) Always abjuring vengeful rage, he responds with composure in the third act, when Wouter is killed by Naaldwijk, the wrathful son of a Cod warrior slain earlier by Schaffelaar (Kate van Loo, 1820: 50). Soon afterwards, Naaldwijk himself is captured in battle and marvels at Schaffelaar's calm, to which the hero replies: 'A pointless revenge Brings nothing to the warrior. – His lofty duty Commends him only towards the good of his fatherland's soil; He is with an enduring vow to their interest bound. And he has consecrated his sword to such a noble aim, Not to avenging those who are fallen in battle' (57).

Naaldwijk is moved by these universalist sentiments, praising his erstwhile enemy as *menschenvriend* (58), and converts then and there to a new sense of duty rooted in these modern values. In a subsequent soliloquy, Schaffelaar curses the aristocracy whose 'self-interest' motivated these civil wars, 'whose cruel compulsion ravaged our dearest Fatherland' (61).

Against feudal self-interest (embodied, in the play, by the bloodthirsty Cod commander, Montfoort), Schaffelaar himself models a new Dutch citizenship, frequently invoking the people of Holland and the village of Barneveld itself as a microcosm of the *demos*. When he barricades himself in the church at the end of the third act, he proclaims 'I look to Holland for help!' (Kate van Loo, 1820: 63). In his final soliloquy, he experiences a vision (somewhat reminiscent of Macbeth's vision of Banquo's descendents) of the Dutch lineage that will proceed from his sacrifice: 'before my eyes the curtain of the future parted: My dearest fatherland, through concord strong and great' (105). This entire speech construes his sacrifice as an act of civic duty to a future Holland. And thus the *volk* appear as future surrogates to noble Schaffelaar himself. By the fifth act, it is the 'noble-minded people' whose faith stands by Schaffelaar (in the person of his 18 soldiers and then beyond) (104). Schaffelaar sacrifices himself, saying to Holland: 'You shall be safeguarded and live by my death' (114). Likewise, young Naaldwijk, converted through Schaffelaar's example, becomes like a surrogate to the slain Wouter, and Schaffelaar like a surrogate father to him. Thus, clan kinship is transgressed in the service of a new national citizenship. Following his release by Schaffelaar in the third act, the young Naaldwijk becomes a Hamlet figure, torn between duty to his oath and his desire to transcend these wars. He asks 'Does not humanity become disfigured by such a revenge?' (59), and when he sets out to try to stop the cycle of vengeance, he proclaims, 'I go only to fulfill my duty, to be worthy of Schaffelaar' (80). Even 'duty' is modernized.

One curious dimension of the play is its insistence on representing the new humanistic nationalism as the exclusive apotheosis of male warrior virtue. Whereas many other nationalist representations (including later Indonesian ones) corporealize the nation as feminine, van Loo aligns femininity with a counterproductive faciality. Schaffelaar must ultimately choose to place his duty to nation above that to his wife, Aldegunda whose decision to join her husband at the front seems a misdirecting claim of kinship. Present at the battle in the third act, she covers her face with her hands, refusing to bear witness to the violence (Kate van Loo, 1820: 65) In contrast, young Naaldwijk's mother, driven by duty to her dead husband, propels the violence. In the most vivid image of the play, she takes a veil stained with blood from clutching her husband's slaughtered corpse, and ties it around her son's arm to remind him of his vengeful purpose. A metonym of the concealed face soaked in his father's blood summons the youth to his atavistic work on the field of civil war. In his final speech, Naaldwijk asks Aldegunda to take it to Schaffelaar: 'This veil, intended that it might guide my people in the field, Must by the same token cover their hero's arm' (110). Young Naaldwijk's gesture comes too late. The veil had already guided the Cod, and Schaffelaar is dead. The Dutch nation will eventually be made whole from these warring factions, but the sacrifice cannot be prevented. If young Naaldwijk, like the Fanon of 'Algeria Unveiled,' imagines the haunted veil screening the nation's heroes from their true enemies, he nevertheless cannot silence its spectral claim. The bloody veil, though reclaimed to an organismic function, remains stained by what it has veiled.

Five months after Ut Desint's production of *Jan van Schaffelaar*, Dirk Hendrik ten Kate van Loo had been named *tooneeldichter*, a sort of dramatist laureate of the colony, no doubt in part for the service rendered by his inspiring play. At a banquet in honor of Ut Desint, he delivered a poetic recitation, invoking the band of faithful 'devotees of Thalia':

> Long last and glisten our temple,
> Sacred to good amusement!
> That each of us, its wide threshold,
> With such feeling for beauty, laid bare!
> And there the art brightly might shine,
> Where we this Peace see disappear,
> And the war sows its destruction,
> So we within, with piety ponder.

(van den Berg, 1904: 163)

Thus, in the midst of the Java War, van Loo imagines the Schouwburg itself as a 'temple' akin to the church at Barneveld, where Dutch patriots must preserve their faith for a future peace. Of course, this future peace will consist in defeat of the feudalism of petty sultans and the civilizing unification of the Indies under colonial rule. Each white man a hero as Schaffelaar was, each youth a Naaldwijk.

Jan van Schaffelaar suggest the specific uncanniness of the Schouwburg Weltewreden itself. Like that neo-classical play, this proscenium stage points

Figure 3.2   An audience at a farewell performance for Poldi Reiff at the Schouwburg, 1912 (Author's collection)

to the influence in nineteenth-century Dutch culture of a French aesthetic, itself haunted by the ancients. Located at the heart of an affluent European neighborhood, the Schouwburg monumentalized the approximation and incommensurability of Batavia to Amsterdam, its imposing pilasters almost the same, but somehow not as white (Figure 3.2). As cryptic space, the Schouwburg has been especially hospitable to transnational hauntings. During the Soekarno era, when Indonesian theatre depended most heavily on Western drama, the Schouwburg was nearly the only venue in use (so much so that one advertisement for a play at the Schouwburg in the mid-1950s wryly adds 'where else?'). In the Suharto era, the construction of Taman Ismail Marzuki (TIM) provided an excuse to allow the Schouwburg to be converted into a more profitable cinema. In 1968, the Schouwburg screened mainly Indian films; in 1970, Chinese. Despite the establishment of a foundation in 1969 to maintain the building's viability as a performance venue, little was done in this direction until the 1980s. In 1987, the Gedung Kesenian Jakarta (GKJ, Jakarta Arthouse) finally reopened. As before, it became the most elite venue in the capital, and appealed to a new rising middle class with more elaborate scenography, more comfortable facilities and stricter Western spectatorial etiquette than could be found at TIM. With the precipitous demolition of three of TIM's stages in 1991, GKJ became a primary venue for theatre festivals. In this capacity, its programming continued to emphasize internationalism. The *Jakarta International Festival of the Performing Arts* (begun in 1992), the *Festival Schouwburg* (begun in 1993, at which STB presented their revival of *Karina Adinda*) and the *GKJ International Festival* (consolidating these two previous festivals in 2004) expressly set out to participate in the global theatre festival circuit. The *Festival Alternatif GKJ* (2003), though responding to charges of exclusivity by providing a forum for local troupes, nevertheless framed this ecumenicism within the aesthetic of global experimental theatre. Finally, the *Jakarta Anniversary Festival* (begun in 1999) embraced the local by presenting Jakarta as a global city, thus emphasizing the Schouwburg's perennial role as the premiere cryptic space for the negotiation of the transnational/national city. This role contrasts tellingly with that of its primary alternative, TIM. In the mid-nineteenth century, when the Schouwburg emerged as the premiere Batavian theatre, the grounds that would become TIM served as a zoological garden (Figure 3.3) in the estate of a Javanese painter.

A zoological garden and an empty frame

Raden Saleh (1816–1880) was an anomaly in the history of Indonesian modern art, a precursor whose orientation towards Europe alienated him from his countrymen at a time when very few shared his sentiments. While growing up as a *priyayi* (minor Javanese aristocracy) youth in Buitenzorg (Bogor) to the south of Batavia, a Belgian painter recognized his talent and arranged

Figure 3.3   The zoological garden on Raden Saleh's estate in Cikini in the 1870s (Author's collection)

a scholarship for Saleh to study painting in the Netherlands in 1831. Over the next two decades, Saleh traveled through Europe, learning to paint in the style of Delacroix, appearing at various Courts and accompanying Horace Vernet (a naturalist painter) to Algiers. He finally returned to Java in 1851 and built a mansion on the southern edge of the Weltewreden district. In 1864, he bequeathed ten hectares of his ample grounds to the city of Batavia for the establishment of a Society of Plants and Animals, featuring a zoological garden. Unsurprisingly, Saleh himself had found his transition back to colonial Java difficult, and struggled in his remaining years to reconnect with his ethnic heritage. He abandoned his Batavian estate in 1867 to marry the daughter of a Yogyakarta aristocrat and live out his days in Bogor. His mansion became part of the Cikini district hospital in 1898, while the gardens remained Batavia's zoo through the 1960s.

The zoological gardens hosted a variety of performance events during those years. Most notably, they housed the Batavian Exposition of 1893 (Figure 3.4), a local response to the contemporaneous global craze for colonial exhibitions. The Exposition lasted three months (from August to November), during which time it dominated the cultural life of the city. Permits for performances elsewhere were curtailed and groups ranging from vaudeville and marionettes to *wayang wong* (an adaptation of shadow theatre with live actors) and gamelan graced the stages. Mahieu quibbled with the financial arrangement, and Komedie Stamboel lost out to a rival company, Abdulrachman's Komedie

Figure 3.4   The Batavian Exposition at the zoological gardens, 1893 (Author's collection)

Bangsawan Permata Johor. Cohen writes enthusiastically of the event as a watershed in Indies performance history, syncretically combining elements of European and native fairground entertainment:

> The exposition was a bringing together of the high and low: crafts, stalls, goods, and people from urban and rural areas throughout the colony [...] Exposition visitors participated in an event that represented the colony as a whole, articulated links between the Indies and other parts of the world, and showed that the world was modernizing.
>
> (2006: 178)

As it would happen, this fairground aesthetic presaged the role that would be served by the Jakarta Art Center at Taman Ismail Marzuki (TIM), built on those same grounds, 75 years later. Whereas the Schouwburg always looked outward towards filling the metropole with the ghosts of distant homelands, TIM looked to instill the municipal culture and its modern theatre with local ethnic cultures, clearing a space for *kampongan* culture within *gedongan* culture.

In the early twentieth century, the estates in the southern area of Weltewreden known as Menteng subdivided into a more affluent suburb. The adjacent Cikini district, which had housed Saleh's estate, was subsequently engulfed by the expanding city. In 1949, the name of the Society changed to Kebun Binatang Cikini (Cikini Zoo) with the grounds being more broadly known as Taman Raden Saleh. A cinema called Garden Hall operated in the zoo during the 1950s, and in 1964 the city government resolved to relocate the zoo to a much larger site in the Ragunan area of Pasar Minggu, a process completed in 1966 under the leadership of Jakarta governor, Ali Sadikin. This relocation of Jakarta's curated wilderness to the new periphery of the metropole fortuitously cleared a space for the first postcolonial arts complex in Southeast Asia.

In building TIM, Sadikin responded to the interest of artists marginalized with the ascendance of the communist Lekra cultural organization in the early 1960s. Many of these artists had been blacklisted as signatories of the *manikebu* (cultural manifesto), a declaration of independence from political ideology published in 1963 (Darmowijono, 1964; Foulcher, 1986; Mohamad, 1993; Foulcher, 1994; Moeljanto and Ismail, 1995; Maier, 2004: 418–20). With the destruction of the Communist Party following the *gestapu coup* in 1965, these demonstrably non-communist artists emerged (or, in many cases, re-emerged) as the Generation of '66, a cultural bloc ostensibly allied to Suharto's New Order. In keeping with their insistence on the separation of arts and politics, Sadikin established the Jakarta Arts Council (DKJ), an independent body of artists fully entrusted with administering the new arts center, and the center itself opened in 1968 as the first independently administrated national arts center in Southeast Asia. Cobina Gillitt describes the 'happening' staged by Arifin C. Noer and his *Teater Ketjil* at the opening ceremony:

> a guerilla take over with a procession of 27 people in bright costumes, including a 4 person barong, masks, and a baptism led by Arifin. A poetic invocation/prayer with such statements as 'When we open this Arts Center what will we have? The wind. Wind neatly packaged and promised to us all [...] This Art Center is a jungle from our Indonesia which is still a jungle and from the edge we pledge forcefully: we want to cut it down.' Then they unveiled the gates, and presented Governor Sadikin with three gifts: a 'self-portrait,' consisting of an empty frame which the governor held in front of his face; a shattered mirror; and a personal letter addressed to the Governor and written in white ink on white paper. The performers scurried away and disappeared behind the crowd.
>
> (Gillitt, 2001: 214–15)

Each of these acts celebrates the clearing of space against the interference of government, convention and locality. Performative metonymies of local traditions are incorporated into an avant-garde ritual procession. Natural metonymies of Indonesia are transplanted and pledged to deconstruction. Finally, the governor is given the blank page, the subverted reflection: the empty portrait. These are all gestures of fluidity and negation proclaiming that TIM will be a cryptic rather than a monumental space, haunted by absent writings, absent representations, absent faces. There would be a similar lingering with negation at the moment of Suharto's resignation in 1998, as artists attempted to begin to imagine a frame not filled with his ubiquitous portrait.

In order to accommodate a full range of modern theatrical activity, as well as local ethnic traditions, TIM incorporated four stages: Graha Bhakti Budaya (a proscenium auditorium seating approximately 800 spectators), Teater Arena (an indoor arena stage), Teater Tertutup (a flexible black-box theatre) and Teater Terbuka (an open amphitheatre seating 1500 spectators, Figure 3.5). However, as the design strove to accommodate traditional and experimental Western and Indonesian spatial paradigms, the configuration of open space evoked a large-scale implementation of a village layout. At Sadikin's prompting, the architect, Tjong Pragantha, visited a modern arts complex in Hawaii and also conducted a survey of architectural styles in Indonesia to arrive at his hybrid design:

> Designing the architecture of PKJ-TIM seemed a difficult challenge for me [...] because it had to reflect the uniqueness of Indonesian architecture [...] We borrowed the basic idea from the architecture of Java and Bali.
>
> (Padmodarmaya, 1994: 31–2)

Although TIM comprised Jakarta's most prominent *gedongan* theatre complex, it did so on grounds modeled after a *kampongan* spatial model.

These two forces were not easily synthesized. The rise of an Indonesian middle class in the 1980s supported the refurbished reopening of the Schouwburg in 1987 as the Jakarta Arthouse, re-establishing that building as the most elite theatrical venue in the city. At the same time, TIM saw a decline in state subsidies leading, with some misgivings, to a greater reliance on corporate sponsorship. Plans to renovate TIM began to circulate, encouraging some perennial activities, such as the Youth Theatre Festival, to cease. In late 1996, anticipating the construction of a new modern theatre building that would incorporate a 2000 to 3000-seat proscenium theatre and several smaller stages, TIM's Arena, Tertutup and Terbuka stages were all demolished (along with various rehearsal and exhibition halls), leaving only the large proscenium theatre for performances. In 1997, the Asian monetary crisis (*krismon*) brought all such grand construction projects to a halt, and so things remained for another decade. When I visited in 1999, the site of these three lost theatres and the interconnecting plaza space so central to TIM's spatial hybridity were a vast pool of use mainly to fishermen and birds (Figure 3.6). Gillitt reports from a 2001 visit 'rumors flying that a mega shopping mall was going to be erected instead' (2001: 103). Indeed, the building that was ultimately erected later that decade is an imposing shell of overlapping glass and metal curves, clearly designed to impress corporate sponsors (Figure 3.7). As of July 2007, only the lobby, a gallery and a *Little/Studio Theatre* were available for use (this last being another proscenium space of approximately the capacity of the old Teater Tertutup). As of 2008, TIM is

Figure 3.5   The Teater Terbuka (Open Stage) at Taman Ismail Marzuki, 1974 (Author's collection)

still considerably reduced from the complement of performance spaces it possessed in the 1970s. Meanwhile, rental costs have increased, and younger theatre artists complain that they cannot afford to take advantage of the new artistic freedoms accompanying the fall of Suharto. Some theatre artists have looked to smaller gallery venues. Others, such as W. S. Dindon of *Teater Kubur*, one of the most promising younger troupes to emerge in the late 1980s, have abandoned *gedongan* theatre culture altogether to work in the urban *kampongan*.

Figure 3.6 View of Graha Bhakti Budaya from across the open pool created by the demolition of the Teater Terbuka, 1999 (Author's collection)

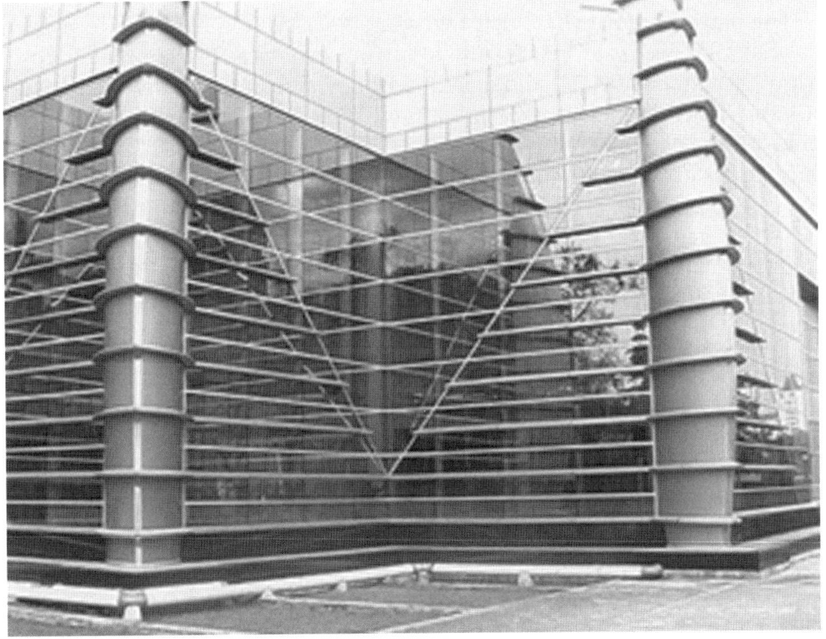

Figure 3.7 The exterior shell of the new theatre building at Taman Ismail Marzuki, 2004 (Author's collection)

Though technically a municipal institution of the special administrative province of Jakarta, TIM was regarded from its inception as a national theatre. As Suharto's New Order centralized the flow of development through the capitol city, so TIM (commanding resources far in excess of any regional arts center), imported a constant flow of regional performance traditions while offering modern artists the best facilities and broadest freedoms for producing their work. This centralization of modern theatre at TIM from 1968 to the 1990s is especially evident in its monopoly on modern theatre festivals and conferences. Whereas in the Soekarno era, major festivals had rotated between Jakarta, Yogyakarta, Bandung and a handful of other cities, this parity disappeared under the New Order, largely due to the allure of TIM. A few months before TIM opened, in June 1968, the model for such meetings was set by a Jakarta Drama Week (*Pekan Seni Drama DCI Djaja*) conducted under the auspices of the Hotel Indonesia, where Teguh Karya's Teater Populer had established itself as a resident company. This event featured lectures by many familiar luminaries of the Soekarno era and presentations of the winning entries in a national playwriting competition in which Arifin C. Noer, Putu Wijaya and Kuntowijoyo took top honors. This was followed in 1969 by a Three City Theatre Conference (*Pertemuan Teater Tiga Kota*) with Arifin representing Jakarta, Rendra representing Yogyakarta and a Teater Perintis representing Bandung.

The participants at these first two conferences would continue to preside over similar events at TIM for the following two decades. Nano Riantiarno, who had attended ATNI and acted with Karya's Teater Populer in the mid-1960s, joined the circle as a prominent director in his own right in the mid-1970s. With Wisran Hadi and A. Alin De (both from Padang, Sumatra) and Aspar (from Ujungpadang, Sulawesi) as regular guests from outside Java, Rendra, Noer, Wijaya, Karya, Anirun and Nano Riantiarno defined the TIM-centered theatre world. The diversity and productivity of their work certainly supports Jakob Sumardjo's designation of the 1968–78 period as a 'second golden age' of modern Indonesian theatre. Nevertheless, this small group of reigning male directors increasingly bore an unsettling resemblance to the Javanese patriarchies ruling the nation. As memories of pre-1968 theatre dimmed, a proliferation of retrospectives on institutions and individual troupes and artists reimagined modern Indonesian theatre vis-à-vis hagiographies of these aging male directors. Like Suharto, who most of them reviled, these directors, in their seeming monopoly over productivity increasingly came to represent an establishment that had failed to provide opportunities for the next generation. Noer died in 1995, as did Karya and Anirun in 2001, but these losses have merely diminished the canon without heralding the rise of a new generation. As of 2007, Wijaya and Riantiarno continue to dominate the productive and discursive life of Jakarta theatre. That empty frame presented by Noer to Governor Sadikin in 1968 had been filled with a cozy family portrait and put on permanent display.

The struggle to fulfill TIM's promise as a safe haven for the development of a national theatre is perhaps most poignantly evident in the fortunes of its greatest initiative to develop artists beyond this celebrated coterie. In 1973, TIM presented the first in what became an annual festival organized by the Arts Council to address the lack of opportunities for troupes outside the established luminaries. The level of participation suggested by statistics presented in a 1985 Council publication indicate a quantity of theatrical activity during the 1970s vastly exceeding the work of these few. At the high water mark, in 1976, 143 theatre troupes participated. However, the workings of this *Festival Teater Remaja* also tell the story of the institutionalization of the golden age luminaries in parallel with the consolidation of Suharto's New Order. The term 'Remaja' (youth, adolescent or junior) carried significant connotations, given that the festival was presented as a means by which 'immature' groups might demonstrate their worthiness to be allowed the opportunity to perform regularly at TIM. Troupes could pass through a 'finalist' stage, to vie to become one of the coveted groups called *dibina* ('promoted' or 'upgraded') in a similar sense to how Suharto claimed to *membina para petani* (upgrade the farmers). This final circle (out of which first, second and third place winners were chosen) was achieved by no more than a tenth of the competing groups in each of these ten years. Troupes that managed to do this three times (a significant feat against so much competition) would be accorded the designation 'senior.' Only troupes that had achieved this coveted designation (and, of course, the established luminaries) could gain permission to perform regularly in the theatres at TIM. Over 30 years of the festival, a total of 22 groups reached this status (Dewan Kesenian Jakarta, 2006: Vol. 2, 4). A few important troupes, such as Teater Sae, managed to navigate this gauntlet. Nevertheless, given the numbers involved, the Festival must be seen as a roadblock to a theatre craze that might have filled the seasons of dozens of playhouses in 1970s Jakarta if such alternatives had existed. The Festival Teater Remaja was evicted during TIM's ill-fated renovations, during which time its function reverted to more local festivals conducted within each of Jakarta's five districts. Indeed, this unsought decentralization presaged the spirit of the post-Suharto era, but did little to diversify participation at the highest echelon of Indonesia's modern theatre.

Although Rendra was arguably the most senior theatre luminary associated with TIM, he was the most reluctant to consider himself a 'member.' He affiliated increasingly with TIM in the mid-1970s due to a police ban that prevented him from performing in his native Yogyakarta beginning in 1974. Thus, he brought his most famous play, *Kisah Perjuangan Suku Naga* (*Story of the Struggles of the Naga Tribe*) to premiere there in 1975. This was a stinging irony given that the play portrays the vitality of development originating in Javanese *kampongan* values rather than proceeding from a condescending patriarchal government in a decadent, alienated and co-opted capitol (Winet, 2005). That same year, Rendra received the first Art Award from the Jakarta

Academy. In his reception speech, he identifies himself with the *punakawan* (clowns) of *wayang* who offer constructive criticism without agitating for regime change. These *goro-goro* scenes are useful, he coyly suggests, for differentiating between noble princes who recognize the value of criticism and coarse ogres who do not. Rendra then proceeds to give the Jakarta Academy a respectful gift in the form of *goro-goro*. He muses on the purpose of an academy by which he further considers the purpose of *gedongan* culture in general. At one extreme, he quips that academies are 'schools impoverished in method and also greedy for the conclusions of foreign thinking without the capacity to digest them well!' (Rendra, 1983a: 79–80). He muses on the Académie Française as a hegemonic force of monarchical neo-classicism that only Molière successfully resisted. Indeed, his own *kampongan* digestion could not stomach this sophisticated academy fare (80).

Nevertheless, the members of the Jakarta Academy could be seen from a *kampongan* perspective as *empu*, defenders of the spiritual values of society. He acknowledges that throughout Indonesian history, there have been times (times of social change, especially) in which the king has called on *empu* to serve in the palace. This is always a partial (and, we might add, uncanny) operation: 'I don't mean that they change the intellectuals into technocrats, but I mean they are incorporated all the same, but only just half-incorporated.' At the same time, there have always been other *empu* who refused to become 'half-incorporated' in this way, and to continue 'living in the air.' For, as Rendra bluntly puts it, 'I can't believe that there is a person who can develop fully while he lives in the air and at the same time lives in the palace or in the council' (1983a: 83) Institutions such as the Jakarta Academy, the Jakarta Arts Council and TIM itself serve a purpose, which is to 'expand spiritual and bodily values until they materialize as a formula that can be implemented' in government arts policies (82). However, this cannot substitute for the true spiritual work of art that can only take place 'in the air.' I was reminded of this rhetoric in June 1999, when I stayed with Rendra at his home in Cipayung, on the rural southern periphery of metropolitan Jakarta. The extensive estate operates as a theatrical commune in which actors work the land amidst training and rehearsal. I spoke to Rendra once upon his return from a conference of artists discussing the shape of Indonesian art after Suharto. He laughed remembering them asking him his position. '*This*,' he spread his arms to indicate the grounds of his estate, its cultivated nature modeling the greater nature, its individual microcosms extending into the cosmos. '*This* is my *position.*'

On 1 May 1978, TIM's role as a safe haven for Rendra to visit from his sojourns 'in the air' ended. Partway through a poetry reading in the Terbuka amphitheatre, someone tossed in six plastic ammonia bombs from outside the walls. Several spectators suffered nausea, but several encircled Rendra, shouting 'we will protect you here.' The poet continued, proclaiming, 'This unwarranted disturbance was [an act of] terror. It was an anti-civilization element. It was an element that embarrasses the nation' (Anon., 1978). As Gillitt chronicles, Rendra was subsequently arrested for three months under Dutch Hatred Articles 'on the grounds of inciting the masses and disturbing the peace. Although Rendra himself didn't instigate the violence through a direct call to the audience, police Lieutenant Colonel Anas Malik reportedly said that his poetry, and especially the "sound" of it was dangerous' (Gillitt, 2001: 197) The actual perpetrator of the attack was never apprehended. In the aftermath, Rendra was banned from performing in Indonesia until 1985. In the following decade, artists presenting at TIM took greater care to submerge controversial social and political stances in abstraction and absurdism. The 'golden age' effectively came to an end.

Tableaux at the ephemeral centers of struggle

The Schouwburg and TIM stand out as *gedongan* venues with enduring roles in the spatial discourse of the city and nation. Various other spaces have played more fleeting or more recent roles. For example, Cohen discusses the Mangga Besar square (in the Chinese district of the old city) as the site where commercial troupes such as Stamboel typically set up their tents in the 1890s. From at least 1911, a Komedie/Gedung Thalia (invoking the neo-classical tragic muse) housed opera derma in the same area, and Dewi Dja recalls Dardanella performing in the same building in the 1920s and 1930s while Miss Riboet's Orion performed in the nearby Pal Merah. Andjar Asmara's most famous play, *Dr Samsi*, premiered in this building, and when Dja and her fellow Dardanella veterans reunited for a post-Independence revival of the play in 1959, they opened in the Schouwburg and then performed three more nights at Thalia (Ramadhan, 1982: 75, 89, 296). This building, which may also have served as a movie theatre, apparently did not survive the Soekarno era. Beginning in the late 1980s, various smaller stages opened in response to the rising costs and limited access to TIM and GKJ. Rendra began sponsoring performances at his compound in 1988, a Teater Dalam Gang Tuti Indra Malaon opened in 1993 (in honor of a leading actress who had worked often with Teater Populer), and Ray Sahetapy opened a performance space called Teater Oncor in 1989 (Bodden, 2002: 302–4). Likewise, various foreign foundations in Jakarta (most notably the Goethe Foundation, Erasmus Huis and the Japan Foundation) began sponsoring performances in their own facilities. In 1995, Goenawan Mohamad joined in an initiative to form another independent art center with funding from the Ford Foundation. The studio theatre of this Utan Kayu Community opened in 1997, and has become a primary venue for experimental theatre and dance. It fills a similar niche to that previously occupied by TIM's Teater Arena. Recognition of the significant roles played by these peripheral spaces in national discourse counters the tendency to locate theatre history entirely within the most prominent and easily legible theatre buildings and complexes.

In the 1920s and 1930s, urban theatre groups such as Dardanella and Orion that lacked European status were not permitted to make use of the Schouwburg. Likewise, to the extent that the *Poedjangga Baroe* playwrights of the nationalist movement saw performances of their works staged, these took place in the peripheral spaces of nationalist congresses, a student culture adaptation of the kind of liminal space associated with festival and carnival. As the nationalist movement at the time was confined mainly to a Dutch-educated elite, it is hardly surprising that what little evidence survives of nationalist theatre performances prior to Independence suggests conditions not far removed from school. Ido had filled out his troupe with native students of the *Dokter Djawa* school in 1913. Effendi apparently had attempted to stage *Bebasari* with his own students around 1926. Yamin's *Ken Arok dan Ken Dedes* was given its premiere by the student delegates of the Second Indonesian Youth Congress, on 28 October 1928. However, none of these pre-Independence venues filled the role of a national playhouse. For its part, the Congress venue (now the Youth Pledge Museum at 106 Kramat Road) was merely a private residence that had previously served as a European school. In the late 1920s, it served as an administrative center for the nationalist movement. However, it would appear that the building's adaptation for performance was makeshift and occasional. It seems likely that many of the '39 performances' of Yamin's play were at subsequent conferences. Insofar as this suggests a nationalist repertoire, it was a repertoire dependent entirely on the circulation of printed manuscripts disconnected from any kind of producing theatrical institution, let alone a theatre building. Michael Bodden cites a teacher and artist named Sunindyo who recalls regular performances of plays by Yamin and Pane at these congresses, and also at celebrations at the end of school years. (Pane, 1953; Bodden, 1997a: 335)

As postcolonial Jakarta represented a 'city of choice' for many Indonesian nationalists, so modern theatre typically took place in the ephemeral sites of conferences and festivals. Government censorship and the lack of adequate theatre facilities certainly contributed to this. At the same time, it was only at such fleeting gatherings that the national culture truly became present. Though direct reportage of nationalist theatre performances is lacking, Alisjahbana imagines a performance of Pane's *Sindhyakala ning Majapahit* (*Twilight over Majapahit*, 1932) taking place on the last night of such a congress in his 1937 novel, *Layar Terkembang* (*Sails Unfurled*). He describes a meeting hall whose walls are covered with red and white banners (echoed on the participants' bodies by red and white cockades) and the writings of the 'Modern Youth.' However, it is the youth themselves who give life to this unpretentious space:

> Through the wide-open doors there streamed an endless procession of
> men and women, most of them adolescents and youths between fifteen

and twenty-five years old. Kebaya of various colors and styles alternated with well-ironed and variously patterned jackets and trousers, increasing the happy and joyful spectacle of this meeting space, which was only becoming more full with each passing minute.

(1995: 113)

At precisely eight o'clock the lights dim. A youth walks onstage and reviews the various resolutions resulting from the preceding conference, wishes the spectators 'beautiful and unforgettable memories' from what they are about to see, and exits:

Not long after he exited back behind the closed curtain, accompanied by boisterous applause, the purple curtain opened, undulating along its entire length. At the same time, the lights in the building went out, and on the platform there was fixed a blue light, illuminating with considerable severity the scene that appeared on the platform; several pairs of youths from throughout the archipelago wearing their assorted national costumes, looking like a large delegation delivering their various tributes. All was silent throughout the building, marveling at seeing this beautiful and absorbing spectacle. When the curtain suddenly closed again, and people were once again illuminated in the room, all the spectators awoke as from a dream. Immediately, as if it were what was intended, the sound of people applauding rose up, interrupted by continuous shouts for an encore.

(115–16)

Alisjahbana intends this parodic scene of the credulous youth taking a tableau for a full performance as part of a critique of Pane's atavism within the context of the cultural polemic. However, he also captures something of the essence of these events. A. E. Teeuw had noted the perplexing choice of Yamin and Pane to express their nationalist sentiments within melancholic historical dramas such as the two previously mentioned. Rather than presenting heroes triumphing gloriously over the colonizers (as does Effendi), these works recuperate old kings, often of dynasties long dead, at moments of painful transition in which old orders collapse, new possibilities remain uncertain and noble princes die needlessly. Then again, such anxious representations reflected the predicament of the Indonesian nationalists in the 1930s, severely restricted by the colonial government yet articulating a mythos with great determination. This brief tableau on an ephemeral stage in a makeshift theatre is a genealogical link connecting these mythic original Indonesians to the assembled youth who will attempt to inspirit the nation with this ambiguous legacy. What the crowd applauds, in Alisjahbana's narrative, is a utopic vision that recuperates an idealized past as a projective future. Suharto would look to replicate a similar vision of

Indonesian unity a half century later with the construction of the Taman Mini amusement park. Like Schaffelaar's vision of a Dutch people unified from Hook, Cod and the rest, this tableau of Indonesia imagines the nation as an organic transcendence of past fragmentation and chaos. However, like van Loo's 'temple to Thalia,' the congresses ironically performed nationalist utopia in sites far removed from the putative origins of national life. Soekarno, faced with the inverse problem, would find different ways to imagine the nation.

Soekarno's theatre in exile

As the nationalist youth struggled to clear a space for Indonesia within the colonial metropole, Dutch authorities exiled their leaders to the peripheries of struggle. Soekarno, who had risen to prominence in Bandung at the heart of the nationalist movement in the mid-1920s, was sent into detention in Ende, Flores in 1934, then moved to Bengkulu, Sumatra from 1938 until the arrival of the Japanese in 1942. As Soekarno recalls in his autobiography, the governor-general turned at this time from the previous policy of exiling troublemakers to the Netherlands, reasoning that 'internal exile' would allow for greater surveillance. During these years, Soekarno maintained his own morale and cautiously attempted to raise nationalist consciousness in the hinterlands by writing and staging 12 plays. This anomalous dramatic output from the man who would become Indonesia's first president received some belated recognition in 2006 with the publication of a study of Soekarno's theatre by Agus Setiyanto, including texts of three plays and synopses of two others. As Bakdi Soemanto notes in his foreword to the collection, Soekarno's drama developed in a direction quite distinct from the contemporaneous historical tragedies of the *Poedjangga Baroe* dramatists (though not, perhaps, so far removed from the melodramas of Hoay and Asmara). What is most striking about Soekarno's theatre, however, is the context of one of the urban nationalist elite being compelled to create works in communities far removed from the cities of Java. Ironically, the champion of a unified Indonesia was brought by detention into greater contact with the outer regions (Flores and South Sumatra) than ever before. However, he clearly struggled with alienation from these local cultures. In confronting such issues as the more orthodox Islam of Bengkulu, Soekarno cast himself as *bapak* (father) and took refuge in such trappings of urbanity as modern theatre.

Soekarno remembers his first exile, Ende, as a small fishing village (it is now Flores' largest town and center for its shipping trade): 'Besides idleness, loneliness, and friendlessness, I was also suffering acute depression. Flores was utter torture in the early days. I needed something stimulating, or I should kill myself. That's when I began playwriting' (Soekarno and Adams, 1965: 130). So, he organized the 'Toneel Klub Kelimutu,' named after Flores' famous tri-colored mountain lakes, and rehearsed his own plays in a church barn. The barn seated 500 spectators and the plays typically performed for three evenings. Soekarno recalls them as big events for Ende that even the Dutch attended. However, he recalls the working conditions with some chagrin. As conservative social values dissuaded women from involving themselves in theatre, Soekarno wrote hardly any female roles and cast men in those that remained. He wrote the plays as mere outlines, accepting the need to teach the illiterate actors their roles in rehearsal. In short, he was like a *dalang* (shadow puppeteer) orchestrating every aspect of these performances himself. Nevertheless, he left the actual direction to a Filipino named Nathan in all the plays except *Tahoen 1945*. This last work, apparently Soekarno's last before being transferred to Bengkulu, predicted that Indonesian freedom would be gained in 1945, under the cover of the coming war with Japan (145). Perhaps Soekarno felt compelled to take the direction for this last work, which presented an anti-colonial narrative more directly than his other works. At any rate, whatever consciousness-raising the 'bapak' had managed to accomplish through the Kelimutu drama club came to an end in October 1938 with Soekarno's transfer to Bengkulu (130–1; Giebels and Oen, 2001: 200; Hurek, 2007).

In contrast to Ende, Bengkulu was already a large coastal town with a more diverse population and some syncretic modern culture. When Soekarno arrived, there was already an established orchestral ensemble led by Manaf Sofiano. The ensemble had adopted the name 'Monte Carlo' to evoke the elite entertainments of the European leisure class, certainly as distant an image from a penal colony as imaginable. The cultural products of this group were typically middle class and urban – 'characteristically non-ethnic, open, urban' and modern (Setiyanto, 2006: 18). Sofiano's group would often play at parties organized by the local high society as well as Dutch officials and elite pribumi. Sofiano himself played saxophone, trumpet and piano, and became one of the leading actors in Soekarno's troupe. As a theatre troupe, Monte Carlo (Figure 3.8) made use of two venues in Bengkulu: the Gedung Royal Cinema and, less frequently, Gedung Gloria. These were both near the Dutch Administrative Center. Setiyanto confirms that Soekarno spent his first year in Bengkulu immersed in social affairs of a non-artistic nature (1938–39), especially amongst the teachers, businessmen and members of Muhammadiyah and Taman Siswa. He tried to reach the youth directly through the education system, to instill a nationalist spirit, but his activities were always restricted by the scrutiny of the *Politieke Inlightingen Dienst* (PID). As in Ende, he would find it easier to engage in consciousness-raising through theatre (20–3).

In 1939, Soekarno involved himself with the Monte Carlo ensemble to change its format more towards theatre. He took advantage of better resources and more amenable social conditions than before. Unlike Ende, Soekarno used complete scripts in Bengkulu. He tried to employ 'realistic'

Figure 3.8 A Monte Carlo performance in the Gedung Royal Cinema at Bengkulu, 1939 (Author's collection)

costuming and setting appropriate to the situations. He also used electric lighting, charged admission, sold tickets, and set age limits and rules of conduct (such as no food in the theatre), all of which were imitative of the kind of conventions of European high-culture spectatorship expected at venues such as the Batavian Schouwburg. As in Ende, Soekarno trained and rehearsed the actors over two to three week periods, generally at the home of Sofiano or that of Demang Karim. Following the conventions of professional urban theatre in Java, Soekarno stock-cast the actors: Sofiano playing protagonists, Bachtiar Karim (father of Roestam Effendi) playing antagonists, and A. M. ('Anak Marhaen') Hanafi (who would later be appointed ambassador to Cuba under President Soekarno), playing female leads. As in Ende, women's roles were always played by men. In one instance, Monte Carlo was invited to perform the play, *Koetkoetbi*, in the city of Curup, 80 kilometers from Bengkulu. Soekarno received special permission from the Dutch resident to exceed his mandated 40 kilometer perimeter, a compelling demonstration of the utility of theatre in circumventing the general apparatus of censorship (Setiyanto, 2006: 35).

Several of the plays Soekarno wrote (or rewrote) during this period represent anti-colonial struggle with surprising directness. In *Rainbow*, Soekarno depicts a female leader, in Bengkulu itself, who protests the removal of a local leader by colonial authorities. In *Chungking Djakarta*, he imagines a coalition against the hegemony of global capitalism negotiated between Jakarta and Peking through the brokerage of the Batavian Chinese. All these are strikingly more topical than the *Poedjangga Baroe* historical dramas of the 1930s, more incendiary than the local social issue plays of Hoay and Asmara, and more global in perspective than either. One might say that they anticipate such works of wartime nationalist propaganda as Abu Hanifah's *Taufan di Atas Asia* (see Chapter 6) and provide some further insight into the mindset that allowed Soekarno to negotiate effectively with the Japanese ideology of a 'Greater East Asia Co-Prosperity Sphere.'

Soekarno also composed two plays that imagine the nationalist struggle through analogy to Hollywood horror movies. Peculiar though this approach may seem, he no doubt took some inspiration in this regard from directors of the professional theatre, such as A. Piedro of Teater Dardanella, who frequently adapted plays from American films. Though it is not clear whether Soekarno first viewed James Whale's *Frankenstein* in Jakarta or Ende, he took this film as the unlikely inspiration for his own first play, *Dr Sjaitan* (*Dr Devil*), in 1936.[14] There are less definite dates for the sequel, *Koetkoetbi*, which may have taken further influence from *The Bride of Frankenstein*.[15]

Soekarno writes of his first play, *Dr Sjaitan*, 'My character was an Indonesian Boris Karloff-type who rejuvenated corpses by transplanting the hearts from living people. Like all my works, it had a moral, the underlying message being that the lifeless body of Indonesia would somehow rise and live again' (Soekarno and Adams, 1965: 130). A pamphlet from the 1938 Monte Carlo performance at Bengkulu's Royal Cinema promotes the production (in a mix of Indonesian and Dutch) in tones evocative of a movie marquee:

'Dr. Sjaitan! A flash of LIGHTNING! Pounding RUMBLES! Rolling like THUNDER! GREAT – MIGHTY – GREAT without EQUAL! [...] *Dr. Mouzaky*, sharp-witted as an angel, typical to one who is not human, attempts to re-animate a thing that has died – thus, people call him Dr. Sjaitan! *Dr. Go Diam Tjoe*, a faithful and noble intellect, wishes to defend his companions, but he himself is destroyed as victim to the savagery of *the Monster*! *Mr. Dr. Amir*, a brilliant doctor-advocate, who pleads before the Hall of Justice, astonishing the entire judicial world! Whose soul is prepared to take responsibility for helping his brother-in-law protect the country from the wrath of the Monster [...] A GREAT STORY that will make all who have souls shudder, and set all hearts pounding!'

(Setiyanto, 2006: 199)

Soekarno deploys an original strategy here against the anticipation of censorship. Insofar as 'the Monster' is legible as a force of nationalist resistance, Soekarno could rightly claim that he depicts it as a force of evil. Insofar as his heroes are depicted as progressive Indonesians (doctors, intellectuals and advocates) who intentionally invoke this Monster, Soekarno could rightly claim that he depicts their efforts as destructive. Furthermore, as the play is explicitly promoted as an adaptation of the Hollywood *Frankenstein* (an association amplified by performing in the Royal Cinema), Soekarno could rightly insist that his play is not set in Indonesia. In any case, as in *Frankenstein*, *Dr Sjaitan*'s Monster is defeated; nationalism is suppressed. However, through the very structure of repeated performance, 'the lifeless body of Indonesia would somehow rise and live again.' It would also rise and live again in the play's sequel, *Koetkoetbi*.

This second play opens in a distant unspecified past in which the woman, Koetkoetbi, is given the death sentence by a priest, Mpu Agni, for claiming a lover of another religion (rather than Agni himself). Agni brutally kills the lover, and, ignoring traditions that stipulate her burial, subjects Koetkoetbi's corpse to a bizarre treatment. Her white funerary robes are exchanged for satanic red (thus crossing over the colors of Indonesian nationalism), her long hair is cut short, a curse written on human skin proclaiming that she will remain buried until the end of the era is placed on her coffin, and the coffin is set upside-down in a sealed cave. The second act brings us to the present day where Dr Mouzaky (recovered from the ordeals of *Dr Sjaitan*) is given an ancient stone by a farmer that indicates a tomb two millennia old. Mouzaky and Amir recover Koetkoetbi's coffin. By reading the ancient inscription, and adding a few jolts of *stroom* (electricity, but also spiritual force), they revive Koetkoetbi. Koetkoetbi detects that Amir is actually a descendent of her adversary, Mpu Agni, and enchants Mouzaky to murder him in her name. Mouzaky resists the influence, and accidentally kills one of Amir's patients. Amir is blamed, and in a lucid moment Mouzaky admits his guilt and attempts to break free of Koetkoetbi. She overpowers him, and the chase resumes. As a last course, Amir recovers the corpse of his ancestor, Mpu Agni, who turns out to be similarly entombed in another cave. They take Agni to the laboratory, and just as they are reviving him with 'stroom,' Koetkoetbi and Mouzaky return. In the ensuing confrontation, Agni kills Koetkoetbi, but then rampages against his 'apostate' descendents. He catches up with all of them at the mouth of the cave. Their various efforts to defeat him fail. He is about to kill them all when Amir's fiancée paralyzes him by uttering the name of Allah. As she uses the same mighty word to restore her fallen companions, Agni begins to recover. They are not afraid, however, for they now know how to control him.

Koetkoetbi moves in strikingly different directions than *Bebasari* or the *Poedjangga Baroe* plays. Whereas Effendi's iconic female figure is simply the object of nationalist desire, Soekarno presents the feminized nation as a reanimated corpse claiming noble youth as surrogates to her ancient vengeance. Whereas Pane and Yamin depict historical dynasties, troubled yet still mighty, Soekarno invokes a brutal past as origin for a genealogy of violence. Mpu Agni afflicts Koetkoetbi, who when reanimated, continues the cycle against his descendent, Amir, until Agni is revived to reciprocate in kind. No doubt thinking strategically of his conservative Muslim Bengkulu audience, Soekarno invokes Islam as the discourse capable of synthesizing the dangerous forces of nationalism that cannot be killed. Curiously, and perhaps strategically, this genealogy of violence is presented as an affair entirely internal to Indonesian history. No foreign characters make an appearance, except perhaps in oblique ways. Hayati relates a prophetic dream in the second act in which the young men go hunting, but a force prevents them from shooting. This force becomes a snake that pursues them. Suddenly, a tiger comes, who is bitten by the snake. The struggle between Dutch and Indonesians was frequently imagined as between a tiger and a buffalo, whereas the snake could allude to the power of ancient pre-Islamic mysticism. Hayati's dream might thereby be taken as a key to the play as parable of ancient spirit of Indonesia subduing the Dutch tiger. That Koetkoetbi and Mpu Agni are reanimated by a combination of spiritual mysticism and '*stroom*' suggests an instrumentalization of Western technology and education towards the spiritual reawakening of the Indonesian nation. In these ways, *Koetkoetbi* suggests Soekarno's distinct mediation of the pre-war cultural polemic.

With Monte Carlo, Soekarno faced very different challenges than the youth who staged nationalist historical dramas in the capital. Performed in a cinema where Hollywood movies were regularly screened, *Dr Sjaitan* and *Koetkoetbi* strategically claimed a status as harmless local surrogates to American entertainment. By presenting nationalism as a monster, he appeared to submit to a colonial narrative. Koetkoetbi and Mpu Agni defy an organicist vision of Indonesia. Instead, however, we see the ancient spectre of a dangerous nationalism that can defeat the Dutch tiger rising repeatedly and unstoppably, and brought under control ultimately by Islam. Soekarno leaves it to his audience to extrapolate what power Indonesian Muslim nationalists might wield.

Eccentrics at Parangtritis

If exile to Ende and Bengkulu peripheralized Soekarno in relation to Jakarta and the other urban Javanese centers of nationalist imagination, other sites invoked by postcolonial theatre artists have directly contested the capital's claim to centrality. One might speak of Yogyakarta and Bandung as such counter-sites. Indeed, these two other Javanese cities have generated resolutely local genealogies of modern theatre since Independence, each with distinct institutions, hagiographies and relationships to local performance traditions. Since Suharto's resignation, the decentralization of arts administration has re-energized theatrical activity in some regional capitals (most notably Makassar, Sulawesi), progressively diminishing the claim of Jakarta-based theatre to speak for the nation. However, the vibrancy of modern theatre in these other cities is generally articulated in terms of the empowerment of locality vis-à-vis the metropole. In contrast, the beach of Parangtritis, on the Indian Ocean to the south of Yogyakarta, has functioned in colonial and postcolonial discourses as an alternative center from which the nation might be haunted, a center that unabashedly connects the national spirit to the dynastic narratives of the majority ethnic Javanese.

Parangtritis becomes a significant site in Javanese *babad* (historical epic) and folk memory through the figure of the second ruler of the Mataram dynasty, Panembahan Senopati Ingalaga (r.1587–1601). Senopati is traditionally hailed as the architect of modern Java, who united disparate kingdoms militarily and consolidated their cultures into a synthetic approach to Islam aligned to *cara Jawi* (the Javanese way). As the popular legend goes, Senopati also fulfilled a prophecy dating to the fall of the Majapahit dynasty that a prince would go to Parangtritis and journey beneath the ocean to spend a wedding night with Loro Kidul, Queen of the South Seas, thereby gaining spiritual authority as ruler of an Islamic Java. After this time, Senopati's descendents would perform an annual rite at Parangtritis to confirm their dynastic betrothal to Loro Kidul, spiritual protectress of the House of Mataram.[16] Thus haunted by greatness, Parangtritis has attracted numerous subsequent performances of devotion, especially by supplicants seeking spiritual legitimacy for political authority. Sultan Pakubuwana IV was arrested there by the Dutch in June 1830, as he communed with Loro Kidul in preparation to join the Java War. Besides such famous examples, John Pemberton notes that many sorts of pilgrims have sought guidance at Parangtritis:

> Beyond the isolated rare instances of royal blessings granted lay a vast spectrum of magical powers and esoteric knowledge (ngelmu) sought by professionals: shamanic dhukun, shadow-puppeteers, thieves, military commanders, religious leaders, court authors, and others whose livelihood depended upon the acquisition of specific skills, both this-worldly and otherwise.
>
> (1994: 272)

Specifically, he describes a pilgrimage in 1982 of retired civil servants (under the guidance of a spirit medium). After repeated fruitless invocations, this group sights a single wave approaching the shore, which the medium interprets as a 'slametan' greeting from Loro Kidul:

> 'Slamet' – safe, free, as it were, from disruptive incidents, perhaps even blessed by a generalized state of security – this was the highly predictable yet no less dramatic dhawuh command imagined in the form of a single watery ripple.
>
> (304)

The power of Loro Kidul and the site of Parangtritis are hereby deployed in a conservative gesture reinforcing the stability and legitimacy of the Suharto regime. At the same time, the notion that such legitimacy might depend on this site of Javanese rather than national significance also implies an incapacity of Jakarta to consolidate all power within its own space. It opens the possibility that the metropole might itself be made peripheral to another, more authentic site of power.

Early in the Suharto era, Rendra made compelling use of the discursive potency of Parangtritis vis-à-vis Jakarta. With his return from study in New York City in 1967, he had already challenged Jakarta's centrality for the modern theatre by heralding a new approach from his kampong in Yogyakarta. In October, 1971, he attracted nationwide media attention by conducting an 'Urakan (Eccentric) Group Campout' for three days at Parangtritis. Attendance was open to the public, and approximately 200 young people participated. Gillitt describes the event:

> It featured a different theme for each day: 'Love and Love Poetry;' 'Flora, Fauna, and the Solar System'; and 'Magnificent Bodies.' Prominent speakers, scheduled to give seminars in the mornings, included cultural critic Arief Budiman, ATNI director Asrul Sani, dancer-choreographer Sardono W. Kusomo, and Rendra. The afternoons were designated for open work periods during which the participants were to create new dance, theatre, poetry, or fine art compositions based on the daily themes using only props and objects on and around the beach. Evenings were devoted to spontaneous poetry readings under the stars. Alongside the scheduled activities, all participants were invited to create posters to be displayed along the beach, with protest messages directed towards anyone or anything, including, according to the flyer, 'clouds, teachers, oneself, women, the sun, the Republic of Indonesia, Vietnam, the God of Love.' Rendra's actors were also scheduled to perform several mini kata [minimal word, Rendra's signature non-verbal style of the period] performances – including *Pip-Pip*, *Rambate Rate Rata*, and *Bip Bop* – in the market, on the beach, by the river, and other open public spaces nearby.
> (2001: 163)

The festivities proceeded more or less peacefully, despite a few police raids. Rendra insisted that the intent of the experiment was not anarchic, but rather to encourage young people to explore individual paths towards joining *kaum urakan* (the eccentric ones).

In an article written shortly after the event, Rendra distinguishes his program as a political and economic 'alternative' to state programs for arts and education: 'We didn't ask for help from the government. Our organizational costs were extremely cheap. And we didn't have a complex committee.' In this simple, self-sufficient non-governmental camp, Rendra and members of Teater Bengkel supervised a very loose program of improvisational and meditative exercises, always stressing 'spontaneity,' a value that Rendra described as crucial for independence and responsibility to self. The young participants were often frustrated, not knowing what to do, and looked for a leadership that Rendra and the members of Bengkel adamantly refused to provide. Rendra reflected that this was precisely the kind of struggle that young Indonesians needed:

> I don't want to become their leader in the course of their maturation. I choose the role of sympathetic witness towards their rebellion, towards their self-definition. My sympathy and dialogue are available, but I cannot provide a prescription for a way out, because I am certain that the one who is involved is the only one who will discover the prescription, but only after fully experiencing the challenges of life.
>
> (Rendra, 1983a: 26)

Whether productive or harmless, the Eccentric Ones Campout (Figure 3.9) modeled this progressive community within Indonesia, but outside the supervision of any state apparatus. In its self-sufficiency, it challenged the notion that Indonesian communities could not function without supervision from Jakarta. In its strict refusal to provide leadership to the participants, it challenged the most fundamental assumption of the New Order: that Indonesia needs a father figure to oversee all forms of development and to safeguard against social chaos. It represented deference to such a leader

Figure 3.9 W. S. Rendra and members of Teater Bengkel at the Urakan Campout on Parangtritis beach, 1971 (© W. S. Rendra)

figure as an erroneous emphasis on the 'authoritarian elements' that have characterized Indonesian political thought since the Javanese courts and the colonial governments. It demonstrated that communities could maintain themselves without leaders and without chaos so long as everyone took responsibility for themselves.

A decade later, Teater Arena, another Yogyakarta troupe under the direction of Fred Wibowo, picked up the genealogical thread of the *kaum urakan* with their own residency at the beach. After studying techniques of 'theatre of liberation' with the Philippines Educational Theatre Association (PETA), the company instituted a series of weekend workshops at Parangtritis from August to December 1980. About 150 young people participated. Eugene van Erven describes the activities:

> In addition to the normal workshop structure, the facilitators took the participants on exposure trips that helped them internalize the socioeconomic and political conditions of the town. The interaction resulted in three public performances of a collectively created play that dealt with issues like the detrimental effects of tourism and Western influence on local culture; ineffectual police protection against crime, youth unemployment, and the control of the Parangtritis economy by a mafia of Chinese businessmen from Yogyakarta.
>
> (van Erven, 1992: 189–90)

Whereas Rendra had summoned the ghosts of Parangtritis to inspire young Indonesians to discover their own individual legitimacies independent of Suharto's developmentalism, Wibowo summoned the same ghosts to inspire awareness of local injustice.

Though it is difficult to imagine two spaces more different than a cryptic theatre building and a beach under the stars, both have allowed modern Indonesian theatre artists to imagine a spectral nation removed from state formulations. The *gedongan* centers of modern theatre in Batavia/ Jakarta facilitate a transnational flow of expatriate ghosts in spaces that mediate between monumentality and ephemerality, in a city that itself remains alien to all localities. Parangtritis functions as a quintessentially Javanese site of disappearance and revenance, whose uncanniness consists in its mediation between locality and peripherality. The Schouwburg and TIM, in contrast, partake of a European tradition of haunting in which ghosts must be summoned to sites of ephemerality, and the local is always already foreign.

4
Despite Their Failings: Spectres of Foreign Professionalism

The last two luminaries

On 11 May 2007, the Jakarta Arts Council sponsored a 'public orientation' on the guidelines for the new Jakarta Theatre Festival, an attempt to reimagine the *Festival Teater Remaja* (Youth Theatre Festival). The Council had initiated the Youth Festival in 1973 to address the lack of opportunities for troupes established since the founding of the Center. Despite a high level of participation, this Festival had achieved mixed success in diversifying modern theatre practice in the capital. Out of hundreds of participants over the years, only 22 troupes ever achieved the 'senior' status needed to perform at the Jakarta Arts Center. Suffice to say that such requirements of continuous success thinned the field. Few troupes stayed together producing work of consistent quality for the minimum three years needed to climb the ladder. Rendra pointedly criticized the infantilizing framework of the Festival in a 1983 article for *Sinar Harapan*, noting that many of the groups vying for recognition were just as 'senior' as the established ones, and that this discourse of professionalization used much the same rhetoric as Suharto's paternalism: adults overseeing the maturation of their children, a conveniently elusive process that somehow never brought the children to the same level as their 'fathers' (Rendra, 1985: 74).

Of the troupes thus 'upgraded,' only Teater Sae (upgraded 1983) and Teater Kubur (upgraded 1988) achieved a status comparable to the established ones. Teater Sae folded when its director, Budi Otong, expatriated to Switzerland in the early 1990s, whereas Dindon, leader of Kubur, left the national stage by retreating from commercial production to work more intimately in the inner neighborhoods of Jakarta. Despite a new creative enthusiasm following Suharto's 1998 resignation, a large portion of the modern theatre performances in Jakarta in the subsequent decade continued to be produced by the same handful of troupes established before 1980. Consequently, in 2006 the Council decided to reorganize the Youth Theatre Festival in line with the spirit of post-Suharto decentralization. Participants were invited from throughout the country (not only the five districts of Jakarta), winners would be funded by the Council for a fully mounted production of their winning works, and they would automatically be granted a production slot in the following year's festival (Komite Teater, 2007: 12). As long-standing council-member Noorca Massardi enthuses in a January 2007 article for *Kompas*, the new changes substantially democratized what had been a very closed system (Massardi, 2007).

For the Council, however, it was not so much quantity as quality at issue. The reforms proceeded from a shared perception that despite a constant flow of new theatre troupes, few had developed into companies that continued to offer new work of a distinct and exciting idiom from year to year. In short, troupes were being formed, but they were failing to professionalize, thus raising the fear that none would be prepared to fill the impending gap when the last of the 'second golden age' luminaries was gone. Thus, at the orientation, the discussion was moderated by the last two of these luminaries still alive and active in the workings of TIM, figures who respectively epitomized avant-garde and commercial paths towards maintaining a professional theatre troupe in postcolonial Indonesia. Seated on the left was Putu Wijaya, whose *Teater Mandiri* (Independent Theatre) had created a unique body of non-linear and socially challenging experimental work attended by small audiences of bohemian devotees. On the right was Nano Riantiarno, director of Jakarta's most (some would say only) commercially successful modern troupe, *Teater Koma* (Com(m)a Theatre).

In the first decade of the new millennium, a panoply of economic and social difficulties (foremost, the dwindling of middle-class audiences and the rise in rent for performance venues due to increases in energy costs and decreases in public subsidies) continued to obstruct the development of new theatre companies. To the group of young Indonesian men in attendance at the FTJ event (no women other than Ratna Riantiarno were there), Wijaya and Riantiarno offered somewhat different visions of the professional theatre artist in a postcolonial nation. Wijaya, it might be argued, is the most successful veteran of Rendra's community of 'eccentric' individuals (*kaum urakan*) privileging their creative visions over adherence to social systems and patriarchal authorities. He presented professionalism to the assembled youths as a matter of personal ethos; a dedication to find ways to continue producing art irrespective of resources. The most fundamental of several key terms and phrases that Wijaya has deployed over three decades is to 'start from what's there' (*bertolak dari yang ada*), an approach that Teater Mandiri has epitomized by maintaining a prolific theatrical output despite disappointingly small audiences and lack of commercial success. After 30 years, 'bertolak dari yang ada' remains evident in Wijaya's recycling of design elements and found objects, and unskilled as well as celebrity performers; a general willingness to incorporate whatever is available. For Riantiarno, in contrast, professionalism is more fundamentally about finding ways to make an artistic life financially sustainable. He had apprenticed in the late 1960s to Teguh Karya, who innovated such commercial strategies as partnering with Hotel Indonesia as a producer and venue, offering season subscriptions and then extending performance runs to accommodate greater demand. Along with his wife and leading lady, Ratna, Riantiarno had run Teater Koma like a family company for three decades, producing well-advertised musical comedies with high production values, whose social and political critiques are rendered marketable by spectacle, dance, song and traditional clowning. As survivors of a dwindling generation, Riantiarno and Wijaya occupy the stage together comfortably. Despite their divergent paths, they clearly share an understanding of professionalism as a state of excellence achieved through the cumulative work of a family of artists within the framework of a long-standing theatre troupe. At the FTJ event, they agreed that such professionalism was required to 'upgrade' the quality of theatre for Jakarta, and thereby Indonesia as a whole. Both, like so many artistic directors throughout the world, have advocated for an iconoclastic collective of individual artists independent from social values, though their troupes would seem to model a fairly conservative family structure, headed by an inevitably autocratic father.

'Gifted queer' amateurs and professional actresses

From at least the *commedia dell' arte* onward in Europe, professional troupes have been distinguished from their amateur counterparts in two key senses: firstly, their members share a specific set of performance skills developed through concerted training;[1] and secondly, the company itself is a commercial entity dedicated to its own longevity through consistencies of quality and approach. On both counts, the example of acting families and troupes (forming stock and touring companies) is crucial, transmitting specific performance skills and styles down through the generations. Amateurism (though lauded within certain contexts) has mainly come to denote (and connote) a mere absence of those qualities affiliated with professionalism. During the eighteenth century, amateur theatrical societies became common bourgeois institutions in European metropoles. A clear distinction thereby proliferated between the art of the seasoned professional and the acculturating entertainments of amateurs. Whereas amateur theatrical societies were formed frequently with the intent of inspiriting national values in an unawakened populace, professional actors were often presented as skilled ambassadors of their nations. In the Dutch East Indies and Indonesia, the performance of modern theatre has taken place primarily under the umbrella of troupes (as distinct, for example, from the prevalent contemporary global practice of hiring casts per production or season), and most of these troupes have aspired to professionalism as a status.

The cultures of European acting and troupe structure reached colonial Batavia in patterns similar to their spread to the cultural peripheries of Europe itself. As Italian opera, French neo-classical drama and Shakespeare dominated European stages in the eighteenth and nineteenth centuries, so they did in nineteenth-century Batavia. As these foreign cultural hegemonies inspired nationalist theatre movements throughout the rest of Europe (including the Netherlands itself), so they did in Dutch Batavia. One crucial difference, however, is that whereas European national theatres exalted their own vernaculars and recovered (or invented) local folk traditions to articulate their sovereignty from France and other cultural hegemons, Batavia contended with a double marginalization in this regard. When moved to cultural nationalism, they asserted themselves as inheritors of a minor European theatrical tradition (that of the Netherlands) to which they were themselves peripheral. From a postcolonial perspective, one could say that Batavian theatre was haunted by the spectre of comparison to a theatre already haunted by the spectres of France and England. Attempts to establish theatre troupes in Batavia devoted to Dutch works did not last long, and throughout, imported European discourses of theatrical professionalism played out to the detriment of local Dutch cultural nationalists. Amateur theatre remained Dutch, professional theatre remained French, and professional opera remained Italian. As the theatrical economy of Batavia became increasingly Europeanized over the nineteenth century, the amateur Dutch theatre perpetually lost out in competition for audiences against higher status professionals from 'more advanced' European cultures.

Under the VOC, the logic of professionalism and amateurism followed a regimentation of space similar to the distinction between courtly and commercial entertainments in early modern Europe. Following the amateur *Hamlet* of 1619, amateur performances of various kinds apparently graced the feasts regularly held in the *kasteel*, and large municipal festivals likewise featured amateur spectacles. However, what scant practices of professional theatre took place under VOC administration took place in the town. Sumardjo mentions a puppet show operated by 'Portuguese' (quite likely *mardijkers*, freed slaves from Portuguese colonies) who, in the 1620s, performed three days per week. Such a constant performance schedule suggests a professional marionette troupe, but this is the only hint at professional theatre in Batavia prior to the nineteenth century (Sumardjo, 1992: 88).[2]

Van den Berg's 1881 history of Batavian theatre is replete with wry laments at the lack of professionalism in local efforts, which he invariably articulates through negative comparison to European examples. He relates the anecdote of Mr de Boer, a nephew of Governor-General Joan Maetsuyker (r. 1653–78), 'who had been a renowned play actor for many years in Amsterdam.' At some point in the 1660s, the actor deigned to visit Batavia, and there surveyed the municipalities to determine whether he might offer some sort of entertainment. At the prospect of operating a professional Dutch theatre in Batavia, De Boer reportedly told his uncle, 'that for him it would be better in Amsterdam once to be a prince, then once a king, and then again an emperor, and for having played all those roles, to be free, then forever to be a slave in India' (van den Berg, 1904: 104–5; Valentijn, 1724, vol. IV). It is interesting that it is not the native colonized population who are being likened to slaves in de Boer's rebuke, but rather the European population of Batavia, supposedly the colonizing elite. In this, he speaks to an anxiety still apparent in the discussion of the Jakarta Arts Council as it was felt by their predecessors in the Batavian theatres of the colonial era. There is a sense of inescapable (because, ultimately, geographic) peripherality to the relevant standards of artistic excellence, whereby no degree of privilege or Europeanization can possibly make up for the fact that Batavia is not Amsterdam, much as no amount of development seems capable of elevating Jakarta from the ranks of the developing world.

As discussed in the previous chapter, the first licensed Dutch schouwburg in Batavia opened its doors in 1757 with a production of de Marre's *Jacoba van Beijeren*, a Dutch nationalist history play about a fifteenth-century precursor to the modern struggle for Dutch independence. The author, de Marre, had premiered the play at the Amsterdam Schouwburg in 1736 to some acclaim, following a 20-year career at sea, whose highlight (evidenced by his six-volume epic poem), was apparently a 1728 visit to Batavia. This celebrated play (because a success at Amsterdam) by 'the Batavian poet-laureate' (who visited and then made his reputation back in Amsterdam) also gives van den Berg occasion for a ghosted review. Though the title role at Batavia was undoubtedly portrayed by a local amateur, van den Berg describes its success in terms of 'the memory it must have evoked' in spectators who had been in Amsterdam 20 years previously.[3] On that prior occasion, the great actress, Adriana Maas (hailed by some as 'a second Clarion'), gave so heart-rending a portrayal that one spectator, in a fit of compassion, flung her jewels onto the stage and began to disrobe before she was restrained (1904: 110–12). There is no record of such a thing occurring at the Bataviasche Schouwburg in 1757; indeed, in the absence of newspapers,[4] there is no record at all of the performance. However, to van den Berg, the mere spectre of such prior professional success gave the 1757 production a luster beyond its own likely merits.

Although no record distinctly indicates it, the experience of Batavia's later amateur theatres raises the question of whether the actor in this leading role was even a woman. In fact, at least as far as van den Berg is concerned, a lack of actresses is the quintessential characteristic of amateur theatres. The Bataviasche Schouwburg did not last long into the 1760s, after which there was apparently a 50-year drought broken by the establishment of a 'Military Bachelors' Theatre' in 1814 by the British soldiers who had occupied Batavia in 1811 (see Chapter 3). Taylor argues that the Bachelors' Theatre served a crucial ideological function for the British colonial administration of Lord Minto and Thomas Stamford Raffles, towards civilizing not the native Javanese population but the largely mestizo 'European' community. By this interpretation, male British soldiers performed English plays largely for the purpose of weaning the local 'Dutch' ladies from their mestizo culture towards a more thoroughly European (and incidentally British) acculturation (Taylor, 1983: 99–101).[5] However, neither British partisanship nor animosity towards the French dissuaded the bachelors from ceding the stage on two occasions to a local performer named Piolle, who presented French afterpieces. After July 1815, the bachelors were exhausted or perhaps lost interest in their ambitious monthly production schedule, and that September they lent their theatre to Piolle. A notice in the 9 September edition of the Gazette announces the program: 'Pygmalion *"Scene Lyrique"* by J. J. Rousseau, to be followed by the Hermitage or Harlequin in Solitude (*Vaudeville*) in one act, with changes of decoration and music.'

In other words, in Batavia, seat of Dutch colonization of the Malay archipelago, British occupiers used amateur theatricals to acculturate the local 'Europeans,' but then ceded primacy to a local specialist, purveying the universal European high culture of France (Britain's contemporaneous enemy). The very idea of professional theatre had been so thoroughly associated with France by this time that a truly Dutch theatre could not be other than amateur. Indeed, the Batavian thespians were not far out of step with the Amsterdammers in the path of such abjection. Both looked to French neo-classicism throughout the eighteenth century, were flooded by visiting English troupes in the second decade of the nineteenth century, and then saw their own theatres decline through the mid-century. However, in Batavia, the Dutch troupes thus marginalized were amateurs, who were threatened by (mainly French) professionals.

Following the departure of the British from Batavia in 1816, a Dutch 'Amateur Theatre at Weltewreden' was established in 1817, which became the resident company of the newly constructed Schouwburg Weltewreden in 1821, under the Ovidian moniker, *Ut Desint Vires Tamen est Laudanda Voluntas* (Despite Its Failings the Best Effort Deserves Praise). The Ut Desint company also turned out to be a primarily male enterprise due to some social stigma (or perhaps simply lack of interest) amongst 'European' women. A Dr Strehler, who attended the Schouwburg on a visit to Batavia in the late 1820s, writes:

When it comes to the players, some lose themselves masterfully in their roles; but others leave sufficient proof that they are only amateurs; and it is a deficiency, the better selves not wishing to contribute to the society, that the men must also take on the female roles: because, however much one who regards their skill might admire them, a man nevertheless has no female countenance, no female voice, no female feet, no female posture, no mark of femininity. As in the rest of our lives lack of this fair half and help to our sex is but a half life, so it is also in this Schouwburg. But all the same, *laudanda voluntas*, the good will is priceless; it is everything.

(Strehler, 1833: 138)

Despite a new commitment on the part of government, and, increasingly, society at large, to offering a Dutch theatre in Batavia, it was from the start a precarious enterprise, built in the shadow of the spectre of comparisons on the fickle foundations of 'laudanda voluntas.' Nevertheless, the Amateur Theatre set out an ambitious program of one production per month, which was then taken up by Ut Desint and maintained into the 1830s. Presently, that same Piolle who had stolen the fire of the military bachelors returned with a rival troupe whose endeavors generally garnered more favorable reviews (in French) in the late teens, reviews frequently featuring the performances of actresses. For example, a production of Piolle's in March 1820 of 'les Folies amoureuses' by Jean-François Regnard, elicited praise on the strength of the performance of Madame Bailly, with no invocations of 'laudanda voluntas' (van den Berg 1904: 152). By the early twenties, Piolle's company appears to have folded for some reason, ceding the field to the nationalist amateurs. These amateurs, however, though ostensively Dutch partisans, did not respond by promoting a Dutch repertoire. Indeed, the Dutch nationalist works of ten Kate van Loo were anomalies to a general preference for German, French and English drama. Only through the dedication of an unusually dynamic figure with recent credentials from the fatherland, and operating at a time of war in Java, was that prevailing logic overcome for a moment.

In 1835, a traveling French professional troupe under the leadership of a man named Minard arrived in Batavia. The Schouwburg was put at their disposal immediately, much as its predecessor, the Military Bachelors' Theatre had been put at the disposal of Piolle. In writing of this competition to Ut Desint, van den Berg returns to a familiar theme:

It was the first time that professional play-actors had appeared before the Batavian public, and what surely made their performances just slightly attractive was the circumstance that the female roles were now no longer 'gifted queer' youngsters but were occupied by more or less unassailable actresses. This would prove a more potent bait for the theatre-minded public than all the talent that the acting members of Ut Desint had given to the female roles; and they attended and soon came to the realization that they would have to endure the Dutch theatre performances [...] so masculine as feminine would have to be overlooked.

(1904: 168–9)

From this point onward, Dutch theatre in the Dutch colonial capital of Batavia took on a distinctly second-class character. French theatre (and soon,

Italian opera) prevailed for the remainder of the century, and remained the examples against which the new mestizo modern theatre would be disparagingly compared in the European press.

Ut Desint was not the only amateur theatrical society to be formed after the example of the British Military Bachelors' Theatre following the restitution of civilian Dutch rule to the East Indies. Similar societies operated in the major colonial cities of Java throughout the nineteenth century. One of these was established in the East Javanese city of Surabaya in 1816 under the leadership of a woman, H. van der Ster. Perhaps thanks to this female director, Surabaya society sometimes employed actresses. Another opened in Semarang in 1817, and another with a Dutch name, *Toneelvereniging Braga*, formed in Bandung in 1882 under the leadership of Pieter Sijthoff, the city's Resident. Each of these societies resembled Ut Desint in that they provided an alternative to the professional French and Italian fare that figured, paradoxically, as both local and oriented towards the Dutch fatherland. J. P. Worp notes that the repertoires of these groups might include mestizo works and original plays and operettas in Dutch (1903: 419). Whereas the professional European troupes commanded foremost cultural status on the basis of their foreign repertoire, the amateur societies, though still restricted by European status, admitted mestizo influence. Though oriented towards Europe, the colonial theatre did nurture its own forms of hybridity. It was not simply a 'pure' European theatre from which Mahieu and his contemporaries borrowed in modeling a native Indonesian theatre.

Although Indonesian postcolonial troupes such as Teater Bengkel, Teater Mandiri and Teater Koma succeeded to a far greater degree than any of these colonial amateur theatrical societies in generating original repertoires and a 'new tradition' of performance rooted in local contexts, they have continued to face similar spectres of a professionalism that is always already doubly exogenous. Insofar as Dutch troupes like Ut Desint attempted to produce Dutch works, they peripheralized themselves in relation to an authenticity located in Europe. Though they struggled to become more professional through rehearsal and adoption of popular repertoires filled with Kotzebue and Ducis's Shakespeare adaptations, they were constantly subject to disenfranchisement by French troupes that were categorically more professional. Likewise, postcolonial Indonesian theatre has constantly struggled against the notion that real modern theatre comes from abroad and no local troupe can hope to attain a comparable legitimacy vis-à-vis foreign professional troupes. Indonesian troupes have always had to navigate between the professional prestige of European dramaturgy and the authenticity of local traditions, both of which threaten to cast modern theatre as relatively amateurish. Indeed, in the formation of Komedie Stamboel, we may trace a fairly smooth transition from the cultural polemics of Dutch theatre in the colony to that of the nascent Indonesian theatre, conducted under the abjective banner of 'despite their failings.'

Mina Kruseman and the nativization of modern theatre

Cohen's recent scholarship looks beyond Komedie Stamboel for the roots of modern Indonesian theatre. His rubric of 'popular theatre' reveals a performance genealogy extending from the Chinese urban troupes of colonial Batavia through Stamboel, Orion and Dardanella to the new commercial theatres of the Suharto era. Such a perspective is especially useful in recovering the Chinese and mestizo contributions to what would become the national culture. However, this genealogy of the 'popular' specifically distinguishes it from 'elite' theatres, whether colonial or postcolonial. Though the claims of such elites to primacy in speaking for the colony or the nation certainly deserve critique, postcolonial historiographies have already gone to such extremes in this regard as to call for serious reassessment. As attractive as it might be, especially from the perspective of the 'new tradition' (*tradisi baru*) movement of the 1970s, to view cultural history as a continuous process of native cultures joining in the elaboration of an Indonesian national culture, we cannot account for the practices of these 'popular' troupes in isolation from the examples of colonial theatres. Most of the innovations commonly attributed to Stamboel and its successors (such as using a common language to attract diverse audiences across localities, touring to reach new markets, adapting plays from print and mass media, employing European theatrical conventions, privileging literary qualities over spectacle and music, and so forth) make little sense outside a negotiation with European traditions. Though offering other worthwhile insights, the 'popular' rubric distracts attention from this crucial relationship. Cohen himself, however, acknowledges the importance of genealogies that lead to Europe rather than the archipelago when he considers Mina Kruseman, a Dutch actress who served as a formative influence on many mestizo theatre artists, possibly including Mahieu.

Kruseman (1839–1922) spent much of her youth in Semarang, where she undoubtedly received some of her earliest theatrical exposure in the amateur society there. She returned to the Netherlands in 1854, and over the following two decades, emerged as a groundbreaking Dutch feminist who employed theatre for political activism. She made her reputation through such works as *l'Homme-Femme* (1872, a rebuttal to the anti-feminism of Alexandre Dumas; *fils*, written under the pseudonym, 'Mlle Oristorio di Frama, Cantatrice'); and *De echtscheiding* (1874, a dramatization of her banned 1873 novel, *Een Huwelijk in Indie*). In 1875, she was praised for her role as Queen Louise in *Vortenschool*, a play by Multatuli (the famous muck-raking author of *Max Havelaar*, an indictment of the colonial plantation economy on Java). In 1877, as her reputation in the Netherlands was on the rise, she returned to the Indies. In October, 1877, she performed 'a dramatic sketch' at the Schouwburg Weltewreden in an evening sponsored by the Theatre Français. She moved on to Surabaya from 1878 to 1883, and became a central figure of the European theatre community there. In Surabaya, Kruseman presented about a dozen 'Soirees Artistiques,' featuring her own work. These were typically performed at the *Soerabajase Komediegebouw*, Surabaya's equivalent to the Schouwburg Weltewreden, under the auspices of the amateur theatrical society. With actors from this local society, Kruseman premiered an original work, *Helene Richard op in de Weelde Geboren*, in 1881 and directed a performance of Multatuli's *Vortenschool* in 1882. To further support the European theatrical life of Surabaya, Kruseman opened a school of theatre and music at the home of W. L. Megenlijk, who Cohen notes was one of the high school teachers of Mahieu. Cohen acknowledges that the link between Kruseman and Mahieu is inconclusive, but highly suggestive nevertheless:

> Mahieu would not have actually attended Kruseman's school (which cost 15 guilders a month) nor taken private lessons from her in piano, song, or oratory (25 guilders a month) [...] it is more than likely that *den heer* Megenlijk, who taught modern languages and geography at Surabaya's HBS from 1875 to 1884, brought to his HBS teaching knowledge culled from direct observation of theatrical instruction and play rehearsals that took place in his own house.
>
> (2006: 64)

Regardless of whether there was 'direct influence,' Kruseman apparently taught many mestizo as well as pureblood (*totok*) Europeans at her school, thereby making a substantial impression on Victor Ido, whose life was so complexly interwoven between the theatres of Native and European status in Batavia (see Praamstra, 2003).

Mahieu constantly strove to be granted legitimacy vis-à-vis European high culture. His deployment of such terms as 'opera' and 'komedie,' his effort to gain admittance to the Schouwburg, his desire to be reviewed in the Dutch language press and his interpolation of European techniques, content and form also served to counter the relegation of hybrid urban theatres to the category of Native. There were practical motivations for this. In Mahieu's time, '*wayang*' (native theatre) laws greatly restricted the free operation of troupes lacking European status. As Stamboel gained legitimacy, it was granted amnesty from these restrictions. Besides such practicalities, however, European (and especially French) professionalism carried its own cultural allure, and the lack thereof its own stigma. Although Mahieu himself and Stamboel's lead actor, Rensing, typically garnered praise, the rest of the troupe were often criticized as under-rehearsed and amateurish. A variety of issues from actors wandering offstage mid-scene to brawls in the audience were attributed to unprofessionalism. The acting style that Stamboel developed, which Cohen perceives as a progenitor of 'the overwrought acting style' seen from Betawi *lenong* to television *sinetron* (soap operas), mimics the acting seen in operetta and burlesque companies at the Schouwburg:

Acting was similarly modeled on the conventions of melodrama: actors were encouraged to 'project movements' (*buang tingkah*) to their audiences and wore white socks on their feet and sequins on their costumes to make their exaggerated postures more visible.

(2006: 85)

Their efforts were apparently effective for mestizo and native audiences but less so for European critics. Cohen notes 'a sympathetic newspaper reviewer' in Batavia who, in 1895, urges the Stamboel actors to attend performances of French opera at the Schouwburg, so that they might witness more sophisticated and effective techniques for conveying emotions to audiences. (165–6, 175, 248). Mahieu's troupe never gained admittance to the Schouwburg nor attained the kind of European legitimacy achieved by Ido. However, by the cruel inverse of this logic, Mahieu would be recovered in postcolonial narratives as a progenitor of modern Indonesian theatre, while Ido would be remembered as a Dutch playwright stuck in the colonial periphery.

Over the final half-century of colonial rule, most of Stamboel's successors would follow a similar logic of looking to European theatre in innovating their own. When Orion emerged in 1925 and Dardanella in 1926, both troupes promoted themselves as *toneel* (Dutch for spoken drama), much as their predecessors had claimed status as 'opera' or 'komedie.' This shift in terminology reflected a change begun with the opera derma troupes of emphasizing literary playwriting over music and dance, mirroring the emergence of literary social dramas in Europe. The works of Ibsen, further mediated through Tagore, were widely imitated throughout Asia, establishing a new standard of modern theatre quite distinct from the repertoires of large traveling variety troupes like bangsawan and Stamboel. As suggested by the text of Hoay's *The Living Corpse*, these new works demanded not only greater memorization of lines, but also a new emphasis on psychological realism in acting. As discussed in Chapter 2, this approach to theatre suited the amateur Chinese opera derma troupes whose members were typically literate but unskilled at improvisation or other performance techniques. In these groups, as in the amateur nationalist troupes that emerged in the 1940s, literary drama served practical as well as ideological needs. However, professional troupes such as Dardanella and Orion continued to resemble Stamboel more than they admitted. They maintained large retinues of skilled entertainers who performed a variety of acts in the interstices of these serious plays. They walked a fine line in this respect between modernizations that increased the troupe's stature with European and elite audiences while remaining marketable to mass audiences. The fact that Oemarjati and others have given Dardanella such pride of place for its innovations over its contemporaries is due largely to the promotions of Andjar Asmara.

Asmara had come to Batavia as a young man, after a childhood in Padang in which he had learned something of 'komedi Melayu' from an itinerant actor, formed his own circus, and at one point acted in a Tagore play alongside Roestam Effendi. Asmara first saw Dardanella on its second tour to Batavia in 1930. He quit his job as an editor for *Doenia Film dan Sport* (*Film and Sport World*) to join them. The artistic director, A. Piedro (alias Willy Klimanoff, a white Russian from a circus family), initially hired him as a publicity manager, but after two months, Asmara presented them with his first and most success-ful play, *Dr Samsi*. Thus, Asmara became a leading member of the artistic staff, and wrote at least eight more plays for them over the next six years (Cohen, 2010: introduction to *Dr Samsi*). Though fervently devoted to the troupe, Asmara would over the following decades interpret its legacy in relation to a nationalism somewhat removed from Piedro's commercial ends. Dewi Dja recalls letters written by Asmara to her and the actor, Astaman, in which he praises Piedro's professionalism, but pushes gently at the implicit colonial patriarchy of the management, which a true Indonesian theatre troupe must transcend:

> Piedro is a dictator, one who cannot be disputed at all, but since everything that he makes and commands is right and can be seen to succeed, then he gets great faith from his theatrical children (*anak-anak wayangnya*). I declare, Piedro has implemented many changes in the world of our stage. Great! Quite revolutionary. But it must be admitted that he will not bring fundamental changes to our culture. This can only take place if we ourselves, native people, Indonesian people, implement it.
>
> (Ramadhan, 1982: 86–7)

Dja aligns the zeitgeist of the troupe with Asmara's interpretation, claim-ing that members of the company took interest in the 1928 Youth Pledge (though she herself was only 15 at the time), and the troupe modeled 'national unity' through its representation of various ethnicities (69). Of course, Dja remembers all this from a post-Independence perspective.

It is clear that Asmara already conceived of Dardanella in the 1930s as a link between Mahieu and a modern native theatre, a theme that he reworked in numerous writings over the following two decades. Nevertheless, at a time when Effendi, Yamin, Pane and even Soekarno were writing plays explicitly within a nationalist milieu, and untrained actors of the nation-alist movement were staging them at youth conferences, Dardanella and Orion remained commercial profit-oriented theatres. In 1934, the company embarked on an Asian tour, which expanded into a world tour, and Dewi Dja and Piedro remained in Los Angeles. We might reasonably wonder whether the 'nationalism' of Dardanella was not mainly a revisionist perspective canonized by its fervent impresario, Asmara. Nevertheless, Dardanella holds a somewhat ironic status in nationalist histories as a 'first nationalist troupe' that never affiliated directly with the nationalist movement. To this end, nationalist meaning is found in Asmara's *Dr Samsi*.

Dr Samsi and Dewi Dja

Soon after joining Dardanella, Asmara saw the Hollywood film *Madame X* (1929, based on Alexandre Bisson's 1908 play, *La Femme X*). The courtroom scene of a lawyer discovering that the woman he has just defended is his long-lost mother reminded Asmara of his first Javanese wife and son who had disappeared when he was compelled by his family to marry a West Sumatran. Asmara combined these elements with urban legends (such as 'the Kemayoran crocodile,' a Batavian gangster) and details from a Batavian murder trial he had once covered as a reporter, and *Dr Samsi* was born. He wrote the play in a few weeks in December 1930, and Piedro rushed it through rehearsals for a premiere in Medan at the end of that same month. The play met with such success that it became a staple of the Dardanella repertoire and launched the acting career of Dewi Dja playing both the young and aged Sukaesih. Two film versions were made (the first in India in 1936, the second in 1952, directed by Asmara's ex-wife Ratna) and it was broadcast as a radio drama on NIROM, the colonial network, in 1939. Asmara revived the play with his *Tjahaja Timoer* troupe during the Japanese occupation, and brought much of the cast together for one last nostalgic performance in 1959 (Cohen, 2009: 105).

In the first act of the play, we learn that while in medical school, Samsi had been involved with Sukaesih, a girl from Buitenzorg (Bogor), and they had a son together. However, when Samsi became a doctor, his parents compelled him to marry a higher status woman of their choosing. Outcast, Sukaesih struggled to survive in the Chinese district of Batavia. At the opening of the play, she brings the son, who is on the brink of death, to the hospital where Samsi works. As he is not there, she leaves the child for him on a bench. At the same moment, Samsi's infant son from his new wife is sick in the same hospital. This second son dies, and Samsi cannot bear to tell his grieving wife. Meanwhile, Sukaesih's son has recovered, and Leo van den Brink, an orderly at the hospital, convinces Samsi to substitute the living infant for his own. Samsi, having no idea who this other infant is but desperate to assuage his grieving wife, agrees, swearing Leo to secrecy. The second act takes us many years later to Samsi's home. The grown son, Sugiat, is about to graduate from law school and marry. Leo van den Brink pays Samsi a visit. After losing his job at the hospital (for drunkenness and tardiness), he has become 'the Kemayoran crocodile,' a gangster engaged in underground enterprises. He reminds Samsi of their terrible secret to blackmail him. Samsi throws him out but not before Leo mentions knowing a certain Sukaesih.

The third act is an extended display of the pathos of Sukaesih. She has sought refuge with Leo who has exposed her to his dangerous dealings. Piun, a gang leader from another district, shows up looking for Leo and demands money of Sukaesih. Leo returns, intimidates this adversary, and then turns to drinking. Samsi arrives, hoping to silence Leo with a payment. Leo tries to kick him out. They scuffle, Sukaesih intervenes, and Leo is stabbed with his own knife. Samsi runs, the police arrive, and Sukaesih is arrested for murdering her own husband. In the fourth act, we see Sukaesih with Sugiat who has just successfully defended her in court, having no idea who she really is. She is grateful, but despondent. She is free, but still poor and a widow without even a family. Sugiat is moved and resolves to help her find a home. He feels he owes a debt since this case has established his own reputation. He leaves for a moment and Samsi appears, looking to reconcile with Sukaesih. Sugiat returns and sees them together, and Samsi finally reveals the truth. Mother and son are reunited in the final moment of the play (even as the future for Samsi and his new family are now called into question).

Besides the numerous specific sources already mentioned, there are obvious similarities between *Dr Samsi* and Hoay's *Living Corpse*, which Hoay had written just a few months previously, and the two plays were performed in repertory on the same tour to Sumatra. Both plays foreground native characters who are medical doctors. Both deal with a weighty philosophical problem of medical ethics whose consequences disrupt healthy traditional family structure and the legacy from one generation to the next. In both narratives, a lapse of ethical judgment is affiliated with the protagonist's submission to degenerate social elements circulating within Batavia (Yang Bwe's friends, Leo van den Brink) that may be interpreted as representing the colonial system. However, the anti-colonial sentiments are far more explicit in Hoay's play. Syphilis is presented as a disease brought about by over-indulgence in European tastes. Lian Gie admires the health of traditional society, uncorrupted by urban Westernization. There is nothing so explicit in *Dr Samsi*, and an anti-colonial reading must privilege more subtle elements, such as when Leo attempts to extort Samsi in the second act, and taunts,

> 'Doctor, I believe your son is intelligent and educated. But Sugiat is like a flag hoisted high on a flagpole: when there's wind, it flutters back and forth and everyone who looks at it speaks good of it. But don't forget that as long as I'm alive, I've got a saw and if I were to cut through that flagpole with my saw the flag will fall in the mud and get dirty beyond recognition.'
>
> (Cohen, 2009: 118)

Through this unusual simile, the hidden son, filled with promise as an agent for justice in Indonesia, is presented as a sign of nationhood whose dignity is held ransom by the corruption of colonial society. Likewise, Sukaesih must be read as Indonesia, a transposition of the allegorical Bebasari who is enchained by Dutch ogres to the milieu of literary realism wherein she appears as an object of melodramatic suffering. Sukaesih evokes a constant stream of *dukacita* (pathos), from the desperate abandonment of her infant child in the first act to the ill-fated defense of her husband in the third act, leading to her false accusation and exoneration to an empty house. She laments to Sugiat, 'If I had a family, children, grandchildren, there would be a source of joy, but I'm all alone in the world […] I'd be better off dead than living in this sort of emptiness.'

However, it is in Sugiat's response to Sukaesih that Samsi's narrative parts most tellingly from that of Hoay (though it may be said to parallel *Bebasari*), and provides some insight into the play's legibility as anti-colonial parable. Whereas Lian Gie heroically interrupts a tainted genealogy through his own suicide, Sugiat counsels the woman he will soon discover is his mother,

'Don't speak of death, Ma'am. That's immoral. We will all die one day, but God tells us: You must prepare for death as if you were to die tomorrow, and exert yourself for life as if you were to live forever. The secret of life does not lie in family or children – which you don't have – but here (*indicating his chest*). Here, in our own hearts.'

(Cohen, 2009: 127)

Whereas *Living Corpse* offers suicide as a noble transcendence of a genealogy terminally haunted by the ghosts of foreign crimes, *Dr Samsi* responds to its own uncanny premise ('replace a dead child with a live one') by an act of forgetting. Sugiat, unaware of his true origins, offers an organicist image in the closing moments of the play, re-inspiriting the degraded nation (in this case, his mother) with a gaze oriented to the future. It is little wonder that the play has become increasingly popular to Indonesian audiences as post-colonial mores have increasingly resembled Asmara's vision. In the following moments, when Samsi returns and Sugiat learns his real identity, we are overwhelmed by the redemptive vision of a mother recovering her progeny, a son who promises to restore the nation to full dignity. Any notion that this revelation has made Sugiat into a ghostly double, a living manifestation of terrible colonial crimes, is banished. We never again see the (unknowingly foster) mother who actually raised Sugiat, nor contemplate how the news of this scandalous deceit affects his family. Instead, we forget. 'Exert yourself for life as if you were to live forever,' Sugiat proclaims.

A more direct reason for the success and longevity of *Dr Samsi* with Dardanella was that it provided an exceptionally compelling role for the young Dewi Dja, who was transformed by the role of Sukaesih from a pretty young dancer into Dardanella's leading lady (Figure 4.1). As Minard's French theatre troupe had drawn audiences from Ut Desint with their professional actresses, so Orion and Dardanella had featured their leading actresses prominently. Indeed, the Javanese actress known as Miss Riboet (who simultaneously commanded a celebrity following as a singer) was so important to the marketing of the former that the troupe was promoted as 'Miss Riboet's Orion.' Orion protested when Dardanella presented its own Miss Riboet (Piedro settled the dispute by christening his starlet 'Miss Riboet II'). Dewi Dja had been

Figure 4.1   An advertisement for Teater Dardanella's production of Asmara's *Dr. Samsi,* featuring the young 'Miss Dja,' 1931 (Author's collection)

a young teenager when Piedro married her into the Dardanella family, and was only 17 when Dardanella started work on *Dr Samsi*. It was assumed that Miss Riboet II would play Sukaesih, a demanding role involving considerable emotional projection and convincing portrayal of the same character as both a young and an old woman. However, Riboet fell ill, and Piedro took a chance on his young wife. Exceeding expectations, she impressed audiences as well as fellow actors with her ability to inhabit the emotional life of a much older woman.[6] 'Miss Dja' became the diva of Dardanella, and when she and Piedro abandoned the troupe on the world tour, the group disbanded. Although Dardanella and other troupes also featured male actors of stature,[7] there was a particular fascination for these female divas whose choice for a life in theatre remained so counter to social norms. As van den Berg lamented in surveying the entire history of Dutch colonial theatre, as Soekarno faced in his theatres in exile, and as the nationalist theatre troupes would encounter again in the coming decades, the presence of headlining actresses went a considerable distance towards separating the professional from the amateur stage.

And so, in 1953, after years of struggling to develop a nationalist theatre troupe out of fervent, but inexperienced intellectuals, who were mostly young men, another theatre artist from West Sumatra who was studying film at the University of Southern California paid a visit to Dewi Dja in her home in Los Angeles. He would introduce her to some of his colleagues of the Generation of '45, who would soon found an Indonesian National Theatre Academy in Jakarta, and were now furthering their own education at UCLA. The next year, he would write in an article on 'The Difficulty of Finding Indonesian Actresses' that whereas he had no difficulty finding American women to act in his thesis film at USC, Indonesian families still 'tremble at releasing their daughters to become film actors' (Ismail, 1954: 14). On the occasion of Miss Dja's return to Indonesia in 1959 for one last performance of *Dr Samsi*, he would mount the stage with Asmara, sharing one last nostalgic vision of the era of professional actresses and troupes. On this occasion in Los Angeles in 1953, however, he simply paid a visit to a legend from a bygone era. Dewi Dja recalls:

> One day a guest appeared, a man with glasses and rather curly hair. I could tell immediately that he was Indonesian. But who? 'Let me introduce myself, Usmar Ismail,' he said. 'I know the name Dewi Dja. But you probably don't know me.'
>
> (Ramadhan, 1982: 278)

The Greater East Asia Co-Prosperity Sphere

Three years of Japanese occupation (1942–45), the subsequent five-year revolution against the returning Dutch (1945–49), and Soekarno's 15 years as the first president of the postcolonial Republic (1950–65) saw a dynamic reversal in the practice of amateur theatre. As amateur practitioners paid greater attention to the craft of acting, they began to articulate notions of psycho-spiritual authenticity in performance. They turned away from the representation of mythically idealized images of anti-colonial and revolutionary heroes, in favor of their own adaptations of Euro-American realistic dramaturgy and acting. Meanwhile, the Indonesian government slipped from a tenuous parliamentary democracy to an authoritarian state under President Soekarno. As the Soekarno regime increasingly represented the *rakyat* through monuments and 'functional groups,' modern theatre continued the revolution in the minds and souls of actors.

Nationalistic and pan-Asian ideologies propelled the rapid imperialistic expansion that brought Japan to Indonesia even as it joined the Axis powers in world war. After the Meiji Restoration (1868), Japanese racial theories had argued that the Japanese people were of a superior, though related, stock to the rest of Asia, and that it was a matter of racial teleology that Japan should occupy a position of hegemony and tutelage over its younger Asian brothers (see Ching, 1998). As Japan came ever closer to international conflict, this sentiment informed state policy in the form of the Greater East Asian Co-Prosperity Sphere (proclaimed in August 1940). According to this doctrine, all Japanese occupation, exploitation and development in the rest of Asia served the noble goal of awakening the region to its rightful modern development, free from the exploitation of European colonialism. To convince other Asian peoples that it acted in this noble spirit, Japan would promote local anti-colonial nationalistic movements in Thailand, Vietnam, the Philippines and Indonesia. Although it soon became clear to the various occupied peoples that Japan sought only to win their own war at terrible cost to their empire, the simultaneous promotions of pan-Asianism and regional nationalism found deep resonance beyond the empty rhetoric. Many people beyond the intellectual elites began to think of themselves as descendents of Asian civilizations as great as those in the West. Simultaneously, they began to imagine their own national sovereignties as Filipinos, Thais, Malays and Indonesians. The Japanese immediately renamed the Dutch East Indies 'Indonesia' even as they renamed Batavia 'Jakarta,' these being outward signs of a postcolonial imagination.

Because Java was deemed the most politically advanced (and least materially significant) region of the Indies, the Japanese *Gunseikanbu* (military government) there emphasized social administration and development. Although these efforts ostensively served to indoctrinate Javanese in Japanese culture and wartime ideology, in practice they also developed a variety of social elements conducive to Indonesian nationalism. It soon became apparent that it would not be practical to conduct instruction in Japanese. Therefore, mass training and propaganda were conducted largely in Indonesian. Nationalist leaders such as Soekarno and Hatta were allowed to speak at large public gatherings and, for the first time, in radio programs broadcast throughout the island. Although these broadcasts were crafted to support the Japanese war effort, the authorities tolerated, and even encouraged, anti-Western messages articulated through Indonesian nationalism.

James Brandon writes that 'the largest concerted effort in modern times to utilize theatre as a propaganda medium in Southeast Asia was that of the Japanese occupation forces during World War II' (1967: 285). In Java in 1943, the Gunseikanbu set up a *Keimin Nunka Shidosho* (*Poesat Keboedajaan*, Cultural Center), which exerted a highly controlled patronage of all major performance genres and media. All the Western cinemas were closed, and many reverted to use as stages for live theatre. Through such policies, the Japanese occupation generated a paradoxical prosperity for nationalist arts in the midst of the general destruction of the economy. Brandon cites a bitter theatre manager looking back at the Japanese occupation from the economic crisis of the late Soekarno years:

> The best time *sandiwara* [theatre] ever had was under the Japanese. We had to do what they said but they got us lights, generators, costumes, and even built us theatres to play in. We were charged a 10 percent 'interest' fee to pay for the equipment we got. Now our government charges us 27 percent tax and we get nothing in return. I'd rather be under the Japanese.
>
> (1967: 237)

At the same time, the Central Office did much to dismantle existing performance economies. By demanding that all theatrical productions submit scripts for scrutiny, they effectively censored any professional groups whose style still depended on unscripted elements. More significant to the shift in power, however, was the fact of the replacement of the commercial theatre economy with an ideological economy conducive to works written by nationalists. To the extent that professional artists had sought legitimacy in the West, they were compelled to adjust. Use of Dutch or other European languages was forbidden (putting an even more absolute halt to colonial theatre of European status), and all European words for theatre and drama were replaced with '*sandiwara.*' A few professionals who had tended towards nationalist literary playwriting, such as Asmara, adapted. Many others, who had switched from the professional theatre industry to the professional film industry in the late 1930s, now found themselves dumped back into a theatre culture that frowned at their old repertoires and had no patience for their commercialism.

On 8 October 1942, the Gunseikanbu had established *Djawa Eiga Kosya*, an arts administration centered in Jakarta that included a drama school to promote the writing of propaganda plays. These institutions were embellished in 1943 with the establishment of a Jakarta arts center (administered by Sanoesi Pane), and in January 1945, by the foundation of the Javanese Sandiwara Association (Perserikatan Oesaha Sandiwara Djawa, POSD), a body more explicitly devoted, in the few months of its existence, to developing a national drama (Sumardjo, 1992: 132, 136–7). Together, these organizations promoted the writing of at least 54 original plays between 1942 and 1945, a productivity that would be recalled wryly from the vantage point of the 1950s (370–4; Teeuw, 1967: 110–14; Kurasawa, 1987: 109–11). As the new administration encouraged the expression of anti-Western ideologies that could be aligned with Japan's military agenda, many of these new plays took nationalist positions of unprecedented directness.

As the Japanese began to lose the war, the occupation government became increasingly sympathetic to the idea of training Indonesian troops and building organizational infrastructure for Indonesian resistance to the returning Dutch. In October 1943, the Gunseikanbu established *PETA* (*Pembela Tanah Air*, Protectors of the Homeland), a volunteer army composed entirely of Indonesian youth. It was through *PETA* and other organizations for Javanese youth that the Gunseikanbu encouraged *semangat* (spirit, soul, zeal) as a sustaining principle of Pan-Asian struggle against Western colonialism, and *pemuda* (adolescent youth) as the principal Indonesian agents of that *semangat*. The Japanese fastened onto this language as analogous to their own modernized notions of samurai *bushido*, and some Indonesian youth drew inspiration from the discipline of Japanese soldiers. At the same time, as Anderson points out, the local model was readily available in Javanese society. Young Javanese men would traditionally seek out masters, such as the *kyai* who administer *pesantren* (Islamic boarding schools) with whom they would undergo physical and spiritual training in ascetic isolation from society before returning to assume the responsibilities and pleasures of adults. In times of crisis, these *pemuda* might utilize the power gained from their discipline to heal social disorder:

> As the meaning of the regular life-arc was undermined by war, oppression, or economic disaster, the asceticism and élan within pesantren-like communities took on a general significance unimaginable in times of peace. Traditional deviant aspects of santri existence – sexual abstinence, fraternal solidarity, selfless devotion, nomadic wandering, and dealings with the supernatural – were now seen as in harmony with the times [...] the society itself became a larger pesantren, in which the pesantren life-style assumed the mode of normality and necessity. For in periods of great crisis the whole society moved to free itself from the cycle of routine and regularity, and accepted the suspended soaring of the spirit which underlay the pesantren's conception of itself.
>
> (Anderson, 1972: 10)

This notion of revolutionary *semangat* as an 'inner order' through which the *pemuda* radicalizes all society into a *pesantren* became manifest during these years and in the early 1950s in the work of theatre artists who articulated their social role as activists whose 'inner truths' point the way to postcolonial subjectivity.

The first (amateur) Indonesian troupe

A few years into the Occupation, a group of young intellectuals who had been conducting informal philosophical salons under the rubric of the *Gelanggang Maya* (Illusion Collective), formed into a theatre troupe. On 24 May 1944, Rosihan Anwar, Abu Hanifah and Usmar Ismail joined together in Jakarta to form *Sandiwara Penggemar Maya* (the Illusion Amateur Theatre), the first organized troupe in the history of amateur nationalist theatre.[8] Although Maya disbanded in 1945, as the beginning of the revolution propelled many of its members into military and administrative roles, it began a movement to develop a commitment to theatre as 'an instrument of culture, an expression of culture with national consciousness, humanity and divinity' (Sumardjo, 1992: 134). These emphases mark a crucial shift for nationalist theatre, which had up to that point represented anti-colonial sentiment through heroic and mythic characters and narratives. Maya set out to develop an Indonesian theatre representing the *humanity* of the Indonesian people, not simply the nobility of *ratu adil* (just prince) figures. With the return of the Dutch and the beginning of the Revolution, some of the professional theatre artists attempted briefly to return to their old practices. However, in 1948, as the process of recognizing Indonesia's independence began, the dormant film industry started up again, and nearly all the old professional actors abandoned theatre for film, leaving the field to Ismail and these young amateurs.

One of the most striking aspects of Maya was that apart from a performance of *Si Bakhil* (Molière's *L'Avare*) and *Djeritan Hidoep Baroe* (an adaptation by Karim Halim of Ibsen's *Lille Eyolf*), both performed in May 1945, their repertoire consisted entirely of original works by Abu Hanifah and his younger brother, Usmar Ismail.[9] Ismail had been working for the Keimin Bunka Shidosho, and quickly emerged as the member of Maya with the greatest theatrical craft. The three plays he wrote for the troupe between late 1943 and early 1945 were published in 1948 under the title, *Sedih dan Gembira* (*Sad and Happy*).[10] Though Ismail would turn decisively at the end of the decade from theatre to film, the three plays in this early collection have been taken into the canon of major Indonesian dramatic works.

This is due in no small part to the fact that H. B. Jassin, a member of *Maya* at the time, emerged after Independence as 'the custodian of Indonesian literature.' Jassin devotes an entire chapter to his colleague, Ismail, in his seminal *Indonesian Modern Literature in Essays and Criticism*, and Mbijo Saleh devotes a quarter of his book, *Theatre and Education* (one of only a few full-length studies of theatre in Indonesia published prior to Oemarjati's history) to an extended analysis of Ismail's plays. Subsequent anthologies and surveys of Indonesian dramatic literature have never failed to consider him as a major figure, all following from Jassin's judgment that Ismail filled a major 'transitional' role in the emergence of the Generation of '45.

Jassin contends that Ismail had still not distanced himself from the '*Sturm und Drang* idealism' of the *Poedjangga Baroe* poets and a sentimentalism still tied to tradition, but that these allowed him to express himself within the parameters of Japanese propaganda. In all the plays, romantic youths are confronted with moral choices to which Ismail presents a correct answer that affirms nationalism and tradition without challenging the role of the Japanese government. In *Api* (*Fire*), there are two scientists, one devoted to personal aggrandizement through development of a new explosive, the other to social welfare through development of a cure for malaria. The humanitarian prevails over the individualist.[11] In *Tjitra*, there are two brothers who each love the same girl (another feminine corporealization of Indonesia) in the context of an East Javanese factory that has just started producing again five months after the Japanese arrival. In reconciling their dispute and saving her from disgrace, they save the nation, incidentally 'inspiring society,' 'developing a work spirit' and 'aiding development' as Jassin wryly notes (1954: 175).

Liburan Seniman (*Artists' Holiday*), produced in the middle of Maya's trajectory, offers a fascinating glimpse into how Ismail viewed the company's role vis-à-vis nationalist and Japanese goals, traditional social values and the values of professional commercial theatre (Figure 4.2). A group of aspiring artists have felt the stirrings of nationalist awakening, but have been frustrated at their menial jobs or inability to serve in the National Defense Force. They rally around Suromo, who has written a play called *From Awakening to Victory*:

> This is the story of the struggle of a young Indonesian man and woman who hope to see realized their nation's ideals but find themselves pulled apart by their own blood. Since they first developed feelings, they've struggled, but when they want to find a place for themselves, they fall victim to the ethnic thinking they've opposed all this time. He goes to the field of battle without being united with his sweetheart, but the two of them make an oath that they'll struggle for a New Homeland.
>
> (Bodden, 2009: 144)

The youths, who share a common feeling that this play expresses stirrings deep within them, dedicate themselves to mounting a production. However, a series of practical impediments threaten the enterprise. They gain and lose the funding of a local businessman (Tahir Malik), gain the funding of Suromo's employer (Raden Hassan) and then lose it as soon as Hassan learns the play is the work of his least reliable employee. Unsurprisingly, they run through a series of difficulties relating to actresses. In one instance, parents prevent their daughter performing and 'Miss Sulastri is afraid her reputation would be stained if she acted in a play nowadays' (141); another is prevented by her fiancé from portraying a middle-aged woman (160); and Rani, who does perform in the play, insists that she wear a traditional *kebaya*,

Figure 4.2 The Maya Amateur Theatre's production of Usmar Ismail's *Liburan Seniman*, 1944 (Author's collection)

'otherwise people will say I'm too westernized' (157). Kartalasmara, an old timer who has 'been working in the theater since the time of *stambul* and *bangsawan*, through to *Dardanella* and on till today,' watches all this unfold and laughs at their inexperience.

It is in the dialogue between the old professional, Kartalasmara, and the young amateur director of the production, Kajiman, that Ismail presents a stark contrast between the nationalist and commercial theatres. Suromo had given this old man a copy of the script in deference to the knowledge of his elder, though Kajiman insists on the need for the young to transcend the old thinking. When Kertalasmara arrives at a rehearsal, the old actor's criticism might just as easily indict all the nationalist literary drama:

> the play is nothing more than a series of conversations, so that just reading it I was already bored. I can't imagine watching it. There's no action, there's no physical movement [...] No, my dear friends, the audience will just laugh at this.

Kajiman replies that this work speaks to different audiences than those who prefer the 'popular theatre': 'Even though we're only talking, still in these conversations there's a friction like a stone rubbed against iron that sparks a flame. And in the same way conversations with deep content will set the hearts of the viewers aflame' (142). Later, Kartalasmara criticizes realistic vocal cadences onstage, urging them to use full Shakespearean voices, and to free the actors to move more by letting them improvise from plot outlines. Eventually, he is bored, and pointedly leaves to go see a boxing match (148). Upon seeing the production, Kartalasmara finds little to admire. He accuses the production of having nothing Eastern in it, to which Suromo delivers a response worthy of Sanusi Pane: 'The East is something with sacred significance. It shouldn't be used to defend one's position or to counter one's opponent' (166). In other words, 'Indonesia' is the inner self-awakening that will find expression through modern artistic developments, not through the pleasing spectacles of the commercial stage.

Of course, there is no small amount of revisionist polemic here on Ismail's part. By collapsing all of 'popular theatre' into one figure who espouses the least literate and most spectacular manifestations found therein, he presents Maya as a radical rupture from all its predecessors. In point of fact, Maya's preference for literary playtexts and realistic acting did not differ much from that of Dardanella. However, *Liburan Seniman* presents the nationalist struggle as a spirit rising within the youth, in relation to which the older generation appears lazy at best, corrupt at worst. As Kartalasmara represents the older generation's obsolete art, so the obsolete social values of the older generation are represented in the figure of Uncle Garmo. He constantly scolds Ratmi and Suromo for wasting their time with a play that doesn't even have dances and songs (and won't make any profit) rather than making a good living and looking after their marriage. However, we learn early in the play that Garmo had made his own profit by swindling his partner, who is the father of one of the actors, Kanto. Kanto wryly describes Garmo as a kind of clever, deceitful actor 'with a poker face' that 'sometimes reveals its cards,' a corrupt contrast to the youth actors whose actions flow from an inner nationalist awakening (Bodden, 2009: 133). At the conclusion of the play, Garmo's corruption is exposed and Raden Hasan arrives to express his solidarity with the young artists. 'I don't want to be put in the same category as Raden Garmoyono' (173). The older generation redeems itself in this final image by repudiating greed and affirming the value of an ideal-driven theatre.

More specifically, Hasan gives his support to a theatre that serves the people 'without lowering yourself into the valley of shallowness and impoverished emotions' (173). He thereby consolidates one of the play's central themes, which would become a guiding principle for Ismail's approach to actor training, and would find expression in several generations of Indonesian educational institutions and troupes. As Kajiman explains in an early scene, the youth find inspiration in the awakening of true feelings and emotions. However, 'Don't think it's you who've awakened. You're still asleep, but something has awakened in your soul, Indonesia has awakened.' It is not a romanticist individualism that is awakening, but rather a power 'concealed within the Indonesian people' (135–6). This is the 'Awakening' of Suromo's play. 'That's the spirit that I want to release from within me' (148). This is the *semangat* that will bring success to amateur nationalist troupes, despite their failings.

In 1948, Ismail participated in a Cultural Congress (*Kongres Kebudajaan*) at Magelang, near Yogyakarta, where he joined in the historic first discussions concerning the future of Indonesian national culture. He urged the assembly that if amateur theatre is to thrive in the new republic, it must be professionalized. Scorning the imitative and improvisational style of the old *commercial* professional theatre, he calls for a 'systematic' approach to training and rehearsal in order to produce more carefully crafted characterizations. This will lead, in Ismail's thinking, to a more profound artistic 'consciousness':

> experience uninformed by consciousness, effort and the quest, both broad and deep, for the foundations of knowledge is like a farmer who works his fields only out of inherited custom without making an effort to find out how he can achieve greater and more satisfying results. Repetition from night to night and from day to day provides the opportunity for directors and actors to become conscious in the moment of the need to study the performance and to execute the needed repairs.
>
> (Ismail, 1983: 41–2)

The 'consciousness' Ismail finds lacking on the professional stage is first and foremost a consciousness of consistent and 'rounded' characterization associated with realism. However, it is also, implicitly, a national consciousness, the same kind of consciousness through which the farmer must throw off the shackles of the nineteenth-century Dutch cultivation system and develop modern and personally beneficial ways of working his fields. In the immediate aftermath of colonialism, Ismail saw only two options for the patronage of modern theatre: some form of state-supported national theatre or the 'commercial pit.'

In his view, Indonesian intellectuals needed to be strong in these years in building a national theatre that would not compromise in moving beyond the craft of acting as practiced previously in the commercial theatre. The actor must achieve a more profound consciousness in relation to his role. Ismail concludes his statement admonishing,

> it must be realized by the amateurs that amateurism is not a solid foundation for an art that may be hoped to grow strong. Our hope is that within a brief time a professional corps may be established, who with full conviction will dedicate themselves to this art, without any more need to fear the near-sighted.
>
> (1983, 43)

Essentially, Ismail hopes for a modern theatrical *pesantren* to train actors with the same *semangat* as that of the *pemuda* currently fighting in the revolution. These truly revolutionary and postcolonial actors would represent a modern Indonesian identity beyond the surface play of idealized heroes, but expressive rather of individual Indonesian souls. Ismail would continue searching for this technique over the next decade through his work in film.

In 1950–1, Ismail took inspiration from the Italian neo-realist filmmakers, and began casting untrained actors in his films as a means to capture a performative authenticity obscured by the histrionic techniques of the old professional theatre. Neo-realism appealed to Ismail as an approach stripped of essentializing conventions, and thus seemingly well suited to the project of representing the true condition of the Indonesian people. As Salim Said puts it, 'PERFINI [Ismail's film company] [...] did its best to show the real face of Indonesia' (1991: 54), a face that Ismail found missing in the films of his rivals, which relied more exclusively on the box-office draw of old professional theatre stars to turn a profit. He conducted general casting calls, attracting mainly untrained students, and rehearsed them until he had selected his principals. In a 1963 article, he laments his early purism: 'One of my problems as a neophyte was that I wanted everything to be authentic, like the original and in the original locations. My official and unofficial advisers increasingly urged me not to deviate from the actual events. Only my opponents understood that the film was actually *make-believe* [...].' Ismail recognized later to his chagrin that however realistic, it was not enough for actors to 'be themselves.' They needed to be themselves as characters. Furthermore, he found that untrained actors had no greater capacity than professionals to portray realistic characters in a simple and consistent manner, whereas they utterly lacked the skills necessary to portray characters that demanded histrionic embellishment: 'After a great deal more experience in direction, I came to realize that acting less than is required, *under-acting*, is not always appropriate for all characters. Sometimes exactly what a role calls for is *over-acting* (Ismail, 1983b: 168).

Asrul Sani, reflecting on the same problem, argues that neo-realism doesn't work in Indonesian film because the actors aren't 'theatrical' enough. If Indonesian actors were sufficiently theatrical, they wouldn't need to 'act' (falsify) in front of the camera. Their 'natural' behavior would be sufficiently compelling. However, he carefully resists a return to the histrionics of the old professional theatre. Instead, he demands a disciplined theatricality animated by 'genuine' impulses (Sani, 1997b: 212–13). In recognizing the failure of Ismail's neo-realism, Sani admits that undisciplined behavior does not produce theatrical authenticity. Instead, the actor must learn to create a more truthful representation, a theatrical artifice that will operate in harmony with his own postcolonial identity (214–16). In short, the 'real face of Indonesia' that Ismail had sought in vain could only be discovered by an actor who looks into the face of his character as at the face of another.

Indonesian method acting

On 29 September 1955, over 39 million Indonesians turned out for the nation's first free democratic election. The Nationalist Party (PNI), the Communist Party (PKI) and the two major Islamic parties took about 20 percent of the vote each, and the remainder was split amongst numerous minor parties. To a society bewildered by the ongoing chaos of political debate, the lack of a definitive victor came as a disappointment. In retrospect, this 1955 election, Indonesia's last democratic election until 1999, may be seen as the beginning of a rapid slide towards President Soekarno's dismantlement of parliamentary democracy in 1957. With this 'guided democracy,' the actual representation of political parties gave way to 'functional groups,' replacing real ideological differences with reductive identity categories: 'the workers,' 'the farmers,' 'the students,' and so forth, to all of whom Soekarno represented himself as a dalang (puppeteer) on the Indonesian political stage. Similarly, the elections marked a turning point in the commitment of the revolutionary intelligentsia to public cultural policy. While President Soekarno replaced civic discourse with his own soliloquies, Sani and Ismail operated Indonesia's 'national' theatre academy as a private institution.

Sani looked to Konstantin Stanislavsky as the answer to Ismail's failure to discover a productive middle ground between technique and spontaneity. He began his formal theatre studies with a brief sojourn at the Theaterschool of the Hogeschool voor de Kunsten in Amsterdam in 1952 (Rosidi and Sani, 1997: xv). Either here or on subsequent trips to the United States in 1954 (to Harvard) and 1956 (to the University of Southern California), he became convinced that Indonesia's path to its own version of Italian neo-realism depended on a Stanislavskian approach to acting. It can be surmised that he was drawn to American Method more specifically at the time of his extended study of dramaturgy and cinematography at USC in Los Angeles in 1956 (1997: xvii). Indeed, the acting manuals that formed the canon of the *Akademi Teater Nasional Indonesia* (ATNI, Indonesian National Theatre Academy) through Sani's translations (Richard Boleslavsky's *The First Six Lessons* and Stanislavsky's American trilogy – *An Actor Prepares, Building a Character* and *Creating a Role*) indicate that he followed the American, rather than the Russian or even European textual traditions.[12] Sani was not content, however, simply to translate. Through his philosophical commitments to individualism, existentialism and postcolonial cultural nationalism, he developed a unique understanding of American Method acting as indispensable to the Indonesian national project. As head of Indonesia's leading theatre academy, Sani built the entire training program around this understanding.

Method allowed Sani to draw an active distinction between the old professional star system that he and Ismail associated with the commercial theatre and a new professionalism rooted in psychoanalytic acting. In the introduction to his translation of Boleslavsky, Sani writes:

An actor is the opposite of a 'Star.' The forte of an actor is not his pretty face or his good build, but his *capacity* to animate and inspire a character before a spectator. We love him not for his persona, but exactly because he succeeds in taking leave of his persona to become another persona. In contrast to a 'star,' an actor is capable of performing different characters [...]. While a 'Star' becomes faded with age, an actor in contrast becomes more mature, and better. But he must purchase all this with concerted diligence, study, analysis and practice. They [actors] pay attention to all matters, not only everyday life, but the effects of other arts.

(Sani, 1960: 8)

Sani imagines the new Indonesian actor as free in a way that movie stars and old professional actors were never free. It is a freedom rooted in the Generation of '45's organicist vision of postcolonial awakening, although ultimately, the craft of Sani's postcolonial actor will depart substantially from an organicist imagination.

As not every politician is equally capable of leading Indonesia into the future, not every acting student will produce the same results from their training. As Ismail writes: '*Bakat* (talent) is a gift that someone receives, possessed from birth as a gift from God that allows him to pick up an art more easily than other people.' Someone who possesses sufficient talent may even outshine the trained actor, while those without talent will progress very slowly. However, the actor who relies on talent alone will be limited to the resources of his own personality, and will not be able to create something new, such as a new national culture (Ismail, 1968: 9). The journey of the Indonesian actor requires not only talent, but the same *semangat* that animated the revolutionary *pemuda*. In describing the Stanislavsky system, Sani invokes a discipline that reaches deep into the actor's soul:

Stanislavsky divides his system into two parts, first 'inner technique' and second 'physical technique.' Bodily movement is derived from a spiritual source. Every movement or outer expression that is performed is the result of a preparation of the soul that is long and penetrating. For a youth who wants to be an actor, it is no longer enough simply to have talent or will alone. These must be incorporated with hard work.

(1960: 6)

If Sani begins with an American version of Stanislavsky's teaching that emphasizes psychological training, he transforms it through a distinctly postcolonial metaphysics. Talent is seen neither as the element that makes discipline superfluous (undermining the need for training) nor as something superfluous itself, but rather as a variety of *semangat*, a mystical potential to be channeled through discipline. Accordingly, the academy training interpolates foreign acting methods made native through patterns of self-epistemology and development consistent with the ongoing *revolusi jiwa*, the revolution of the soul.

ATNI's emphasis on training Indonesian actors to perform characters in plays from the Euro-American canon has struck most critics as an abjection vis-à-vis the West. As Sani and Ismail frequently replied, they never encouraged Indonesian actors to imitate Western actors. Sani insists that it is the mastery of a more authentic creative *process* that is desired. Explaining the use of Boleslavsky for Indonesian actors, Sani writes:

> in his way of thinking, it is not a graceful gesture that makes someone into an actor, but the consistent inner aspect that makes the gesture genuine. He does not instruct us in the way that we smoke, sit and so forth on the stage. But he wants to point out that the inner aspect is how we generate a specific way of smoking, and how we go about discovering that inner aspect. What Boleslavsky presents are the first problems that must be tackled by an actor before he performs a gesture. And these first problems are valid for every actor, regardless of his nationality. Because of this, we can also make use of him for our purposes.
>
> (1960: 5–6)

In Boleslavsky, as in most American Method acting theory, realistic action onstage derives from truthful psychological impulses on the part of the actor. Sani appropriates the psychology of this process as simply a 'consistent inner aspect.' This subtle recasting abstracts the Method from the American fascination with individual feelings in order to interpolate it into Sani's 'revolution of the soul.' Psychological truth in service to representational realism becomes a personal mystical truth in service to postcolonial subjectivity.

To put it another way, the psychology of identification with the character becomes, for Sani, an internalization of anti-colonial struggle. He writes that 'for actors, the basis for truth is the struggle between their own personalities and the personalities of the characters they wish to portray.' It is a 'struggle' that will not result in complete identification. 'A one hundred percent identification surely cannot be achieved, because within ourselves we keep substances that reveal our identities, and which it is not possible for us to escape, no matter how much we wish it.' The struggle for identification trains the actor to recognize his own 'substance,' and to be able to construct personae to achieve specific actions beyond that basis. Sani views this process of struggle with a character that is insurmountably Other, that cannot be identified with 'one hundred percent,' as a path to a creativity consisting of identification co-ordinated with artificial construction. He believes that a true characterization can be achieved across the spectrum of identification and construction, from the rare cases of pure identification – 'a correspondence between the actor and the character, such that the two make use of the same emotion' – to combinations of identification and construction (the vast majority of cases) to pure construction when 'the situation portrayed by the actor is indeed foreign' (1960: 13–14). Indonesian actors, in their inalienable 'substance,' continue the inner revolution in confrontation (not merely identification) with foreign roles. The actor interpolates the colonial ideology inherent in Western characterization as a means to discover his own soul.

Sani's profoundly individualistic understanding of Indonesian cultural nationalism increasingly parted ways with state policy. Mohamad cites Sani in 1955 describing Indonesian nationalism as 'a nationalism still in search of its foundations,' and he was certain that these foundations lay not with any easy national chauvinism, but with a difficult individualism. In this, Mohamad credits Sani with moving beyond the essentialist rhetoric of the day, and anticipating Edward Said's criticism of Orientalist essentialism a quarter-century later. He cites Sani on the failures of cultural policy towards the individual, stemming from this narrow essentialism: 'This is something disavowed by those who want to turn us into a group of soldiers who get spurred on from right to left. This is something that people are protected from in this variety of democracy that wants to strangle all inner nationalisms' (Mohamad, 1997: 50). Sani declares that Indonesia must turn now to the 'inner revolution (*revolusi jiwa*)' that 'will not end' (cited in Mohamad, 1997: 44). In this stage of the revolution, in the *revolusi jiwa*, the leadership of actors will outstrip that of soldiers or politicians, because only they will achieve the requisite inner discipline through methodical training. Furthermore, in Sani's view, only Jakarta could serve as an appropriate site for this struggle. This frontier of the soul, this *pesantren* city to which he invites the disciplined actor, offers rebirth into freedom from all the feudal and colonial hierarchies, all the 'characters' of old.

When in 1948 Ismail called for the establishment of 'a new communal house' in the service of Indonesian theatre, he expressed the aspirations of a generation expectant that the new Republican state would catalyze an authentic postcolonial culture. By 1953, the general disillusionment of the artistic intelligentsia towards state cultural policy was also reflected in thinking about modern theatre. Sani, in a series of magazine articles written between June and September 1953, progressed from a general dismay towards the insufficiency of Ministry funding for theatre groups to a conviction that a private League of Dramatic Arts would be the most dynamic catalyst for a modern Indonesian theatre culture (see Sani, 1997c). In the early 1950s, the Ministry had established numerous academies of traditional arts, music and dance as ministerial sub-divisions. By the middle of the decade, Sani and Ismail both argued that a national theatre academy must be private, or at least claim a greater degree of sovereignty from state bureaucracy.

Three weeks before the General Election, on 10 September 1955, Asrul Sani, Usmar Ismail and D. Djajakusuma established ATNI privately through a special arrangement with Jakarta's mayor. By the early 1960s, ATNI would find itself on the losing side of an ideological confrontation with the increasingly influential Lekra (the communist cultural council). Their production activities ground to a halt after 1962, and their academic program closed soon after the 1963 'Cultural Manifesto' affair in which Generation of '45 artists asserting their freedom from ideology were denounced and blacklisted. In retrospect, it appears that ATNI was created in the eye of a gathering storm at one of the last moments in which it was possible. That said, ATNI accomplished a great deal in a short amount of time. Although they stressed pedagogy over production, ATNI produced 23 productions between 1958 and 1963 (some in the Schouwburg, others in a lecture hall of the University of Indonesia).[13] If one were to include the independent productions of ATNI students such as Steve Liem (Teguh Karya), Wahyu Sihombing and Pramana Padmadarmaya, ATNI's production history would encompass the majority of modern theatrical performances in Jakarta over the second half of the Soekarno era. It was undoubtedly the example of ATNI's productions at various Soekarno era theatre festivals that inspired the spread of similar Method-based 'acting courses' to STB in Bandung and Rendra's Youth Theatre in Yogyakarta.

ATNI's numerous productions of realist drama might seem the best indication of their success at staging Method. However, Sani's celebrated 1958 production of Jean-Paul Sartre's *Pintu Tertutup* (*Huis Clos*) provides a more intriguing example. Whereas in most psychological realism, environment progressively reveals identity, in Sartre's play identities struggle in an explicitly superfluous environment. Sartre's characters, much like Sani's revolutionary souls, are figures who must forge a new identity beyond history, in a room strewn with the ridiculous debris of cultural history. Sartre depicts figures who must give rebirth to themselves in order to survive. The topography of Sartre's stage may be psychological, but both psychology and ontology are subordinated to these subjective epistemologies. As Sani repeatedly affirms in his own writings, the world created by European domination is the given stage for all contemporary inner revolutions, but it is up to us to perform those revolutions. The deceased characters, Garcin, Inez and Estelle, all reject the hideous 'Second Empire furnishings' of their shared prison cell as having nothing to do with themselves, but individually recognize that this will nevertheless be the background for their postmortem performances. When Indonesian actors portray this rejection and *anagnorisis*, the situation takes on a clear postcolonial significance. The hideous colonial infrastructure is the stage on which the postcolonial revolution must take place.[14] The characters famously conclude that 'Hell is other people,' and the play ends with mad laughter.

Ever since this premiere, *Pintu Tertutup* has served as a staple of Indonesian modern theatre, and a proving ground for actors. In particular, the character of Inez has always attracted Indonesian actresses.[15] There are relatively few opportunities for actresses to play assertive roles on the Indonesian stage, making exceptions such as *Pintu Tertutup* particularly striking. Since many young Indonesian women are uncomfortable portraying the character's sexual aggression, they work with available local archetypes of Jakarta prostitutes and other women who flaunt dominant sexual moralities. In these cases, the process of identification leads Indonesian actresses into intracultural struggles with marginalized Indonesian identities. In a 1999 performance of the play by student actors of the *Institut Kesenian Jakarta* (IKJ, Jakarta Art Institute), actors took great delight in the play's final moment. This exuberant terror, this tragicomic hysteria, might be seen as the cathartic rejection of that militaristic notion of postcolonial Indonesia as a corps of the like-minded. The Indonesian actors portraying these defiantly individualistic characters confront dangerous images of the self, measuring their own souls against cultural values that they have learned to see as foreign.

In the Suharto era, a string of institutions continued ATNI's tradition. ATNI itself resumed operations for a few years at the end of the decade, by which point Teguh Karya's *Teater Populer* had begun to operate as a kind of producing master class, building on the same theoretical foundations. In 1976, The Institut Kesenian Jakarta (IKJ) opened at TIM, offering college-level education in all the arts. Wahyu Sihombing, a graduate of ATNI's first class in 1955, who had already assumed a leading role in educational programming in 1973 through the Youth Theatre Festival, took on new duties organizing the new Institute's theatre department. As various critics have commented, ATNI had served as a kind of theatre troupe under the direction of Asrul Sani. Similarly, Sihombing formed his *Teater Lembaga* (Group Theatre) from IKJ's department of theatre. By Sumardjo's estimation, Sihombing staged 14 productions with his group between its founding in 1975 and his death in 1989, including works by Ibsen, Arthur Miller and Tennessee Williams (all of whom are still staged frequently by IKJ students; see Sumardjo 1992: 209). Sihombing transferred Stanislavsky-based training and a focus on the Western dramatic canon (especially the modern realists) from ATNI to IKJ, a continuity that he clearly outlines in his discussion of Teater Lembaga's production of Ibsen's *Musuh Masyarakat* (*Enemy of the People*) for TIM's *Pertemuan Teater 1980* (Sihombing, 1980). Despite some changes over the course of the New Order, such as the promotion of ensemble improvisation by Bengkel veteran, Jose Rizal Manua, Stanislavsky has remained at the core of actor training at the nation's leading theatre institute. Teguh Karya and Suyatna Anirun continued to promote work of similar aesthetic commitments through the remainder of the Suharto era. Despite a frequent refrain in Indonesian cultural discourse that the arts must find more authentic roots in local cultures, Sani's commitment to a *revolusi jiwa* accomplished through application of an imported acting method to an imported repertoire still informs much of modern theatre's search for 'the real face of Indonesia.'

Dewi Dja recalls in her autobiography having asked Andjar Asmara one night in the days of Dardanella to tell her about Mahieu. Asmara responded that Mahieu was a Westerner whose innovations provided the model for a Chinese practitioner named Tio, whose innovations inspired more innovations by a Westerner named Piedro, and that the time would come for Indonesians to make their own innovations and create a true modern Malay theatre. In Ismail's *Liburan Seniman*, the 70-year history of popular urban theatre from *bangsawan* to Dardanella becomes the professional commercial theatre, in opposition to which the time had come for idealist amateurs to create a true Indonesian theatre. These myths of rupture, these needs for the syncopation of the gap that separates past from present practices have recurred with each new moment in which artists seek to re-inspirit a degraded national culture. They are always attended by a binary that makes of the past a racial or ideological other so that the subjects of the new present may emerge whole as from a *jahilliyah*, a time of ignorance. So a new Generation of '66 would look to W. S. Rendra and begin to say that all prior modern Indonesian theatre was shackled to Western dramaturgy. Many ghosts were silenced in the Suharto era, but not entirely exorcized. Even New Order theatre artists committed to a new local organicism nevertheless turned to imported techniques and repertoires again and again in confronting lives that only became more profoundly influenced by the flows of global capitalism. By the late 1960s, few artists were interested in colonialism as a direct theme. Nevertheless, foreign ghosts were summoned to the stage again and again to haunt the ongoing failures of the revolution.

5
Hamlet and *Caligula*: Echoes of a Voice Unclear in Origins

The wandering woman

Under the Japanese occupation, dramatists with pre-war reputations (such as Asmara and Pane) and a younger generation including Ismail and Hanifah all wrote nationalistic plays couched primarily within the aesthetics of social realism. Apart from a few works such as Kartakusuma's *Prabu dan Puteri* (1950) and Moertono's *Genderang Bratajuda* (1953), post-Ibsenite realism remained the prevailing style of new Indonesian drama through the Soekarno era. Though there were mild experiments in existentialist, absurdist and mythic aesthetics, the new generation of playwrights, including Utuy Tatang Sontani, Sitor Situmorang, Kirdjomulyo, Motinggo Busje and Nasjah Djamin, populated their works with ordinary Indonesians facing contemporary social issues in recognizable contemporary Indonesian settings. In relation to this norm, Sontani's first play, *Suling* (*Flute*), written in 1948 in the midst of the revolution, provides a startling contrast. It is an allegorical work that sets the emergent challenge of postcoloniality within a genealogy of oppression.

The story proceeds in the style of an allegorical morality play, following a man and woman (Panji and Sri) through a series of five encounters with different 'comrades' or 'friends.' The play begins with an angel placing this man and woman in an empty landscape, a cleared space within which they may cultivate the 'fire in their souls.' Young and unfettered, they enjoy a pure mutual love through their respective creativities; Panji plays a *suling* given to him by the angel, and Sri dances to the music. There can be little doubt that this couple represents Indonesia as the garden before the Fall, prior to civilization and history. In this imagined state of primordial origin, they joyfully express their sacred freedom. However, such a state of innocence cannot last long.

A first comrade arrives offering extended companionship. At this point, critics have differed greatly in interpreting Sontani's allegory. Jassin, Teeuw and Luigi Santa Maria consider this figure to be representative of Indic cultural influence (though there is little detail in the text on which to base such a reading; Jassin, 1954: vol. 2: 185–9; Santa Maria, 1954: 4–7; Teeuw, 1967: 190–1). Harry Aveling's view is somewhat clearer. He suggests that this figure stands for the ethos of mutual co-operation (*gotong royong*) heavily promoted by cultural nationalists as a fundamental component of the Indonesian character. As bearer of community traditions, this first comrade makes the couple aware of gendered proprieties: 'a woman's responsibility is to quietly fence her body' (Aveling, 1969: 332; Sontani, 1948: 18). Panji accepts the rules. Sri stops dancing. A second comrade arrives, asserting the supremacy of God. So Panji affirms his faith, and now that they are believers they must be properly married, which in turn brings further social restrictions upon Sri: 'The face of your wife must be hidden, veiled, not seen, covered by cloth' (Aveling: 335; Sontani: 28–30). What had begun with restriction of her movements, now extends to her countenance. This third figure clearly has brought them organized religion (Jassin and Teeuw say Islam specifically, thus to follow the Indic comrade), though Aveling sees him more as a social elaboration of the first comrade, from community to social integration through institutions such as marriage. The third comrade brings finance, espousing the virtues of 'an exchange economy, backbone of prosperity.' Though this comrade's 'gift' might be taken broadly as economic development, Jassin and Teeuw note the unequal brokerage of the deal as a clear reference to a global capitalism controlled by foreigners. The third comrade thereby represents the coming of Western colonization. He offers Panji food, but alas the price is high. Sri must sacrifice her bracelets in payment. Things are starting to get rough for the couple, as the basis of their communication is progressively legislated and traded away.

Whereas the first three comrades had solicited Panji to join their respective institutions, the fourth demands obedience. Under his leadership, the playing of the flute is transformed from a choice to a privilege. Panji must obtain permission from this new 'government' before engaging in any free expression. With the very impulse to free expression thus fettered to a state apparatus, Panji no longer feels like playing. Sri, who can no longer even hear the music to which she once danced, abandons Panji and leaves the stage.

If Sri (like Bebasari, Sukaesih and Tjitra) is the female embodiment of Indonesia, and Panji (like Bujangga, Sugiat etc.) the male youth given agency to strive for the nation, then Sontani's play rests at this penultimate moment in an unusually dark vision of the nationalist struggle. The fourth comrade, bearer of government, silences art and ultimately ends the 'relationship' between the nation's youth and the nation. Sontani portrays social 'development' as a progressive alienation from authentic expressions of the self and authentic communication with the 'fire in their souls.' Progress brings to Indonesia alienation of the body, followed by concealment of the face, followed by a stripping of treasure, and culminating in total absence. In the end, politics reigns triumphant over a truly barren and sterile landscape. Jassin, following a brief gloss set out by Sontani in the midst of his short story, *Mengarang* ('Writing,' see Sontani, 1951), associates the first three friends with the respective cultural polemic philosophies of Dewantara, Mansur and Hatta, but cannot bring himself to follow Sontani in viewing the last figure as Soekarno. 'I would much rather see the Japanese fascism as revealed in this friend,' he writes (Jassin, 1954, vol. 2: 188). Aveling, in contrast, credits Sontani with predicting that postcolonial governments would fail to exorcize the spirits of prior regimes (1951: 339–40).

In *Mengarang*, Sontani writes that he had written this much of the play prior to Soekarno's proclamation of Indonesian Independence on 17 August 1945, and could not imagine how to finish it. He found inspiration in an encounter with a young lady who treated him rudely (1951: 26). This wandering woman (*perempuan pengembara*) appears to Panji as the play's fifth and final figure. She cares little for any of the gifts of the previous friends, rejecting community, marriage, materialism and the authority of the state. In short, she answers only to herself, and this makes her invulnerable. She asks Panji to become her companion forever and offers him an extraordinary gift: 'the world shall become a field where you can enjoy yourself' (Sontani, 1948: 78). He kisses her, but declines her offer. However, the kiss has given him a kind of transcendence. He asserts himself over the four comrades and takes back his flute. He tells the wandering woman that her pleasure is not enough. The only truth she knows is negation. Panji turns from her and draws Sri back to the stage with the music from his flute.

Aveling puzzles at the meaning of this extraordinary final figure, this 'mixture of divine woman and prostitute' (1969: 342). Jassin states simply that she is 'the inspiration of the artist which gives him strength' (1954: 185). Aveling is dissatisfied by the implication that the artist must reject his inspiration as a negative force. He offers his own reading: 'Is it too fanciful, following through the historical interpretation to see in the woman the Revolution itself, with an awareness on Utuy's behalf of the double nature of war, beneficial in bringing freedom, harmful in taking life?' (1969: 342). Further than this, is it too fanciful to see in the woman an alternate vision of Indonesia itself who occupies the stage as an uncanny double of Sri? At the moment in civilization shown with the arrival of the fourth comrade, Indonesia as primordial origin has already left the stage. It would seem an enactment of Alisjahbana's view of pre-colonial origins as 'dead as dead can be.' And yet, the play ends happily in a vision of organicist unity, the restitution of a true national community in which the original dances can be danced to the original music. However, the road to this nativist modernization passes through a disturbing incident that must be repeated in every performance. The nationalist youth must kiss the wandering woman who stands for the negation of all truths. Can Panji simply forget this affair and return to his Sri, or will the wandering woman always haunt the dancing nation?

Over the course of two decades following *Suling*, Sontani emerged as the most prolific and celebrated playwright in the new Indonesian republic.

His works, which were performed frequently at home and translated and celebrated in the West, explore a variety of responses to the nativist predicament presented in his first play. Although most of his works explore familial relationships in a realistic idiom that is never far removed from the *universalisme* of the Generation of '45, he also looks for inspiration to local ethnic communal life (*Bunga Rumahmakan*, 1948) and traditional Sundanese narratives (*Sangkuriang*, 1953). In this, his work suggests the approach advocated by Lekra, the communist 'People's Cultural Association,' to pay sincere attention to local ethnic traditions as a more authentic basis for the modern national culture (once their counter-revolutionary aspects are refined away). Ironically, with the absolute vilification of communism after 1965, Lekra came to be associated with atheism and censorship, and those impulses that would seem to presage New Order nativism were forgotten.

On the night of 30 September 1965, when six Indonesian generals were murdered by an inept communist *coup*, Sontani was in Beijing with a PKI delegation honoring China's national liberation day. He would never return to his homeland. He watched from China as hundreds of thousands of members (and presumed members) of the Communist Party were murdered in reprisal, and Lieutenant General Suharto cautiously assumed control of the nation. As China's own Cultural Revolution made life increasingly difficult for foreigners, Sontani boarded a Trans-Siberian train for Europe in 1971, disembarked in Moscow, and lived out the rest of his days in the Soviet Union. In the 1950s, at a time when most theatre artists, like Asrul Sani, were producing works by foreign (and mostly Euro-American) playwrights in translation, Sontani wrote original plays that experimented with local settings and regional narrative traditions. Nevertheless, from the perspective of the Generation of '66, he was not only a representative of a Westward-gazing generation, but a communist. As of 2007, the plays of Utuy Tatang Sontani, the foremost playwright of the 1950s, were not listed in the drama inventory of the H. B. Jassin Documentation Center at Taman Ismail Marzuki. The Jassin Center is the most extensive repository of dramatic manuscripts in the nation, to which theatre artists in other major cities turn to research their dramatic heritage. Thus, absence from their lists is a significant indication of absence from the archive in general.

Anxieties over the authenticity of modern theatre's repertoire cannot be laid to rest in a spectral nation perpetually haunted by foreign dominance. As with successive avant-gardes in the West, each generation of Indonesian theatre artists have created new myths of rupture that relegate their predecessors to a less authentic connection to the true origins of the nation. Barbara Hatley notes that Rendra has commanded respect from the beginning of the Suharto era on as 'founder of and model for' a 'dominant trend' in modern theatre on Java:

> one which drew strongly and directly on local Javanese theatre tradition.
> Narratives, characters and scenic conventions from the wayang tradition

were invoked in modern plays; gamelan music, traditional dance and shadow puppetry provided a common store of stage devices.

In that first decade of renewed activity with Teater Bengkel after his return from America, Rendra commanded an unprecedented respect as both leading counter-cultural innovator and man of the people. However, by the late 1980s, younger theatre groups looked at Rendra in terms surprisingly similar to how Rendra's generation had viewed Asrul Sani and his circle. Central Javanese troupes such as Jeprik, Gandrik and Gapit asserted stronger claims to Javanese locality than Rendra ever had, by using conventions of rural folk theatre to depict situations in ordinary local people's lives. Jeprik and Gandrik actors interspersed a great deal of colloquial Javanese into their Indonesian dialogue, while Gapit performed entirely in Javanese, effectively abandoning the project of a national theatre in the name of local relevance rooted in the ethnic language (Hatley, 2007: 95–6). In the other direction, avant-garde troupes resisted New Order discourses of paternalism, nativist modernization and commercialization of society by embracing confrontational postmodern aesthetics. From the avant-garde camp, Rendra, who had increasingly accepted corporate sponsorship, appeared co-opted by global capitalism. From the Javanist camp, Rendra appeared insufficiently rooted in the *kampongan* he so often claimed, and overly devoted to Western techniques and repertoires. One might say that in both cases he was accused of having been recolonized.

Although the old cultural polemic did not continue to dominate critical discourse in the New Order, Bodden argues that 'a nativist ideology was strongly present in determining the "structure of feeling" in New Order society' (Bodden, 2002: 209). In its most hegemonic formulation, this 'nativism' took the form of the state enforcing normative cultural policies to outlaw any behaviors or practices inconsistent with their definitions of native traditions. This would be used to ban 'harmful' outside influences (Bodden mentions 'break dancing and rap music') as well as counter-cultural practices by Indonesians. As one would expect, most theatre artists have strenuously disassociated themselves from this kind of legislative nativism. Nevertheless, discourses that privilege *kampongan* over *gedongan* and local tradition over foreign imports also proceed from a nativist ideology. Arifin C. Noer and Putu Wijaya both developed their craft in Yogyakarta and in collaboration with Rendra before moving to Jakarta early in the New Order. They both separated themselves from the ATNI family, claimed roots in local ethnic *kampongan* (Noer from Sundanese Cirebon, Wijaya from Balinese Tabanan), and built their reputations on prolific outputs of original works that rarely looked to foreign repertoires. Wijaya deployed the terms 'tontonan' (an Indonesian mode of attending spectacles different from Western reception of dramatic theatre) and 'tradisi baru' (the 'modern tradition' that connects nativist modern theatre to its authentic roots in local culture).

Although he has often written and spoken ironically about being a Balinese 'contaminated' by many other influences, he has increasingly acknowledged local culture as a fundamental point of reference. Noer filled his productions with a *porak-poranda* (disorganized mess) of elements taken from foreign and local sources, even as he campaigned against uncritical acceptance of Western technique. He rejected ATNI's legacy as a 'realism' alienated from what is real in Indonesian experience. He writes: 'We are truly already trapped – even colonized – by a Western way of conceptualizing about the arts and aesthetics' (Gillitt, 2001: 218; Noer, 1983: 19) and takes up the project of training his actors in traditional performance techniques.

However, despite his search, more deep and profound perhaps than either Rendra or Wijaya's for an Indonesian theatre that is not shackled to the West, he finds himself perpetually haunted by the old polemic: 'More and more I refuse to allow myself to become only an echo of a voice that is unclear in origin. I have a voice. Indonesia has a voice. Sanusi's and Takdir's cultural polemic continues to reverberate. The two of them are Indonesia in process, engaged in continuous dialogue' (Gillitt, 2001: 233; Noer, 1983: 18). Though insisting on a distinction between the generative practices of Rendra, Noer and Wijaya and the restrictive policies of state-sponsored nativism, Gillitt acknowledges the difficulty of completely disentangling their projects. Both partake of an ideology of nativist modernization that has seemed inextricable from national culture.

Noer and Wijaya both sought to create new traditions, theatres of roots with more authentic connections to local life, and to this end they created works independent of Western repertoires much more than either Rendra or Riantiarno. However, paradoxically, it is they who have been seen as highbrow and intellectual artists whereas Rendra and Riantiarno were always popular. Wijaya began working in the United States in the mid-1980s, expressing frustration with his lack of success at home. In a different irony, Noer replaced Sontani as the Indonesian playwright most admired and translated in the West, and it was Noer, who had inaugurated TIM with his installation in 1968, who also inaugurated the renovated GKJ in 1987. Both of Jakarta's top *gedongan* theatre venues were 'baptized' by Noer. Indeed, it is hardly surprising that an artist of Noer's stature would have been granted this honor. It is not possible 'to search for an Indonesian aesthetic prompted by a desire to enter the world stage with a unique Indonesian vision' (Gillitt, 2001: 306) without repeating colonizing gestures that are 'unclear in origin.'

'A stretch of beach binding dry land to a spiritual sea'

In 1875, Veth had written with irritation about the enduring 'French craze' in nineteenth-century Batavian entertainment, as noted earlier writing sarcastically of the repertoire at the Schouwburg Weltewreden that 'as Java is a Dutch colony, it is, of course, French drama they prefer' (Veth,

1896, vol. 3: 53). In a 1956 issue of *Budaya*, one of the major Soekarno era cultural journals, Subagio Sastrowardojo muses on the question of 'a crisis in Indonesian playwriting.' He opines that Indonesian drama is 'not yet fertilized with our nation's blood,' to which Sukarno Hadian advises patience while admitting that 'we have not yet given birth to great plays of the caliber and popularity of works of Shakespeare, O'Neill, Ibsen, Sartre or Maeterlinck' (Sastrowardojo and Hadian, 1956: 97, 107). In 1966, in the second issue of *Horison*, the dominant New Order literary magazine, J. M. Ang Hiap Lee urges Indonesian dramatists to take advantage of post-Lekra artistic freedom by liberating themselves from Western dramatic influence: 'Recently there is a mania for foreign repertoires such that it lowers or disparages our own national repertoire' (Lee, 1966: 55). An article published in the cultural magazine, *Sagang*, in January 1999, proclaims theatre still 'shackled to Western theory' (Nurcahyoab, 1999). Indeed, it would seem that anxiety, or perception of 'crisis' regarding the dependence of the national dramatic repertoire on foreign repertoires, has persisted throughout the history of modern theatre in Java. More specifically, despite a variety of cultural initiatives to counter such dependence, modern theatre remains haunted by imperial powers; France to nineteenth-century Dutch Batavia, Europe and the West in general to postcolonial Indonesia.

As Noer laments, some Indonesian 'shackling to Western dramaturgy' proceeds from an uncritical preference for things Western. However, as most colonial and postcolonial theatre practitioners have acknowledged, the foreign dramatic canon remains relevant because it carries a history of associations that cannot easily be substituted. Once it is acknowledged that the nation's origins are indeed disparate, and that the postcolony remains haunted, we can begin to regard the staging of foreign drama and the 'contamination' of native drama with traces of the foreign as specific cultural strategies rather than merely symptoms of abjection.

As I argue in the first chapter, the first production of Shakespeare's *Hamlet* at the VOC castle in 1619 was not simply a repetition of European culture, but rather a complex appropriation of a work from the civilization of the besieging enemy by the newly christened Dutch nationalist enclave of Batavia. Apparently, the next production of *Hamlet* in Batavia occurred nearly two centuries later in 1816 as what would turn out to be the final performance of the Military Bachelors' Theatre during the British interregnum. However, this amateur performance by English soldiers was interrupted by a Dutch mob that demolished the bamboo playhouse, apparently in a patriotic display at the news that the Indies would be returned to Dutch rule. The *Java Government Gazette* referred to these vandals as 'mercenaries of Jan Pieterszoon Coen,' casting the attack as a reperformance of the founding of Batavia itself. From this perspective, the British military production of *Hamlet*, which might itself be understood as a more typical 'colonial' Shakespeare (universalizing the high culture of the colonizing civilization), precipitates a postcolonial counter-discourse from the Dutch Batavians. The Batavians patriotically 'deconstruct' *Hamlet* in violent fashion.

Peculiarities of circumstance give these two productions a postcolonial character vis-à-vis Dutch Batavia. There were certainly more typically 'colonial' literary and theatrical discourses implemented by the Dutch during their time in Batavia. However, for the reasons demonstrated by these productions, Shakespeare never operated comfortably as part of the culture of the colonizers in the Dutch East Indies. Indeed, when Dutch partisans first attempted in the late eighteenth century to establish a Dutch theatre in Batavia, they ran into difficulties that would recur throughout the nineteenth century, and indeed still plague the ongoing struggles to establish an Indonesian theatre in Jakarta. Better-funded, more professional foreign repertories keep the nationalist repertoire at a disadvantage. In colonial Batavia, this most commonly took the form of French theatre and opera troupes against which Dutch thespians constantly struggled to attract audiences and sponsors. Against military and cultural dominance from the British and the French, Dutch Batavians paradoxically remained marginal even at the center of their own colonial empire. In the two aforementioned instances, *Hamlet* served as a battleground for that sense of dislocation, marking the difference between Elsinore (and London and Paris) and Batavia.

Cohen records various instances of Komedie Stamboel and other popular urban troupes incorporating *Hamlet* and other Shakespeare plays into their repertoires in the late colonial periods. The European press recorded these practices sometimes with disdain, and sometimes with amusement. A German account of a Stamboel *Hamlet* in Menado in 1922 describes 'the prince of Denmark and his mother singing a duet to the strains of the "Blue Danube" played on violin, piano and flute.' Similarly, Koks records watching a Stamboel performance in 1931 in which Hamlet appears 'robed in something between a dressing-gown and the uniform of Napoleon's grenadiers, discussing the merits of a dusky Ophelia, who violently agitates her Japanese fan, with the rollicking ghost of his father in turban and top-boots.' Cohen concludes that 'an enjoyment of travesty accounts for much of the reason why casual European observers repeatedly privileged stamboel treatments of Shakespeare and Goethe over other plays performed' (2006: 350–1). Nevertheless, such canonical Western texts could infiltrate early Indonesian drama in more subtle ways. For example, Muhammed Yamin, the poet and nationalist leader who would become a leading architect of the cultural platform of the postcolonial state, interpolated elements of *Hamlet* into the play he wrote for the Second Youth Congress in 1928: *Ken Arok dan Ken Dedes* (*Lord Arok and Lady Dedes*).

The story of Ken Arok, thirteenth-century founder of the Majapahit dynasty, constitutes half the text of the *Pararaton*,[1] a fifteenth- to sixteenth-century Javanese text rediscovered by archaeologists in the early 1920s. According to the *Pararaton*, Kertajaya, king of the East Javanese kingdom of

Kediri, had been persecuting his Indian Brahmin minority. Ken Arok, king of the neighboring Tumapel kingdom, comes to their aid, and kills Kertajaya in the ensuing war. Tunggul Ametung ascends the throne of Kediri with his wife, Ken Dedes. Ken Arok falls in love with Ken Dedes, and determines to win her. He commissions a magic *keris* (ritual sword) to assassinate his rival, but grows impatient before its completion. He kills the *keris*-maker and takes the weapon, but not before the maker lays a curse on it. Ken Arok kills Tunggul Ametung, marries Ken Dedes and combines the two kingdoms into a new mighty clan, which would claim the rulers of the Majapahit and Mataram dynasties as descendents. The *keris* remains cursed, however, and Ken Arok will eventually be assassinated by a descendent of Tunggul Ametung.

Along with the rediscovered *Nagarakrtagama* (which chronicles later Majapahit rulers), the *Pararaton* inspired the nationalist literati in the 1920s and 1930s as testaments to the vitality of earlier Javanese empires.[2] For Yamin in particular, these stories would form the basis for an argument that the idea of Indonesia was not in fact a foreign imposition, but had its true origins in pre-colonial dynasties. In his first history dealing with Majapahit, *Gajah Mada* (1948, written in-between histories of the Java War, 1945, and the American Revolution, 1951),[3] Yamin writes of Arok's Singasari kingdom as 'mother to the Indonesian nation' (Yamin, 1945: 18). As a reviewer of a 1953 revival of *Ken Arok* comments, what is most striking about Yamin's revision of the *Pararaton* is that these dynastic warlords are 'depicted as men who sincerely assume responsibility for their actions with resolve towards the future' (Anon., 1953: 33). Ken Arok shows an idealized concern for the unity of the nation (rather than merely his own passion and power), and Ken Dedes and her son Anusapati act not from vengeance but rather from consideration of what is best for society. 'Voila, a jurist's sense of justice!' (35). In structuring the play and giving it a postcolonial emphasis, Yamin drew on various 'native' elements. Court scenes are reminiscent of *wayang* shadow theatre, and Yamin himself recalls historic costuming and gamelan accompaniment (Yamin, 1951: 5). However, the dramatic structure of the play is most strongly reminiscent of Shakespeare's *Hamlet*. With a Dutch education, Yamin would have had ample opportunity to know the play. Indeed, he had already written an Indonesian translation of *Julius Caesar*, another of Shakespeare's plays with strong affinities to *Ken Arok*. This intertextuality certainly reflects comfort with a foreign canon, but also enables the play to transform its feudalist subject into a vehicle for universalist sentiments.

Like *Hamlet*, Yamin's play begins after the inciting act of regicide. Tunggul Ametung is already dead, and Ken Arok has already had another son with his new wife, Ken Dedes. In the first act, the future (of Indonesia) is being discussed under the guise of dynastic succession. Which of Ken Dedes's sons will rule Kediri after Ken Arok? Will it be Wong Atelang, son of the new king, or Anusapati, son of Tunggul Ametung and (again like Hamlet) beloved of the people. Ken Dedes and her two sons arrive. Ken Arok gives his own son a seat of honor by his side, but Anusapati is given no space. In the next act, Anusapati expresses his frustration at the snub to the Brahmin priest, Lohgawe (who acts as a less buffoonish sort of Polonius). Lohgawe convinces Ken Dedes to reveal to Anusapati that it is Tunggul Ametung, not Ken Arok, who was his true father, and that his grave is here in Tumapel. Apparently summoned by the revelation that they stand on a site of paternal disappearance, the ghost of Tunggul Ametung 'rises behind them.' Though his message, as a ghost, is remembrance, Tunggul Ametung calls on the crowd to look to the future. 'You high ministers, I do not forget. Continue working towards justice. Do not run! You and I are the land of Daha! Aid the descendants of old Tumapel that is no more!' All but Anusapati and his Horatio-like companion depart as Lohgawe delivers an epigram on the function of spectrality itself: 'ghosts are a stretch of beach binding dry land to a spiritual sea.'

Once effectively alone with his descendant, the ghost delivers his full message of spectral surrogation; that he is indeed Anusapati's father, and what's more, the victim of regicide. He delivers a fairly unambiguous riddle: 'He who uses the knife will suffer the knife, he who uses the keris will suffer the keris.' However, unlike the elder Hamlet to his son, Tunggul Ametung does not directly set Anusapati on the road to vengeance. Rather, in departing, he calls for genealogical continuity and remembrance of the roots of the present in the autochthonous past. 'O, mankind, show respect to the earth, where the dead are buried' (Yamin, 1951: 29–30). Of course, Anusapati proceeds to kill Ken Arok and to avenge his father, but here Yamin steers his narrative away from *Hamlet*, the revenge tragedy, and closer to *Hamlet*, the proto-existentialist problem play. The entire Court, including Ken Arok himself, accepts the bloody retribution for the earlier crime as a way to 'show respect to the earth' and get on to the business of building a just society. As in *Jan van Schaffelaar*, an organicist national vision is asserted over claims of kinship.

Rendra, *pemuda* of Denmark

In the 1950s, as emerging theatre troupes began to stage the Western dramatic canon, Sani and Trisno Sumardjo gained some recognition as translators of Shakespeare. Sumardjo, whose translations are still regarded as the literary standard used in most Indonesian productions, was almost single-handedly responsible for establishing a reverence for Shakespeare in Indonesian literary circles. His universalizing assessment of *Hamlet* is typical:

'This work of Shakespeare is considered the best drama in all of English literature up to now. Thoughts that are lofty and penetrating, the poet's resources of beautiful language, portraying a time of constant suffering, and above all the extraordinary romantic power of the imagery all combine to give the play a special place in the world of literature. This tragedy consists in the tragedy of an individual filled with ideas, but gloomy and sorrowful, feeble in coming to a decision, and unwilling to fulfill the heavy duty with which he has been charged. Then Hamlet only fulfills his destiny in the final pressing moment, when he himself is beyond all hope.'

(Machdan, 2005: 557)

Despite Sumardjo's enthusiasm, the performance records of the Soekarno era evince only occasional interest in producing these works. Rendra's more colloquial translations and locally colored productions in the 1970s inspired numerous Shakespeares 'with local color' (a Balinese *Macbeth*, a Batak *Romeo and Juliet*, and so forth). Nevertheless, the overall record of Indonesian production, publication and criticism shows a paucity of specific interest in the Bard that challenges the universality of his postcolonial relevance. Soemanto, in one of the more extensive recent Indonesian surveys of Western drama, *Jagat Teater* (*World of Theater*, 2001) considers absurdism, *Oedipus* and realism (in that order), referring to Shakespeare merely for comparison. Saini, another leading New Order theatre historian, sandwiches a discussion of *Hamlet* between *Tristan and Isolde* and *Ibsen and Chekhov* in his 1981 monograph on Western drama, *Beberapa Gagasan Teater (Several Ideas of Theatre)*. There is, in these works, what might appear to Western observers a shocking indifference to periodizations and notions of style. It might be seen as an inversion of Orientalist interculturalism, leveling the foreign culture into a banquet of available texts, shorn of complex historical contexts, none of any greater intrinsic value than the others. One young Jakarta-based director suggested to me in 2007 that Shakespeare reminded him of the poetry of Kahlil Gibran (a comparison that tellingly situates Shakespeare within the domain of an aesthetics of beauty rather than as a master of psychology or any of the other typical Western views), but that economic considerations preclude frequent production of his plays. With huge casts, and difficult language, they are simply too colossal for most Indonesian theatre troupes.

In light of this situation, the three productions of *Hamlet* undertaken by Rendra and his Teater Bengkel (in 1971, 1976 and 1994) cannot be seen as 'representative' of Indonesian Shakespeares. On the contrary, they demonstrate a convergence of exceptionalisms: that of a play frequently regarded as beyond the reach of Indonesian troupes, and an actor often lauded (paradoxically) as the singular epitome of modern Indonesian theatre, the one actor whose personal mystique has been regarded as commensurate to the role.

Rendra began experimenting with intercultural techniques for adapting Western plays in the early 1960s. In 1962, for example, he adapted Eugene Ionesco's *Les Chaises* in a work he called *Kereta Kencana (Golden Chariot.)* *Kereta Kencana* preserves the basic structure of Ionesco's parable, but fills the imaginative world of the play's elderly couple with imagery more congenial to Rendra's own romantic and mystical palate and verbal etiquette more closely aligned to Javanese and Indonesian conversation patterns. The culminating suicidal defenestration of *Les Chaises* becomes for Rendra's couple a more mystically optimistic passage. They ascend via a 'golden chariot,' invoking the wondrous vehicle of Krishna that carries Prince Arjuna in the *Bhagavadgita*. Although Rendra's theatrical work of this period was not overtly didactic, he did publicly criticize President Soekarno and communism. He was harassed and imprisoned twice more in 1962 and 1963, which apparently influenced his departure. In 1964, he attended an international humanities seminar for anti-communist youth at Harvard University, and afterwards connived to remain in New York. Thus, Rendra lived in the United States throughout the succession of events that catapulted Suharto to power. He studied social sciences and humanities at New York University where he first began to think of art in relation to 'structural analysis' and communal activism.[4] At the same time, he received his first (and only) formal theatre training at the American Academy of Dramatic Arts. Although he had already been exposed to Method acting through the work of ATNI and STB in the 1950s, it was here that Rendra first became acquainted with improvisational rehearsal techniques.

When Rendra returned to Indonesia in 1967, he began to produce a kind of modern theatre Indonesia had not seen before: ensemble-based, improvisational, abstract and theatrical; a theatre that privileged action over text, visual over linguistic composition and the company over the individual actor. Goenawan Mohamad called the style *mini-kata* (minimal word). The bulk of critics saw it as pointing to a significant shift from the literary, realistic Indonesian theatre of the 1950s and early 1960s. There are certainly historical affinities between Bengkel's early experiments and the contemporaneous work of Jerzy Grotowski, Peter Brook and Eugenio Barba. Nevertheless, it would seem that Rendra came to his own methods from the admixture of his training in American social sciences and Method acting with the *kampongan* culture of Yogyakarta. This was not so much an imitation of currents in the Western avant-garde as an original Indonesian intercultural and intracultural experiment. Indonesian artists and political activists had met the first years of Suharto's presidency with optimism following the political turmoil of the preceding decade. They hoped that Suharto would put the nation back on course towards development and democracy, and Suharto, for his part, seemed eager to inspire confidence in his new regime. The mini-kata aesthetic suited such times. It was political, but in an exploratory rather than an ideological mode. It gently represented what many Indonesians regarded as the enduring political and social question for the nation (that is, how to balance leadership and liberty) without controversial language. Rendra came to be regarded as an artistic prophet. In this extraordinary transitional moment, people in Yogyakarta claimed him as 'our Rendra,' academics praised him as a cultural hero, and, in 1969, the Indonesian government presented him with a National Arts Award.

However, by the early 1970s it became clear to progressive students that Suharto had assumed a familiarly paternalistic and authoritarian stance, and was settling into the role of a latter day Javanese king. They began to demonstrate against the same sorts of political and economic abuses and 'prestige projects' seen under Soekarno. In particular, the construction of the Taman Mini amusement park on the southern outskirts of Jakarta and the open manipulation of the first post-Soekarno election in 1971 convinced many student activists that the new regime was not committed to improving the plight of the poor. In these years, Rendra allied himself with the student movement and its critique of Suharto. Once again, so soon after being hailed at all levels of society as a cultural treasure of the nation, Rendra found himself at odds with official state nationalism. He was detained briefly in 1970 for taking part in a 'night of prayer for the nation,' and thus began a new period of police harassment. Rendra would face escalating state opposition during this most productive period of his career. From around 1971 to 1978, he produced his most acclaimed work and faced his most severe persecution. Police authorities banned him from performance in Yogyakarta (1973) and ultimately throughout Indonesia (1978).[5]

Rendra staged *Hamlet* twice during this period: once in 1971, and then again in 1976. The 1971 staging reflected the simple, contemporary aesthetics of mini-kata. A setting primarily characterized by green and orange acting areas, with an ordinary wooden chair representing the throne. Claudius wore a simple star on his chest to signify his rank, the Queen wore a simple contemporary nightgown, and Ophelia dressed like a contemporary Indonesian student. Rendra, in the role of Hamlet, wore blue jeans and a sweater, looking like a student, or as if he had just come from one of his own poetry readings. What impressed the critics (and apparently audiences) most about this production, however, was a liberal use of colloquial dialect (especially Javanese words). Many critics, no doubt raised on Sumardjo's literary translations, were shocked, and reacted like conservative European critics bemoaning an avant-garde outrage. Audiences found the production entertaining, prompting some reviewers to denounce Rendra's lack of gravity and others to praise him for bringing the modern theatre closer to such populist genres as *lenong, ludruk* and *kethoprak* – a connection heightened by the fact that it had been staged in TIM's open amphitheatre, Teater Terbuka.

The 1976 staging was different in many respects. It played for two nights (rather than three, as previously) in TIM's Teater Tertutup (a medium-sized proscenium stage) – a much smaller audience in a more intimate and controlled environment supporting a more carefully composed *mise-en-scène*. Indonesia's eminent scenic designer, Roedjito,[6] used bamboo scaffoldings, ten blocks and multi-colored lights to create numerous specific delineated acting areas. One reviewer described it as reminiscent of a traditional *wayang orang* stage mixed with contemporary elements. Likewise, the costuming was more suggestive of Javanese traditional garb, and Rendra himself (again as Hamlet) wore the batik *kain* (wrapped cloth) of an aristocrat from the Javanese traditional stage. A gamelan ensemble led by Rendra's wife, Sunarti, provided music (whereas the previous production had featured an ensemble singing Simon and Garfunkel tunes). Various explanations might be given for this shift in approach. One significant factor, however, was that between 1971 and 1976, government pressure on Rendra had increased such that he took greater care to frame his social criticism within traditional culture. Whereas in October 1971, he had held a meditation and improvisation workshop at Parangtritis beach explicitly as an 'alternative' to the absent civil society of Suharto's regime, his 1975 play, *Kisah Perjuangan Suku Naga* (*Story of the Struggle of the Naga People*), had adopted the frame of *goro-goro* (clown scenes) from the *wayang* shadow theatre to defend against anticipated censorship. In the 'play within a play' scene (III:ii) of his 1976 *Hamlet*, for example, the king asks, 'Isn't this play of yours dangerous?' to which Hamlet/Rendra replies:

> This play clearly is not dangerous, Sire. It's nothing but shadows. Only make-believe. Just look, the one who plays the king just feigns kingliness, the one who plays an adviser just gives pretend advice. Also that throne is just a play-throne. So, *enggak berbahaya dong* (it's no problem, man!).

After 1978, Rendra's credentials as an oppositional figure lost some of their luster. After the performance ban was lifted in 1985, a prominent investor, Djody Setiawin, sponsored Bengkel's relocation to Depok, a relatively upscale community on the outskirts of Jakarta. Many critics and old admirers judged Rendra hypocritical for accepting the aid of an investor and moving into an exclusive development. However, in 1991, Rendra moved a little further out from Depok to the village of Cipayung where he re-established a *padepokan* (training compound). Since then, new Bengkel recruits have trained and worked in the extensive grounds while numerous old Bengkel actors have settled nearby, partially transforming kampong Cipayung into kampong Bengkel. Meanwhile, a period of self-censoring depoliticization of the arts accompanying the New Order's height in the early 1980s started to change by the end of the decade. A growing Indonesian middle class began clamoring for greater freedoms and real civil society. Suharto, responding to Soviet President Mikhail Gorbachev's *glasnost*, declared '*keterbukaan*' in 1990. Artists immediately began testing this 'openness,' and some censorship and performance bans followed. Angered and frustrated by the hollowness of *keterbukaan*, many artists kept pushing. From the early 1990s to Suharto's resignation in May 1998, such theatre artists as Emha Ainun Nadjib, Ratna Sarumpaet and Butet Kartaredjasa gave voice to a growing consensus of dissatisfaction with the regime, and began to call for reform and real democracy. Despite the doubts against him, Rendra was very much a part of this movement when he staged *Hamlet* a third time in 1994.

The 1971 production had been striking for its colloquial language, and the 1976 production for its more extensive Javanization – each of these an early example of approaches that would become commonplace to staging Western drama in Indonesia. The 1994 production, however, heralded a new trend in corporate sponsorship that previously had been seen only with Teater Koma. Rendra's 1994 *Hamlet* was sponsored by Djarum clove cigarettes, a fact marketed through a special edition cigarette packet with an image of Rendra in the starring role (see frontispiece). The economics of theatre production had changed in the intervening years, with government subsidy for the arts minimal, and rental costs for rehearsal and performance space in Jakarta on the rise. *Hamlet* played for five performances at TIM's Graha Bhakti Budaya (a large proscenium space) at a cost of 150 million rupiah, at that time one of the most expensive productions ever staged. This expense did not, however, translate to elaborate design. Setting and costumes were as simple, if not more so, than before. The setting was simply a series of platforms providing acting areas at different levels. The costuming suggested a greater mixing of styles than in previous productions. Rendra (as Hamlet, of course) was once again in blue jeans, but was also the only character to carry a *kris panjang* (a long sword believed to channel mystical princely power), indicating (as Dahana suggests) his connection to traditional Javanese society (Dahana, 2001: 124). Claudius (like Gertrude and the rest of the Court) wears a mix of Betawi, Javanese and contemporary Western upper-class garb, but instead of a scepter, wields a military crop – an indication that he is an army man, like Suharto, but also recalling the crop Soekarno habitually brandished. Thus, the radical student still rooted in Javanese tradition opposes the military dictator who has no authentic connection to the people.

One thread running through reviews of all three productions is the force and unique authority of Rendra in the title role. There is an awareness, implicit and sometimes explicit, of the role of Hamlet as the 'ultimate test' for Western actors, and hence of Rendra's attempt as the ultimate test of how Indonesia's best actor measures up. Sani had written, in the introduction to his 1960 translation of Boleslavsky's *Acting: The First Six Lessons*, that the Indonesian postcolonial actor encounters the difference between these canonical Western roles and his own experience, and in this very difference finds the substance for a new modern identity as an Indonesian. Rendra, likewise, had filled the role of Hamlet with his own existential doubt and humor, and located the role in his own *habitus* as modern Western-educated youth (in 1971 and 1994) and traditional Javanese man (1976 and 1994). In the 1994 production, however, the additional element of his advanced age added a new dimension of complexity and difference between actor and role. E. H. Kartanegara describes the image of Rendra in the role with some trepidation:

Rendra's chubby body, his sluggish movements, the furrowed skin of his face (remember, Brother, Rendra is already 58), reveal some difficulty at

portraying the seething soul of Hamlet, who is surely just in his twenties [...] The face of Hamlet-Rendra now has more the kneaded look of a
'native.' Putting on his bell-bottom jeans and jacket, sometimes wearing
an *overcoat* (like a New Yorker in December), juxtaposed with a *keris* and
fan, the meaning of which is unclear.

(Kartanegara, 2005: 631)

For some reviewers, however, this complexity added another dimension of
political meaning to the portrayal. For Hari Prasetyo, this Hamlet is simultaneously Danish noble, Javanese revolutionary aristocrat and contemporary
middle class, all looking for a way out of their social cages (Prasetyo, 2005:
627). Muji Sutrisno goes further to see this last *Hamlet* as Rendra's depiction
of widespread Indonesian social stagnation. In these latter days of Suharto's
Indonesia, the aging actor paradoxically dons the blue jeans of youth and
takes up the traditional Javanese sword, warning Indonesian society to
shake off its 'Hamletization' and recover its progressive culture (Sutrisno
cited in Anon., 2005: 624).

Postcolonial artists and critics have often looked to Shakespeare's disenfranchised black men, Caliban and Othello, and their marginal realms as
sites of anti-colonial resistance. However, there is a more intimate disenfranchisement available in the figure of Hamlet and a more complex site
of resistance in Elsinore. There is Elsinore as the *polis* of Jayakerta/Batavia/
Jakarta, a palimpsest of loss ever poised between existential crisis and the
imagination of a nation built on ruins, reaching back to some enabling
spectre from a nobler time. There is the disenfranchisement of a prince
approached by his usurping uncle, who calls him 'cousin' and 'son.' Hamlet
knows, as did Rendra, that he can never truly claim a place in a family built
on such violence, on such suppression of the ghosts of his fathers. He has
inherited a richness of cultural, political and intellectual traditions, which
he wears in a clashing *gado-gado* (mixed salad) of styles. And yet, what power
does he have to 'set things right' in this endlessly 'out of joint' postcolonial
moment? From the kings in Jakarta and London and elsewhere, he has been
guaranteed equal human rights, but systematic limits on change and his
own lack of stamina to fight for change ensure a comfortable stagnation. To
those in power in Indonesia, the represented people remain 'a little more
than kin and less than kind.'

Caligula in the wake of Soekarno...

Obviously, colonial and postcolonial Indonesia have participated in a
global Shakespeare economy. However, as a postcolony of the Netherlands,
Indonesia has been haunted less by the dramatic legacy of a specific
European nation than have English and French postcolonies. In the remainder of this chapter, I will discuss a peculiar attraction of Indonesian theatre

artists to Albert Camus's *Caligula*, evident in clumps of productions and adaptations around two significant moments of postcolonial history: the mid-1960s around the anti-communist massacres, the fall of Soekarno and Suharto's rise to power; and the early to mid-1990s as tensions mounted between a Suharto regime that had effectively dismantled civil society and a re-emergent culture of criticism expressed in the arts through a return to political content and radical uses of postmodernist aesthetics.

The French existentialists had enjoyed particular favor amongst the Generation of '45. T. Heraty Noerhadi, looking back on this generation from 1967, explains the attraction as arising from an ambivalent will to 'sophistication' amongst the educated class, but also to a shared sense of humanity living in a 'state of emergency' in which traditional explanations of the meaning of life no longer suffice. However, she concludes with a distinctly post-1966 critique of the Soekarno era, warning that the 'pessimistic-nihilistic' spirit of rebellion in Sartre and Camus cannot provide the faith in development and reason that Indonesians require in order to transcend what Mochtar Lubis called the 'mytho-mystical' basis of traditional society. Skepticism, in other words, provides no way forward from superstition (Noerhadi, 1967: 316–17). Mohamad, in a short response to Noerhadi's analysis, counters that though the 1950s enthusiasm for existentialism was certainly modish (he likens it to a fad for 'mini-skirts'), it nevertheless was part of the postcolonial struggle to transcend the conservatism of local social traditions:

> In my opinion, this issue was not originally born out of a doubtful attitude towards reason or positivism or modern technology. In my opinion, this issue registered the effects of a crisis that took place with our spiritual lives, in a society that was giving up our traditional ways of life. We were in the process of questioning authority, our old connections and associations. I refer to one important matter: the rigidity of our spiritual life – reflected in the manner of our religious lives – was being rejected. Openly or not!
>
> (Mohamad, 1967: 318)[7]

As he would often do in later writings, Mohamad here defends the radicalism of Generation of '45 writers against a revisionist New Order perception of them as Westward-gazing elitists whose approaches were merely alienated from the real needs of the nation and the concerns of 'ordinary' Indonesians.

Nevertheless, there were no productions of *Caligula* during the Soekarno era. Despite the fact that by 1956, Sani had already written what Mohamad would describe as a 'beautiful' translation of the play, there is no record of this translation having been performed by anyone prior to the famous ATNI production of 1966. This lack is not difficult to explain. By 1957, when Soekarno imposed 'guided democracy' and began increasingly to resemble a whimsical tyrant himself, *Caligula* surely would have been seen as a dangerous play, insulting to 'the father of the proletariat' and contrary to the escalating rhetoric of state ideology. By the same token, it is not difficult to understand why the text commanded such appeal as soon as Soekarno's government had become 'the Old Order.' However, *Caligula* may not have attracted so much attention in the wake of Soekarno if it were simply a depiction of a mad tyrant. The play's alignment of Caligula's radical freedom to atheism was of considerable significance to Indonesian audiences as well. Muslim leaders had stepped forward quickly in the weeks following the failed *coup* on 30 September 1965 to depict the reprisal against the communists as a *jihad*, openly expressing hopes that this chaos would resolve into the transformation of Indonesia into an Islamic state. During the first half of 1966, as the mass killings of hundreds of thousands of presumed communists subsided and Suharto's more cautious gambit of maneuvering Soekarno from power proceeded, articles appeared in *Kompas* (Jakarta's leading newspaper after the banning of all leftist periodicals), advancing a crucial new principle for the New Order: communists are evil atheists. With such claims as 'Atheists [...] are not humans, but devils' and 'Atheism is the source of savagery,' pundits explained the violence that had just taken place as a necessary response to the dangerous social forces implicit in communism itself.[8]

The ascendance of this anti-communist denunciation of atheism is likewise apparent in post-1965 reflections on existentialist works, including Camus's *Caligula*. Noerhadi, writing in 1967, imagines Indonesians shuddering at the Camus whose 'Caligula declares God dead, filled with arrogance and denial,' and that if there is any existentialist voice amenable to Indonesians, surely it would be the Kierkegaard who claims: 'Faith is a miracle, and yet no man is excluded from it; for that in which all human life is unified is passion, and faith is a passion [...]' (317). In a 1968 issue of *Horison*, Said analyzes *Kebinasaan Negeri Senja* (*Destruction of the Twilight Nation*) a one-act play by Mansur Samin written in 1964, but unpublished for reasons that should become obvious. The play depicts confrontations between opposed political parties destroying the fabric of a central Javanese community. One of the play's culminating arguments occurs between a sympathetic *ulama* (who may represent a religious party) and Sobat, an atheist who Said connects to the communist party. The dialogue is clearly adapted from a conversation in the first act of Camus's play in which Caligula's wife, Caesonia, questions her husband on his absurd ambitions. Sobat refuses to believe anything he does not prove for himself and resolves to resist death. The *ulama* replies that to resist death is a madness akin to resisting God, to which Sobat replies that he has no interest in resisting a God he does not believe in and that he is only interested in creating a world that is equitable for all people. When the *ulama* replies that the world exists according to God's will, Sobat declares:

> The mission of my party is precisely to put an end to this dispute. The cadres of our party must alter the inequality of the world. We must create

a new history for the peoples of the world. We will not submit to hardship. A new era, in which the people will be judges, must be achieved! We must shape a new world, where the people will not know death, because they are always happy!

(Samin, 1968: 117)[9]

By inspiriting the speech of a communist pundit with the ghost of a foreign atheistic tyrant, Mansur indicts the Indonesian Communist Party not only as irreligious, but as rooted in extreme foreign philosophies. The organicist project that Sobat espouses is undermined, partly in keeping with Camus's existentialism, but also from associations specific to an anti-communist stance in 1960s Indonesia.

In mid-1966, Indonesian national culture began to recover from the state of emergency. On May 16, *Kompas* announced this rebirth with a front-page proclamation differentiating the Generation of '66 from the follies of the Generation of '45 as decisively (and dubiously) as that generation had differentiated itself from the Generation of '33. Two days previously, the first post-*gestapu* theatre announcement had been printed, for a production of Jef Last's *Djaja Prana* at the Hotel Indonesia, under the auspices of its 'cultural division' to be staged that August. On 9 July, an article announcing that 'dramatic activities live again' began with an assurance that artists could return to the theatres without fear of censorship by Lekra/PKI (outrageously implying that the communists, even while being exterminated, were responsible for the closure of theatres over the preceding year). Over the following month, the Hotel Indonesia would sponsor five different productions directed by Asrul Sani, Aiwi As, Deddi Sutomo, Steve Liem (Teguh Karya) and Galeb Husein. On 30 October, Boen Oemarjati and Peter Daniels directed a production of Ismail's *Api* in a hall of the Jakarta Cathedral. Two separate reviews in *Kompas* pay respects to the play and Oemarjati, celebrating the accomplishments of the revolutionary generation as it gives way to the next.

From 8 to 10 November, Asrul Sani directed a production of his translation of *Caligula* at the Hotel Indonesia (Figure 5.1) with a cast including Sukarno M. Noor (as Caligula), Ismed M. Noor, Steve Liem, Galeb Husein, 'and dozens of other thespians famous in the Capital.' It was billed as a joint production of ATNI and the Hotel Indonesia, and clearly signaled the return of the academy into public life. As ATNI promised structure for the arts after a reign of terror, so the posters for the production featured a woodblock print dominated by two columns with a Roman figure staggering underneath in an actorly pose. Indeed, as production photographs confirm, a fairly realistic design was employed, with Roman togas and classical architecture. The historical milieu of the production was reinforced somewhat differently by the fact that the Bali Room doubled as a cinema at the same time. They were apparently inundated at that time by American and Italian costume dramas. In July, *The Giant of Rome* and *The Fall of the Roman Empire*

Figure 5.1 The ATNI production of Camus' *Caligula* in the Bali Room of the Hotel
Indonesia, with Sukarno M. Noor as Caligula and Steve Liem (Teguh Karya) as Scipio,
1966 (Author's collection)

were screened. Two days before the premiere of ATNI's *Caligula*, an Italian film called *Maciste in the Land of Cyclops* screened in the same space.

The production was received as a welcome return of Asrul Sani to the cultural life of the capital. The academy's adherence to old 'Generation of '45' aesthetics was not yet criticized; indeed, in 1966 no real alternatives were apparent. Thus, the production has entered the theatrical memory primarily in terms of its professionalism (this being a respect paid to Asrul Sani) and also as a tour-de-force role for Noor in the title role. Anwar's review for *Kompas* on 14 October, 1966, consists mainly in such praise (Anwar, 1966). In contrast, Edward Liem, in another *Kompas* review published two days previously, considers why a play by a French existentialist spoke to the current moment. He cites Wiratmo Sukito (one of the principal signatories of the 1963 cultural manifesto and an architect of the 'PKI-Gestapu' conspiracy theory of the events of 30 September 1965) who had commented that *Caligula*, 'shows a declaration from Camus, who was earlier attracted to revolutionary philosophy a la Marx, but was later frustrated in relation to the implementation of that revolutionary philosophy because it resulted in a despotic power whose basis of government is cruelty.'

Camus's loyalty to the Generation of '66 thus confirmed, Liem glosses the play's narrative as a cautionary tale with obvious application to Soekarno and the communists:

> With the loss of hope in a disordered world, his desire emerges to execute power through his political influence. Such that finally he becomes cruel, mad, and alone. Like the communists. Caligula then denies God and places himself above Him. Thereby, there is no longer any power higher than himself, and so he becomes the most free of human beings [...] Caligula dies not as a fighter seeking to establish heaven on earth – he says 'Humanity dies: and they are not happy' – but rather as a dictator, as an ordinary tyrant. But even though he dies, his impossible qualities and dreams do not die. He passes into history. And so in the twentieth century, Caligula emerges – a new Caligula. And with this emergence there also emerges a transferable force. Thus the struggle between the just and the unjust will continue throughout the era.
>
> (Liem, 1966)

Dick Hartoko, editor of *Basis* magazine, published an article in *Horison* early in 1967, criticizing the rudimentary understanding of existentialism in the Anwar and Liem reviews. He then presents a more informed understanding of existentialist philosophy; and yet, this misses the point (Hartoko, 1967). Liem grasps very well the moral of the play to the emerging New Order ideology: a heightened political culture leads to madness and the denial of God; likewise, he who pursues freedom too dearly, becomes a tyrant, a menace to society. Lastly, Liem calls attention to the terrifying final image of the play in which the tyrant, covered with stab-wounds, claims the last word: 'I'm still alive.' So Indonesians must be forever vigilant against the resurgence of latent communism.

ATNI's production clearly struck a nerve within the Indonesian theatre community. The production was broadcast on TVRI (the national television network) shortly afterwards, where it was seen by a far broader audience than any previous Indonesian modern theatre performance. Jim Adilimas directed the play in Bandung in a joint production of Studiklub Teater Bandung and Teater Perintis, and Arifin C. Noer directed a production in Yogyakarta in 1967, while still affiliated with Teater Muslim (before he moved to Jakarta and founded Teater Ketjil). Riantiarno remembers traveling to Bandung from Cirebon to see the Adilimas production when he was just 16 years old. As he recalls, Adilimas staged it in a fairly realistic style, using Roman costuming in a historically precise manner, but this was nevertheless interesting. He remembers slogans inscribed into the scenery. One said 'I revolt, therefore I am.' Riantiarno also witnessed the Teater Muslim production: 'Arifin's production was different again. He utilized local color (*warna lokal*), central Javanese and from Cirebon. Peculiar. For instance, in the music and some aspects of blocking, choreography. Nevertheless, he used Roman costumes too' (Riantiarno, 2007).

Bakdi Soemanto remembers watching the 1967 Teater Muslim production, and criticizes it for depicting Caligula's madness as a psychological condition rather than as an embodiment of the 'absurdity' of the human condition in general (in the sense Camus elaborates in *Le Mythe de Sisyphe* and anticipating Beckett *et. alia*) (Soemanto, 2001: 60). Like Hartoko, Soemanto appears to privilege a 'correct' interpretation of the play internal to Western discourses, and in this he misses the real attraction of the play to artists at this specific moment. After seeing two of these three major productions, Riantiarno returned to Cirebon and played Scipio in a production of the play by *Teater Tunas Tanah Air*. All this experience with the play influenced his decision to move to Jakarta, where he began his theatrical career.

Putu Wijaya was also inspired by viewing the Teater Muslim production of *Caligula*, which provided a basis for his own one-act play, *Lautan Bernyanyi* (*Singing Oceans*), one of the works that launched his theatrical career. Wijaya recalls the Teater Muslim production:

> I was greatly drawn in by that production. I didn't read too well, but I learned existentialism from watching that production. I liked it a lot and that influenced me when I wrote plays [...] So what I saw onstage, especially in Albert Camus' *Caligula* greatly influenced me when I wrote *Lautan Bernyanyi*. Then, Habib Hamzah, if I'm not mistaken, wrote a review that it was like I was putting existentialism into practice. Whereas I didn't really understand it.
>
> (Soemanto, Wijaya, 2000: 171–2)

At the time, he, like Nano Riantiarno, had participated in student drama, but had not yet struck out on his own. He had acted a fair amount, and wrote his first play, *Dalam Cahaya Bulan* (*In the Light of the Moon*) in 1966. It was shortly after this that he saw *Caligula*. Wijaya recalls being especially impressed with Noer himself in the title role. Though he claims to have understood little about existentialism at the time, Caligula's views seemed to him very familiar from a Balinese philosophical perspective: 'If you believe it, it will exist. If you don't believe it, it will never exist.' 'Black and white' magic must balance each other as must tragedy and comedy. In reflecting on this moment in his career, Wijaya describes it as yet another example of his 'cultural predicament,' 'whereby Indonesians see him as Western and "absurdist" whereas Americans see him as "traditional"' (Wijaya, 2007).

Wijaya took the inspiration for the story of *Lautan Bernyanyi* from a mysterious incident that had occurred a few years previously. A ship had been discovered anchored off the beach at Sanur, Bali, near one of the hotels, with no trace of a crew. Putu wrote a short story about this, which he then developed into the play. The story opens with a ship, 'The Ocean Tiger' that has run aground on a Balinese beach known as a center of 'black magic.' The captain, Leo, approaches the situation rationally and refuses to believe in such superstitions, whereas his child believes whole-heartedly. The Captain and his chef abandon ship, confident that it will eventually work itself free. He waits calmly for the arrival of a tug boat, but is tempted by voices in the wind. As one *Kompas* reviewer puts it, 'a sputtering sea wind is like singing oceans and a black cloud leaves an impression like the ghost of a sea spirit' (Nada2, 'Lautan Bernjanji,' 1968). Furthermore, they are plagued by *leyak* (Balinese witches) and accusations from the local natives that the ship had violated restricted waters and a sea spirit had retaliated by afflicting the region with smallpox. All these forces drive Leo mad, such that he becomes convinced of a new belief. He continues to hold his ground, even as the ship breaks free as he had predicted. His new state of conviction prevents him from recognizing the truth. The play concludes with an image of Leo, like the mad Caligula, who has set a personal vision of rationality above communal social values and thus is driven into his own personal and highly ironic reality.

The play's central theme is summarized in the proceedings of the 1968 *Art Week* conducted at the Hotel Indonesia, where *Lautan Bernyanyi* was performed as third prize winner in the festival's play competition: 'A story that mediates between two worlds that are severed, yet are intertwined through one event, that is, the world of magic/belief and the world of practicality/rationality' (Noer, 1968: 28), As Wijaya himself has reflected, the paradoxical severing of these worlds – of belief and rationality, of tradition and modernity, of native and foreign – has haunted his own career. With *Lautan Bernyanyi*, Wijaya uses Camus's *Caligula* as a springboard for advancing his own 'new tradition.' Professing ignorance of existentialism, he simply internalizes what he found exciting in the Teater Muslim production of *Caligula*.

The Roman emperor becomes a solipsistic sailor negotiating his destiny in the New Order on 'a stretch of beach mediating between dry land and a spiritual sea.' In the 1968 *Art Week* production that constituted Wijaya's debut on the Jakarta stage, his original adaptation of Camus to a Balinese sensibility, inspired by Noer's production with Sundanese and Javanese local color, the 1966 ATNI production which Putu had not even witnessed was also spectrally present. Sukarno M. Noor played the role of Leo, the sea captain. By appearing again in such a related role, Noor carried memories of that post-massacre *Caligula* into the beginning of 'new tradition' theatre.

...and in the twilight of Suharto

In 1988, Mohamad contributed a prologue to a new collection of Indonesian translations of Camus's essays published by *Yayasan Obor*. Here, he reflects at greater length on why the general Indonesian attraction to existentialism manifested in a clear preference for Camus over other French existentialists. He recalls reading essays advocating the relevance of Camus to Indonesia by the Dutch writer, Jan Lamaire, Jr., included in an April 1954 issue of the Jakarta-based cultural magazine, *Zenith*, and published letters by Sani about encountering the writings of that 'dangerous and captivating' Camus while traveling to Europe in the early 1950s, after which he 'translated, most beautifully, the Camus play that has become most famous in Indonesia, *Caligula*.' French writers were attractive in general at the time, because 'France is a place that is unproblematic for Indonesians: the nation has no connection with their colonial era' (Mohamad, 1988: 372). In explaining the preference for Camus over Sartre or Maurice Merleu-Ponty, Mohamad begins with accessibility (the dense metaphysical tracts of the others were simply too abstruse for Indonesians without philosophical backgrounds), but concludes with an argument that expands on his 1967 rebuttal of Noerhadi. Mohamad claims that Camus is attractive to Indonesians precisely because he offers a moral vision that retains 'a smell of the earth', 'and a relatively unthreatening philosophy vis-à-vis traditional values.' He re-affirms 'our existence in the midst of chaos and the destruction of purpose and meaning.' Although his voice is not 'traditional' in an Indonesian context, 'Camus does not frighten us. On the contrary, his gospel of rebellion may be heard as heroic and at the same time without overturning intent' (373). Rather than offending traditional sensibilities, as Noerhadi argued, Camus might be seen as offering a different branch of tradition proceeding from those 'mytho-mystical' foundations: 'Camus claims to be on the side of a tradition that declares ignorance. He, like his Mediterranean world is on the side that receives the limits of the world and the limits of humanity, the beloved face, and again, beauty' (374). Though ostensibly a reflection on the roots of Indonesian postcolonial fascination with Camus, Mohamad's analysis here also hints at the need that would be perceived to reclaim and fragment *Caligula* after two decades of the New Order. If, as Mohamad writes, Camus had become safe and easy, then it, like the rest of the depoliticized rhetoric of the New Order could be deconstructed.

After Rendra was banned in 1978 from performing in Indonesia, a decade of relatively depoliticized arts followed. Asrul Sani, Teguh Karya and Arifin C. Noer abandoned theatre for film, Wijaya continued to develop a personal aesthetic mediating between Balinese and avant-garde milieus, and Riantiarno developed a theatre of entertaining but relatively unthreatening social commentary that drew large audiences from Indonesia's emerging middle class.[10] Following a decade of confrontations with disillusioned elements of civil society, the New Order had largely succeeded in silencing its political opposition. Over the following decade, Indonesia traded democracy and liberal freedoms for political stability and a substantial measure of economic prosperity. By late in the 1980s, however, artists and intellectuals were emboldened to express dismay at what their national culture had become. Bodden describes a range of artistic practices emerging at this time that adopted Western postmodernist aesthetics in order to express resistance to Suharto's authoritarianism and the commercialization of society. From Bodden's perspective, such practices specifically challenged the New Order's ideological nativism as a manipulation of the old discourse of cultural nationalism to promote social conservatism and suppress radical politics. In these works, we see typical postmodern techniques, such as fragmentation of character, nonlinear narrative, deconstruction of the distinction between high and low culture, and so forth. However, unlike Euro-American postmodernists who specifically challenged all forms of 'universalism,' these Indonesian artists often 'seem concerned to construct a new, holistic vision beyond the deformations of the New Order (and perhaps those of its Reform Era legacies).' As Bodden notes, this conflict, though confronted through the aesthetics of postmodernism, is more fully legible as postcolonial:

> In each case, the tension between deconstructing the legitimating discourses of the New Order state with its **'nativist modernization'** and the effort to formulate universal principles or visions of meaning, identity and community represents the postcolonial dilemma of Indonesia's postmodernist cultural workers. Wary of creating new master narratives, yet championing ideas (equal rights, individual identity and freedom) long associated with the modern nation-state, it is not so easy for these artists to leave behind the informing ideologies of a national community.
>
> (Bodden, 2002: 318)

The need to challenge the univocality of Suharto's Indonesia is animated partly from a spirit of individualism, but also from the ongoing postcolonial desire to re-inspirit a degraded national culture.

Afrizal Malna emerged at this time as an inspirational voice for the next generation of theatre practitioners. Having grown up in the neighborhood of TIM, he and his peers had savored an eclectic array of traditional and modern arts. Beginning in 1983, he started having conversations with director Budi Otong and wrote a manifesto asserting two principles that would inform their work with Teater Sae: 'First principle: We are of an insane generation. Second: I will open my body to the most impossible possibilities.' Malna explains that they formulated these principles in opposition to a New Order government that had standardized the Indonesian body in terms of sumptuary norms (batiks for men, kebaya for women). They sought to avoid the paternalistic structure of other Indonesian theatre troupes by organizing more as a 'network of artists' (although Otong was very clearly the director, and Malna a spiritual and literary manager) (Malna and Usman, 2007). Malna wrote, or as frequently *compiled*, texts for the Teater Sae productions using techniques legible as postmodern, but chosen specifically in opposition to New Order hegemonic discourses. As Bodden records, Malna rejected the unified characters of classical European drama, which were also assumed by the Stanislavsky-inflected actor training. For him, such characters did not reflect the condition of the individual 'in an era of globalization, industrialization, the standardization of New Order culture and the increasingly monolithic nature of its social institutions' (Bodden, 2002: 304). Echoing the fragmentation of character in late modernist and postmodernist Euro-American drama, Malna called for replacing the old character- and plot-driven drama with 'installations of ideas' (*instalasi gagasan*) presented in disjunctive frameworks that denied the experience of cohesive identification with a personality 'type.' Joining a common complaint of the time that the New Order had stripped the Indonesian language of meaning, Malna defined his performance texts in opposition to the style of popular magazines such as *Tempo* that advertised themselves as *yang enak dibaca* (language that's fun to read). In contrast, Malna intentionally presented a language *yang-tidak-enak-dibaca* (that's not fun to read) as part of an attempt to cultivate discomfort in audiences anaesthetized by market and government rhetoric. Nevertheless, Malna and Otong both remained committed to the notion that they were promoting the development of a new kind of community 'occurring in spite of and in opposition to the New Order's socio-political organization of life.' For Malna, this would need to be a community of 'complex, fragmented individuals' (305). Though Teater Sae would disband in 1993 when Otong moved to Switzerland, their aesthetic opened the door for a new generation of theatre artists who would similarly distance their works and organizational principles from the 'second golden age' luminaries.

In late 1991, Teater Sae presented *Pertumbuhan di atas Meja Makan* (*Things Growing on the Dining Table*), by some estimations its most successful work and one chosen for inclusion in the *Lontar Anthology of Indonesian Drama*. Sae regulars, Zainal Abidin Domba and Margesti played the married couple who recur in all six scenes.[11] Bi Sari'ah appeared (as herself), disrupting the flow of Indonesian texts at seemingly random intervals by chattering in Sundanese.

Busro Yusuf played 'the delivery boy' and Dinaldo served as an 'all-purpose' player, further disrupting the identification of actors with roles by portraying a variety of characters as needed. Wijaya, in a review for that 'fun to read' publication, *Tempo*, describes the opening moments of the performance at TIM:

> The entire space of the Teater Tertutup [...] is wrapped in the works of Roejito. To the left, right, above and behind are curtains. Entering the space, it is as if we are invited into the head of someone who is thinking. On the stage, the curtains are open. The actors have already taken their positions. Sitting on the floor of the stage, there are several people engrossed in watching television. Far in the back, there is someone putting on a black costume with a *caping* [bamboo farmer's hat] on his head, jumping around like a frog. A cellist faces away from the audience. A garbage collector in white *kain*, bare-chested, body caked with white powder, sweeps as if he is offering a prayer. The performance has already begun before the gong sounds the third time. The broom, which parodies a vacuum cleaner sounds in the ears. This person ritualistically herds the dust to the back. He shakes the broom so that dust falls from it. His gestures are devout, intentional and controlled. The spectators are absorbed in anticipation with a question mark: What is going to happen? For a little longer, nothing happens. What appear to be small gestures increasingly make the question greater. So then, one by one, the actors change positions, taking their next poses. One of them sleeps, then lifts his body with full tension. Finally shouting, 'Newspaper, newspaper!' Then we see that there is indeed a stack of newspapers at his side.
>
> (Wijaya, 1991: 110)

Malna's manuscript describes this opening scene as a moribund tableau: Husband and Wife asleep, morning sun shining, dining room setting as a still composition and the only sound coming from an electric fan by the bed, '*buzzing with a sound that seems to be trying to give life to a space that feels dead.*' A woman denounces the 'Indonesian' values of 'consultation and discussion' declaring to the hired help (the maidservant, apparently) that it is only through the exercise of power that everyone knows their place in society (Gillitt, 2009: 438). In this composite opening scene, familiar tropes of traditional Indonesian life are transformed into an empty ritual of maintaining a 'clean and orderly' society. Televisions usurp theatrical spectacle while the role of inspiriting a dead space has fallen to an electric fan. This opening scene, titled 'Jakarta 1988' in Malna's manuscript is followed by a second, titled 'Jakarta 1988–1963' in which the delivery boy sells subsequently banned leftist newspapers from the late Lekra period and the husband and wife converse by exchanging quotes from a 1963 speech by Soekarno on the need to limit freedom of the press: 'I am of the opinion now that I will not permit absolute freedom, which would allow the press to destroy the head of state in front of the entire world' (439). Though presented with stage figures apparently representing ordinary Indonesian people and a married couple (staple of domestic drama), their voices seem haunted by a combination of direct censorship and media saturation. In the third scene, entitled 'A Fatal Impossibility,' they are inspirited by selections from Sani's translation of *Caligula*.

The scene combines dialogues between Caligula and three other characters from different parts of Camus's play. In each case, the 'Husband' speaks Caligula's lines and the 'Wife' each successive interlocutor without any textual cues to demonstrate changes in characterization. As the scene opens, the Wife is in a nightgown regarding her husband from the bed, whereas the Husband directs his lines to a large painted portrait of his Wife's face. They exchange Caligula's first dialogue with Helicon in which he explains that he is fatigued from looking for the moon. Because current reality is unsatisfactory, he wants something impossible, 'something that sounds nonsensical. Something that can't be included as part of this world' (440). He reveals to his Wife/Helicon the truth he has discovered, 'that people die and they're unhappy,' and that the apparent happiness around them,

> only proves that I'm surrounded by lies and self-deception. I want humanity to live in the light of the truth. And I have the power to make that happen. If everyone agrees that wealth is the most important thing, then the human soul is of no importance whatsoever. The sentence has already been pronounced. This world is of no more significance.
>
> (Gillitt, 2009: 441)

At this, Malna's text cuts (without any apparent change in characterization) through a few later fragments of Camus's dialogue between Caligula and Caesonia in which Caligula weeps at the painful 'ritual of creating humanity.' The scene then continues with most of a later dialogue in which Caligula compels Scipio to read a poem about achieving harmony with the earth, a poem whose imagery Caligula intuitively knows already. Nevertheless, he tells Scipio (the Wife, that is) that 'there's no real lifeblood in your poem,' that she does not understand that humanity is never alone (442). At this point in Malna's text, the delivery boy returns and places a newspaper on the table. The Husband turns from the portrait and applies make-up to the actual face of the Wife, '*and adorns her with jewelry, until she resembles a queen, or a dancer, or a bride whose outfit is a bit overdone*' (442). While this happens, they exchange dialogue between Caligula and Caesonia from the end of Camus's play. Caligula insists that he must kill to be alive. 'Only the dead can make reality palpable for me' (442). He predicts that his end will come at the hands of those he has ridiculed. The stage directions read: '*The* WIFE *is now fully dressed. The* HUSBAND *carries her to the middle of the room and arranges her like a display. The* HUSBAND *tries to hide himself inside the* WIFE *who poses like a mannequin.'* He sees his death coming at the hands of a world full of 'sinners.' 'Seeking the impossible to the last, I stretch out my hand and enter history' (443). The scene ends.

The remaining three scenes of the play build on themes of responsibility, censorship and the evacuation of meaning from language. Scene four, 'Majapahit at 11pm,' takes dialogue from Sanusi Pane's *Sandhyakala ning Majapahit* in which the nation-building protagonist, Damar Wulan (the Husband), interrogates the wise Maharesi about the nature of the universe and his *dharma* as warrior for his country. Then we see witnesses testify against him, using his introspection as grounds for charges of atheism. The delivery boy rides through, collecting for his newspaper. In Scene 5, 'The Moral Responsibility of the Intellectuals,' the Husband delivers excerpts from a speech by Vice-President Mohammed Hatta given at the University of Indonesia in June 1957, calling for universities to train the character of the youth to link experience with creativity, and warns that the revolution failed to carry out its social ideals. The delivery boy rides through crying 'Newspaper! Newspaper! Newspaper!' A vocal group comes onstage and sings 'Langit Hitam' ('Black Sky,' a well-known song by Franky Sahilatua that speaks of the denial of love as an empty sky 'without stars, without a moon'). In the final scene, 'Jakarta at 11pm,' the themes culminate in a domestic scene. The Wife eats at the dining table. The Husband reads the newspaper. The Maid scrubs the floor. The delivery boy rides back and forth across the stage. They do not communicate, but simply quack meaninglessly. The scene repeats several times (449). In his review, Wijaya describes an additional spectacle and final line:

> Towards the end, the rear black curtain opens. The burden of various philosophical questions pressing since the beginning are swallowed by a fantastic perspective. In the background, lights swirl around, refracting off plastic. Then, one human figure wrapped in plastic approaches. Not long afterwards, the character of the Husband repeats the sentence spoken at the beginning of the story, 'Hello, ready to talk, we are a cultural people.'
>
> (Wijaya, 1991: 110)

These descriptions of the final moments, somewhat at variance with each other, may reflect alterations over the course of production. In any case, both versions provide unsettling visions of an Indonesian society descended into madness; distracted, irresponsible and meaningless.

The creative process for *Pertumbuhan* began with actors improvising around abstract concepts, in the course of which Malna chose and arranged the texts. He started with the image that change in the late Suharto era might begin over a dinner table between a husband and wife. Hatta, Caligula and others might come to the table. Otong brought *Caligula* into the process as a work that he had been interested in staging previously. He had used scenes from Sani's translation to stimulate improvisations in rehearsal, but never staged the play in its entirety. Malna was inspired by Noer's understanding of the play 'as a poetic statement about a human body suffering the loss of the moon,' which he connected to the loss of vitality in creative expression. They staged a powerful scene that partially found its way into the production, in which Caligula makes up his own wife in *lulur* (Javanese yellow rice-powder cosmetic) and then strangles her as she washes herself (Malna and Usman, 2007).

Malna also credits Noer with recognizing the affinity between Caligula and Adolf Hitler. Within an Indonesian postcolonial discourse, such an association should not be read as a simple condemnation of the character. On the contrary, as Wijaya argued in relation to the mix of black and white magic in *Lautan Bernyanyi*, such powerful allusions may be utilized as correctives to serious lacks in the other direction. The terrors of a Hitler, or of a Caligula, are not met with approbation, so much as evoked as a source of fervent energy that might disrupt the status quo, much like punk rock invokes violent imagery that the singers in no way intend to carry out in real life. Whereas ATNI's Caligula was a Soekarno whose reign of terror needed to be ended by any means necessary, Teater Sae's Caligula speaks for the 'mad generation' that has been denied the 'impossible,' whose bodies suffer the mystical imbalance of a lover gazing at a moonless sky. This Caligula peers desperately into the painted features of a portrait of the beloved and then turns to paint her face himself, while the true face of the beloved remains inaccessible to him. These shifted concerns are evident in two other productions that drew on *Caligula* later that decade.

In 1995, Yudi Ahmed Tajudin directed an adaptation of *Caligula* for his Yogyakarta-based Teater Garasi (Figure 5.2), which would emerge a few years later as one of Indonesia's leading avant-garde theatre troupes. Tajudin insists that he did not see Teater Sae's *Pertumbuhan*, though he had seen their *Migrasi dari Ruang Tamu* (*Migration from the Guest Room*) in 1993, and took inspiration from their style of combining texts. Indeed, he subtitles the manuscript for his play, *Or Anyone Else…*, 'a COLLAGE, a VERSION, an INTERPRETATION' (Tajudin, Camus and Sani, 1995).[12] Tajudin's play consists of a cropped condensation of the play, interspersed with original ensemble interludes that are somewhat reminiscent of Rendra's mini-kata scenes.

The play begins with a 'Big Bang!!' followed by horrifying rolling thunder descending into silence and darkness at which voices narrate embodied reactions to violence: 'Rustling breath, choked sigh, sluggish stride, stinging curse, overgrown body, stifled cry, desperate growl that is caught in the throat […],' and then Caligula's voice calls out 'Eureka!,' at which point flames leap up from urns around the stage: the inciting event of Caligula's madness. The stage is filled with the undifferentiated ensemble exclaiming in abbreviated form the growth of confidence and passion between a wife and husband culminating in free and authentic movements, animated by love. However, their movements 'exceed the limits of authenticity.' The light grows more intense and they are burning. Darkness descends again and

Figure 5.2   A scene from Teater Garasi's production of *Atau Siapa Saja...* with Yudi Ahmed Tajudin as Caligula, 1995 (©Teater Garasi)

obscures the space. *'People's faces are bowed in defeat.'* They discover a cord that is attached to their bodies that they believe will lead them to 'Happiness, Truth, Beauty, Eternity...' They 'seize the day,' *'fervently mumbling the terms/ concepts that represent the results of humanity's intellectual accomplishments and explorations through reason.'* However, their expressions of inspired thought dwindle ultimately into 'Production, Market, Capital,' and before they know it, the rope is looped around their necks and they are bound fast, recognizing in confusion that 'What I earlier thought liberating... / became a prison.' They fall silent and the play moves directly into the first act of *Caligula*.

Next, there is a brief interlude in which the ensemble affirms the universality of Caligula's yearning: 'His is also the same desperation as that of Faust, Zarathustra, Or the stubbornness of Jenar and Hallaj. / So, he is also the same as us... / Or anyone else...' (Tajudin, Camus and Sani, 1995: 14). Caligula returns to the stage in a strange, frightening mask that startles the people. A smiling mask; perhaps the mask of Suharto, 'the smiling general.' He calls for a party to begin. He takes hold of the cord wound round the necks of the people and holds it taut as Caesonia dictates lines of bloodless poetry that they repeat back to their leaders with increasingly frantic 'idolatrous gestures.' Caesonia hysterically shouts 'Buy! Shop!' as the crowd's frantic movements pull the cord tight and they collapse, suffocated. The smiling mask of the

Emperor laughs and the play continues with the dialogue in which Caligula proclaims himself an atheist. We see the final conversation between Caesonia and Caligula and then comes a scene remarkably evocative of *Pertumbuhan*:

> *The morning paper and a glass of black coffee are delivered. The people are wearing dark sunglasses, reading the newspaper and watching tv. Caligula stands stupidly in front of the mirror. Then walks slowly, rolling a stone up a hill, and watching it roll back down again. Raising the stone to the top of the hill and watching it roll back down again. He continues like this and smiles. The people look around.*

(19)

Tajudin concludes the play, however, with a startling, unexpected image. A pregnant woman runs out seeking her inaccessible beloved: 'Last night, I dreamed of meeting my Groom. He smiled. His face was white and smiling, although he bore a large stone that was very heavy on his shoulders. He smiled. His face was white and smiling' (20). As Teater Sae's Husband (Caligula) is denied the face of the Wife, so an unnamed figure – an everywoman, perhaps another surrogate of the feminized nation pregnant with its future generations – is denied the face of her husband who has become Caligula. Or anyone else whose love and imagination have been strangled by the political and economic authoritarianism of the contemporary era. A gruesome mask fixed in an unwavering smile has replaced the face of the beloved.

A 1996 production of *Caligula* by Teater Payung Hitam (just then emerging as Bandung's leading avant-garde theatre troupe) follows fairly similar lines. Director, Rachman Sabur signals his radical editing of the text (and freedom from the structure of authorship, perhaps) by taking his production's name from Caligula's haunting final line: 'Aku Masih Hidup!' ('I am still alive!'). In this 'version' cut to about an hour and a half in performance, the actors already perform in the dimly lit auditorium as the audience enters the proscenium theatre at the Bandung Arts College. There is a shrouded corpse stretched out along the apron, and a couple already stands abreast at center stage. Lights play on the back scrim as Caligula regards the corpse. He pulls the shroud from the body and the set pieces disassemble in different direction to an industrial music 'as the voice of a train that carries the dead who knows where' (Dimyati, 1996: 341). Along this 'industrial' theme, Alex Poerwa comments on the thematic use of metal in this and other Payung Hitam productions: 'Hundreds of cans that are hanging from the building's heavens, an actor who is imprisoned in a steel cabinet, stiff cable unrolled as a border to the stage (in *Kaspar*) or used cans just scattered around (in *Musik Kaleng*).' Poerwa associates this use of metal with the company's 'steel-like' discipline achieved through long training and rehearsal in defiance of commercial markets: 'This sort of theatrical spirit is an endangered class, such that it is often valued as a utopia. So, Caligula, who is isolated in his dream of utopianism amidst the logic of society resembles a portrait of Payung Hitam' (Poerwa, 1996: 346). Like Sae and Garasi, Payung Hitam might well find resonance in Caligula's dismay at 'bloodless poetry' produced by artists who have become lazy. The theme of metal might also be seen as analogous to the electric fan and televisions in Sae's *Pertumbuhan*: an expression of the mediation of contemporary life through machines. Throughout the performance of *Aku Masih Hidup!*, no proper names are uttered. Likewise, the Payung Hitam actors eschew any trace of period costuming, but instead wear jeans, broad belts and dirty shoes. 'Altogether, they are like a gang of thugs' (Dimyati, 1996: 342). As in Tajudin's version, these events are universal to our contemporary predicament, and the mad emperor could be anyone.

In an interview with both Tajudin and Malna in June 2007, I asked them what independently had drawn them to Camus's *Caligula* in the 1990s. Both recalled the novels of Iwan Simatupang, who effectively internalized Camus's existentialism to a local milieu in the late 1960s.[13] Tajudin recalled that he had read Camus's novels, 'The Myth of Sisyphus,' Sani's translation of *Caligula* and Goenawan Mohamad's essays on existentialism, all while still in high school. He agreed with Mohamad's assessment that Camus seemed 'more of a humanist, not so much of a dark, dead end' as Sartre. When he directed *Or Anyone Else…*, he had been reading the philosophy of Theodor Adorno, and was attracted to the idea that rationalism was itself another mythos, a potentially powerful idea in critiquing the rationalism of New Order developmentalism. Malna replied that he was attracted to *Caligula* in much the same way that he is attracted to *Hamlet*, which, for him, accesses similar issues. 'They both possess madness, and they both confront a history that wants to die,' as the New Order had nurtured a madness whereby Indonesia had murdered the memory of its own history and replaced it with global market capitalism. As Rayner writes, considering Jacques Lacan's description of Hamlet living 'always at the hour of the Other':

> I take it to mean that Hamlet's deferred action has something to do with being caught in the temporality of an impossible demand, a paternal demand, that holds his attention and suspends him in time like 'John a-dreames.' When his time becomes his own, which is to say when his consciousness turns from the demand to his own 'readiness,' he begins to live his own life.
>
> (2006, xxx)

It would be several more years before the Indonesian Hamlets and Caligulas could transcend the impossible demand of the Suharto regime, break back into the flow of time and attempt to recover the forgotten faces of the past.

6
Umat as *Rakyat*: Performing Islam through Veils of Nationalism

Devotions of the revolutionary youth

In Malaysia, during the early 1980s, proponents of an Islamic theatre, such as playwright Noordin Hassan, constituted an influential faction of its national theatre community. This is unsurprising to Malaysian theatre scholar, Krishen Jit, who connects the emergence of an identity-based theatre alternative to secular nationalism with the fragmentation of a decolonial discourse; that is, with a progression from universalist postcolonial nationalism to a de-centered critique of state neo-colonialism. However, lest such 'progression' seem teleological, he calls attention to a very different situation amongst Malaysia's close ethnic and cultural kin to the south: 'Although plays revealing Islamic themes have sprouted in contemporary Indonesia, they have been eschewed by the major and influential figures. And no signs of a similar movement are to be seen in Indonesia' (Jit, 2003: 73–5). In Malaysia, Muslim artists challenged the nationalist presumption that Malaysians were the people (*rakyat*) before being members of the global Islamic community (the *umat*). Despite the existence of a vast Muslim majority, despite the rise of political Islam from the late Suharto era onward, and despite the fact that most Indonesian theatre artists self-identify as Muslims, there has never been a similar attempt to acculturate postcolonial Indonesian theatre to Islam.

Islam has indeed mattered to the development and practice of modern theatre in Indonesia more than nationalist and materialist histories have acknowledged. Despite a substantial legacy of Islam to Indonesian arts, most Indonesian Muslim artists have demonstrated a reticence to claim Islamic credentials. Neither Islamic iconoclastic indictments against figural representation nor Clifford Geertz's distinction between devout (*santri*) and nominal (*abgangan*) Javanese provide sufficient explanations. Conservative censorship (on iconoclastic or ethical grounds) has rarely prevailed in Javanese history, yet not all the positions taken by Muslim artists can be explained simply by *abgangan* syncretism. A few Indonesian dramatists, such as

Mohammed Diponegoro, have viewed their work as a form of proselytization (*dakwah*); however, there are others such as Emha Ainun Nadjib who have used theatre to explore Islamic contexts and experiences of faith, yet make no claims to *dakwah*. Although the Suharto regime generally promoted a kind of depoliticized religious syncretism, many progressive Muslim artists, such as Ratna Sarumpaet, have argued that art as *dakwah* cannot be reconciled with the critique of power nor the advancement of democratic ideals.

Nevertheless, modern theatre and other arts following Indonesian independence have advanced certain Islamic interests over rival ideologies. The Maya amateur theatre, usually understood as one of the first nationalist troupes, also launched the careers of several artist-intellectuals committed to Islamist[1] cultural and political advancement. Abu Hanifah argued that the embrace of Western progress must be rooted in Eastern culture and spirituality, a formula vindicated (though not in a manner Hanifah envisioned) by the rise of intracultural nativism as a prevailing mandate for many of the leading theatre artists after 1966. Jassin, remembered by Rosihan Anwar as 'the historian' of Maya, devotes a chapter in his 1954 *Kesusasteraan* to Hanifah, his friend and mentor, but gives no such consideration to leftist Indonesian intellectuals. The H. B. Jassin Documentation Center (established in Jakarta in 1977 from Jassin's personal archives) compiles the most complete and heavily cited list of Indonesian drama in the nation.[2] There is, nonetheless, a conspicuous absence in this list of works by leftist dramatists of the 1950s and 1960s. Even starker is the absence of leftist works at Jakarta's Usmar Ismail National Film Archive. Established in honor of Ismail – who in the 1950s had been a member of *Lesbumi*,[3] the cultural wing of Nadhlatul Ulama (Indonesia's largest Muslim organization), and then administrated by the outspoken Islamist critic and artist, Misbach Jusa Biran – the archive contains no leftist films from the Soekarno era. To be sure, these erasures of the memory of leftist thought and art were facilitated by Suharto's criminalization of the communists; however, both Jassin and Ismail cast their lot against the Left in the 1950s, long before it was politically expedient to do so. Whether through programmatic effort or ideological omission, their works brought official histories of Indonesian nationalist arts closer to the interests of orthodox *ulama* (Islamic scholars).

The relation between Indonesian modern theatre and Islam is not, however, simply a narrative of erasure. Despite Jassin's effort to avoid naming as Islamic all Indonesian theatre, it could be argued that Islam has significantly shaped the peculiar character of Indonesian performance traditions in general, preceding and including the postcolonial national theatre.[4] Islam makes Indonesian performance traditions legible, not only as local, but also as already global and transnational. For example, Qur'anic recitation – *tilawah* (Arabic) or *pengajian* (Indonesian) – has been practiced as a performative form of devotion in South Sulawesi since the earliest Islamic states at the turn of the seventeenth century, circulating a variety of aesthetic elements common to the Abrahamic religions into expressive practices.[5] Qur'anic aesthetics arguably include a tendency towards poetry and abstraction over colloquial, quotidian language and imagery; recurrent concerns with familial and interpersonal morality; concern with genealogical connections in linear, eschatological (as opposed to synchronic or cyclical) time; and concern with interiority and the distinction between outward behavior and inner conviction.[6]

Likewise, the pedagogy of modern Indonesian acting also evinces a strong connection to Qur'anic *pengajian* by way of the modern art of *deklamasi* (poetry recitation). In Indonesia, as in the Arab world, renowned poets are public celebrities whose recitations are as popular as rock concerts. In the Arab world, literati are typically poets first, infusing their other literary endeavors with the sensibilities of this primary genre. Likewise, most of the leading Indonesian modern theatre artists are poet-playwrights, and some who have explicitly proclaimed a Muslim identity (such as W. S. Rendra, Noer and Nadjib) are especially renowned in the art of *deklamasi*. Rendra and Noer have both written primers for would-be poetry declaimers that read much like acting manuals in the tradition of psychological realism. Both emphasize the need for declaimers not only to master vocal technique, but also to know their material intimately and to begin by establishing a personal rapport with the thoughts and feelings of the poet (not unlike the confrontation with character advocated by Sani for actors). Both Noer and Rendra have spoken in quite similar terms about the training of actors (Noer, 1987; Rendra, 1976: 86–90). Indeed, Indonesian dramaturgy, though it clearly draws directly from Euro-American examples might be traced, at least in part, to such poetic, and ultimately Qur'anic heuristics.

However, Indonesian governments from the post-VOC colonial era onwards have tended to view Islam's ethnic and transnational appeals as a threat to their own hegemony. Robert Hefner notes that Islam has historically been so linked to Malay identity that when non-Muslims in neighboring populations converted to Islam, they were said to be 'entering Malayness' (*masuk melayu*). Similarly, in pre-nineteenth-century Java, to become Javanese was frequently associated with becoming Muslim (Hefner, 1999: 212). Nevertheless, as colonial and postcolonial Indonesian governments looked to forge unity out of vast cultural, ethnic and religious heterogeneity, Islamic identity was consistently marginalized. In the early nineteenth century, the colonial government promoted a 'prophesy' that without the restraining presence of their central administration, Islam would act out of an intolerance of Indonesian heterogeneity, leading to disorder and mass killings in the name of establishing an Islamic state. Islam was thereby set in opposition to order and justice. During the Java War (1825–30), the Dutch used this prophesy as part of a negative campaign against the *jihadis* (religious fighters) of Prince Diponegoro.[7] Although

Islamic organizations had played various crucial roles in early anti-colonial and nationalist movements, Soekarno had attempted, in the 1920s, to subsume political Islam into an ecumenical nationalism. Although many Islamic political organizations accepted such pragmatism, others did not. In 1948, in the midst of the revolutionary war, one group generally known as 'Darul Islam' ('House of Islam') went so far as to establish an 'Indonesian Islamic state' in West Java and South Sulawesi. The fact that the Indonesian army was compelled to turn from fighting the Dutch in order to crush this insurgency left a lingering distrust of hard-line Islam after independence and throughout the Soekarno regime. Militant Islam enjoyed some stature in the overthrow of Soekarno during 1965–66, as a rallying point for demonizing the 'atheistic' communists. Although the new president, Suharto, would allow a greater scope for conservative Muslims to influence cultural policy, he soon quelled any hopes for a revival of aspirations in the mold of Darul Islam. There would be only one political party under Suharto and an ideological dismantlement of most other aspects of civil society, including Islamist ones. The political thaw during the 1990s that allowed democratic parties and activists freer reign to operate in Indonesia similarly released political Islam from restraints that had limited its influence through much of colonial and postcolonial history. Although the capacity of Indonesian Islam to unify disparate peoples has proved useful to colonial and postcolonial regimes, its more local and alternately foreign (that is, Middle Eastern) sources of authority have posed an implicit challenge to Batavia/Jakarta.

The limits of anti-theatricalism

The record of Muslim anti-theatricalism in Indonesia (not to mention in the Middle East) is far from consistent. Indeed, conservative Islamic authorities in Indonesia have never suppressed theatre to the extent achieved by Christians in first-millennium Europe or in Puritan England. A. S. Al-Haggagi finds little evidence for theatrical censorship on the basis of iconoclasm in the pre-modern Islamic Middle East. When Arab leaders did censor theatre on iconoclastic grounds (that is, on the grounds that representation itself is immoral), it appears that they borrowed their rhetoric from Christian Byzantium. What anti-theatrical censorship did recur in Muslim Arabia was on moral grounds, against representation of immorality (Al-Haggagi, 1980). In Java, Islamic iconoclasm is credited in some narratives not with silencing theatre, but rather with shaping the modern aesthetics of *wayang* shadow theatre.[8] Although there is some evidence of Islamic anti-theatricalism from the sixteenth century onward, Javanese Muslims generally preferred to infiltrate and negotiate with popular performance (see Sears, 1996: 34–74). Reformist movements emerged in Sumatra and Java during the eighteenth century, denouncing all sorts of 'impurities' attending these local negotiations of

Islam. As the 'origin' of Europe haunted Batavians throughout the colonial period, so Arabia as the 'authentic' origin of Islam, came to haunt Indonesian Islam. It would be overly simplistic, however, to view all such movements as enemies of theatre. Indonesian cultural traditions continued to negotiate with competing visions of Islam over the past two centuries, during which time *wayang* has remained popular throughout Muslim Java. Meanwhile, as Michael Francis Laffan points out, the same nineteenth-century Islamic reformist movements that some Indonesians would come to view as Arab neo-colonialism also profoundly influenced the early discourse of anti-colonial nationalism, shaping the emergent framework of Indonesian national culture (Laffan, 2003).

In contrast, orthodox Muslims have frequently attacked modern theatre practices on the grounds of immoral content. During the Soekarno years (1950–65), when Jakarta stages were filled with productions of the European modernists and native works inspired by them, critics mixed their dissatis-faction with the lack of creative originality with denunciation of the frank depiction of sexuality, violence and unrestrained emotions. In the works of playwrights such as Ibsen and Sartre, such criticism, however, is not in itself religious censorship (indeed, we might recall that critics had expressed shock at the immorality of Ibsen and Sartre when their works were first performed in Europe and the United States); instead, it is an indication of ideological complexity in Indonesian national culture, and a yearning for the national culture to forge closer connections to the spiritual life of the Indonesian people. When Rendra founded his Teater Bengkel in 1967, it was in part a response to this desire for a theatre rooted in the spiritualism of popular Islam.[9]

That said, accusations by Muslim authorities of immorality in theatre and dance performances did instigate an institutional policy of self-censorship at Taman Ismail Marzuki beginning in the mid-1970s. The Jakarta Arts Council, a body consisting of artists elected by their fellow artists, had been established in 1968 by Jakarta governor, Ali Sadikin, in response to demands within the artistic community for protection from the sort of ideological interference suffered during the early 1960s from Lekra, the communist cultural organi-zation. Nevertheless, this independent arts board soon decided of its own accord to assuage the concerns of conservative Islamic authorities. As Gillitt (2001) chronicles, it began with a confrontation over a production directed by Arifin C. Noer in 1974:

> At first, the objection was not to the performance itself, but to the poster design, which included sacred Arabic calligraphy illustrating the wayang punakawan character Semar. The combination of the sacred and secular was highly criticized and debated in the press. Claiming concern for the safety of the performers, the [Jakarta] Arts Council ordered the show closed.

This incident was followed by two more: an objection to a 1975 Putu Wijaya piece called *Lho*, 'which contained nudity and mimed acts of defecation,' and a 1976 dance piece by Farida Faisol called *Putih-Putih* (*So White*), whose 'movements were perceived as too erotic,' and that utilized a call to prayer. In response to a request from the Jakarta Council of Ulamas following this last performance, the Jakarta Arts Council agreed to review all future programming to avoid further incidents (Gillitt, 2001: 193–5). Insofar as this policy of self-censorship has not been abandoned since the 1970s, one could say that all contemporary productions at TIM have passed through a *de facto* orthodox Islamic filter.

Such self-censorship on the basis of religious sensibilities is not peculiar to Indonesia or any other Muslim societies. When new theatre cultures emerged in Turkey, Egypt and Lebanon during the early twentieth century, Arab Muslims sought to bar women from the profession of acting on moral grounds, associating it with prostitution. The Sheikh al-Islam declared this ban an official doctrine in 1918. Of course, association of actresses with immorality is an extremely ubiquitous prejudice in the global history of theatre, and hardly one that requires the peculiar imprint of Islam. Nevertheless, Islamic moralism might explain the extension of this prejudice to the early theatre of Indonesian nationalists, whereas it would seem to have little to do with nationalism itself. Female actors were prominent, headlining attractions in the professional urban theatre of the 1920s and 1930s; in stark contrast, the nationalist theatre had considerable difficulty attracting the talents of women, and thus seemed an almost exclusively male enterprise.

Nevertheless, such religiously inspired restrictions on theatrical activity have affected a relatively small and predictable section of modern Indonesian performance culture. In contrast to the self-censorship of theatre artists and institutions that have elected to privilege the concerns of religious authorities, government officials have exercised inevitable and seemingly capricious authority over theatre practices. No *ulama* in Indonesia has ever had the authority to censor, suppress, ban, harass or imprison theatre artists directly as various police and government agencies have done.[10] Further, as demonstrated in the profiles below, many Muslim theatre artists have not disavowed their faith, but instead have separated their views of Islam from those of these orthodox *ulama*. Modern artists throughout the Islamic world have adopted similar strategies, avoiding religious discourses heavily tainted with political conservatism in order to avoid being instrumentalized against liberal and progressive agendas.

The nationalist as perfect man

Teeuw echoes Jassin's assessment of a paucity in pre-independence Indonesia of 'literary works which could be regarded as satisfactory renditions of Moslem conviction.' However, he singles out Hanifah, who, on the strength of six plays and one novel written during the 1940s, 'was probably the most aware and at the same time most creative Moslem author of his time' (Teeuw, 1967: 138). Hanifah (who wrote under the Arabic *nom-de-plume*, El Hakim, 'the scholar') was a founding member of the Maya cultural collective and the theatre troupe of the same name that formed during the final year of the Japanese occupation. Four plays written by Hanifah during this time and performed by Maya have secured the author's place in the history of Indonesian dramatic literature (see Hanifah, 1949b). These works, however, are rarely performed, and Indonesian critics writing during the New Order (beginning with Oemarjati) have dismissed them as being mired in the pre-war *polemik kebudayaan*, lacking in good form and being programmatically Islamist (an accusation effectively redundant with having 'lack of good form').

Hanifah was a leading apologist among the revolutionary generation for the implementation of an Islamic cultural policy in Indonesia. As Teeuw notes, he revived the polemik during the revolution, assuming Pane's side of the argument against Alisjahbana.[11] However, unlike many pre-war syncretists such as Pane, Hanifah was uninterested in plumbing Indic origins; rather, he defended Islam as the sole wellspring of a national ethic and aesthetic. Following his work with Maya, Hanifah became a member of the central executive body for *Masjumi*, Indonesia's leading Muslim party at the time, in which capacity he held a variety of significant diplomatic and administrative positions, including as one of the conveners of the 1948 cultural conference at Magelang, which laid the groundwork for the first Indonesian national cultural policy. He represented *Masjumi* as Minister of Education in Hatta's first cabinet (1949–50). During these fervent years at the dawn of the postcolony, he published numerous polemical works arguing the cultural nationalist position that Western progress must be embraced, but only on the terms of local, traditional values (see Hanifah, 1945, 1946, 1948, 1949b). To him, this meant on the terms of Islam, the majority religion and source of a native idealism more in tune with Indonesian society than Western materialism. Nevertheless, Hanifah, like so many of the Dutch-educated elite, came to be viewed by his own party as too sympathetic to the West, and out of touch with postcolonial cultural nationalism. The 'most aware Moslem author of his time' was not 'Indonesian' enough for the 1950s. He was relegated to a succession of overseas diplomatic posts (chairman of the United Nations delegation, 1953–57; ambassador to Italy, 1958–60; ambassador to Brazil, 1961–64), which effectively removed him from the domestic political and cultural scene. Whereas his younger brother, Usmar Ismail, emerged from the revolution to become a leading voice of the Generation of '45, Hanifah's artistic works remained tied, in the perspective of critics and artists, to pre-independence paradigms.

There is a certain disconnect between how Hanifah himself and fellow Maya founder, Rosihan Anwar, would remember the four occupation-era plays of 'El Hakim' and the critical consensus regarding these same works from the 1950s onward. In his 1972 memoir (written, tellingly, in English under the title, *Tales of a Revolution*), Hanifah reflects on the formation of the Maya collective, firstly as a salon for appreciating Western luminaries – 'I studied Ibsen and Strindberg but also Pirandello. I didn't like Shaw too much but could go along with O'Neill' (Hanifah 1972: 137) – and secondly as a nationalist rejection of Japanese cultural imperialism. Thus, of the four plays, he tends to dwell on *Dewi Reni*, the most popular and the most straightforwardly nationalistic. The play's eponymous beautiful maiden is one among many feminine embodiments of the Indonesian nation, but one that evokes the land itself more directly than Effendi's Bebasari, Ismail's Tjitra or Sontani's Sri. Dewi Reni is the earth goddess or goddess of the homeland, closely analogous to *ibu pertiwi* (the earth mother or motherland). However, having studied such Euro-American realists as Ibsen, Strindberg and O'Neill, Hanifah did not simply evoke the traditional young *ksatriya* (the Indic warrior hero of the *wayang* theatre) as Dewi Reni's lover, but rather called on a cast of representative social types. Hanifah's characters are less like the mythic nobles in works by the pre-war nationalist playwrights (such as Roestam Effendi, Mohammed Yamin and Sanoesi Pane), and more like the ordinary Indonesians in the plays of pre-war commercial playwrights such as Andjar Asmara and Khee Thek Hoay. Their locale is contemporary; they struggle to come to terms with the Japanese occupation. Indeed, there are numerous hints that Dewi Reni herself lives in the vicinity of Pasar Baru, the Jakarta neighborhood by the Schouwburg Weltewreden where the play was performed. We meet a doctor, a politician, a youth, a businessman and a soldier, each of whom are preoccupied with their relation to the current political situation. Dewi Reni compassionately inspires and encourages them to channel their respective efforts towards the nationalist struggle. In sharing their love for her, these 'factions' (somewhat prefiguring Soekarno's 'functional groups') join together in fighting for Indonesia. In his memoir, Hanifah fondly remembers Rukmini Singgih, the actress who played Dewi Reni so effectively in 1945 that strangers in the audience wrote love letters to her. Hanifah, Anwar and Jassin all recall confrontations with the censorship board of the Japanese *Sendenbu* (propaganda department) over this play, and regarded their eventual success as a victory for nationalist expression.

In a sense, however, the story of national aspiration is only the outer shell of the play. The second act (out of three) is dominated by Ki Alwali, a *dukun* (a local Sufistic shaman) who lays out Hanifah's program for a revolutionary struggle rooted in religious faith. After presenting his vision of returning Indonesia to the 'freedom' known under the pre-colonial Sriwijaya and Majapahit dynasties, Ki Alwali turns to Dewi Reni, and explains that the nationalist struggle depends upon religious method:

KIALWALI: My child, Dewi Reni, always remember that you are the symbol of
the aspirations of your nation, from the past (*indicates her mother*)
to the present (*indicates the soldier*) to what will come (*indicates*

> *the others*). Protect yourself, your inner and outer purity, meaning
> the inner and outer purity of your nation. And never let your
> attention slip. May Allah, the Most Holy, protect you and bring
> pleasure and happiness to you that will not be broken by the
> waves of your life.
>
> (Hanifah, 1949b: 126–7)

In the contexts of the Japanese occupation, the revolutionary struggle and the Soekarno regime to follow, an outer shell of nationalism conferred legitimacy and legibility to Indonesian (as well as Japanese) observers. For Hanifah, however, as for Effendi, the *pemuda* could only draw spiritual strength from their own 'inner purity' in submission to God. Once again, the *pemuda* (revolutionary youth) had to be Muslim.

Similar themes inform Hanifah's other three plays for Maya. In *Taufan Diatas Asia* (*Storm over Asia*), a play set amid Asians at the beginning of the South Pacific war, Abd Azas, the Indonesian protagonist, appears as the complete person (*manusia seutuhnya*) insofar as he embraces Western progress with local faith:

> For us children of Indonesia, children of the East, what matters is: *Firstly*:
> The religion of Islam is the flesh and blood of the Indonesian people [...]
> in that difference lies our strength to free ourselves from the shackles
> of Western influence all around us. Thus we can proceed, with Western
> knowledge, but an Eastern soul.
>
> (Hanifah, 1945: 36)

A third play, *Intelek Istimewa* (*Remarkable Intellect*), depicts a doctor who, upon losing his family, rejects his self-centered (Western) materialism in favor of a similar sort of ideal 'completeness.' Finally, the last of his plays from this era has the title *Insan Kamil* (*The Perfect Man*), directly invoking a Sufi concept, popular in Indonesia, of the individual who reaches an ideal state of ethical behavior in submission to God.

Given such thematic consistency over his four occupation-era plays, it is striking that Hanifah, in his memoir, remembers his art primarily in relation to nationalism. There is only one statement regarding faith in his narrative of his work with the Maya collective: 'I was not a pious man but I believed deeply in the existence of God and the justice of God' (Hanifah, 1972: 137). Herein, perhaps, lies the source of his reticence; even as he distanced himself from Alisjahbana's call for total Westernization, he was also at odds with both the right- and left-wing Islamist camps. As L. M. Penders puts it in the introduction to Hanifah's memoir:

> Rejecting the legalistic and scholastic approach of the traditionalist *ulamas*
> (Muslim teachers) as well as the puritan and fundamentalist approach of

many reformists, he became a modern, Western-orientated, liberal Muslim, who strongly believed in the right of individual interpretation of the sacred scriptures.

(1972: ix)

These differences rapidly alienated him from the nativist mainstream in *Masjumi* during the 1950s (as well as from many less educated Indonesians), while the exegetic Islamist structure of his plays alienated him from the emergent mainstream secular nationalist theatre. For Oemarjati and subsequent critics, 'El Hakim does not succeed in presenting the problem of the story in a dramatic fashion' (Oemarjati, 1971: 149). In other words, from the perspective of the secular universalist consensus of postcolonial Indonesian drama critics, Hanifah's proseletization was in poor form. This would be the prevailing view of the Soekarno era, with a few fleeting exceptions.

Teater dakwah (theatre with the explicit aim of promoting Islam) enjoyed a brief moment of prominence in the history of modern theatre during the early 1960s when many of the leading theatre practitioners associated themselves with religious, leftist or nationalist theatres. Indeed, Arifin C. Noer, who would become one of the theatrical luminaries of the Suharto era, began his career through affiliation with *teater dakwah*. Noer, Mohammad Diponegoro, Hemy Nasution and Ajip Rosidi established Teater Muslim in Yogyakarta in 1960. In the 1950s, there had been a Coordinating Body for Islamic Culture in Yogyakarta (BKKIY), 'whose purpose was to promote Islamic cultural activities amongst the Islamic umat.' This body spawned separate organizations devoted to the arts, including Teater Muslim.

Teater Muslim premiered on the Yogyakarta stage with a production of Diponegoro's play *Iblis* (*Devil*) on 25 September 1961. The play relates the story of Abraham's sacrifice, which, in the Qur'anic version, is Ibrahim's sacrifice of Ismail, his son by Hajar. The play is a didactic presentation of how Ibrahim and, ultimately, Hajar resist devils who tempt them to disobey God's commands. A female devil and a male devil directly challenge the audience to ponder whether there are any among them as faithful as Ibrahim. The choice of the story of Ibrahim is also significant within an Indonesian Muslim context. As Diponegoro acknowledges in his reflections on Teater Muslim, anxiety about representing the Prophet Muhammad prevented them from dramatizing any *hadith* (direct accounts of the Prophet's life) (Diponegoro, 1984: 60).

For Muslims, the story of Ibrahim is not only about the origins of monotheism (as it is for Judaism and Christianity), but of a specific covenant with the (Arab) *umat*, who is seen as descending from Ismail. As with Budjangga in *Bebasari*, Ibrahim, and especially Hajar, wrestle with doubt and temptation, but ultimately emerge as *pahlawan* (heroes) of religion. In relation to Islamic mysticism, they demonstrate themselves to be *insan kamil* (perfect/ideal people), a righteousness that allows Hajar, at the end of the play, to predict the coming of the Prophet: 'I see your downfall now, Devil. Your mouth screams loudly only to conceal your cowardice. I now believe that God has adopted Ismail as his beloved. And in time Ismail will give rise to a great one who will save this world from your dirty tricks' (Diponegoro, 1984: 58). Ibrahim and Ismail reconcile their own warring emotions and the chaos around them to bring order to the world.

Arifin C. Noer's *Sumur Tanpa Dasar* (*The Bottomless Well*), which was originally composed in 1963 under the auspices of Teater Muslim, deals with the *insan kamil* ideal in more philosophically ambivalent ways. The protagonist, Jumena Martawangsa, is something of a Shavian anti-hero – an intellectual who, as Noer puts it, 'has faith in Thought, but somewhat less in God' (Noer, 1987: 37). Jumena had been a self-made man; like Bujangga (and the Prophet), he had been an orphan (a useful literary predicate to social transcendence). He was once a politician in Jakarta (Noer, 1989: 36), but left it all to find some peace in the countryside by shutting his eyes, ears, heart and dreams. He never had any children, but had four wives whom he never trusted or loved. In contrast to Ibrahim, who was rewarded for his faith with children late in life, Jumena addresses God in a spirit of distrust, and squanders his capacity to change the world. He is an old, paranoid man who never found happiness. At the end of the second act, there is one of many recurring gunshots. An *ulama* attending Jumena hears a leaf fall – Jumena hears a bomb. There is a character in the play who is actually named Kamil (ideal), and who claims extraordinary mystical powers; however, in Jumena's world, he is merely a madman. He dies in a fire that destroys Jumena's factory. Meanwhile, Marjuki, who had been like a brother to Jumena, has no moral center; he betrays Jumena and his wife, Euis, whom Marjuki loves. He is meaninglessly slaughtered by bandits, which drives Euis mad. When the bandits confronted him, one of them presented the nihilistic theory that wind, food, women and nothingness are all the same, to which his partner ironically commented, 'Lodod is truly a genuine man (*manusia sejati*). He is truly a hero for all ages' (1989: 154). There is no ultimate deliverance or redemption from such travesty. *Sumur Tanpa Dasar* (Figure 6.1) is the tragic inverse of *Iblis*: a parable of human isolation and despair resulting from misplaced faith.

Noer's play has enjoyed critical international success (indeed, it may be the most performed of all Indonesian plays) and several domestic revivals. It was chosen to inaugurate the grand reopening of the Jakarta Arthouse in 1987. It is one of the defining works of the modern Indonesian dramatic canon; as such, it is not typically viewed as an Islamic play. The religious content of the play, as of many other Indonesian plays, is difficult to distinguish from the supposedly 'secular' existentialist individualism that pervades much modern drama. Many canonical works of Indonesian drama productively invoke an ambiguity between modern existentialist alienation and a more Islamic spiritual struggle – a symbiotic ambiguity

Figure 6.1   Teater Ketjil production of Arifin C. Noer's *Sumur Tanpa Dasar*, 1970 (© Teater Ketjil)

whereby Islam can pass as modernism (and thereby as national culture), and modernism can pass as Islam (and thereby as popular indigenous spirituality).

The lonely path of the liberal infidel

Emha Ainun Nadjib, more than any other contemporary Indonesian public figure, is respected within both religious and artistic spheres. His role with Teater Dinasti, which became Yogyakarta's leading theatre troupe during the late 1970s soon after Bengkel moved to Jakarta, is somewhat akin to that of Malna with Teater Sae. Nadjib was not a founding member of Dinasti, and has even belittled his own accomplishments as a playwright, estimating that there were only about ten productions in which he was involved (Nadjib, 2007). However, as troupe founder Fajar Suhardjo readily acknowledges, Nadjib's role as playwright and editor provided intellectual and spiritual guidance for the group throughout the 1980s (Suharno, 2007). During this period, Nadjib rose to prominence as a musician (with the ensemble *Kiai Kanjeng*, with whom he still travels), poet and counter-cultural activist against the Suharto administration, gaining him a following amongst foreign scholars and observers that is disproportionate to his domestic fame. During the early 1990s, he turned from working with Dinasti to running an informal television talk show called *Gardu* (*Guardhouse*). Here, and on radio, cassette recordings, and in live performances, Nadjib channeled his individual style of collective performative spirituality (drawing heavily from his own training in Javanese Sufi mysticism as a youth in Yogyakarta) into dialogues in the style of town meetings – a kind of grassroots, revivalist democracy. In the new millennium, Nadjib has led such discourses in monthly gatherings in Jakarta, Yogyakarta and several other Javanese cities. Although animated by Nadjib's substantial charisma and spiritual authority, the message of these gatherings is always that young Indonesians must take responsibility for the progress of Indonesian democracy.

By the late 1990s, Nadjib had become a leader of the Yogyakarta counter-cultural arts scene (a more local version of what Rendra had become nationally) and a respected liberal Muslim speaker throughout the nation and abroad. He had begun to move in very influential Muslim circles, conferring often with the future Indonesian president and leader of Nadhlatul Ulama, Gus Dur (Abdurahman Wahid). However, he still considered himself a marginal figure with minimal access to power, a self-perception belied somewhat by the role he played in the final moments of the Suharto regime. In a lecture in 2004 entitled, 'The Nation of the Laughing People,' he recalled the scene in May 1998 in which a 'suggestion' (*husnul khotimah*) for Suharto to step down was drafted. Upon making his decision, Suharto 'asked for "senior" people to accompany and guide him. Rather spontaneously, nine people were chosen.' Nadjib, to his own surprise was among them:

> Starting that afternoon and until this very day, many people hold a grudge and even want to burn my house just because I met Suharto that day. 'Which faction does Emha represent?' Even a couple years later, Malik Fajar – who served a few times as the Minister of Education – was asked by a university student. 'How did Emha become one of the nine?' Malik answered lightly with his Eastern Javanese accent, saying: 'I have no idea how that little kid tags along all the time.'
>
> (Nadjib, 2007)

Nadjib's feigned humility here in casting himself as a 'little kid' in relation to other influential Muslims is typical. Having established himself as an anti-establishment figure, he has responded awkwardly to his recent prominence. The notion that he would be among a coterie of nine spiritual advisers to the Indonesian president (a number intentionally evocative of the nine *wali sangga* who are held to have introduced Islam to the country) seems beyond belief. His modesty is not entirely disingenuous; despite his successes, Nadjib has avoided the mainstream in both theatre and Indonesian Islam, paradoxically remaining marginal to dominant discourses in both these spheres even as his star has risen as a national figure. Indeed, the unusual combination of his art and faith has something to do with his ongoing marginality.

In June 2007, I interviewed Nadjib at his home and workshop in Yogyakarta, where he explained that the primary goal of Teater Dinasti productions was to 'contribute information to society,' a very different purpose from that of Rendra's artistic theatre. Whereas Bengkel took inspiration from the Greeks, 'Dinasti only staged plays that were taken from their own history with a political aspect **against** the mainstream.' To illustrate, Nadjib described a production called *Geger Wong Ngoyok Macan* (*House Pursues the Tigers*). In the 1980s, as the anti-communist paranoia that had legitimized the Suharto regime lost its edge, military and local police had increasingly turned their attention to local crimes, often of a vague or confusing nature, whose alleged perpetrators were often dealt with in extrajudicial executions (see Siegel, 1998b). In 1989, members of Teater Dinasti learned of an immanent initiative by the local police to engage in a mass eradication of such alleged criminals in the Yogyakarta area. The troupe mounted a quick response:

NADJIB: So all the criminals who were listed at that time – there were 189 criminals all over Yogyakarta – were to be executed. The government orders were issued in a mysterious way, [so that] the army would secretly arrest [them] at their homes, kill [them]. Now, the play *Geger Wong Ngoyok Macan*, in which Butet [Kartaredjasa][12] participated, was an informing of society that there were these *macan,*

> TIGERS that were to be sought out and executed. Thus, the title [in Javanese, rather than Indonesian]: 'Geger' means 'house.' 'Wong Ngoyok': 'pursuing to kill.' 'Geger Wong Ngyoyok Macan.' Now, it happened that the play was staged one day before the first shooting [...] For me personally, that was monumental. Above all, because it succeeded in informing the public about what was going on.
>
> (Nadjib, 2007)

For Nadjib, it is this insistence on local and immediate relevance that made Dinasti's work more radical than that of Bengkel; informing people in Yogyakarta about the abuses of the national government in their own neighborhood, and explaining the situation in colloquial Javanese rather than Indonesian.

Such an aesthetic distanced Teater Dinasti not only from the political interests of the nation-state, but also from mainstream theatre. It is not that mainstream theatre artists did not embrace oppositional and counter-cultural politics – many certainly did. However, in locating themselves resolutely in Yogyakarta within a Javanese cultural framework, Dinasti declined to occupy the stage of the Indonesian nation. Teater Dinasti marginalized itself vis-à-vis mainstream Indonesian national culture. In advocating such self-marginalization, Nadjib has struggled to articulate alternative localism, globalism and even nationalism for progressive Indonesian artists. In a series of statements on 'The Future of Art' printed in his 2006 collection, *Kerajaan Indonesia* (Indonesian kingdom), Nadjib writes:

> [They must] do two things at once. *First,* to open the door as wide as possible to the global community. *Second,* to work on [their] maturity and independence. Just opening the door won't guarantee personal maturity. At the same time, mature work is impossible to bring into being if the door is closed [...] What I mean is that they must be competent enough so that the works they deliver are complete and give inspiration as well as an enriching inner experience to society. On the issue of Indonesianness, which is increasingly complex and this rapid development of scientific knowledge and technology, the challenge for our artists is just becoming greater [...] I am certain that our artists remain competent to create. What is required is that they must combine three capacities: *First,* technical artistic skills. *Second,* their capacity for social understanding. And *third,* their sensitivity *vis-à-vis* space and time in history.
>
> (Nadjib, 2006: 268–9)

Of course, Nadjib identifies issues facing all artists vis-à-vis globalization. However, he also re-articulates Hanifah's call for an embrace of Western progress rooted in local cultural history, tradition and values.

Ian Betts has paradoxically called Nadjib's public life as a Muslim leader a 'lonely pilgrimage.' As Nadjib reflects in a dialogue titled, 'Yang Saya Lakukan,

Melawan Arus' ('What I do is to resist the tide'): 'In Islamic activities, it is so; in politics, it is so; in art, it is so. Although I have many poetry collections, perhaps the most of any Indonesian poet, it is nevertheless so, their contents embarrass everyone' (2006: 84). From his own perspective, this is because at a moment in which anxieties and uncertainties about rapid change and instability are strengthening conservative voices in Indonesian Islamic discourse, Nadjib still calls for tolerance of local and global complexity, skeptical opposition towards power and critical artistic engagement with the history of Javanese authoritarianism. Against right-wing Islamists, Nadjib has called himself a *'kafir liberal'* (liberal atheist), provocatively allying himself with other Indonesian leftists branded as atheists, including even the communists. By claiming such a derogatory epithet, Nadjib challenges the authority of *ulama* dispensing *fiqih* (Islamic legal opinions) ascribing their opposition simultaneously to apostasy and treachery. He reminds his fellow Muslims that *pesantren* originally flourished in Indonesia as radical institutions when the struggle against Dutch colonialism could not be conducted in the open. He thus defends the religious legitimacy of the margins against corrupt governments past and present; further, he defends the spirituality of art regardless of its adherence to *fiqih* – indeed, that art may convey a religious purity that many *ulama* have foregone out of desire for greater authority:

> In truth, nearly all poetry has a religious aspect. Poetry from whomever. The thing is, what do we mean by religious perspective? For myself, a poet who has written about 'The Morning Sun,' that is religious. Someone who writes about 'Poor People,' that's religious. Because, with the religious perspective that I intend, there can be no element in this life that is not included in the religious perspective, as long as the instigator, the worker, or the writer, positions all those elements within an aspect, according to Islam, of *tauhid* [the oneness of God].
>
> (2006: 1)

Despite such pronouncements, Nadjib also avoids making connections between his social engagement and his religious faith. During our interview, he adamantly maintained that Teater Dinasti's work had nothing to do with religion. At one point, he resisted questions about Islamic imagery in his plays, saying, 'I never argue my position in a manner muddled by questions of religious idiom' (2007). He explained that he is concerned about being able to speak not only to Muslims of a particular perspective, but to any audience, using whatever idiom most suits it. Given that in recent years, Nadjib has expanded his touring circuit not only to Hindu Bali but also throughout Asia, Europe and the United States, he is extremely conscious of presenting on global stages images of Islam that are counter-discursive to those of conservative and militant Islamists.

Nadjib's typically Javanese pragmatism has been taken by some American and Australian scholars as sufficient grounds to represent his religious views as subordinate to leftist sympathies and genealogies. For example, van Erven's *Playful Revolution* (1992) was a quite popular survey of modern Asian theatre in the Anglophone world. By emphasizing the 'theatre of liberation' movement (inspired in the region primarily by the Phillippines Educational Theatre Association, PETA), van Erven links the region to a Freirean tradition legible and of interest to American theatre scholars. His chapter on Indonesia deals extensively with Nadjib. Van Erven acknowledges that connecting with the 'grassroots' in Indonesia means connecting mainly with Muslims and that Dinasti and Nadjib have succeeded to the extent that they directly engage with Islamic discourse. However, for van Erven (as for many Euro-American observers of Nadjib and other leftists artists), Indonesians are clearly the *rakyat* to be reached *by means of* the *umat*. He implies that the Islamic community serves primarily to assemble the proletariat, and that Qur'anic scripture is not an ends in itself, but a gateway text leading to Paolo Freire (van Erven, 1992: 184–206).

Herein lies another violence to the complex episteme of liberal Muslim artists in Indonesia. Nadjib is not simply a counter-cultural artist who happens to be Muslim; rather, Islam is an inalienable aspect of his intellectual and artistic vision. If he has problematized his own faith, it is out of a desire to reach more broadly to eclectic audiences in Indonesia and abroad, and to clarify his distance from orthodoxy. In a dialogue titled 'Religiosity and Piety,' he claims that his nickname 'Emha,' formed from the initials of his actual given name, 'Muhammed' (M plus H), has, in itself, helped him avoid presumptions of conservatism: 'If I use the name Muhammed, it makes the realm of cultural politics seem more primordial for my activities. With the name Emha, a door that might be closed for me will be more open' (2006: 13–14). During the 1980s, Nadjib did not dissuade observers from representing him primarily as a leftist artist. Since his emergence in the 1990s and as his claim to a unique vision of liberal Indonesian Islam has become a basis of his credibility, both domestically and abroad, he has endeavored to keep his own art and that of his compatriots independent from any kind of presumption of Islamic authority. Although, as Nadjib himself readily affirms, such modesty conforms to Javanese syncretist traditions, it was a counter-cultural move to claim such a discourse in resistance to the national government. Further, in an era of resurgent Islamic reformism, what may seem conservative from a traditional Javanese perspective has taken on an edge of liberality.

An actress haunted by martyrs

Given the link between an Islamic moralism and male hegemony amongst the Indonesian theatrical elite, it is striking that Ratna Sarumpaet, the most prominent female playwright and director of the New Order, has foregrounded Islamic identity in her politically inflected works. She first became involved in theatre in 1969, upon seeing Rendra's *Karsidah Barzanji,* a theatrical adaptation of a sung collection of Islamic verse that marked his own conversion to Islam from Catholicism. Sarumpaet established her company, Satu Merah Panggung (One Red Stage) in 1973, and started working on her first piece, an adaptation of Omar Khayyám's *Rubáiyát*, which was staged in 1974. Sarumpaet had converted to Islam with her marriage to her husband, and reasoned that this work would bring her closer to Islamic traditions. It is worth considering that she was drawn to the theatre by the only explicitly Islamic work that Rendra would produce until 1991, and that her own first production was an adaptation of an Islamic work. Unlike Rendra's conversion to Islam, which, over the course of his career, has seemed practical, functional, and often subsumed in slippery intercultural eclecticism, Sarumpaet has shown a consistent concern with Islam throughout her career. This becomes even more apparent in her recent work, though it has gone unremarked by Euro-American observers who have concentrated on her feminist and leftist sympathies.

Sarumpaet achieved sudden celebrity in Indonesia and abroad in 1994 with *Marsinah: Nyanyian dari Bawah Tanah* (*Marsinah: Songs from Beneath the Earth*) (Sarumpaet, 1997). The title character of this full play and several subsequent monologues titled *Marsinah Menggugat* (*Marsinah Accuses*) written and performed by Sarumpaet was an East Javanese factory worker and labor activist who was abducted, raped and murdered by Indonesian soldiers in 1993, apparently in retribution for her activities organizing her fellow factory workers to demand higher wages. The Indonesian courts never brought the perpetrators to trial, and Marsinah became a martyr for the labor and women's movements and a symbolic victim of state violence and corruption. Sarumpaet was one of many artists and activists who was moved to respond to this crime and injustice (Rendra reportedly considered creating a new piece on the subject), but for her, it was the culmination of a long development in her work towards confronting human rights abuses against women in the context of a corrupt Indonesian national culture. Consequently, Sarumpaet came to be associated with Marsinah more than any other Indonesian artist or activist, and in the process developed a style of documentary theatre new to Indonesia.

Sarumpaet was frequently harried and persecuted by local police authorities who interfered with performances of *Marsinah Menggugat* in Surabaya, Bandung and Lampung (Sarumpaet, 1999, 2000). In March 1998, Sarumpaet and several fellow artists and activists were arrested at a peaceful demonstration. Laura Harvey, who had come to know Sarumpaet through her participation in the Fourth International Women Playwrights conference in Galway, Ireland in 1997, organized 'Readings for Ratna' around the world. Copies of a new English translation of *Marsinah: Nyanyian dari bawah Tanah* by Robyn Fallick (Sarumpaet, 1998) were made available *gratis*, and the events were used to raise awareness and promote a letter-writing campaign to get her released from prison. In May, hours before Suharto resigned,

Sarumpaet was set free. Although the charges against her were never fully cleared, and she suffered a variety of forms of government persecution during the following years, she immediately became one of the new luminaries of post-Suharto Indonesia. Her political activities, already significant before her arrest, rapidly expanded.

Before her arrest, Sarumpaet had created an organization (SIAGA) that supported anti-establishment political figures Amien Rais and Megawati Sukarnoputri in an effort to bring down the Suharto regime, and her ties (especially with Megawati who would become Indonesia's fifth president) continued into the new era. She also initiated the Forum for Justice and Democracy, a major non-governmental organization in the sudden scramble to root out corruption, collusion and nepotism. One of the most concerted efforts she has undertaken since 1998 is an initiative called 'Trace' (*'Jejak'*). She intended it as an independent institution for fostering reconciliation by opening up selected human rights cases ignored under the Suharto regime. Sarumpaet also imagined Jejak sponsoring 'theatres of the real' to provoke testimonial evidence. Sarumpaet hoped to collect all the evidence gathered through Jejak in a museum where Indonesia's youth would be able to view what went wrong so that the next generation could be spared a repetition of the dark sides of their history. The first case actually taken up by Jejak was a thorough investigation into the unresolved murder/rape of Marsinah. Thus far, it has met with little success.

In media coverage of all this activism, Sarumpaet has been portrayed as a feminist and social activist concerned with workers' rights.[13] However, in this and all of her subsequent 'activist' plays, the Islamic identity of her protagonists is consequential. In all of Sarumpaet's plays about Marsinah, this character challenges and ultimately seeks solace in Allah, as do the female protagonists of *Alia: Luka di Serambi Mekah (Alia: Wound on the Doorstep of Mecca)*, Sarumpaet's 2003 play about the conflict in Aceh, and *Anak-Anak Kegelapan (Children of Darkness*, her 2004 play about children of communists killed in 1966). In these plays, as in much Islamic literature, Allah is a mystery though also the ultimate source of justice in a highly corrupt world. In the Marsinah plays as well as in *Alia*, Sarumpaet employs choruses that bear clear affinities to Greek tragic choruses, but are specifically women who mediate through prayer between Sarumpaet's tragic Antigone-like figures and Allah. This is a dramaturgy that moves beyond her drama and into her activism through which she takes on the role of protagonist, gathering choruses of citizens to activate liminal spaces of justice.

In contrast to *teater dakwah*, however, Sarumpaet does not look to inculcate Muslim values, but rather to call for divine justice as she draws the spirits of righteous Muslim women through her own body in performance. In interviews with her in 1999 and 2004, Sarumpaet emphasized the extraordinary intimacy and responsibility of playing these female martyrs. In her *Marsinah* plays (Figure 6.2), she makes little attempt to *represent* any historical

Figure 6.2   Ratna Sarumpaet performs in front of a portrait of murdered labor activist, Marsinah, 1999 (© Ratna Sarumpaet)

particularities regarding the life of Marsinah herself because these are not 'documentary plays' in that sense; instead, she makes a theatrical claim to be inspirited by the martyred activist. Sarumpaet performs through and in proximity to Marsinah's image. Portraits of Marsinah often figure prominently in the scenic design, and journalistic photographs embellish programs and other supporting materials. Wielding the moral authority of the murdered Marsinah (akin to the enduring moral authority of the revolutionary youth), Sarumpaet condemns New Order corruption, paternalism, and, above all, its arrogance and violence towards women. If, as Siegel claims, Javanese ghosts are traditionally tied to sites of disappearance, Sarumpaet disrupts this convenient marginality to bring Marsinah directly into prominent performance spaces in Jakarta and other major cities in Indonesia and abroad. In contrast to Nadjib's insistence on locality, Sarumpaet nationalizes and globalizes the forgotten local crime.

The idiosyncratic portrayal of religious experiences in each of these plays makes sense in light of this spectrality in the author/actor's own experience. Voices of such personal suffering, speaking from the graves of the Suharto era, could not help but cross the barrier between public politics and personal piety. At the same time, there is a strategic dimension: by framing her representations of controversial New Order victims as acts of piety (for example, the program to her first Marsinah play opens with a Muslim prayer and the performance ends with one; *Alia* opens with women reciting from the Qur'an), she cast censorship thereof as impious. As in *Kisah Perjuangan Suku Naga* (*Struggles of the Naga Tribe*), Rendra playfully cast the Suharto administration as *wayang* ogres censoring his goro-goro clown scenes, so Sarumpaet, though more sternly, casts the same administration as unjust in the eyes of God. In *Alia*, the Acehnese protagonist who defies the Indonesian military has little faith that any human institutions will bring about a just resolution from Jakarta's neo-colonial aggression. Instead, she tells the Commandant,

> But don't forget Sir,
> In the great Beyond, before the Last Judgment,
> You will stand face to face with Allah
> And in the face of Allah, there won't be any other words
> But 'to Account for'

(Sarumpaet, 2003: 183)

Thus Islam enters into Sarumpaet's plays at the point at which the political sphere denies the possibility of justice, and justice becomes spectral. The authoritarian state may greet the moral claim of its victims' faces with a gruesome smiling mask, but beyond the grave, God will rend all such veils.

Like preceding generations of Indonesian Muslim theatre artists, both Sarumpaet and Nadjib have preferred to subsume aspects of Islamic discourse and imagery in their work to the outer framework of secular local and national politics. This should be understood as a tactic in relation to the cultural politics of Islam in postcolonial Indonesia, and not an indication that Islam is merely an incidental source of inspiration. Instead, Islam and its disparate genealogies enter national discourse from a different angle than colonialism, producing distinct hauntings and uncanny contradictions. For contemporary artists such as Noer, Nadjib and Sarumpaet, religion provides vocabularies for contesting injustice as well as for challenging official state discourses of nativism and Indonesian identity. For Effendi, Hanifah and Diponegoro, the *pemuda* (youth) had to be devout Muslims, and the *umat* ultimately preceded the *rakyat*. For Rendra, Noer, Sarumpaet and Nadjib, *dakwah* seems too much the polarizing tool of the orthodox *ulama* and the image of 'insan kamil' or 'manusia sejati' colors the search for truth with too much of the absolute.

For these contemporary Muslim artists, Islam must be softened and individualized so that it may transcend both locality in favor of a national discourse, and nationalism in favor of a global discourse. Whether this stance is conservative or radical is ultimately a matter of perspective. In promoting the Javanese syncretic approach to Islam, they have implicitly sided with the dominant ethnic culture and the Suharto regime against conservative Islamist *ulama*. However, after 1998 these same conservative Islamic factions have endeavored to influence government social agendas, introducing a range of censorship initiatives unimaginable under Suharto. For example, beginning in 1999, orthodox Muslims promoted an anti-pornography bill that threatened, in its broad language, to criminalize numerous forms of traditional performance. Ratna Sarumpaet and Goenawan Mohamad contributed to a vigorous campaign against the measure. However, the Indonesian parliament, quite possibly looking to attract Muslim voters in advance of national elections, finally passed the bill into law in October 2008. The struggle over the bill exemplifies a significant strengthening of the local representatives of a global Islamic Right in Indonesian cultural politics that was paradoxically enabled by Suharto's departure. In light of this shift, the traditional syncretism of many post-independence Muslim theatre artists has begun to appear radical. As Nadjib would have it, such syncretism and ecumenicalism are merely a reappropriation of the tradition of nineteenth-century Islamic *pesantren*.

7
Teater Reformasi: The Lingering Smile of the Absent Father

Performing the face of Suharto

In the preceding chapters, I have discussed a variety of practices belonging to the period immediately following Suharto's resignation in 1998 that might be taken as evidence of vitality. The lifting of restrictions on representation of Chinese culture has reintroduced traditional performances (such as New Year 'lion dances'), new works dealing with minority issues and the role of Chinese in Indonesian history by major playwrights and poets such as Seno Gumira Ajidarma and Remy Sylado, and a new interest in major figures such as Kwee Thek Hoay. Taking inspiration from figures such as Ratna Sarumpaet and Ken Zuraida (Rendra's wife), women have begun forming their own theatre troupes and writing plays (see Bain, 2005). Despite a crisis in available venues for performance after the demolition of most of TIM's stages, institutions such as Teater Utan Kayu and foreign organizations such as the Japan Foundation and the Alliance Française have gone some distance to filling the need. A proliferation of festivals in combination with the reformation of the guidelines for the seminal Jakarta Theatre Festival suggest an expansion of opportunities for younger troupes to let their works be seen. Furthermore, the political and economic decentralization of Indonesia, which has allowed regional centers to keep a larger share of their economic and human resources to use according to their own political interests, has also allowed regional theatres to develop independently. There can be little doubt that in the coming decades, observers of Indonesian modern theatre will need to travel not only to Bandung and Yogyakarta, but also to Makasar, Medan and other cities beyond Java to see the most groundbreaking work.

However, despite all these apparent causes for optimism, there is a widespread sense amongst practitioners and critics that the theatre of the '*reformasi*' era has somehow underperformed. This perception would seem to parallel a lingering sense of despair attending the economic and political fortunes of the nation as a whole. Despite the general enthusiasm in the West for post-Suharto Indonesia as a demonstration of the compatibility between Islam and democracy, Indonesians tend to dwell more on the persistence of corruption, the failure of the economy to recover, and the rise of cultural conflicts that nationalism never resolved. Likewise, apart from those few remaining luminaries who established their reputations in the 1970s, Indonesian theatre artists to whom I've spoken feel that conditions have not improved since the 1990s.

From 1966 to 1998, Suharto maintained the legitimacy of his New Order by promising development and modernization against the spectre of latent communism. Under this rationale, he had transformed the boisterous Indonesian civil society of the Soekarno era into empty 'festivals of democracy.' He had silenced the anti-colonial discourse of the revolution to open Indonesia to global capital investment, and with a new coalition between an emergent Indonesian middle class and Western business, acquiesced to a course of development and modernization laid out by the IMF and World Bank. In place of Soekarno, 'mouthpiece of the revolution' and 'father of the proletariat,' Indonesia now had a 'father of development' who appeared on billboards and currency as the smiling general.[1] As the economic indicators of Indonesia's well-being steadily improved in the 1970s and 1980s, the capacity and instinct of the public to question the legitimacy of the New Order waned. As sacrifice to this managed Indonesian future, generations that came of age during these years were asked once again to forget a great deal about their past. First and foremost, of course, they were asked to forget any positive contributions that the political Left had ever made to the creation of an Indonesian nation so that they could remember an honor roll of Indonesian heroes all committed simply and unproblematically to the nation. They were asked to forget the deaths of hundreds of thousands of presumed members of the Communist Party at the hands of soldiers and mobs in early 1966 so that they could remember only the heroic six generals martyred for their nation on the night of 30 September 1965. They were asked to forget political prisoners like Pramoedya Ananta Toer, removed from public sight and mind so that no articulate voices would remain who had thrived under the Old Order. They were asked to forget the hypocrisy of a 'republic' that governed unwilling 'citizens' in East Timor, Aceh and Irian Jaya through military occupation. They were asked to endure a police state, in which citizens might be arrested, detained, persecuted, censored or simply murdered with no recourse to an independent judiciary. They were asked to accept the banning of Chinese media for no better reason than its implicit association with communism, and the censorship of any independent media that criticized the government. They were asked to forget the syncretism and ideological complexity of their cultural heritage so that these could be transformed into colorful dioramas for the 'Beautiful Indonesia in Miniature' amusement park.

This is all to say that over the course of 33 years in power, the Suharto regime filled Indonesia with new 'sites of disappearance' superceding and overlapping already rich palimpsests of forgetting in the capital and throughout the nation. The persistent discourse of *pembangunan* (development) covered over the gaps in the national memory where inconvenient pasts lay deeply buried. Other than the *Lubang Buaya* (*Crocodile Hole*) in which the bodies of six murdered generals had been dumped in 1965, the 'holes' of New Order history were forgotten, an amnesia justified by an ongoing state of emergency. From the uncounted casualties of 1965 to three decades of 'state enemies' or 'latent communists' killed from Aceh to East Timor and West Papua (Irian Jaya), and from the factories of East Java to the streets of Jakarta, the death toll exacted by the New Order in the name of progress was staggering. By the late 1970s, the New Order had become so thorough in its evacuation of the public sphere that these acts went largely unresisted and uninvestigated. As steel and glass skyscrapers in the capitol heralded the rise of a glorious future, the past receded into patriotic silence, an ever-deepening well of absence.[2]

By the late 1980s, however, an increasingly affluent and educated Indonesian population began to question their leader's bargain with greater insistence. Events such as the rape and murder of the East Javanese labor activist Marsinah in 1993, by military police under the protection of corrupt courts, generated outrage and ongoing protest. Workers organized into unions and campuses became safe havens for radical anti-government discourse. Beginning with the Marsinah plays of Ratna Sarumpaet in the mid-1990s and continuing with Butet Kartaredjasa's *The Tongue is Paralyzed* (*Lidah Pingsan*) monologue in 1997, theatre artists began to represent that which Suharto had removed from sight. In the decade following Suharto's resignation in May 1998, victims of the New Order haunted the modern stage. However, unlike previous theatrical ghosts called into being as uncanny doubles through the bodies of actors, these ghosts of silenced histories often remained pointedly absent. They were invoked as the missing reporter whose fate could not be discovered, the gravestone that could not be located, or simply as silent bodies moving obscurely on dark stages. After living in a state of terror for their entire lives, the young activists who brought down the Suharto regime appeared to move forward with some trepidation and confusion. Some critics worried that Indonesia had lost its entire population to the deadening ideology of the New Order (other than those elders who could remember a time before 1965), and that the revival of national culture couldn't take place until an untainted generation came of age.[3]

With expectations heightened for a radical rupture from the old 'new tradition' of theatre in the Suharto era, critics expressed disappointment almost immediately at the extent to which this *Teater Reformasi* failed to transcend the Suharto era. An article in *Sagang* in January 1999, disappointingly echoed critics of the past half century in proclaiming that Indonesian theatre was 'still shackled to Western theory' (Nurcahyoab, 1999). The avant-garde theatre seemed largely a continuation of postmodern and deconstructive aesthetics pioneered by Teater Sae a decade earlier. Many asked whether it was still possible for theatre to be radical after the fall of the 'status quo' (see Bain, 2000). R. Anderson Sutton, a longtime observer of Indonesian popular culture, attended a few performances by the leading theatrical satirists during the summer after Suharto's May 1998 resignation. Nano Riantiarno's *Opera Sembelit* (*Constipation Opera*), written the previous November and restaged in July and August 1998, depicted Suharto as a 'Dr Salim' whose clinic got rich by faking a cure for a mass epidemic of constipation. Butet Kartaredjasa, whose *Lidah Pingsan* (*The Tongue is Paralyzed*, 1997) had portrayed a reporter braving the corrupt Indonesian justice system to find someone abducted by the police, returned in 1998 with *Lidah (Masih) Pingsan* (*The Tongue is [Still] Paralyzed*), in which nothing much has changed under the new President Habibie. Although Sutton finds that both works criticize the New Order more scathingly than either artist had previously, he wonders reasonably whether such criticism is actually radical any more, and whether it could possibly serve as a basis for a new 'theatre of reform':

> Riantiarno and Butet were derisive, to be sure, but they were taking little risk. One wonders what level of provocation Indonesian theatre might have to reach nowadays in order to stir immediate political action, whether by the audience or by 'the authorities.' For the moment, I would simply argue that live performance has had a tradition of bold expression and now, no longer under the repressive eye of the New Order, such expression has continued, but because it no longer risks repressive measures, it is, in effect, less bold.
>
> (Sutton, 2001: 8)

With the dismantlement of much of the apparatus developed under the New Order to silence criticism, including the requirement dating back to colonial times for performances to obtain official permission, politically invested theatre artists faced a paradoxical freedom. At the same time, these freedoms have allowed various kinds of decentralization in the practices of modern theatre. Bodden and Lauren Bain have both written of collaborations between theatre artists and non-governmental organizations. In addition, some NGOs, such as the Union of Indonesian Workers for Prosperity (SBSI) have taken the opportunity to begin organizing their own theatrical endeavors (see Bodden, 1997c; Bain, 2003). Similarly, modern theatre groups based in urban communities other than Jakarta, Bandung and Yogyakarta have declared independence from these dominant theatre cities. Makassar, Sulawesi, in particular, has emerged as a major regional theatre capital, with its annual *Journal of Moment Arts* (JOMA) outdoor festival boasting a vitality rivaling any arts events in the post-Suharto capital (see Tajudin, 2004; Bain, 2005).

Some critics of the vitality of '*teater reformasi*' have viewed the lingering obsession with deconstruction and abjection as a failure to move boldly into some unprecedented generative aesthetic. Despite the euphoric moment of '*reformasi*,' many troupes seem to have taken the New Order's evacuation of meaning, already explored in the work of Teater Sae and Teater Kubur, to an extreme of despair. For example, Aritonang pointedly contrasts Rendra's 'mini-kata' performances that seemed so revelatory at the beginning of the Suharto era with the aesthetic of Teater Payung Hitam in their 2000 production, *DOM Dan Orang Mati* (*DOM And People Die*):

> This is not *teater minikata* [minimal words], but rather *teater tanpa kata* [without words], a theatre of interjection (to borrow a linguistic term). Why? Because there are no longer any words to be said, words or expressions are already dead themselves; death or pressure, oppression, tyranny, and power, there only remains space and moaning. Human freedom colonized to the extreme, all become mute. What remains, disturbed movements, furious thoughts, furious consciousness, sighs, murmurs, tears, groaning, shouts, sickness, all of which merely reveals the interjection of humanity.
>
> (Aritonang, 2004: 301)

Bain similarly describes a scene in *Aku Pinjam Baju Baru* (*I'm Borrowing a New Shirt*) a 2004 performance by Teater Kita Makassar, in which costumes taken from a coffin are like a 'Pandora's Box' of ills unleashed on Indonesia since Suharto:

> One character wears a head piece crowned with a huge crucifix and a Muslim crescent moon and star, and a breast plate instantly recognizable as Indonesia's national symbol, the Pancasila shield, but without the symbols it usually contains. He's the hero of emptiness, his values stripped of meaning. This character presides over the costume-changing ceremony, mumbling a mantra of magic spells as catastrophe unfolds.
>
> (Bain, 2004)

Such imagery reflects widespread disappointment at the unfulfillment of the era of '*reformasi*' itself; its many continuities from the Suharto era mixed with a plethora of new challenges, from Islamic militants to natural disasters. Nevertheless, there is some trace of euphoria in these enactments, and it might be argued that their negative representation or refusal to represent a new surrogate in the genealogy of Indonesian progress actually constitutes a quintessentially democratic gesture. As Slavoj Žižek points out (invoking Claude Lefort's *Democracy and Political Theory*):

> *the Name must remain empty* [...] democracy implies the distinction between the empty symbolic locus of power and the reality of those

who, temporarily, exercise power; for democracy to function, the locus of power must remain empty; nobody is allowed to present himself as possessing the immediate, natural right to exercise power.

(Žižek, 1993: 190)

By lingering with the critique of Suharto, theatre and performance artists of 'Era *Reformasi*' have clung to the most vital moment of democracy itself, that moment in which a space is cleared before the desire for order and stability demands that it be filled.

During the three-decade span of the New Order, images of Suharto's face had pervaded Indonesian society. Some of these representations were larger than life, as in ubiquitous billboards and posters featuring the 'father of development' beaming over some scene of modernization and progress. However, Suharto studiously avoided the monumentality of his predecessor, Soekarno. Suharto's face did not shine out from massive banners unfurled over city plazas like that of Mao Zedong. Rather, it was reproduced infinitely in miniature, in the far more pervasive and integrated mode typical of corporate logos. Modest, standardized portraits of the smiling general hung from walls in private homes and offices. Unlike Soekarno (or Chairman Mao), Suharto eschewed public spectacle in favor of private proliferation. Suharto ceded monumentality to the murdered generals of September 1965, but his portrait stared out at every Indonesian from the 50,000 rupiah note. What bolder means of giving the president representational currency than through the overt commodity fetishism of bank notes? As the New Order stripped Indonesia of much of its postcolonial memory, Suharto's face re-inspirited the nation in the manner of the *wahyu* (facial radiance) of an old Javanese king; and in the manner of a Javanese king, he consolidated the vitality of the nation into his own person. The *rakyat* (the people), in the New Order, were *masih bodoh* (still ignorant). To weather the unceasing threats of social chaos (most likely through latent communism), the *rakyat* required constant guidance from their smiling father. Given the pervasiveness of Suharto's portrait as icon of the New Order, it is hardly surprising that some of the most compelling images generated during the demonstrations of May 1998 involved the defacement of Suharto, both in the usual sense of vandalizing the image of his face on posters, and in street installations with mockups of official portraits of Suharto whose faces had been cut out, leaving a hole for anyone to insert his own face.[4]

In July 1999, a group of University of Indonesia students occupied an intersection in Jakarta wearing photocopied images of Suharto's face. When they were arrested and brought before a judge, they identified themselves only as Suharto (Figure 7.1), and insisted that they would not remove their masks until Suharto himself removed the mask of 'father of development' and submitted to justice for his numerous crimes against the Indonesian people.

Figure 7.1 The Suharto face demonstrators appear in court, 1999 (Author's collection)

This tactic posed a difficult dilemma for the judge, who hesitated to treat students roughly at a moment when demonstrating *pemuda* (noble youth) had supplanted the defending soldiers and military police in public sympathy. However, without unmasking the students, there seemed little option but to credit the disturbance to the name of the ex-president. The students dispersed in the confusion before their actual names could be discovered. This act of civil disobedience on a public thoroughfare of the capital was ultimately filed under 'Soeharto.'

These 'Suharto faces' worn by the students were full face-covering masks, but were also cheap photocopies of a readily available image. No doubt, pragmatics had dictated as much as design here. Nevertheless, it was a productive efficiency. The photocopied faces invoke the shallowness of Suharto's authoritarian project. His avowed program to develop the *rakyat* holistically (*manusia seutuhnya*) is shown as a mechanical proliferation of his own superficiality. Once confronted by the state legal apparatus, the students resisted not by ripping off their masks to reveal 'the real face of Indonesia,' but by performing anonymously through the *wahyu* of the ex-president. This courtroom performance demonstrates that as Suharto's 'children,' they should receive as much justice as he would, and inversely, he should receive as much justice as them. Rather than recapitulating the old organicist dramaturgy by presenting their own faces, the Suhartoface demonstrators summoned the smiling general, acknowledging spectrality as a more appropriate metaphor for post-Suharto Indonesia.

The Suharto face demonstrations performed a focused act of resistance against the lingering epistemic violence of the neocolonial, patriarchal state, and a near perfect metonym for the ironic heuristic of Indonesian *reformasi*. Levinas, in explaining his concept of the transcendent face as the basis for a philosophy that begins with ethics, writes:

> The way in which the other presents himself, exceeding *the idea of the other in me*, we here name face. This *mode* does not consist in figuring as a theme under my gaze, in spreading itself forth as a set of qualities forming an image. The face of the Other at each moment destroys and overflows the plastic image it leaves me, the idea existing to my own measure and to the measure of its *ideatum* – the adequate idea [...] It *expresses itself.*
>
> (Levinas, 1969: 50–1)

The Suharto face demonstrators ironically claim freedom in the act of indicting the plastic image of Suharto's ubiquitous face. His paternal smile, which had presided for 33 years over a depoliticized, infantilized populace empowers these performers to transcend that 'ideatum' made to the state's measure. In appropriating that one facial 'set of qualities' whose demand for justice was respected by the Indonesian judiciary, the demonstrators parody the egalitarian 'blindness' of the Indonesian legal system. By making their identities invisible, they compel the courts to heed the ethical claim of their Levinasian faces. By performing the interchangeability of the face of every citizen of the republic with that of the president, they indict the disjuncture between the postcolonial ideal of respect for the irreducible other and the surrogation of 'human rights' by the plastic visage of an authoritarian state. However, one might reasonably wonder whether such appropriation, depending as it does on the persistence of the plastic image of epistemic violence, does any work towards 'clearing a space' for a form of life after colonialism.

During the transitional presidency of B. J. Habibie (May 1998 to November 1999), Suharto was seen as the face animating the mask of Habibie, or Habibie was seen as the puppet prodigy of Suharto, his 'professor' and *dalang* (puppetmaster) and each subsequent president has struggled to demonstrate that he (or she) is not merely a repetition of the old.[5] That smiling countenance, like the terrible mask worn by Tajudin as Caligula in Teater Garasi's *Or Anyone Else...*, continues to haunt Indonesia in the age of reform. A nation does not easily transcend a legacy that has encompassed several generations. Like a new colonial past, the Suharto regime is uncannily present in *reformasi* performance. It is through this paternal mask that many theatre artists struggle to find the faces of their lost genealogies, the faces desperately needed to re-inspirit a mad generation wandering confused on the sites of their own disappearance.

The haunted graveyards of Payung Hitam

Bandung's Teater Payung Hitam (Black Umbrella Theatre) interpolated this facial metonymic into several spectacular performances early in the *reformasi* period. Payung Hitam's works are typically highly physical and imagistic with text and character deployed in the manner of choreography and composition rather than in service to a linear narrative. In the pieces of this era, their spectacles reflected chaos and lingering terror from the old regime. *Katakitamati (Ourwordsaredead*, 1998*)*, the troupe's first production following the fall of Suharto, opens with televisions flanking the stage, screening news clips 'thick with fetid blood' of the violence and demonstrations of May 1998. Five orators wheel podiums around the stage, orating competing fragments of text in a chaos of free expression that builds into a blunt, percussive rhythm, reinforced by the pounding of metal chairs. Political freedoms ironically 'filled the stage space, aggressively forcing all other activity into the margins and silence' (Bodden, 2008: 137). Reviewers interpreted the orations as 'the cheap expressions of belated heroes' (S.J.S., 2004: 271) and 'a terror all in itself ready to claim victims' (Maulana, 2004: 265). Another piece performed in 2000, called *DOM, Dan Orang Mati* (*And People Die*) redefines an acronym typically used to designate 'military operation zones' (Daerah Operasi Militer) to denounce the ongoing abuses by the Indonesian military in the North Sumatran province of Aceh. Beginning from a scene of an Acehnese grandmother looking through a picture album, *DOM* takes the form of a series of 'portraits' or 'stolen scenes' from the 'black history' of military killings in the region.

Corpses, severed heads, headless figures and the national flag appear in these and other productions of the period, mixing imagery of the unnumbered dead with the loss of national identity metonymized in the separation of faces from bodies. Such images of absence contained within national symbols are already apparent in their 1997 piece, *Merah Bolong Putih Doblong Hitam (Red Perforated White Perforated Black)*, which in its very title invokes a flag imbricated with violence and death. In *Tiang ½ Tiang* (Flag at Half Mast, 1999), we see 'a naked boy seeking solace from a headless giant dressed in red and white (as though representing a nation without direction) who is unable to offer any comfort' (Bodden, 2008: 134–5). Similarly, Katakitamati features a large headless carcass. There is also a pregnant woman who sees through the empty rhetoric of the *reformasi* orators. However, she is a Cassandra, who staggers, alone, unheeded. Images of (her?) malnourished baby in a hospital play on the television screen at the end of the play. In DOM (Figure 7.2), many related images build over the course of several scenes. The stage is dominated from the start by the faceless silhouette of a four-star general on the back screen.

Figure 7.2   A general appears before an empty silhouette of Suharto in Teater Payung Hitam's production of *DOM, Dan Orang Mati*, 2000 (© Rachmann Sabur)

There are sprawled corpses that cannot be revived. In one scene, the faceless leaders proliferate:

> With the illustration of thundering music, the background of the stage changes to present three posters without faces. The first poster is red, the second white with its picture upside-down and the third is green depicting the figure of the leader of that era. Then, three figures dressed all in black appear and deliver expressions of protest against the dead figure.
>
> (Wirawan, 2004: 298)

Leadership becomes an empty portrait for a succession of surrogates who only arouse a continuing stream of protest. A man grasps the Indonesian flag and dances with a carcass. A woman weeps into the flag and is reprimanded by a soldier. Another man marks out a graveyard with tombstones while singing an Acehnese song.

> The gravestones grow, chatter. The mass graves rise up suddenly, the victims go on with grit in their eyes. The hero has no more power to determine the suffering of the people, he can only cast off the helmet, the boots that all this time he has been carrying.
>
> (Aritonang, 2004: 304)

Amidst sounds of battle and a proliferation of sprawled corpses, a masked man in a red jacket and bow tie dances with someone in military dress. They pay no attention to three severed heads lying on the table. At the end of the play, a small child circulates between the gravestones, but he cannot find what he is looking for. He expresses his sadness and solitude by playing a *suling* as the performance comes to an end.

This final image in *DOM* brings the central allegory of Sontani's *Suling* to its melancholy antithesis. After 50 years of the organicist project in Indonesian modern theatre, the *suling* sounds not the hopeful assertion of a nationalist youth synthesizing tradition and modernity, but rather the loneliness of a child amongst the forgotten dead. The pregnant woman of the play, like the bride in the startling final image of Teater Garasi's *Atau Siapa Saja…*, is the antithesis of Sontani's wandering woman. Disempowered, disconnected and all too mortal, she despairs of ever finding the face of her beloved again, the nation that she would inspirit. In all these scenes, the spectral nation lays bare the failure of the organicist project. The dead proliferate under icons of faceless leaders, while soldiers and nationalists dance amidst the severed heads of the people. Women and men wander in confusion and the moment in which people might look into each other's faces and answer their claims for justice is always deferred. In stark contradiction to the 'euphoria' of *reformasi*, we see a people incapable of imagining the future as they mourn over severed links to the past. Instead, there is one ghost from the all-too-recent past who proliferates and haunts each of these performances.

In *Katakitamati*, there is a wall constructed of tightly packed bales of black cardboard on which a huge image of Suharto's face is painted, beside which a huge 'windmill' has been fitted with muscular arms ending in fists over each blade, 'like the threatening presence of potential violence ready to pummel and batter any and all of those acting in its shadow' (Bodden, 2008: 137) Above it all, an electric fan hangs, fitted with severed feet in army boots. The fan and the windmill turn from time to time, creating a composite image of the fragmented body of the state, mechanized into a grotesque automaton hovering over all the scenes of empty *reformasi* rhetoric. The performance ends, like Pink Floyd's *The Wall*, and with obvious intimations of the Berlin wall, with the set piece being torn down. Suharto's portrait is fragmented, his New Order dismantled. However, as might be signaled by the fact that it is the headless giant who does the smashing, this accomplishes nothing. We see through the ruins of the old wall, the white shadow of another Suharto visible behind it. Like a collage on a June 1999 issue of *Tempo* magazine of Habibie's face as a mask worn by Suharto, this final image presents the old president's face as a hall of mirrors, or an inescapable procession of surrogates. In *DOM*, when the three faceless posters appear (which Bain interprets as Suharto, Habibie and General Wiranto), a group of actors join the banners onstage. They are all dressed as government officials, 'all wearing the same mask: a smiling face, one the audience became very familiar with during the 32 years of the New Order regime' (Gintini, 2000). Indeed, what 'generative' new aesthetic could speak with greater clarity to the surrogation of the smiling general throughout the *reformasi* era? After three decades of the ideological evacuation of national memory, artists such as Rachman Sabur are in no great hurry to forget.

Like the Suharto face demonstration, Payung Hitam's repetitions of Suharto might be understood as an appropriation of the plastic image of the phenomenal countenance that permits the free expression of the transcendent, Levinasian face of the Other. However, they might better be understood in relation to Deleuze and Guattari's concept of faciality as that 'white screen' upon which authoritarian regimes project their deterritorializing substitutions for citizenship. In the optimistic window of 'era *reformasi*,' it appeared as if the logic of Levinasian transcendence prevailed. As 'era *reformasi*' settled into the 'post-Suharto' era, a more Deleuzian logic emerged. As Deleuze and Guattari present it in their chapter on 'faciality' in *Milles Plateaux*, the face becomes a 'horror' instrumentalized by fascism to insert uncanniness into lived experience (Deleuze and Guattari, 1987: 190). The post-Suharto era is simply another phase of that postcoloniality that Cheah describes in relation to spectrality. The claim for a new organic life remains haunted by the lingering prefix, and the unsettling, ghostly face of the father speaks through the alienated faces of a new generation of Indonesians.

President of the Republic of Dreams...

While Sarumpaet accused Suharto through the ghost of Marsinah and Teater Payung Hitam staged the proliferation of Suharto's countenance through landscapes of death, Butet Kartaredjasa ascended to national celebrity by doing presidential impersonations. As Malna's modernist eclecticism had been shaped by growing up next to TIM, Butet grew up steeped in traditional Javanese dancing, theatre and visual arts thanks to the fact that his father, Bagong Kusudiardja, was one of Yogyakarta's leading traditional dancers. Nevertheless, he was inspired to become an actor by watching Rendra's 1975 production of *Hamlet* while still in high school. He was attracted to Rendra's charisma, his infusion of Javanese character into the play and his ability to mix humor with serious material (Kartaredjasa, 2007a). That year, he wrote a short play, in the form of Javanese *kethoprak*, about the annexation of East Timor. After a lackluster attempt at art school, he started working in the Yogyakarta theatre scene in the 1980s, acting with Teater Dinasti beginning in 1983 and joining Teater Gandrik (Lightning) in 1985. He became the leading actor of Gandrik, and has continued to work with members of the troupe even after branching off into independent work in the late 1990s.

Teater Gandrik is one of the groups that had begun to move beyond Rendra's nativism in the 1980s. Embracing their Javanese locality more extensively, Gandrik presented plays about ordinary kampongan people in styles based on folk theatre. Though still performing in Indonesian, they rely on Javanese for much of their humor. Also, eschewing the dominant troupe structure, they cultivate an ensemble creative ethos that 'mirrors the democratic spirit of traditional folk theatre' (Hatley, 1999a). Their work in the 1980s consisted mainly of 'light-hearted social satires,' variously described as *mencubit tanpa membikin rasa sakit* (pinch without causing pain) or *guyon parikena* (making a serious point while seemingly only joking) (Hatley, 1999b: 276). Critics often invoke the term *sampakan* (war music) to describe Gandrik's style of criticism couched in traditional humor, and Kartaredjasa, like Rendra, compares it to the spirit of the *punakawan* (the clown characters of *wayang* shadow theatre). In 1993, some members of Gandrik signaled a shift to a more aggressive political engagement by collaborating in a production called *Pak Kanjeng*, protesting dispossession of local people for construction of the Kedung Ombo dam (see Samson, 1994). Though never departing from their signature style, many of Gandrik's subsequent productions have targeted government policies and injustice more directly. For example, in their 2008 production, *The Trial of Susila (Sidang Susila)*, Indonesian President Susilo Bambang Yudhoyono is lampooned as 'Susila' (decency), a character arrested for infringement of the new Decency Laws.

In Gandrik productions of the 1980s, Kartaredjasa typically portrayed ridiculously bombastic and aloof government officials. In 1987, this led him to his first experience impersonating President Suharto in the guise of an 'exalted leader' of the world of *djin* (spirits) in a Teater Gandrik piece called *Spirit* (*Demit*):

> This was staged in 1987, in the times when Suharto was still powerful. Whenever I was accused, I would say, I'm just playing a *djin*, a ghost! If this ghost has a voice like Suharto, then maybe that's just a coincidence! But they weren't going to ban a story about a ghost. There was no problem, and people enjoyed it. It was performed a hundred times on campuses, from 1987 to 1990. People knew. But the police couldn't ban it. This was a story about a ghost.
>
> (Kartaredjasa, 2007b)[6]

In this and subsequent performances as 'not-Suharto,' Kartaredjasa would summon the (ex-)president's spirit by deploying highly characteristic speech patterns and quirks while ostensively playing an unrelated character. Hatley explains some of these characteristics in a description of a monologue performed by Kartaredjasa at *Ruwatan Bumi*, an Earth Day manifestation in April, 1998:

> Butet dons a *pici* (Indonesian fez cap), assumes a sombre demeanour, and prepares to give a speech. Although he refers to himself simply as a *saudagar*, a trader, his opening words *saudara-saudara* (brothers), pronounced in a deep nasal tone, identify him unmistakably as President Suharto. The audience explodes with mirth. Throughout his address on the subject of the Indonesian environment, the earlier themes of language, power and dominance are maintained. The President's characteristic speech errors are evident – wrongly-placed usages of *daripada*, *ken* in place of *kan*, the notorious *semangkin* – plus his familiar throat-clearing and slightly wheezing, menacing laugh.
>
> (Hatley, 1999b: 276)

Though Kartaredjasa first developed this skill at impersonating the president in productions with Teater Gandrik in Yogyakarta, he became famous when he began performing it within his monologue, *Lidah Pingsan*, which played at theatre venues, university campuses and other sites where the democracy movement gathered in opposition to the New Order, beginning in December 1997.

In *Lidah Pingsan (The Tongue is Paralyzed)*, the New Order's repression of free speech at the national level is transposed to a Javanese village where journalist Aji tries to uncover what has happened to the only son of Pak Mardiko, a man who has been protesting outside the house of the village *lurah* (headman) for 30 years, believing that the *lurah* is complicit in his son's disappearance. The journalist discovers that this is indeed the case, but cannot publish his story because the *lurah* controls the press. Besides invoking recurrent abuses and 'disappearances' of the Suharto regime in general, Javanese audiences made connections to the story of Udin, a Yogyakarta-based reporter who had been murdered in 1996 while investigating a regional official. The *lurah*, performed as Kartaredjasa's 'not-Suharto' character, meets all inquiries with deflecting rhetoric.

Shortly following Suharto's resignation in 1998, Kartaredjasa developed a sequel to his first piece, *Lidah Masih Pingsan (The Tongue is Still Paralyzed)*, in which Aji is roused from his euphoric *reformasi* era activities (such as founding new political parties) by the continuing laments of Pak Mardiko. Newly emboldened by the regime change, Aji sets out again to look for answers. He follows the chain of command, and so confronts both the old lurah and the new lurah, who is an outrageous parody of the interim president, B. J. Habibie. At the point in the monologue when Aji confronts this 'not-Habibie,' Kartaredjasa produces a *wayang* puppet of the clown character Gareng (who, like Habibie, is short with big round eyes).[7] He places the Gareng/Habibie in a stand and faces off with him in silhouette (like the warring sides in a shadow play), as he demands answers to his questions. As Gareng/Habibie responds, Kartaredjasa takes the puppet down and assumes the character into his own body. With wide eyes and a bobbing head, Kartaredjasa ruthlessly caricatures this new president's affectations: his frequent interjections of 'okay?,' 'his usual diatribe of Anglicised abstractions (*konstitusionil, proportionil, proaktif*), irrelevant to the case in point' (Hatley, 1999b: 280). At one point, Gareng/Habibie acknowledges that Suharto is his 'professor' and that he is indeed a 'puppet' of the old regime. However, despite freedom of the press, both *lurah* are unconcerned by Aji's investigation. Nobody takes responsibility. Aji is free to print his story, but with little confidence that it will do any good for Pak Mardiko and his son. Like Teater Payung Hitam's post-Suharto performances, *Lidah Masih Pingsan* expresses disillusionment with *reformasi* and a widespread perception that Indonesia is still a long way from becoming a liberal democracy. However, it also constituted a specific declaration from Kartaredjasa that he was ready to apply his acting skills to summon the spirits not only of Suharto, but also of any of his surrogates. This readiness took him into the next phase of his career, as president of the Republic of Dreams.

In December 2005, Effendi Gazali, a veteran of the 1998 student movement and professor in politics and marketing at the University of Indonesia, hosted the opening of a radical new Indonesian television show: *The Truly Drunken Republic (Republik Benar-Benar Mabuk)*. Inspired by Jon Stewart's *The Daily Show* in the United States as well as the genre of American late-night talk shows, Gazali conceived of the show as presenting *Republik Mimpi (The Republic of Dreams)* as a kind of 'mirror-image' of Indonesia (always referred to as 'the neighboring country') in which a 'cabinet' composed of actors portraying past and current heads of state would discuss current events, parodying the behavior of those in power, and gently suggesting policy. Gazali brought in Kartaredjasa to portray the sitting president, Susilo Bambang Yudhoyono (or 'SBY,' which Kartaredjasa jokingly redefines as 'Si Butet Yogya'). He has subsequently ridden the edge of post-Suharto censorship with his fellow television actors. The television broadcaster, Indosiar, discontinued the show in June 2006 (due to corporate and political pressure) and Gazali started a new show on the same premise called 'Newsdotcom' (Figure 7.3). Newsdotcom itself was threatened on 1 March 2007,

> when the Minister of Communications and Informatics, Sofyan Djalil, told journalists that he considered issuing a 'somasi' (legal notice) against the program, because he did not agree with 'the president being mocked.' A day later, the program's main sponsor, the cigarette company Sampoerna, announced it would not renew its sponsorship, which had expired at the end of February.

Three days later, President Si Butet Yogya of the Republic of Dreams responded on the show, by declaring that the Republic would revert to a Kingdom. During the episode the new king cynically joked that he preferred living in a kingdom, as 'everything was comfortable and nice.' Various

Figure 7.3 SBY (Butet Kartaredjasa) and the 'cabinet' of Republik Mimpi, 2006 (© Effendi Ghazali)

government officials (of the neighboring country of Indonesia) expressed support, and Amien Rais, a prominent figure in *reformasi* politics, appeared on the show to call on the Indonesian government to accept open criticism. On the 18 March show, Kartaredjasa restored the Dream Republic (Juriens, 2007).

This new, highly politicized role on a popular national television program brought Kartaredjasa into a new kind of celebrity. As Ratna Sarumpaet had been transformed into a labor activist through her representations of Marsinah, so Butet Kartaredjasa suddenly acquired a kind of stature as surrogate president within a variety of Indonesian cultural spheres. Ironically, he has viewed his experiences with Gazali's show as his first portrayal of a president as a character:

> When asked to parody SBY, I was aware that my face didn't resemble his. I said, I am an actor, a stage player. It's possible for me to interpret a character. Such that it will appear as an image of SBY. I don't know whether it has succeeded or not. All this time, I have never performed a character. I imitated the voice of Soeharto, rather than playing Soeharto as a character. For example, I portrayed a *lurah* with a character that resembled Soeharto. More of an association. It's all in the realm of imagination.
>
> (Kartaredjasa, 2007b: 32)

Thus, 'Republic Mimpi' signals a shift in Kartaredjasa's conception of his impersonations. Though in most of his theatre work, he continues to present his unmistakable characterizations merely as available associations, he has increasingly acknowledged and made use of his celebrity as Indonesia's foremost presidential surrogate.

This recent celebrity has opened the door to numerous acting engagements in which the ambiguities of his portrayal are somewhat less ambiguous than in his earlier monologues. He tells a *Playboy* interviewer of situations in which he used his ability paratheatrically:

> I've often sold my voice for a ring *back tone*. There was a time when Wismoyo Arismunandar was the commander of kostrad, the soldiers were mustered in the yard in the middle of the night. The lights went out, *sound* turned on, I imitated the voice of Pak Dirman [General Sudirman], Bung Karno and the voice of Pak Harto. Messages to motivate the soldiers. Maybe those soldiers were fooled.
>
> (Kartaredjasa, 2007b: 39)

When I spoke to Kartaredjasa in early June 2007, he was rehearsing for Teater Mandiri's latest production, *Cipoa* (*Lies, Bullshit*), which played at TIM later that month. This piece consisted of a combination of one of Putu Wijaya's short stories, 'Raksasa' with a script he had written for television. Wijaya, as

Semar, tells the story of a country inhabited by demons and humans ambitious to become demons. He then becomes captain of a golden ship that exploits nature for personal fortune, tricking and deceiving his workers. He declares that deception is necessary for development, as is violence to keep people oriented towards 'the truth.' At the end of the play, following a declaration that in the new era everyone in the Fatherland will say everything honestly, Kartaredjasa walks onstage. He is not clearly portraying any character in particular, but he wears his SBY suit from *Newsdotcom* and recites Sutardji Calzoum Bachri's poem *Tanah Air Mata*. Bachri's well-known poem plays on the slippage between three Indonesian words, 'earth,' 'water' and 'eye,' that form two overlapping compound words for 'nation' (*tanah air*) and 'tears' (*air mata*). Kartaredjasa speaks these words about the doubleness of nation and sorrow, written by Bachri for the victims in Aceh, in his SBY voice.[8] Thus, this figure who is not the president, but clearly not merely Butet from Yogya either, concludes Wijaya's parable on the deception underlying state developmentalism.

In June 2007, Kartaredjasa also mentioned a large private poetry reading for President Yudhoyono being held the next week at the MegaBlitz, a new premiere shopping mall in central Jakarta that was not yet open to the public. He had been invited to read poetry there in front of businessmen, officials and ministers. He would, of course, be wearing this same SBY suit from his television persona. And SBY will be there also, I asked. Yes, of course, Kartaredjasa replied.

...and bridegroom to global capitalism

Kartaredjasa's celebrity as surrogate president has also colored his post-Suharto career performing in the theatrical productions of other established troupes. Indeed, the unique sovereignty and individuality that has attended Javanese and Indonesian rulers seems to find its analogue for the 'universal surrogate president' in his nearly unique capacity to work as a freelance actor, unfettered by the familial structure of a troupe. As such, Kartaredjasa has appeared in a variety of productions of Riantiarno's Teater Koma and Wijaya's Teater Mandiri in the post-Suharto era. In such a capacity, he performed in Teater Koma's lavish 2007 production of Friedrich Durrenmatt's *The Visit* (rendered into Indonesian as '*Kunjungan Cinta*,' the Rendezvous). Here, Kartaredjasa plays Ilak Alipredi (an Indonesianization of the character Alfred Ill or Anton Schill), leading citizen of the town of Goela ('Sugar,' a felicitous transformation of the original, *Guellen*, meaning 'manure'), opposite Ratna Riantiarno as Klara Zakanasian. As Kartaredjasa frequently repeated in interviews, he was merely an actor playing a role here, subsuming his familiar improvisatory skills to Nano Riantiarno's precise directorial concept. That said, it is undeniable that Jakartan spectators watching him in the role experienced the double-vision that always accompanies watching a celebrity in performance (see Quinn, 1990), if not a triple-vision appending Kartaredjasa's very specific association to the portrayal of Indonesian presidents.

There would be various grounds on which to dismiss Riantiarno's production of *Kunjungan Cinta* as an example of Jakarta *gedongan* theatre at its most elite and Westernized. Indeed, Nano Riantiarno acknowledged to me that he had taken on the project at the request of the Swiss Embassy. He and his wife, Ratna, both marveled that it was the most expensive production Teater Koma had ever mounted, and that most of this expense had gone to the building of a complex realistic set. This included Alipredi's general store (with detailed 1930s wares), a train station, a two-storey hotel, and a large rolling proscenium stage unit that appears in the final scene (shown on the cover of this book). Nevertheless, Riantiarno enthusiastically interpolated references to a contemporary Indonesian context, and through Kartaredjasa, a distinct range of topical associations. The result was a production of greater immediacy and urgency than is often achieved with this staple of the modern European dramatic canon.

From the opening moments of the play, Riantiarno departs from strict verisimilitude to confirm that Goela is indeed Indonesia caught in the seemingly interminable moment of *krismon* (the 1997 Asian monetary crisis). A signpost shows the directions to the centers of global power: Paris, England, the Pentagon. As the various express trains blast through the station without slowing, we hear that they are traveling between Los Angeles and Paris, between Melbourne and Manila, and that ten years ago (before the monetary crisis, we might think), the 'train' stopped in Goela. Now, however, it has been left behind by progress. The leaders of the community, awaiting Klara's arrival, recall her youthful relationship to Ilak, 'forty-five years ago.' Back, that is, in the days of the revolutionary generation (further invoked by the number 45), back in days of postcolonial innocence and optimism. Then Klara arrives, and we see at once that she represents the deathly arrival of global capital. Her seventh husband, a factory owner from Havana, dances like a monkey. She has bought a pair of gangsters from New York to bear her palanquin (a gift from the French president). And, of course, she carries with her everywhere she goes, a funeral procession complete with a brass band that later breaks into a rendition of 'When the Saints Come Marching Home.' Even post-Katrina New Orleans is part of the global retinue owned by this corporate empress who will ask Goela to sacrifice its leading citizen to satisfy her dignity.

Through most of the play, Kartaredjasa simply plays the prominent citizen, not unlike roles he had played with various Teater Gandrik productions. In one scene, however, Riantiarno gives him some creative license for his accustomed improvisation, which invokes the double/triple-vision to his celebrity. In an interview, Riantiarno makes the familiar comparison to a goro-goro scene in which the *wayang* clowns speak their criticisms freely.

At this point in the play, all the citizens of Goela have been bought off by Zakanasian (indicated in Koma's production by the wearing of yellow shoes, incidentally the color of Suharto's Golkar Party), and will soon sacrifice him to her justice. This includes Alipredi's own wife and children. His son, dressed like James Dean (apart from the yellow sneakers) takes them all for a drive through town, during which Alipredi/Kartaredjasa comments freely on what he sees. He bears witness to the various bittersweet 'developments' of Jakarta. He marvels at the skyscrapers like stacked houses. They watch a *bajaj* (a three-wheeled pedicab) go past: *tuktuktuk!* They hit a nasty pothole. Kartaredjasa (only nominally still Alipredi at this point) cracks jokes about the traffic and the governor who never steps down. He sees a monorail (a prominent boondoggle project in the capital at the time): 'Oh, wait, it's only a mirage!' This 'supplement' to the play, in which Kartaredjasa inserts his own brand of routine deriding the ongoing failures of urban development ten years after the fall of Suharto predictably functioned as the kind of interlude seen in the professional theatre a century earlier. Predictably, audiences responded with the big laughs to which Kartaredjasa is accustomed in his solo monologues.

Next, Alipredi meets Klara in a forest that is dying of pollution. They smoke *Romeo y Julieta* cigars (from her Havana husband, perhaps – Klara has not seen fit to distribute Indonesian clove cigarettes). Two of Klara's henchmen play a tune called 'Revolution.' It plays sweetly but briefly, and Alipredi (slipping, perhaps, into Kartaredjasa as he says it), comments 'Now, Reformasi.' A similar tune plays out, again all too quickly. Alipredi submits to Klara's death sentence, and she promises to build him a mausoleum in her Mediterranean villa. The body of the martyr to development will be 'disappeared' to Europe. She tells him:

> I will live there forever. Your love died decades ago. My love cannot die, but it cannot live either. My love changed from the evil inside me. Like pooling rains can turn a stone, as the unseeing face of the forest interrupts the spreading flow of my wealth that wants to fight against you [...] In a little while, there will be nothing left remaining, except someone approaching that which is dead to recollection, a shadow of a domesticated ghost in a receptacle that is broken.

The forest has already receded, and as Klara gets up to leave, Alipredi is left alone on a bare stage, sitting on a dead log. Judgment is passed and the town kills its foremost citizen, the popular Javanese actor, the President of the Republic of Dreams.

However, Alipredi had died already in the polluted forest, graveyard to ideals of revolution and reform. Klara, another terrible inverse to Sontani's 'wandering woman,' returns to Indonesia to give the leading citizen a kiss of death. Appropriately, the kiss that to Sontani was the ambivalent but necessary spirit of revolution becomes in Riantiarno's production the sacrifices of a weak developing nation at the altar of global capitalism. The final scene of the play is, then, an obscene festival of democracy bought with blood. Si Butet Yogya lies in state in an open casket draped with red and white chains of flowers as a chorus builds rapidly from a solemn ritual (as at a memorial for national heroes) to a musical revue (like a performance on Indonesian Idol) in a theatre within the theatre. Klara watches from her throne, the citizens of Goela tap their yellow-shod feet, Alipredi's own family eats popcorn from cinema seating, and a large mirror reflects out to the auditorium as concert lighting flashes throughout the auditorium. Above the corpse, a chorus of white-faced citizens screw their faces into broad mask-like smiles.

Conclusion: forgetting the monotonous nation

In Agus Noor's *Matinya Toekang Kritik* (*The Death of a Critic*, 2006), Kartaredjasa casts himself as Raden Mas Suhikayatno. The name appends 'Raden Mas' (a Javanese aristocratic honorific) to the word '*hikayat*' (a traditional Malay genealogy) embedded between two common Javanese phonemes that evoke Presidents Soekarno and Suharto. Suhikayatno is a social critic who, like one of the ancient elders of Ionesco or Samuel Beckett, has fallen from the experience of time and looks back at history from the threshold of his own demise. He is unsure what day it is, and voices from the *rakyat* tell him that it is 17 August, Indonesian Independence Day. On the back screen, we see images of slums being cleared, and then of the Presidential Palace. 'Clearing that too? My, the governor is ambitious!' He is unsure what year it is, and a booming voice from above replies '1998!,' repeating the word with bludgeoning force, as if it is not possible to move beyond that year. The voice tells him that these are 'the forces of *jihad*' and images of Islamist militants and East Javanese 'ninjas' fill the screen. Suhikayatno shakes his finger at the sky, and reflects wearily to his young audience:

> I was condemned to be the Indonesian president. To become the president of Indonesia, one must be the object of a curse. The job of being Indonesian president isn't interesting. From year to year. All you clever, innovative people out there, you don't want to be president of Indonesia. The duty, destiny, responsibility of the president is monotonous. From year to year, it's just the same work.

Thus the critical genealogist warns the *reformasi* generation of the endless repetition, the sheer monotony of Indonesian patriarchy. As in the Generations of '45 and '66, the *pemuda*, the radical youth, is invoked in the name of hope. The hope of breaking the endless cycle, refusing to be inspirited yet again with the ghosts of (neo-) colonialism. However, as in each prior moment of historical rupture, the inexorable presence of the same old ghosts upstages any competing memories. The re-entry of forgotten pasts onto the stage of Indonesian history is always already upstaged by a paternal apparition.

In the modern theatre, as in the national political life, Suharto lingers. More to the point, democratization has revealed the irony that only such father figures embody Indonesia as a coherent unity. Thus, it is hardly surprising that many artists and intellectuals seek post-nationalist frameworks for cultural identification. Some such identifications are animated by 'glocality,' such as Nadjib's itinerant ecumenical civic forums that promote global citizenship with a Javanese spiritual core and Sarumpaet's claim to TIM and GKJ as glocal spaces for women's theatre. Others, such as Mohamad, have looked to negotiate 'more local' globalizations through regional partnerships with other Southeast Asian and Asian societies. In a 2008 conference on 'Islam and Popular Culture in Indonesia and Malaysia' at the University of Pittsburgh, for example, Ariel Heryanto called for scholars studying Indonesia to move beyond not only nationality, but even globality and glocality to observe the history and rise of truly post-nationalist social formations. In this, he heralds a pervasive fatigue with nationality as a source of social life and cultural inspiration. In order to move beyond 1998, and to counter the erasure of many alternate histories and social formations wrought by the nationalist episteme, perhaps the spirit of 1945 must be laid to rest.

It remains to be seen, however, whether these trends will constitute a true paradigm shift or merely a reconfiguration of persistent cultural elements. As argued previously, the trope of diachronic rupture to radically new frameworks has repeatedly abetted claims by Batavian/Jakartan regimes to build a *novum ordo* on a site of disappearance. The colonial Batavians inspirited their theatre with spectres from the *schouwburgs* of the Netherlands by way of forgetting pre-colonial Jayakerta. The *Pudjangga Baroe* playwrights inspirited their plays with spectres from ancient Javanese dynasties by way of forgetting colonial Batavia. Likewise, the Generation of '45 theatre artists and dramatists looked to the French to forget the Dutch, and the Generation of '66 looked to intraculturalism and absurdism to forget the communists. Foulcher's view of postcoloniality via Bhabha's description of a direct confrontation with colonial legacies is indeed missing from many of these practices. Nevertheless, the national theatrical culture of the Indonesian metropole has revived itself at successive moments of crisis through a hermeneutics of forgetting that reveals a lingering concern with exogenous sources of political power and cultural legitimacy that extends back at least as far as 1619. Ghosts have been 'unforgotten' repeatedly on the cleared stages of the *schouwburg* and the art center, and the organicist idea of Indonesia has remained uncannily co-present with apparitions of foreign spectres in the faces of Batavian and Jakartan actors.

As I discussed in the opening chapter of this book, the term 'postcolonial' is useful in speaking of the predicament of Indonesian theatre precisely in the ways in which the term remains problematic. As the anxious epithet, 'post-Suharto,' has supplanted the more hopeful 'era *reformasi*,' so the term 'postcolonial' signals the lingering of past histories beyond the presumption of historical watersheds. The New Order model of a *'tradisi baru'* or a 'trans-ethnic theatre' had appeared to move substantially beyond 'the shackles of Western theory' that Suharto era practitioners ascribed to the preceding generation. However, as we have seen, each generation perceives itself as facing the same crisis. The desire for cultural authenticity that Cheah associates with an 'organismic metaphor' in postcolonial nationalist discourse gives way to the return of old ghosts. This is a kind of return which the national theatre is especially well equipped to represent. The site of postcolonial Jakarta, haunted by colonial Batavia, connects the national theatre to the surrogative imagination of Javanese dynastic pasts and ancient European tribal pasts. Although various mechanisms of censorship may have been dismantled, there is still something in postcolonial Indonesian theatre that is still informed by the Organic Law of 1854, which divided the Dutch colony into Natives and Europeans. If this theatrical genre whose special exigency lies in its capacity to transcend ethnicity and tribalism is to play a productive role in a democratic Indonesia, it must clear a space not only for the 'native' but for the Chinese, the Muslim and, perhaps most challengingly, the mestizo.

Appendix: A Timeline of 'Indonesian' and 'Batavian' Histories

58BC Romans occupy the Low Countries. Batavians apparently settle in the area around the same time and serve in the Roman army.

AD640 Earliest Javanese state enters the historical record as 'Ho-Ling' thanks to a trade delegation that arrived in China. Small communities of ethnic Chinese settle throughout the Malay archipelago.

7th C Sriwijaya empire forms in coastal southeast Sumatra and northwest Java. It is a Buddhist state whose rulers adopt Sanskrit titles and conduct trade with China. French scholar George Coedès would recover the existence of this forgotten kingdom in the early twentieth century, providing inspiration to the nationalists.

930 Earliest inscription documenting performance of shadow puppetry (*wayang*) in Java. However, Javanese accounts such as the *Babad Tanah Jawi* credit the Sunan Kalijaga with introducing shadow theatre. Kalijaga is one of the nine *wali sangga* (Islamic saints) credited in Javanese tradition with bringing Islam to the region. He lived in the fifteenth or sixteenth century.

1222 Ken Arok of Tumapel conquers the kingdom of Kediri, unites East Java into the Singhasari empire (predecessor of Majapahit). Muhammed Yamin, among other nationalists, takes Arok as a pivotal figure in the pre-colonial formation of an Indonesian civilization.

1292 Kertaredjasa, a prince in the royal lineage of Singhasari, emerges from Court intrigues to found the Hindu Majapahit dynasty, whose power at its height extends from Sumatra to New Guinea (according to the *Negarakrtagama*). Along with Sriwijaya, Majapahit will serve as a core touchstone for Indonesian nationalists.

1365 *Negarakrtagama* records the history of the Majapahit dynasty to this point. Rediscovered in the 1920s, this document becomes a major inspiration for nativist Indonesian nationalists. Along with the *Pararaton*, these will become the major sources for the 'historical' drama of the *Poedjangga Baroe* dramatists in the 1930s.

14th C Aceh, at the northern tip of Sumatra, becomes the first kingdom in the archipelago to adopt Islam. Aceh continues to be regarded as a 'doorstep to Mecca' through its fierce guerilla resistance to the Dutch in the nineteenth century and the Indonesian state in the twentieth century.

1480 Following the trade routes to the Moluccas (Spice Islands) from Aceh, the Central Javanese Demak Dynasty converts to Islam.

1511 In a campaign to bypass the Muslim domination of the spice trade, Portuguese merchants capture the mainland port of Melaka, and a year later establish a base on the island of Ambon. Thus, the European struggle for the spice trade begins.

1525   Banten, in West Java, converts to Islam.

1527   The Islamic Demak Dynasty conquers the Majapahit Dynasty, the remains of which flee to Bali. In the same year, Fatahillah defeats a Portuguese party and founds Jayakerta (glorious/perfect victory) at the port of Sunda Kelapa as vassal to Banten. Most of Java is now governed by two Islamic states.

1548   Charles V grants the Netherlands, which he had united over his reign through inheritance and conquest, a degree of autonomy under Hapsburg rule.

1567   Following two centuries of restrictions on foreign travel in China, official contact with Southeast Asia resumes. Emigration of ethnic Chinese to port cities in the Malay archipelago increases.

1568   Revolts against persecution of Calvinist Protestants by Philip II of Spain begins the Eighty Years' War.

1581   Seven rebellious Dutch provinces formed in the Republic of the Seven United Netherlands issue the Act of Abjuration declaring independence from the Spanish king.

1587   Senopati Ingalaga ascends to the throne of the Central Javanese Mataram Dynasty (established in 1581). According to Javanese tradition, he goes to the beach at Parangtritis to spend a wedding night with Nyai Loro Kidul, Queen of the South Seas. The Queen places her spirit powers at his disposal, and at the disposal of all his descendents down to the current sultans of Yogyakarta.

1591   First English expedition to the East Indies.

1595   First Dutch expedition to the East Indies.

1600   English East Indies Company founded.

1602   The major Dutch overseas trading companies combine to form a single joint-stock company, with a board of 17 directors in Amsterdam. The 'United East India Company' (VOC, *Vereenigde Oost-Indische Compagnie*) administers Dutch interests in the Indies until their bankruptcy in 1799.

1603   The first colony in the history of English empire is established on the island of Run in the Moluccas.

1605   VOC forces sieze Ambon from the Portuguese, their first major regional victory in the Dutch–Portuguese war for control of Asian and American trade that extended through the mid-century.

1610   VOC builds their first warehouses at Jayakerta.

1619   Jan Pieterszoon Coen breaks a siege by Bantenese and English forces on the Dutch warehouses at Jayakerta, razes the town and establishes Batavia, henceforth the base of VOC and Dutch colonial administration.

1628   Sultan Agung, in the midst of consolidating the influence of his Mataram Dynasty over the entire island of Java, lays siege unsuccessfully to Batavia. This results in a prolonged stalemate. The VOC, primarily concerned with maritime trade networks, makes no attempt to conquer Mataram while Mataram views Batavia as a nuisance more than a serious rival.

1648   At the Treaty of Münster, Spain finally recognizes the independence of the Dutch Republic, which had been operating for the prior 60 years.

1667 At the Treaty of Breda, the Dutch give Manhattan to the English in exchange for Run.

1669 VOC forces defeat the last major fort at Makassar, consolidating their control of the spice trade. This marks a significant moment in their transition from mere traders to regional power.

1682 The Sultan of Banten grants the VOC exclusive trading rights through his port, effectively expelling the English East India Company from Java.

1733 A five-year epidemic in Batavia kills 85,000 VOC personnel. The company begins a long decline towards bankruptcy.

1740 Responding to the rapid increase in Chinese workers arriving from the mainland coupled with decline in their own numbers from disease, the VOC begins forced transmigration of Batavia's Chinese population. Fearing genocide, Chinese-Batavians riot. In reprisal, European forces kill as many as 10,000 ethnic Chinese. The resulting decline in Chinese businessmen compounds the VOCs financial woes for the remainder of the century.

1749 At a low point of Javanese civil war, Pakubuwana II cedes sovereignty over the entire Mataram dynasty to the VOC. It is telling that this document brought about no significant change. Still concerned only with maintaining advantageous trade arrangements, the Dutch continued to manipulate Javanese politics behind the scenes for the remainder of the century.

1754 The Batavian administration passes 'Measures for Curbing Pomp and Circumstance' aimed at instituting class-based codes for public display of wealth and status. A significant

moment in the marginalization of *Indisch* Batavia.

1755 Treaty of Giyanti. Mataram kingdom split, under Dutch brokerage between Surakarta and Yogyakarta. Javanese Court poets begin composing *babad* incorporating Dutch figures and histories into Javanese genealogies.

1796 Following decades of corruption and declining finances, the VOC is nationalized by the new Napoleonic Batavian Republic. Four years later, the company's charter runs out and is not renewed. The Dutch Indies become colonies directly administered by the (French) Netherlands government.

1808 Governor-General Herman Willem Daendels relocates the administrative center of Batavia to the southeast to enable the construction of new civic complexes on a French Republican model. Daendels also initiated more aggressive military relations with the Central Javanese Courts, annexing their lands.

1811 As part of the colonial theatre of the Napoleonic wars, British forces conquer the Dutch colonies in the Indies. Sir Thomas Stamford Raffles becomes adminstrator of Batavia, during which time he writes his *History of Java*, and introduces various aspects of Britain's more insidious model of colonial government. The *Java Government Gazette* inaugurates a tradition of municipal periodicals continued by the Dutch and Indonesians.

1812 In response to political defiance, the British take Yogyakarta with artillery fire on the palace, plunder the treasury and library, exile the Sultan to Penang and install his son, Hamengkubuwono II as the new sultan. This marked a turning point in colonial history, the first military takeover of a Javanese Court by a European power.

1816   Britain relinquishes the Indies to Dutch administration.

1818   Eurasian mestizos granted universal education privileges.

1825   Prince Diponegoro of the Yogyakarta Court leads a guerrilla rebellion against the Dutch in central Java. He is motivated by Dutch interference in his own royal birthright, but also frames his rebellion as a *jihad* against the colonizers. It is for this reason, the nationalists would recuperate him as a national hero.

1830   With Diponegoro's surrender at Magelang, the 'Java War' officially concludes. Ricklefs marks this as the last stand of the Javanese aristocracy and the start of 'the truly colonial period of Javanese history.' The Courts are now administered as bureaucratic regencies subject to the Batavian administration, and colonial bureaucracy is instituted down to the village level. The *cultuurstelsel* replaces the pre-existing system of colonial taxation with a colonial plantation economy. Each village is compelled to set aside land to produce export crops for sale to Batavia at fixed prices. Through this policy, the agricultural basis of local economies is integrated into the colonial system.

1848   Inspired by the socialist revolutions in Europe, an Indo-European 'People's Assembly' is formed.

1850   British anthropologist J. R. Logan coins the name 'Indonesia' from the Greek words *indos* (India) and *nesos* (island) and in ethnographic analogy with 'Polynesia'. The name is popularized by German anthropologist Adolf Bastian in his book,

Indonesien (1884), adopted in 1917 by the 'Indonesian Students Association' in the Netherlands, and subsequently claimed by the nationalist movement. Dutch authorities resist the term for its implied ethnic unity.

1851   Raden Saleh returns from Europe and builds his mansion and gardens in Batavia.

1854   The Organic Law explicitly lays out a separate legal and justice system for 'natives' and indigenous non-native Muslims and Chinese, to which Europeans were obviously not subject. The ramifications of this law for Eurasian mestizos continues to be debated for the remainder of the century.

1870   The so-called 'Liberal Policy,' in the sense of economic liberalism, replaces the Culture System. Villages no longer must produce export crops. However, the government monopoly on plantations is opened to European entrepreneurs. Private European businesses start operating in the Indies.

1873   After the Anglo-Dutch Treaty of 1871, in which Britain abandons its stake in Sumatra and the Netherlands its stake in South Africa, the Dutch instigate the 'Aceh War' to quell the rising economic wealth and power of the region. They declare victory in 1881 and continue to govern, whereas many Acehnese guerrilla forces continue to engage in warfare and never acknowledge an end to the war.

1891   Eugène Dubois discovers the fossils of 'Java Man', one of the first known specimens of *homo erectus* on the banks of the Bengawan Solo River. This adds to the scientific discoveries claimed by Indonesian nationalists as evidence of an ancient precolonial civilization in the region.

1893 Inspired by the Chicago Columbian Exposition and similar colonial fairs in Europe, the colonial government holds a Batavian Exposition in Saleh's zoological gardens.

1898 The *Indische Bond* forms, a proto-nationalist social organization for the mestizo population that will serve as a prototype for similar native organizations.

1900 Beginning of the 'Ethical Policy,' whereby the colonial government acknowledges a 'debt of honor' to develop the native population towards eventual independence. Although these policies certainly enable the formation of political organizations that would be significant to the anti-colonial movement, it is also clear in retrospect that there were no clear intentions that it would ever lead to actual political power, let alone native sovereignty.

1908 *Budi Utomo* forms, a socio-political organization for Javanese *priyayi* minor aristocracy. *Balai Pustaka* established as the first government-sponsored publishing company in the Indies.

1911 Publication of R. A. Kartini's letters in Dutch, *Door duisternis tot licht* (*From Darkness into the Light*).

1912 *Indische Partij* forms, the first independent political party in the Dutch East Indies, which is devoted to the advancement of mestizo rights. Muhammadiyah, Indonesia's most significant modernist Muslim organization is formed. Sarekat Islam (The Muslim Union) forms. Though all these organizations are seen as proto-nationalist and anti-colonial, they are generally very circumspect about representing themselves as 'social' organizations and not broaching open confrontation with the Dutch.

1913 Kartini fund established for education of Javanese women.

1918 Founding of the Batavian *volksraad*, the most obvious political expression of the 'Ethical Policy.' Though native Indonesians served on the council, membership was entirely at the discretion of the Dutch and the body was understood to have, at most, an 'advisory role.' Such ineffectual gestures towards civil society would be imitated in the postcolonial regimes.

1920s Rediscovery of the *Pararaton* (fifteenth/sixteenth-century Javanese text chronicling the East Javanese kingdom of Kediri, Kertajaya and Ken Arok). Also rediscovery of *Nagarakrtagama* (chronicling later Majapahit rulers).

1920 Indonesian Communist Party (PKI) established.

1926–7 Premature communist insurrections against Dutch rule across Java and a major uprising in West Sumatra are quickly suppressed. Communist leaders and members, including Roestam Effendi, are exiled to Europe. Destruction of the PKI creates a space for the founding of the Indonesian Nationalist Party.

1927 Soekarno and his Bandung Study Club take the initiative in establishing an Indonesian Nationalist Association (PNI), which is emboldened enough by 1929 to call itself a Party (same acronym). This crosses a line, and Soekarno and other leaders are arrested.

1928 At the Second All-Indonesia Youth Congress, delegates pledge themselves to one language, one people and one nation that is Indonesia.

1931 Soekarno is released and *Partai Indonesia* is founded by ex-PNI members.

1933 Soekarno is re-arrested and sent to Flores, then in 1938 to Bengkulu where he remains until the arrival of the Japanese. The nationalist movement continues through the 1930s largely through less threatening activities such as the cultural polemics of the *Poedjangga Baroe* authors.

1942 The Dutch government abandons their Indies colonies to the advancing Japanese. 1943 Japanese occupation government establishes *PETA* (Protectors of the Homeland, a native militia that will become the nucleus of a revolutionary army).

1945 Japan surrenders and departs Indonesia. Soekarno proclaims Indonesian independence. The Dutch maintain their colonial claims. British troops invaded, but soon looked to extricate themselves against fierce resistance. Dutch look to divide and conquer setting up puppet states in various regions.

1946 A brief treaty with the Dutch back in control in Jakarta and the Republican government in Yogyakarta dissolves as fighting re-escalates. Dutch launch major offensives in 1947 and 1948, which turn the tide of world opinion and move the United Nations to intercede on behalf of Indonesia.

1948 The 'Darul Islam' group establishes an 'Indonesian Islamic State' in West Java and South Sulawesi, and continues to resist Republican power into the 1960s. Separately, communist troops attack the Republican forces in Surakarta and Madiun. The Indonesian revolutionary army is thus diverted from fighting the Dutch to quell these internal insurrections, leaving lingering distrust of both factions after Independence.

1949 Dutch officially acknowledge Indonesian sovereignty. Soekarno becomes the first president of the Republic of Indonesia.

1955 The Bandung Asia-Africa Conference in which President Soekarno presides over the formation of the Non-Aligned Movement. In the same year, Indonesia holds its first free general election. The resulting split between nationalist, communist and Islamic parties confirms anxieties regarding the chaos of civil society.

1957 Amidst growing civil unrest, Soekarno begins implementing 'guided democracy,' transforming parliamentary democracy into a more totalitarian executive system in which 'functional groups' represent predetermined sectors of society in a token fashion.

1963 The annexation of Dutch West Papua 'completes' Indonesia's territorial integrity from the perspective of the nationalists.

1964 Kartini accepted into the registry of National Heroes.

1965 On 30 September, a small group claiming to act on behalf of the Indonesian Communist Party abducts and murders six top-ranking generals. This alleged *coup* is rapidly contained by the military under the leadership of Lieutenant-General Suharto. In the ensuing months, the Communist Party is dismantled, hundreds of thousands of suspected sympathizers are killed or imprisoned and the effective powers of President Soekarno are transferred to Suharto.

1967 Because of the association of Chinese with communism, the Suharto regime bans Chinese schools and other organizations and all public printed or written materials using Chinese characters. Many Chinese-Indonesians adopt Indonesian-sounding names.

1971   First post-Soekarno general election is openly manipulated. Historians typically date the consolidation of Suharto's 'New Order' to around this time.

1975   Indonesia invades East Timor and, despite ongoing guerrilla fighting and the absence of any kind of plebiscite, claims it as a state of Indonesia.

1993   The rape and murder of Marsinah.

1997   Asian monetary crisis. More than half of all Indonesians fall below official poverty lines as economic growth and development grind to a halt.

1998   Civil unrest from the failure of the government to respond to the Asian monetary crisis escalates into confrontations with the police and riots against the Chinese-Indonesian population. In response to mounting pressures within civil society and within his own government, President Suharto resigns, leaving his vice-president B. J. Habibie in power.

1999   Following a United Nations sponsored Act of Self-Determination, East Timor becomes a sovereign nation. In the period of voting and withdrawal, militias sponsored by the Indonesian military engage in extensive killings and domestic terrorism. Indonesia holds its first free general election since 1955. Megawati Soekarnoputri (daughter of Soekarno) wins the popular vote, but the parliament, claiming that she is unready, installs Abdurachman Wahid as president with Megawati as vice-president.

2001   In response to waning confidence in Wahid's ability to respond to ongoing economic and political crises, parliament installs Megawati as Indonesia's fifth president.

2002   A bombing by Jemaah Islamiyah (an al Qaeda affiliated group) at a tourist bar in Bali propels Indonesia into the War on Terror and plunges the economy into deeper straits.

2004   Despite international concerns at the strengthening of political Islam in Indonesia, religious parties do not make substantial gains in the general election. Susilo Bambang Yudhoyono, Megawati's vice-president, wins the presidency. In December, the Indian Ocean earthquake causes a tsunami that devastates Aceh on the north coast of Sumatra. This causes even further damage to the Indonesian economy.

2008   After years of debate and parliamengary maneuver, a broad anti-pornography bill is passed into law. By banning images, gestures and speech deemed pornographic, artists and cultural groups fear that the law will be used by hardline Muslims to criminalize many traditional and modern cultural activities.

Notes

Chapter 1   Introduction: Colonial Foundations and Precessions of Postcoloniality

1   Shannon Jackson makes much the same point that performance studies specifically marginalizes contemporary postcolonial drama in *Professing Performance* (Cambridge: Cambridge University Press, 2004: 25).

2   Following Foulcher's 1995 article, a 1998 conference at the University of Sydney led to the publication of *Clearing a Space: Postcolonial Readings of Modern Indonesian literature* (Foulcher, 2002). *Kalam*, a literary journal that emerged in the late New Order with a more 'cultural studies' orientation than *Horison*, devoted its fourteenth issue (1999) to 'Pascakolonialisme dan Sastra' ('Postcolonialism and Literature').

3   Much has been written regarding how *hikayat*, *babad*, *sejarah* and other Malay forms of genealogical or historical narrative adapted into Javanese contexts proceed from different premises and towards different goals than modern Western history. For an overview, see C. C. Berg, 'The Javanese Picture of the Past' and H. J. de Graaf, 'Later Javanese Sources and Historiography,' in Soedjatmoko (ed.), *An Introdcution to Indonesian Historiography* (Ithaca, NY: Cornell University Press, 1965): 87–136. Nancy Florida explores the exigencies of *babad* form in her study of the *Babad Jaka Tingkir* (a nineteenth-century work that retroactively 'prophesizes' the arrival of Islam in the sixteenth century): *Writing the Past, Inscribing the Future: History as Prophecy in Colonial Java* (Durham, NC: Duke University Press, 1995). Henk Maier reflects on the various perspectives from which such texts may be viewed as literature or annal (Maier, 2004: 84–6).

4   The competing autocthonous narratives regarding the identity of Fatahillah are as fascinating as one would expect, and suggest various visions of a true native founder of the Indonesian capitol. The most significant and contested question is whether Fatahillah was simply an alias of Sunan Gunungjati, first Sultan of Banten and founder of the Demak dynasty – an interpretation that would align the founding of Jakarta to Javanese dynastic genealogies. Another story holds that he was a devout Acehnese who returned to the archipelago from the *haj* in 1525. Another says that he was actually Arabic, a son of the Meccan king who married into the Pajajaran dynasty. One even dubiously claims that he helped the Turks capture Constantinople; this took place in 1453.

5   In 1749, at the height of the Javanese civil conflict that culminated in the Treaty of Giyanti, the Sultan Pakubuwana II had, startlingly, signed a document ceding sovereignty over the entire Mataram dynasty to the VOC. It is revealing of the interests of both constituencies that this document brought about no real change and was never invoked again by the Dutch or Javanese (see Reid, 1994; Ricklefs, 2001).

6   This story is engagingly, though flamboyantly, rendered in Giles Milton's *Nathaniel's Nutmeg, Or, the True and Incredible Adventures of the Spice Trader Who Changed the Course of History* (New York: Farrar, Straus & Giroux, 1999). This popular non-fiction work, like Charles Corn's *The Scents of Eden: A History of the Spice Trade* (New York: Kodansha International, 1998) relies primarily on English records with little consideration of Dutch, let alone Indonesian narratives. Thus, it

is hardly surprising that Jan Pieterszoon Coen is invariably portrayed as a tyrant, whereas the English (who were, of course, equally engaged in pursuing advantageous trade monopolies) appear as cunning heroes. What's more, the English, who were engaged in establishing the first holdings of the British Empire (Run was Britain's very first colony) are portrayed as underdogs struggling bravely against a Dutch foe depicted as simultaneously disdainful and boorish.

7 *Taman Mini Indonesia Indah* (the 'Beautiful Indonesia in Miniature Park') was a major prestige project of the early New Order years. President Suharto's wife, Tien, had been inspired by Disneyland on a trip to the United States, and commissioned the Harapan Kita (our aspirations) foundation to build an amusement park on the outskirts of Jakarta, not far, incidentally, from the Lubang Buaya memorial for the six generals killed in the October 1965 *coup* attempt. Taman Mini is something of a latter-day colonial exposition and Epcot Center rolled into one, with pavilions memorializing the 'beautiful' ethnic traditions of each of Indonesia's 26 provinces. Notably, as the park was completed in 1975, there was no pavilion for Indonesia's twenty-sixth province, East Timor. Criticized immediately from within as a flamboyant display of Suharto's indifference to real Indonesian lives outside the capitol, Taman Mini has become a canonical referent in the global cultural studies and heritage industry literature. See Shelly Errington, 'The cosmic theme park of the Javanese,' *Review of Indonesian and Malaysian Affairs* 31:1 (1997): 7–35. Also Pemberton, 1994: 152–61.

8 These estimates are based on a census of the *kasteel* taken by VOC Head Merchant, Pieter van den Broeck, in December 1618. Van den Broeck's records are reprinted in Volume 4 of *De Opkomst van het Nederlandsch gezag in Oost-Inde* (de Jonge, 1862). Jean Gelmen Taylor discusses these figures in the context of the demographic make-up of early colonial Batavia. (1983: 3–20).

9 It is not altogether certain that the play was *Hamlet*. The vague reference in the 1619 journal does leave room for doubt. Dutch theatre historian, J. A. Worp, suggests that it was more likely a familiar play by a Dutch playwright, J. J. van Wassenburgh, called *Historiaalspel van koningh Reynier van Norwegen ende de schoone Langerta* (first printed in Rotterdam in 1612) but offers no argument other than this play's familiarity. Indeed, the named relation between kings of Denmark and Sweden would seem closer to the story of *Hamlet* than of this other play. In either case, the players mistook Norway for Sweden.

10 The *Ramayana* along with the other major Hindu epic, the *Mahabharata*, came to Indonesia along with Hindu and Buddhist migrations and empires in the first millennium. Although most of the Indonesian peoples who adopted these religions subsequently converted to Islam (the Balinese are a significant exception), the narrative traditions survived in a variety of theatrical genres, including *wayang* shadow theatre. The fact that these stories still form a significant portion of the *wayang* repertoire would seem to be compelling evidence that Islam did not bring with it the draconian suppression of theatre that is so commonly ascribed to it.

11 I have not been able to find information regarding the first public performance of *Bebasari*. It would seem that it was suppressed long enough for its ideological and aesthetic moment to have passed. After Independence, its depiction of the rise to anti-colonial struggle would have appeared overly cautious. Its hybrid, but still clearly binary aesthetic (modern content in a *wayang* narrative) also would have appeared heavy-handed and old-fashioned compared with a post-war drama fascinated with realism (socialist and psychological and existentialism).

12 Most accounts follow Jassin in assigning 1926 as its date without considering distinctions between composition and publication. Effendi himself, however,

offers contradictory dates in the respective introductions of the second editions of *Bebasari* and *Pertjikan Permenungan*. In the former, he cites 1928 as the publication date; in the latter, he claims that the style of *Pertjikan Permenungan*, which was published in 1925, was shaped by censorship of *Bebasari*. Ikranagara (1998) attempts a reconciliation by separating the 1928 publication date from a 1926 composition. One further synthesis of Effendi's accounts might be achieved by surmising that some version of the play already circulated prior to the 1925 publication of *Pertjikan Permenungan*, and that Dutch censorship delayed its publication until 1928. Teeuw relates the disparity as it had played out in literary circles by 1967 in a footnote on p. 18 of *Modern Indonesian Literature*. Every mention I could find of *Bebasari* concerned with its place in the history of Indonesian *teater* (as a performance rather than a literary genre) places it in 1926. (See Jit, 1987: 3; Kosim, 1998/1999: 178; Mohamad, 1973: 92; Rafferty, 1989; Sumardjo, 1992: 123.) In his unpublished history of Indonesian *teater*, Ikranagara assigns 1928 as the date of publication, but claims that it was written in 1926 (Ikranagara, 1996).

13 The titles of Effendi's many treatises published between 1930 and 1950 give some indication of his admixture of nationalism and socialism: *Colijn verdwijn. Rede in de Tweede Kamer* (1933), *Indonesia's jeugd in trijd tegen Hollandsche heerschappij* (1933), *Van Moskou naar Tiflis. Mijn reis door de nationale Sowjet-republieken van de Kaukasus* (1937), *Recht voor Indonesiee! Een beroep op democratisch Nederland* (1937), *Indonesia Vrij!* (1940), *Quo Vadis* (1945), *Revolusi nasional* (1947), *Demokrasi dan Demokrasi* (1950), *Perspectip dari finansiel-ekonomi kita* (1950), 'Pidato-pidato tentang soal-soal 'negara demokrasi' dan 'diktatur proletar' (1950), *Soal-soal mengenai sistem kapitalis* (1950), *Soal-soal disekitar krisis-kapitalis* (1950), *Strategie dan taktiek* (1950).

14 Teeuw explains the debate succinctly (1967: 35–8). Foulcher elaborates its role within the trajectory of the *Poedjangga Baroe* journal (1980). The most significant text for Indonesian understandings of the debate is Achdiat Karta Mihardja's *Polemic Kebudajaan* (1954). Maier, however, warns that as with so many aspects of Indonesian cultural debate, simple binaries (in this case, Alisjahbana vs. Pane) have radically simplified complex debates (2004: 292–6).

15 The sheer proliferation of epithets ascribed to his new aesthetic suggests the excitement with which critics greeted Rendra's work. Goenawan Mohamad coined the term that ultimately prevailed: *mini-kata* ('minimal word'). Dami N. Toda called it *teater puisi* (referring to the poetic quality of the theatrical movement itself.) Trisno Sumardjo called it *teater abstrak*, Subagio Sastrowardoyo called it *teater murni* ('pure'), and Arifin C. Noer called it *teater primitif* (Toda, 1984: 39).

16 Nevertheless, Effendi himself dedicates the play in its second 1953 edition to 'the brazier of the *Malay* language,' making no distinction between this and the Indonesian language.

17 Foucault introduces Deleuze and Guattari's preceding work, *Anti-Oedipus* (1977) in these terms, as a 'non-fascist' epistemology.

18 The first of these was Bhabha's introduction to the 1986 British edition of *Black Skin, White Masks* ('Remembering Fanon: Self, Psyche and the Colonial Condition'), subsequently reprinted in Kruger and Marianni (eds), *Remaking History* (Seattle: Bay Press, 1989), and in Williams and Chrisman (eds) *Colonial Discourse and Post-Colonial Theory: A Reader* (New York: Columbia University Press, 1993). Better known in the United States are the two essays on Fanon in Bhabha's collection, *The Location of Culture* (New York: Routledge, 1994).

Chapter 2   Unimagined Communities: Theatres of Eurasian and Chinese Batavia

1   Cohen writes: 'The flip side to this attention, one is tempted to say fetishization of the authentically indigenous performing arts, was the devaluation of everything hybrid or mixed' (2006: 349).

2   Frederik de Haan, the foremost Dutch historian of colonial Batavia, points out that the period from 1690 to 1730 was, ironically, both the beginning of the Company's economic decline and the time of its greatest prosperity (1935: 348). Leonard Blussé agrees with de Haan, and finds the explanation in the breakdown of the economic partnership between the Company and the Chinese community, a breakdown that was determinitive, though not immediately apparent in the operations of Indisch society (see Blussé, 1981).

3   The period termed 'liberal' in Dutch colonial annals reflects the arrival of European economic liberalism to the colonies. With the Agrarian Law of 1870, the previously centralized plantation system admitted free enterprise. As in Europe and the United States, such liberal economic policy was linked to progressive rhetoric that such free market capitalism would ultimately raise the working poor (in this case, the colonized natives). The colonial administration turned to the 'ethical policy' in 1900 in response to the rise of socialist factions within Dutch society, who recognized that the liberal policy was not delivering its promised social benefits. Under the 'ethical policy,' the colonial government created economic, educational and political opportunities for native Indonesians that had not previously existed. Of course, from a postcolonial perspective, neither policy could possibly succeed for the simple reason that the colonial system required that economic and political agency ultimately remain within European hands.

4   For example, *The Lombok War* and *The Cakranegara Battle* (1896, works dealing with the recent Dutch campaign in Lombok) and *Teuku Umar's Traitorous Work* (1896, about the leader of Aceh's guerilla resistance against the Dutch). (See Cohen, 2008: 256–7, 267.)

5   On the significance of the *Nyai Dasima* story to turn-of-the-century urban literary discourse in Batavia, see Taylor, 1996.

6   The nearby river whose imanent flooding drives the action of the play is identified as Brantas, a major waterway that flows down through Malang and wends west through much of East Java. The Dutch colonial administration used weirs and floodgates to control the powerful confluence of the Brantas and Ngrowo rivers near Tulungagung. This might be a reasonable locale to imagine Wiriosari.

7   In Jose Rizal Manua's 2007 production of *Abang Thamrin*, in which I participated, a similar ensemble provided a distinctly colonial color to the scene changes.

8   The *Dokter Djawa* school was established in the Weltewreden district of Batavia in 1851 for the children of Javanese *priyayi* aristocrats. It served, for several generations, as the foremost venue for Dutch education of the Javanese elite.

9   The original of this anecdote may be found in Valentijn, 1724: 536. Ann Kumar describes a similar fascination with Chinese performances in the letters of Clas Fredrik Hornstedt from his 1783–84 visit to Java (1989: 252–4).

10   As of this writing, the three-volume *Lontar Anthology of Indonesian Drama* is still awaiting release. Matthew Isaac Cohen's discussion of the development of Chinese urban performance culture appears in his introduction to the first volume.

11   As Cohen puts it: 'The pattern of Chinese 'exploitation' of non-Chinese performers also largely began with stambul. Chinese bankrolling of Indonesian artists and

culture workers continues to be characteristic of nearly all forms of Indonesian entertainment involving large sums of money, including the recording industry, television, and film' (2006, 344).

12 Hoay's introduction to the play was originally published in *Panorama* No. 192, 30 November 1930.

13 This was published in Hoay's own literary journal, *Moestika Panorama* in 1931 and then reprinted as a book later that year.

14 Cohen, in the Introduction to Volume 1 of *Lontar* (2009), writes of the two companies, 'Both companies emphasized in publicity that they were not *stambul* but rather *toneel*, the Dutch term for theatre (also spelled *tonil* or *tunil*). Plays featured few songs or poems, and while music and dance were still to be found in the extra-numbers inserted between scenes of the main story, there were new notes of psychological realism in acting and a raft of new plays dealing with contemporary social issues. The appeal of these companies cut across all ethnic groups; for the first time since the heyday of Mahieu's Komedie Stamboel troupe in the 1890s, Malay popular theatre was taken seriously and actually reviewed in the Dutch-language press. Both companies fielded soccer teams that engaged local teams wherever they toured as a gesture of affinity with local audiences. When Miss Riboet and Dardanella simultaneously played Batavia in 1931, they famously mounted an advertising war that consumed 6000 guilders on newspaper ads alone' (Cohen, 2009: xiii).

15 Michael Bodden notes a renewed theatrical interest in Hoay after 1998 (2008a: 121). Kwee Tek Hoay's adaptation of a Philip Oppenheimer story, *Allah Jang Palsoe* was staged by Mainteater Jakarta in late May 2003 (see Aryanto, 2003). An adaptation of Kwee's 1926 novel, *De Roos Van Tjikembang*, was staged less than a year later in February 2004 by Teater Bejana under the title *Bunga Roos dari Tjikembang* (see Muhtarom, 2004).

16 Pamela Allen notes that as of 2003: 'On the customs forms to be filled in upon entering Indonesia "Chinese printed material" is still listed next to weapons, ammunition and drugs, suggesting that the language was/is perceived as being very dangerous indeed' (2003: 3).

17 Ariel Heryanto points out that the circulation of this 'fact' in itself reinforced an undifferentiated racial perception of *tionghoa* privilege, unnuanced by the vast class disparity between *tionghoa* tycoons and small shopkeepers (1999).

Chapter 3   Sites of Disappearance: Expatriate Ghosts on Ephemeral Stages

1 Goenawan Mohamad traces Asrul Sani's passion for Jakarta as a place of great cultural possibility back to the first years of Independence: 'Jakarta,' writes Asrul Sani in an editorial for the magazine *Zenith* in June 1951, is a place 'where all values are as the breaking of waves,' in which one might discover 'an arena for a new Indonesian culture and life' (Mohamad, 1997: 41).

2 This is an indefatigable refrain, for example, in the English language daily newspaper, *The Jakarta Post*, which, following the typical concerns of middle-class Westerners, is especially concerned with Jakarta's failure to measure up to Kuala Lumpur, let alone Singapore, in terms of green space.

3 Later that summer, Fauzi Bowo defeated his rival, Adang Daradjatun, to become the first directly elected governor of Jakarta.

4 Additional stipulations included that all spectators would require approval of Elders, Guardians or Chiefs to attend; they would be expected to subscribe in order

to cover the theatre's expenses; they would be seated in the theatre according to rank 'in the most distinguished or convenient Places'; no non-paying 'Slaves, Servants or Livreymen' would be admitted (excepting one Slave each for the Ladies); and the theatre itself would be responsible for maintaining public order and barring admittance to the intoxicated. The actors would be contracted for at least three years, and liable for any breach thereof.

5 To pay for all this, the Regents would set up a tender of 50 Ryksdalers to be paid to the public coffers over the course of a year by each renter. Should renters not take up all the available places, Pouget himself would be held responsible to the Regents for the difference. Regardless, Pouget would pay a monthly tax of 25 Ryksdalers.

6 Thorn corroborates this opinion in his 1815 *Conquest of Java*: 'The higher circles, however, have to boast of ladies as well as gentlemen of rather superior achievements, who are for the most part Europeans, either by birth or education. These meet frequently in convivial parties, entertaining themselves with sprightly dances and elegant suppers. But there are no places of public amusement at Batavia; nor a single theatre of any kind, and what is still more extraordinary in such a populous capital, there is not a single assemblyroom' (2004: 249).

7 In describing the camp in more detail, Stockdale describes the barracks as built of 'wood and stone' (1911: 300). Thorn describes, 'several ranges of excellent barracks, some of which have been finished, and are occupied by our troops' (2004: 259). Thorn makes quite clear that these fine barracks in Weltevreden were begun under Daendels. It would thus appear that the 'bamboo theatre' was a throwback to a cruder style of military architecture, of which examples may still have survived in the walled city. There is another note in this section of Stockdale which may describe the bridge connecting the site of the Schouwburg to the area that would become *Pasar Baroe*: 'An avenue, forming the left front of Welte-Freden, leads to a large Chinese village only separated from the barracks by a ditch, over which is a bridge. A large general market is held there daily' (1911: 301).

8 The 22 October 1814 edition of the *Java Government Gazette* printed, alongside its official review and reproduction of the original prologue to the Theatre's inaugural performance of *The Heir at Law*, an extensive letter of gratitude from 'a devotee of the stage' named Dienaar (*Java Government Gazette* 3: 139, 22 October 1814).

9 See Sumardjo 1992: 90. As of this writing, I have found no additional corroborating accounts or evidence.

10 In Cohen's very thorough survey of Komedie Stamboel, he cannot confirm any instance in which they actually performed at the Schouwburg. He mentions a possible performance of Komedie Stamboel at the Schouwburg for a charity benefit in October 1892, but acknowledges inconclusive evidence (Cohen, 2006: n. 116, p. 411). Despite the increasing popularity of the troupe, Mahieu was denied permission to perform there for a benefit in 1900 (304), and in 1894 he tried to garner publicity by advertising a Stamboel performance at the Schouwburg attended by the governor-general, which the press confidently dismissed (209).

11 There has been much scholarship on the Java War, and various interpretations of its significance. John Pemberton has a particularly nuanced take in *On the Subject of 'Java,'* where he argues that the Javanese Courts had already reimagined their realms as a kind of 'floating world' imagined through the perpetuation of a 'Javanese way' as early as the 1740s. Thus 1830 simply marked the political necessity of a worldview already enabled through transformations of ritual practice in the preceding century (Pemberton, 1994: 61–7).

12   There have been many version of the story, following from the oldest written account by historian Antonius Matthaeus of Utrecht (1698) – an account no doubt also penned in the context of the Batavian republic. The story is elaborated in *De Schaapherder een verhaal uit den Utrechtschen oorlog van 1480-'83* (1838) by J. F. Oltmans (1806–1854).
13   Van Loo's subsequent play with Ut Desint, *Petronella van Saxen, Gravinne van Holland* (November 1827), goes even deeper into the distant 'origins' of the Netherlands. It chronicles the twelfth-century founder of the Abbey of Rijnsburg, regarded as one of the 'founding mothers' of Holland.
14   Soekarno first wrote *Dr Sjaitan* in Ende in1936, but the manuscript was apparently not forwarded to Bengkulu with his belongings. This suggests that he rewrote the play from scatch for a performance with Monte Carlo in Bengkulu on 6 December 1938. The colophon of the Bengkulu manuscript is dated the 24th of that same month.
15   Soekarno may have seen *Frankenstein* prior to his arrest. The film was released in the United States in1931, and reached theatres in Asia beginning in 1932. He may have arrived at the idea of a female counterpart for *Koetkoetbi* simply from hearing of *Bride of Frankenstein*, which was released in the United States in 1935, though it is possible that he saw the film in Ende or Bengkulu.
16   The prophecy of the Goddess of the Southern Ocean is related in the *Babad Tanah Jawi* (see Florida, 1992). As Pemberton notes, Parangtritis is but one of three major foci of Javanese power (the other two being Lawu and Dlepih), but it has captured modern imaginations somewhat more than the others, in large part due to the special association with Ratu Kidul (Pemberton, 1994: 271).

Chapter 4   Despite Their Failings: Spectres of Foreign Professionalism

1   For example, in a recent global history of acting, Daniel Meyer-Dinkgrèafe presents 'professionalism' primarily as a goad to superior pedagogy: 'With the rise of professionalism in European theatre, training became more and more sophisticated' (2001: 159).
2   It is a pity that there is so little evidence of this troupe, as they apparently enjoyed the most extensive performance calendar of any production in the history of colonial Batavia or postcolonial Jakarta.
3   Van den Berg uses such evasive grammar in insinuating the example of the Amsterdam premiere onto the *Bataviasche Schouwburg* production that when I showed this passage to Jenneke Oosterhoff at the Department of German, Dutch and Scandinavian at the University of Minnesota, she had to reread it carefully several times before being certain that Adriana Maas had not actually performed in Batavia.
4   After a newspaper briefly run from the naval academy in the 1740s, continuous newspaper publication only began in Batavia in 1811 with the *Java Government Gazette*, printed by the occupying British administration. With the return of Dutch control in 1816, the *Bataviasch Nieuwsblad* became the newspaper of record, and at least one newspaper has been printed in Batavia/Jakarta ever since.
5   From my own examination of notices in the *Java Government Gazette* from the first offering in October 1814 through December 1815, the military bachelors offered a total of 11 performances to the Batavian public, of which five were 'comedies' (including *The Rivals* and *She Stoops to Conquer*), three were 'farces,'

one a 'mock tragedy.' They performed Shakespeare's *Henry IV* (Part One) twice as they did a comedy of *John Bull*.

6 Curiously, when she revived the role in 1959, Asmara shortened the earlier scenes to limit the incongruity of an aged Dewi Dja portraying the young Sukaesih.

7 Dardanella's Tan Tjeng Bok, for example, was hailed as 'the Douglas Fairbanks of Java' (see Suryadinata, 1996: 180–1).

8 Other members of the company included D. Djajakusuma, Surjo Sumanto and H. B. Jassin. Jassin also notes the contributions of composers Cornel Simanjuntak, Hario Singgih and Tjok Sinsu, who wrote original music for the plays. There were at least two female members of Maya, Mien and Ida Sanawi, who married Usmar and Rosihan respectively, thus continuing the pattern of the professional troupes wherein leading actresses were socially legitimized through marriage to the male leaders of the troupe.

9 An advertisement in the 12 May 1945 issue of *Asia Raya* announced production on 24 and 25 May of 'Djeritan Hidoep Baroe,' an adaptation (by Karim Halim) of Ibsen's *Little Eyolf*. Rosihan Anwar transcribes the programme notes of this production in his autobiography, *Menulis Dalam Air* (1983: 71).

10 The dates included with the texts in *Sedih dan Gembira*, which typically record an archival version compiled shortly after the premiere, are as follows: *Tjitra* (November 1943); *Liburan Seniman* (23 December, 1944); *Api* (April 1945). A note hand-written by Jassin himself on the title page of the copy of *Sedih dan Gembira* held at the H. B. Jassin Documentation Center notes that *Api* was performed at the Schouwburg on 22 and 23 March 22 1945.

11 Anwar also remembers performances of Hanifah's *Insan Kamil* and Usmar's *Api*. He claims that Usmar was influenced by reading Ibsen's *Enemy of the People* (*Vijanden van het Volk* in Dutch) when writing *Api* and also was influenced by reading Japanese authors such as T. T. Kwan's *Chichi Kaeru* (influencing Usmar's film, *Dosa tak Berampun*).

12 Richard Boleslavsky (1889–1937) was one of the first of Stanislavsky's actors to introduce Method to the United States in the 1920s. His *Acting, the First Six Lessons* (1933) is a canonical text of American (not Russian or European) psychological realism. The trilogy, which has provided the only writings by Stanislavsky available in the United States until quite recently, were not published in that form in the Soviet Union. These books have been criticized recently as placing undue emphasis on Stanislavsky's psychological experiments without acknowledging the equal importance he placed on physical training (see Carnicke, 2008). A curriculum based primarily on Boleslavsky and this trilogy almost certainly derived from exposure to American training.

13 ATNI's five Indonesian plays were: *Malam Jahanam* by Motinggo Boesje, *Titik-titik Hitam* by Nasjah Djamin, *Domba-domba Revolusi* by B. Sularto, *Mutiara Dari Nusa Laut* by Usmar Ismail and *Pagar Kawat Berduri* by Trisnoyuwono. The foreign plays included works by Chekhov, Ibsen, Strindberg, Sartre, Lorca, Gogol and Molière (Sumardjo, 1992: 151–2).

14 Jean-Paul Sartre himself recognized the postcolonial condition as the greatest problem for social philosophy after the Holocaust. Although he may not have begun to recognize this as early as 1944 when *Huis Clos* was first staged (at the time, the occupation of France was more pressing), he actively supported the development of postcolonial theory in the 1950s, particularly through his promotion of Frantz Fanon and the publication of North African literature.

15 Interview with Eka Sitorus, director of the theatre school at the Jakarta Art Institute, June 1999.

Chapter 5   *Hamlet* and *Caligula*: Echoes of a Voice Unclear in Origins

1   This text is also referred to as 'The Book of Genealogy or the Recorded Story about Ken Angrok' ('Serat Pararaton atawa Katuturanira Ken Angrok') and its Sanskritic name, *Pustaka Raja* (*Book of Kings*).

2   The story of Ken Arok and Ken Dedes belongs to the cultural memory of Java, and as such has found its way into numerous forms of expression from traditional texts subsequent to the *Pararaton* to various forms of popular performance such as *kethoprak*. Pramoedya Ananta Toer wrote a novel, *Arok Dedes*, completed in 1976 while still a prisoner on Buru island, which looks at Ken Arok as progenitor to a succession of Javanese rulers who took power through violence (such as, most recently, Suharto; see GoGwilt, 2006). Arahmaiani, in contrast, in her poem, 'Kisah Percintaan Ken Arok dan Ken Dedes,' views the narrative as a love story between Arok and Dedes, pitting Arok's youthful ambition and lust against the old authority of Bupati Tumapel (2004: 41–4). Where Pramoedya sees illigetimate siezure of power, Arahmaiani (writing in the third decade of Suharto's regime) chooses to see a younger generation seizing its place in the sun from the old.

3   *Sedjarah Peperangan Dipanegara* (1945) and *Revolusi Amerika* (1951). Yamin would return to the first theme in his final years with a seven-volume history of Majapahit, published beginning in 1962.

4   In a forum at Taman Ismail Marzuki in 1982, Rendra reflected on his development from his poetry in the early 1960s at which time he says, 'My spirituality and intellectuality were still quite stoned.' In New York, he became acquainted with 'social and political science and economics.' He describes the influence of these disciplines on his theatrical work in terms both architectural and developmental: 'Only after 1971 was I able to begin seeing the problems of social, political and economic injustice in terms of structures. With the *Bengkel Teater* (*Theatre Workshop*) I began to develop myself, holding discussions and small, restricted seminars, keeping newspaper clippings as documentation and making study tours to the villages' (Rendra, 1983d: 63, 65; Also see Rendra 1983c).

5   Ironically, this ban in his native country greatly augmented Rendra's stature in the West, and most especially in Australia, where translations of *Suku Naga* and *Mastodon*, prominent mention of his contributions in seminal articles and book chapters on modern Indonesian theatre by Barbara Hatley and others, and frequent updates on his activities in the Australia-based monthly journal, *Inside Indonesia*, greatly surpassed coverage of any other theatre artists who actually continued to generate work from 1978 to 1985.

6   Roedjito is reknowned as a foremost set designer of the New Order, having created environments for the early works of Rendra's Teater Bengkel as well as those of Teater Sae two decades later. He also collaborated on artistic design for the films of Garin Nugroho. In 2003, he received the Jakarta Arts Council's Art Award for lifetime achievement, commemorated by a book, *Warisan Roedjito*, which, perversely lacks any illustrations of his work.

7   *Horison*, the leading Indonesian literary journal of the Suharto era, continued to register an interest in Camus. Albert Camus, Engl. trans. Brian Selby and Ind. trans. Sapardi Djoko Damono, 'Seniman Dan Dunia,' *Horison*, III:8 (1968), pp. 238–9; Camus, Albert, 'Orang-Orang Bercintaan Yang Terpisahkan (A Section of *La Peste*),' trans. Nh. Dini, *Horison* (1985), pp. 25–8.

8 The first citation is from 'Orang Atheis adalah setan,' *Kompas* (9 February 1966, p. 3), reporting Major General Professor Doctor Mustopo proclaiming to students of the University of Indonesia: 'Atheists, those who don't believe in the existence of God, are not human but devils. The only ones who are truly human are the Godly ones.' The second is from 'Atheisme sumber biadaban,' *Kompas* (29 April 1966, p. 2), similarly reporting statements from the Catholic Youth Council of Yogyakarta equating *gestapu*, Marxism, class warfare and PKI with a rebellion against *pancasila* rooted in the moral degradation of atheism. Also see Roger K. Paget, 'Djakarta Newspapers, 1965–1967, Preliminary Comments,' *Indonesia*, 4 (October 1967), pp. 211–26.

9 Compare with the following lines from Stuart Gilbert's 1948 English translation on which Asrul Sani's 1956 Indonesian translation and most subsequent Indonesian uses of the play are based: 'And I'm resolved to change them [...] I shall make this age of ours a kingly gift – the gift of equality. And when all is leveled out, when the impossible has come to earth and the moon is in my hands – then, perhaps, I shall be transfigured and the world renewed; then men will die no more and at last be happy' (Camus, 1958: 16–17).

10 In 1990, Riantiarno and *Teater Koma* suddenly found themselves at the center of national debates on censorship when their production, *Suksesi*, which dealt fairly directly with the sensitive issue of presidential succession, was banned by Jakarta police after previously being passed by the censor board. Riantiarno subsequently enjoyed an increased stature, especially amongst Western observers, as not merely a pseudo-Brechtian gadfly but a more radical provocateur working against the Suharto regime. To glimpse this shift in perception, one might compare two articles in American academic journals from the late 1980s and late 1990s respectively: Zurbuchen, 1989, and Bodden, 1997. However, this elevation of Riantiarno's political credentials reflects changes in government and civil society more than Riantiarno's own commitment to raising social questions gently within a popular, commercial milieu.

11 Zainal Abidin Domba had engaged in a somewhat iconoclastic bit of nationalist canon-formation a decade earlier by writing, directing and starring in a television drama titled 'He tried to reach the stars' ('Ia Coba Meraih Bintang') as the anti-Dutch, pro-native, pro-Islam *Indisch* insurrectionist, Pieter Elberveld (executed in 1722, and his skull put on display near the *stadhuis*). As William Horton writes, this television play, which aired on TVRI in June, 1981, followed the mainstream binarism in erasing the character's ethnic hybridity and presenting him as a sympathetic foreigner. See William Bradley Horton, 'Pieter Elberveld: The Modern Adventure of an Eghteenth-Century Indonesian Hero,' *Indonesia* (October 2003): 147–98.

12 The manuscript provided to me from the Teater Garasi archives still carries an earlier title of the same work: 'Metamorphosis of the Bride/Groom'.

13 Iwan Simatupang (1928–1970) gained prominence amongst the *Gelanggang* group when he joined the staff of Jakarta's *Siasat* magazine in 1954, working under Rosihan Anwar and Soedjatmoko. He began working in theatre and reading existentialist philosophy. He was dissatisfied with Indonesian attempts at existentialist drama, and deepened his own knowledge through study in Europe in the late 1950s, during which time he began writing plays. When he returned to Jakarta in 1959, he continued to defend an existentialist commitment to individual freedom against the emerging politicization of the arts. Malna, however, spoke of his novels – *Merah Merahnya* (1968), *Ziarah* (1970) and *Kering* (1972) – as having shown the way for Indonesian existentialism.

Chapter 6 *Umat* as *Rakyat*: Performing Islam through Veils of Nationalism

1 Acknowledging that in the current political climate no terminology is politically neutral, I use the term 'Islamist' in a broad sense to distinguish individuals and activities that seek to Islamicize political and social institutions in a programmatic fashion. Inclusive of liberal and reformist approaches, this is a considerably broader term than Islamic 'conservatism,' 'fundamentalism' or 'extremism.' At the same time, to say that a public figure is 'Islamist' is not simply equivalent to saying that he is a Muslim. Since the Bali bombings, many (especially Javanese) Indonesians have been at pains to promote a moderate, peaceful Islam as mainstream and unproblematic, and many will find my use of the term 'Islamist' counterproductive in this regard. Nevertheless, there are and have been significant disagreements between Muslims (whether liberal or conservative) committed to greater integration of religion into all aspects of social life, and others who prefer more ecumenical approaches. It is this general difference, and no other implicit agenda or ideology, that I intend to convey through the term 'Islamist.' For a useful discussion of this terminological issue, see 'Abd al-Hakeem Carney, 'Analysing Political Islam: The Need for a New Taxonomy,' in *Yearbook on the Organization for Security and Co-Operation in Europe* (Hamburg: Institute for Peace Research and Security Policy/University of Hamburg, 2003), pp. 199–207.

2 This *daftar* drama at the Jassin Archive is invoked well beyond the Jakarta-based theatre community. I have heard theatre scholars and artists in Bandung and Yogyakarta, who otherwise insist on their independence from the capital, nevertheless defer to 'the list' in speaking of dramatic history.

3 In the early 1950s, *Lesbumi* (*Lembaga Seni Budaya Muslim Indonesia*, the Indonesian Muslim Arts and Culture Organization) directly countered the cultural wing of the Indonesian Communist Party, *Lekra* (*Lembaga Kebudayaan Rakyat*, the People's Cultural Organization). With the scapegoating of the communists under Suharto, past membership in *Lesbumi* could retroactively be taken as a sign of political correctness.

4 If one expands the category of *teater dakwah* to include not only explicitly proselytizing works but works that deal with spiritual themes of interest to Islam, a large percentage of modern Indonesian drama is potentially legible as 'Islamic.' Indonesian theatre historian, Jakob Sumardjo, looking at 55 plays staged between 1950 and 1969, identifies only two as *dakwah* plays, but sees 18 as dealing with themes of *kejiwaan* (spirituality) in one form or another (Sumardjo, 1992: 328–40). Many Indonesian plays addressing spiritual themes channel Western psychology and modern philosophy through religious mysticism of which Islamic (particularly Sufi) mysticism is a significant component. Sumardjo sees the emphasis in Indonesian drama shifting in the 1970s from *kejiwaan* to 'more abstractly metaphysical themes.' Nevertheless, the metaphysical theatre to which Sumardjo refers (often discussed as a turn towards absurdism and surrealism) might be understood simply as the channeling of religious concerns into more ecumenical aesthetics.

5 On the introduction of Qur'anic recitation to Makassar and South Sulawesi in the sixteenth and seventeenth centuries, see Cummings, 2002. For discussion of the role of Quranic recitation in the 1990s revival of Indonesian Islam, see Gade, 2004. Makassar, incidentally, has arisen as one of the major new centres for Indonesian modern theatre following the decentralization of the arts in the decade since Suharto's 1998 resignation.

6 Although his distinction of Qur'anic aesthetics from pre-Islamic Arab poetics presupposes an Arab literacy that never developed to a high degree in Indonesia, Adonis (one of the progenitors of modern Arab poetry) argues that the Qur'an introduced a proto-modern sensibility to the arts. In his view, post-Qur'anic poetry was expected to eschew previous models, draw from vast cultural expertise, aspire to universality, and privilege experimentation and semantic ambiguity; 'texts which "the spirit can approach in all manner of ways," as al-Rummani expresses it' (Adonis and Cobham, 1990: 52).

7 The Java War (1825–30), though led by Prince Diponegoro of Yogyakarta, is generally seen by Indonesians as a popular uprising against the advance of Dutch bureaucratic colonization. The nationalists in the 1920s invoked it as a glorious precursor to their own struggle. At the time, the suppression of the uprising gave the Dutch a pretext to incorporate the Javanese courts into their administration and extend their plantation economy throughout the island. It is worth noting that Diponegoro himself had spent considerable time in religious *pesantren*, and conceived his struggle as a *jihad*. One of the reasons he failed was that he alienated non-Muslim supporters by his religious exclusivity, and ultimately lost the support of Muslim *ulamas* by claiming personal religious authority.

8 James Brandon relates one version of this: 'The Moslem Sunan of Giri is supposed to have ordered a nonrealistic puppet set made in order to circumvent the Islamic proscription against the portrayal of the human form in art, a proscription which for a time had led to the Islamic authorities' banning of wajang kulit' (Brandon, 1970: 6). This sort of narrative is more revealing as a legitimation of theatre vis-à-vis Javanese Islam and its leaders than as an objective chronicle of aesthetic change – there is scant evidence that *wayang* was 'more realistic' prior to Giri's sixteenth-century reign.

9 The issue of Rendra's faith tends to be muddled by the conventional wisdom in the political arts community, especially since the mid-1980s, that he is more committed to his own celebrity than to any beliefs. From this view, his conversion to Islam in 1971 merely served to facilitate his second marriage, and his Islam-themed productions (*Qasidah Barzanji*, *Kantata Takwa*) were chosen for sensational rather than spiritual reasons. Regardless of these accusations, the *pesantren*-like structure of Rendra's theatre has inspired much imitation. His appearances in the 1990s with Rhoma Irama, a popular Muslim *dangdut* star, are indicative. His *Kantata Takwa*, in which Rendra declaimed mystic poetry alongside activist Muslim pop star, Iwan Fals, filled the Senayan Stadium in 1992. *Qasidah Barzanji* inspired Ratna Sarumpaet to begin her career in theatre, and even Emha Ainun Nadjib has acknowledged in a personal interview that only Rendra could have produced a modern play baseed on such sacred material.

10 In claiming that *ulamas* have had no direct authority over the national theatre culture, I make no broader claims regarding religious tolerance by orthodox Muslims throughout Indonesian history. This would indeed be a startling achievement. Indeed, Indonesian religious leaders have persecuted other believers for heresy and apostasy, and some of these victims have become revered martyrs as a result. Siti Jenar, for example, was executed for promoting a Sufistic understanding of Islam in sixteenth-century Java, and is now revered by some as a *wali*.

11 Alisjahbana reopened the discussion in issue 9:9 (1948) of *Pudjangga Baroe* (28–32). Several months later, issue 9:12 printed a response by Hanifah, a reply by Alisjahbana and another response by Hanifah (65–74).

12 Butet Kertaredjasa went on to be one of the founding members of Yogyakarta-based *Teater Gandrik*. Since the mid-1990s, he has become one of Indonesia's most

popular comic actors, largely on the strength of his hilarious impersonations of the president and other public figures (see Chapter 7). In a personal interview with Butet in 2007, he confirmed that overtly and ideologically, Teater Dinasti had nothing to do with Islam.

13   In a thoughtful article written in 1997, Michael Bodden consider's Sarumpaet's first *Marsinah* play against the context of actual Indonesian workers' theatres. One workers' theatre group affiliated with an NGO devoted to women's rights had written their own *Marsinah* play shortly after Sarumpaet's. This one had been banned (a common experience for workers's theatre under a New Order government suspicious that anything to do with workers was Marxist). Bodden correctly notes that Sarumpaet's play avoids censorship through formal conservativism, intellectual generalization and general avoidance of the specific details of Marsinah's case. Of course, Sarumpaet knew what she needed to do to bypass the censors and had played it safe in writing *Marsinah*. Bodden concludes that though signaling a promising new political commitment, Sarumpaet's play nevertheless operates entirely within the economy of middle-class New Order theatre (Bodden, 1997b).

Chapter 7   *Teater Reformasi*: The Lingering Smile of the Absent Father

1   In 1993, Suharto's government had issued a series of 50,000 rupiah banknotes with a portrait of the smiling president and the epithet 'Bapak Pembangunan Indonesia' (father of Indonesian development). This most ubiquitous of images of Suharto's face, was, of course, in somewhat shorter supply when the monetary crisis hit in 1997, generating a plethora of sarcastic remarks. A new series was released in 1999 with a portrait of Soepratman (composer of 'Indonesia Raya,' the national anthem), and another series came out in 2005 with Ngurah Rai (a Balinese revolutionary hero). Naturally, it takes some time for the old notes to leave circulation, and with inflation making 50,000 denomination notes even more common currency, the smiling face of 'the father of development' continues to make constant appearances in everyday Indonesian life.

2   One prominent example of the censorship of media dissent under the Suharto regime was the much publicized banning of *Tempo* magazine. Goenawan Mohamad had begun publishing *Tempo* in 1971 as the first non-governmental news magazine on the model of the American *Time* magazine. *Tempo* was widely praised as one of the most critical news sources within Indonesia. Though there were skirmishes, the magazine managed to navigate New Order sensibilities for 23 years before the information minister, Harmoko, banned it in 1994 over an article criticizing a government purchase of former East German naval warships. The magazine immediately launched an online edition, which inevitably reached a much smaller portion of the Indonesian population, and resumed publication upon Suharto's resignation in May 1998. See Janet E. Steele, *Wars Within: The Story of Tempo, an Independent Magazine in Soeharto's Indonesia* (Equinox Publishing, Jakarta, 2005).

3   Afrizal Malna spoke with particular eloquence on this issue in a conversation I had with him in June 2007. He recalled his collaborations with Teater Sae as a small counter-cultural window against a general eclipse of the Indonesian capacity for dissent. He despaired of the expansion of a materialistic urban culture, especially in Jakarta, and a youth content to ignore all forms of injustice so long as their

consumption was not interrupted. This is a topic that Yudi Ahmed Tajudin also readily discussed with me a month later in Yogyakarta, and a frequent point of concern at Emha Ainun Nadjib's gatherings. It is, no doubt, related to the old Javanese theme of a local spiritual vitality that exceeds Western materialism (also evident in Sanoesi Pane's opposition of the Arjuna model to the Faust model). From this perspective, materialistic Indonesian consumers have truly become inferior imitations of Westerners.

4 Special thanks to Laine Berman who observed the May 1998 demonstrations in Yogyakarta first-hand and showed me photographs of several installations mentioned here while we were both in residence at Australian National University in Canberra in 1999. These included a faceless clapboard portrait subtitled 'Aku ini Presiden RI' ('I am the President of the Republic of Indonesia').

5 For example, the cover of the Indonesian print edition of *Tempo* magazine for the week of 28 June to 4 July 1999 displays an image of Habibie whose face is hinging forward from his head to reveal a smiling Suharto face embedded beneath. The caption reads, 'Suharto is responsible for Habibie's politics' ('Soeharto Beban Politik Habibie').

6 Later in the interview, Kartaredjasa elaborated this same point: 'On the issue of imitating Suharto's voice, but not performing him as a character: After Reformasi, I could give free reign to imaginative play. I told stories as a *lurah*. The *lurah* stood for the structure of power. If I made the *lurah* speak in the manner of Suharto, people would see him as Suharto in their imaginations. However, from a legal perspective, I would be safe, because I wasn't talking about Suharto. This was a *lurah*. But it might have the voice of Suharto. People were free to imagine that it was Suharto. For instance, a tiger engages in dialogue with the other animals, but this tiger has the voice of Suharto. I did this as a tactic, a strategy. I couldn't be blamed for insulting Suharto because I was talking about a tiger, I was talking about a *lurah*. If people thought it was Suharto, that was their imagination, and imagination couldn't be forbidden.'

7 Helen Pausacker has noted a proliferation around the fall of Suharto of similar representations of the Indonesian president as one or another of the *punakawan* (the *wayang* clown servant characters) (Pausacker, 2004), while Marshall Clark notes a turn to other *wayang* characters to represent alternate leadership models arising from a post-Suharto society (Clark, 2004).

8 Putu Wijaya told me that he had originally intended to ask Bachri himself to read his own poem at the end of the performance, but Bachri wasn't available. It was then that he decided on Kartaredjasa (as SBY) as a felicitous alternative (Wijaya, 2007).

Works Cited

Abdulkadir, T. S. and Rosdy, Z. (1963) *Sejarah seni-drama*, Pustaka Melayu, Singapore.

Abeyasekere, S. (1987) *Jakarta: A History*, Oxford University Press, Singapore and New York.

Adonis and Cobham, C. (1990) *An Introduction to Arab Poetics*, University of Texas Press, Austin, TX.

Ajidarma, S. G. (1999) *Iblis tidak pernah mati: Kumpulan cerita pendek*, Galang Press, Yogyakarta.

Ajidarma, S. G. (2001) *Mengapa Kau Cilik Anak Kami: Tiga Drama Kekerasan Politik*, Galang Press, Yogyakarta.

Ajidarma, S. G. and Zacky, A. (2001) *Jakarta 2039, 40 tahun 9 bulan setelah 13–14 Mei 1998*, Galang Press, Yogyakarta.

Al-Haggagi, A. S. (1980) 'The Attitude of Muslims Toward the Art of Theater', *Ba Shir: Journal of African Language and Literature*, **11**, pp. 72–81.

Alisjahbana, S. T. (1995) *Layar terkembang*, Balai Pustaka, Jakarta.

Allen, P. M. (2003) 'Contemporary literature from the Chinese "diaspora" in Indonesia', *Asian Ethnicity*, **4**, pp. 383–99.

Anderson, B. R. O. G. and Cornell University. Modern Indonesia Project. (1972) *Java in a Time of Revolution: Occupation and Resistance, 1944–1946*, Cornell University Press, Ithaca, NY.

Anirun, S. and Sugiyati, S. A. e. (1996) *Catatan Perjalanan Studiklub Teater Bandung (1989–1995): Memoir Suyatna Anirun, Jilid 3*, Studiklub Teater Bandung, Bandung.

Anon. (1953) *Untitled newspaper article*, in *Kompas* (Jakarta), Vol. 3, pp. 33–5.

Anon. (1978). 'Rendra diganggu amoniak,' *Tempo*, Jakarta, p. 6.

Anon. (2005), Untitled newspaper article, in *Menonton Bengkel Teater Rendra*, Ed. E. Haryono, Kepel Press, Yogyakarta, pp. 623–6.

Anwar, R. (1966) 'Sekali lagi Caligula', *Kompas* (14 October), Jakarta, p. 3.

Anwar, R. (1983) *Menulis dalam air, di sini sekarang esok hilang: Sebuah otobiografi*, Penerbit Sinar Harapan, Jakarta.

Arahmaiani (2004) *Roh terasing*, Bentang Budaya, Jogjakarta, Indonesia.

Ardan, S. M. and Jakarta, K. T. D. K. (1985) *Gejolak teater remaja di Jakarta, 1973–1985*, Dewan Kesenian Jakarta, Jakarta.

Aritonang, D. (2004) '"DOM" Teater Payung Hitam: Sebuah Manifestasi Kesakitan Sosial Politik Negeri', *Teater Payung Hitam: Perspektif teater modern Indonesia*, Ed. R. Sabur, Kelir, Bandung, Jawa Barat, Indonesia, pp. 301–5.

Aryanto, D. (2003) 'Keserakahan yang (Pasti) Tenggelam', *Tempo* (1 June), Jakarta, pp. 102–3

Asmara, A. (1958) 'Suka Duka dibelakang lajar Sandiwara: Memories dari Andjar Asmara', *Pedoman* (3, 10 September; 1, 8, 15 October), Jakarta.

Aurelius, C. (1517) *Die cronyke van Hollandt, Zeelandt ende Vrieslant beghinnende van Adams tiden tot die geboerte ons heren Jhesu voertgaende tot den iare M.CCCCC. ende xvij. Met den rechten oerspronc hoe Hollandt eerst begrepen en bewoent is gheweest van den Troyanen ... bi mi Jan Seversz, Voleynt tot Leyden.*

Aveling, H. (1969) 'An Analysis of Utuy Tatang Sontani's "Suling"', *Bijdragen tot d Taal-, Land- en Volkenkunde*, **125**, pp. 328–43.

Bain, L. (2000) 'Confused? Some directions in post-New Order theatre', *Inside Indonesia* (September).

Bain, L. (2003) 'NGO theater in the post New Order', *Inside Indonesia*, 1:46, pp. 29–30.

Bain, L. (2005) 'Writing back', *Inside Indonesia*, 1:46, pp. 29–30.

Balme, C. B. (2007) *Pacific Performances: Theatricality and Cross-Cultural Encounter in the South Seas*, Palgrave Macmillan, Basingstoke and New York.

Batubara, A. F. (1993) 'Pementasan "Karina Adinda" STB: Sepenggal Cinta pada Zaman yang Berubah', *Kompas* (26 September), Jakarta.

Biran, M. J. (1971) 'Roby alias Ibnu Saad & Nandi, Pengabdi Seni Drama', *Keadjaiban di Pasar Senen*, Pustaka Jaya, Jakarta, pp. 9–18.

Blussé, L. (1981) 'Batavia, 1619–1730: The Rise and Fall of a Chinese Colonial Town', *Journal of Southeast Asian Studies*, **12**, pp. 159–78.

Bodden, M. H. (1997a) 'Utopia and the Shadow of Nationalism: The Plays of Sanusi Pane, 1928-1940', *Bijdragen tot d Taal-, Land- en Volkenkunde*, **153**, pp. 332–55.

Bodden, M. H. (1997b) 'Teater Koma's *Suksesi* and the New Order Government: Norms of Taste and the Pressure for Democratic Change', *Asian Theatre Journal*, **14**, pp. 259–80.

Bodden, M. H. (1997c) 'Workers' Theatre and Theatre about Workers in 1990s Indonesia', *Review of Indonesian and Malaysian Affairs*, **31**, pp. 37–78.

Bodden, M. H. (2002) 'Satuan-satuan kecil and uncomfortable improvisations in the late night of the new order', *Clearing a Space: Postcolonial Readings of Modern Indonesian Literature*, Verhandelingen van het Koninklijk Instituut voor Taal-, Land- en Volkenkunde 202, Ed. K. Foulcher and T. Day, KITLV Press, Leiden, pp. 293–324.

Bodden, M. H. (2008) 'Languages of Traumas, Bodies, and Myths: Learning to speak again in post-1998 Indonesian Theatre', *Arts, Popular Culture, and Social Change in the New Indonesia*, Ed. Leaf, M. and Kusno, A., UBC Institute of Asian Research, Centre for Southeast Asian Research, Vancouver, pp. 119–51.

Bodden, M. H. (2009) *The Lontar Anthology of Indonesian Drama*, Vol. 2, Lontar Foundation, Jakarta.

Brandon, J. R. (1967) *Theatre in Southeast Asia*, Harvard University Press, Cambridge, MA.

Brandon, J. R. (1970) *On Thrones of Gold: Three Javanese Shadow Plays*, Harvard University Press, Cambridge, MA.

Camus, A. (1958) *Caligula & Three Other Plays*, Knopf, New York.

Carnicke, S. M. (2008) *Stanislavsky in Focus: An Acting Master for the 21st Century*, Routledge, New York.

Cheah, P. (2003) *Spectral Nationality: Passages of Freedom from Kant to Postcolonial Literatures of Liberation*, Columbia University Press, New York.

Ching, L. (1998) 'Yellow Skin, White Masks: Race, Class, and Identification in Japanese Colonial Discourse', *Trajectories: Inter-Asia Cultural Studies*, Ed. K.-H. Chen, Routledge, London and New York, pp. 65–86.

Clark, M. (2004) 'Too Many Wisanggenis: Reinventing the Wayang at the Turn of the Century', *Indonesia and the Malay World*, **32**, pp. 62–79.

Cohen, M. I. (2006) *The Komedie Stamboel: Popular Theater in Colonial Indonesia, 1891–1903*, Ohio University Press, Athens, OH.

Cohen, M. I. (2009) *The Lontar Anthology of Indonesian Drama*, Vol. 1, Lontar Foundation, Jakarta.

Cook, C. (1968) *Captain Cook's Journal, 1768–71*, Libraries Board of Australia, Adelaide.

Corn, C. (1998) *The Scents of Eden: A Narrative of the Spice Trade*, Kodansha International, New York.

Crow, B. and Banfield, C. (1996) *An Introduction to Post-Colonial Theatre*, Cambridge University Press, Cambridge and New York.

242 *Works Cited*

Cummings, W. (2002) *Making Blood White: Historical Transformations in Early Modern Makassar*, University of Hawai'i Press, Honolulu.

Dahana, R. P. (2001) *Homo Theatricus*, Indonesiatera, Magelang.

Darmowijono, R. D. (1964) *Uraian Manipol, garis-garis besar haluan negara: Dihimpun dan disusun*, Madjelis Luhur Taman Siswa, Jogjakarta.

Deleuze, G. and Guattari, F. (1987) *A Thousand Plateaus: Capitalism and Schizophrenia*, University of Minnesota Press, Minneapolis.

Dewan Kesenian Jakarta and Komite Teater (2006) *FTJ 2006: Media festival teater Jakarta*.

Dharwadker, A. B. (2005) *Theatres of Independence: Drama, Theory, and Urban Performance in India since 1947*, University of Iowa Press, Iowa City.

Dimyati, I. S. (2004) 'Catatan 'Aku Masih Hidup' Teater Payung Hitam', *Teater Payung Hitam: Perspektif teater modern Indonesia*, Ed. R. Sabur, Kelir, Bandung, Jawa Barat, Indonesia, pp. 339–44.

Diponegoro, M. (1984) *Iblis: Drama satu babak*, Pustaka Panjimas, Jakarta.

Dorléans, B. (2002) *Les Français et l'Indonésie*, Kailash, Paris.

Effendi, R. (1953a) *Bebasari: Toneel dalam 3 pertundjukan*, Fasco, Djakarta.

Effendi, R. (1953b) *Pertjikan permenungan*, Fasco, Djakarta.

Effendi, R. (1967) 'Author's Introduction to "A Sprinkling of Stray Thoughts" (Pertjikan Permenungan)', *The Development of Modern Indonesian Poetry*, Ed. B. Raffel, State University of New York Press, Albany, NY, pp. 203–5.

Esten, M. and Hadi, W. (1992) *Tradisi dan modernitas dalam sandiwara: Teks sandiwara 'Cindua Mato' karyo Wisran Hadi dalam hubungan dengan mitos Minangkabau 'Cindua Mato'*, Intermasa, Jakarta.

Fanon, F. (1967a) *Black Skin, White Masks*, trans. Charles Markmann, Grove Press, New York.

Fanon, F. (1967b) *A Dying Colonialism*, Grove Press, New York.

Feinstein, A. and Workshop Performing Arts in South-East Asia (1994) *Modern Javanese Theater and the Politics of Culture: A Case Study of Teater Gapit*, Workshop KITLV, Leiden.

Florida, N. (1992) 'The Badhaya Katawang: A Translation of the Song of Kangjeng Ratu Kidul,' *Indonesia*, **53**, pp. 20–32.

Foucault, M. (1998) 'Nietzsche, Genealogy, History', *Aesthetics, Method, and Epistemology, Essential Works of Foucault, 1954–1984*, Vol. 2, Ed. J. D. Faubion, New Press, New York, pp. 369–91.

Foulcher, K. (1968) 'A Check List on Indonesian Literary Criticism', *Review of Indonesian And Malay Affairs*, **2**, pp. 19–22.

Foulcher, K. (1980) *'Pujangga Baru': Literature and Nationalism in Indonesia, 1933–1942*, Flinders University, Adelaide.

Foulcher, K. (1994) *'The Manifesto is Not Dead': Indoensian [sic] Literary Politics Thirty Years On*, Centre of Southeast Asian Studies, Monash University, Clayton, Victoria.

Foulcher, K. (1995) 'In Search of the Postcolonial in Indonesian Literature', *Sojourn*, **10**, pp. 147–71.

Foulcher, K. and Day, T. (2002) *Clearing a Space: Postcolonial Readings of Modern Indonesian Literature*, KITLV Press, Leiden.

Foulcher, K. and Monash University. Centre of Southeast Asian Studies. (1986) *Social Commitment in Literature and the Arts: The Indonesian 'Institute of Peoples' Culture' 1950–1965*, Centre of Southeast Asian Studies, Monash University, Clayton, Victoria.

Freud, S., McLintock, D. and Haughton, H. (2003) *The Uncanny*, Penguin Books, New York.

Gade, A. M. (2004) *Perfection Makes Practice: Learning, Emotion, and the Recited Qur'an in Indonesia*, University of Hawai'i Press, Honolulu.

Gauch, S. (2002) 'Fanon on the Surface', *Parallax*, **8**, pp. 116–28.

Giebels, L. and Oen, I.-K. (2001) *Soekarno: Biografi 1901–1950,* Grasindo, Jakarta.

Gilbert, H. and Tompkins, J. (1996) *Post-Colonial Drama: Theory, Practice, Politics*, Routledge, London and New York.

Gillitt, C. (1995) 'Tradisi Baru: A "New Tradition: of Indonesian Theatre"', *Asian Theatre Journal*, **12**, pp. 164–74.

Gillitt, C. R. (2001) 'Challenging conventions and crossing boundaries: A new tradition of Indonesian theatre from 1968–1978,' unpublished doctoral dissertation, Department of Performance Studies, New York University, New York.

Gillitt, C. R. (2009) *The Lontar Anthology of Indonesian Drama*, Vol. 3, Lontar Foundation, Jakarta.

Gintini, T. (2000) 'Teater Payung Hitam paints black picture of troubled Aceh,' *The Jakarta Post* (1 September), Jakarta.

GoGwilt, C. (2006) 'Writing to the World,' *Inside Indonesia*, **88**, pp. 22–3.

Grotius, H. (1610) *Liber de antiquitate reipublicae Batavicae*, Lugduni Batavorum.

Haan, F. de (1935) *Oud Batavia*, A. C. Nix, Bandoeng.

Hanifah, A. (1945) *Taufan diatas Asia*, manuscript submitted to Gunseikanbu, H. B. Jassin Documentation Center, Jakarta.

Hanifah, A. (1946) *Kita berdjoeang, goebahan koeltoer politis*, Merdeka, Djakarta.

Hanifah, A. (1948) *Kedudukan agama dalam negara_p2_s modern dan merdeka,* Kementerian Agama R. I., Jogjakarta.

Hanifah, A. (1949a) *Soal agama dalam negara modern*, Tintamas, Djakarta.

Hanifah, A. (1949b) *Taufan diatas Asia, dan tiga buah sandiwara lain*, Balai Pustaka, Jakarta.

Hanifah, A. (1950) *Rintisan filsafat, filsafat barat ditilik dengan djiwa timur*, Balai Pustaka, Djakarta.

Hanifah, A. (1972) *Tales of a Revolution,* Angus & Robertson Education, Sydney.

Hartoko, D. (1967) 'Pengaruh Filsafat Existensialis Dalam Drama 2 Europa Modern', *Horison*, Vol. 1, pp. 68–9.

Hatley, B. (1999a) 'Cultural Expression and Social Transformation in Indonesia', *Reformasi: Crisis and Change in Indonesia*, Ed. A. Budiman, B. Hatley and D. Kingsbury, Monash Asia Institute, Clayton, Australia, pp. 267–85.

Hatley, B. (1999b) 'Lightning!', *Inside Indonesia*, **58**, pp. 27–8.

Hatley, B. (2007) 'Contemporary and Traditional, Male and Female in Garasi's *Waktu Batu*', *Indonesia and the Malay World*, **35**, pp. 93–106.

Hatta, M. (1952) 'Pidato kepada Kongres Kebudayaan Pan-Indonesia, Bandung', *Indonesia: Madjalah Kebudayaan*, **3**, pp. 20–30.

Hefner, R. W. (1999) 'Religion: Evolving Pluralism', *Indonesia beyond Suharto: Polity, Economy, Society, Transition*, Ed. Emmerson, and Asia Society, M. E. Sharpe, Armonk, NY, pp. 205–36.

Heryanto, A. (1999) 'Race, Rape, and Reporting', *Reformasi: Crisis and Change in Indonesia*, Ed. A. Budiman, B. Hatley, D. Kingsbury and Monash Asia Institute, Monash Asia Institute, Monash University, Clayton, Australia, pp. 299–334.

Hurek, L. L. (2007) 'Bung Karno Bina Teater di Flores', http://hurek.blogspot.com/2007/03/bung-karno-bina-teater-di-flores.html.

Ido, V. (1913) *Karina Adinda: Oost-Indisch zedenspel in drie bedrijven,* Bataviasche Tooneelvereeniging, Batavia.

Ido, V. (1921) *De paria van Glodok: Episode uit het indische paupersleven in drie acten,* Boekhandel Visser, Bandoeng.

Ido, V. (1922) *De paupers: Roman uit de Indo-europeesche samenleving,* N. V. Boekhandel Visser; Valkhoff, Weltevreden, Amersfoort.

244 *Works Cited*

Ido, V., Lan, G. L. and Bandung, S. T. (1993) *Raden Ajeng Karina Adinda*, Bandung: Studiklub Teater Bandung.

Ikranagara (1996) 'The Making of Indonesian Theatre: From Globalization to Pluralistic Interaction,' *Tenggara*, **38**, pp. 1–21.

Ismail, U. (1949) 'Sandiwara Indonesia dan Masjarakat', *Indonesia*, **1**, pp. 144–8.

Ismail, U. (1954) 'Susah Tjari Aktris Indonesia: Meski Tak Kurang Wanita Tjantik', *Starr News*, Vol. 3, pp. 14–17.

Ismail, U. (1968) 'Beberapa segi dalam memenuhi hasrat para peminat Seni Peran', *Buku Pekan Seni Drama DCI Djaja 1968*, Panitia Pekan Senidrama DCI Djaja, Jakarta, pp. 8–11.

Ismail, U. (1983a) 'Film Saya Yang Pertama', *Usmar Ismail mengupas film*, Penerbit Sinar Harapan, Jakarta, pp. 164–71.

Ismail, U. (1983b) 'Meletakkan Dasar-dasar Baru', *Usmar Ismail mengupas film*, Penerbit Sinar Harapan, Jakarta, pp. 40–3.

Jassin, H. B. (1954) *Kesusasteraan Indonesia modern dalam kritik dan essay*, Gunung Agung, Djakarta.

Jit, K. (1987) 'Modern Theatre in Indonesia,' *Performing Arts (Singapore)*, **4**, pp. 15–21.

Jit, K. (2003) 'Islamists and Secularists Spar for the Soul of Drama', *Krishen Jit: An Uncommon Position*, Ed. Rowland, K., Contemporary Asian Arts Centre, Singapore, pp. 73–5.

Jonge, J. K. J. de, Deventer, M. L. v., Roo, L. W. G. d., Tiele, P. A., Heeres, J. E., Meinsma, J. J. and Haarst, J. W. G. v. (1862) *De Opkomst van het Nederlandsch gezag in Oost-Indie. Verzameling van onuitgegeven stukken uit het Oud-Koloniaal Archief*, M. Nijhoff, 's Gravenhage.

Jurriens, E. (2007) 'Battle royal: Challenge to political parody on Indonesian television', *Inside Indonesia*, **90**, pp. 23–4.

Kahin, G. M. (1952) *Nationalism and Revolution in Indonesia*, Cornell University Press, Ithaca, NY.

Kartanegara, E. H. (2005) 'Hamlet "Pribumi" di Antara Dengkuran Penonton', *Menonton Bengkel Teater Rendra*, Ed. E. Haryono, Kepel Press, Yogyakarta, pp. 630–2.

Kartaredjasa, B. (2007a) Personal interview conducted by E. D. Winet, Bandung, Jakarta.

Kartaredjasa, B. (2007b) 'Playboy Interview: Butet Kartaredjasa', *Playboy (Indonesian Edition)*, pp. 31–41.

Kate van Loo, D. H. t. (1815) *De Gardes d'Honneur: In vier zangen*, Johannes Allart, 's-Gravenhage.

Kate van Loo, D. H. t. (1820) *De dood van Jan van Schaffelaar: Vaderlandsch treurspel*, R. J. Berntrop, Amsterdam.

Kate van Loo, D. H. t. (1827) *Petronella van Saxen, gravinne van Holland: Oorspronkelijk vaderlandsch treurspel*, Lands drukkerij, Batavia.

Kayam, U. (1981a) 'Sang Lenong', *Seni, tradisi, masyarakat [karangan-karangan]*, Penerbit Sinar Harapan, Jakarta, pp. 118–28.

Kayam, U. (1981b) 'Tradisi Baru Teater Kita?', *Seni, tradisi, masyarakat [karangan-karangan]*, Penerbit Sinar Harapan, Jakarta, pp. 92–9.

Kemasang, A. R. T. (1985) 'How Dutch Colonialism Foreclosed a Domestic Bourgeoisie in Java: The 1740 Chinese Massacres Reappraised', *Review (A Journal of the Fernand Braudel Center for the Study of Economies, Historical Systems, and Civilizations)*, **9**, pp. 57–80.

Komite Teater, D. K. J. (2007) *Pedoman Umum Festival Teater Jakarta*, Dewan Kesenian Jakarta, Jakarta.

Kosim, S. (1999). 'Teater Indonesia, Sebuah Perjalanan dalam Multikulturalisme,' *Jurnal Seni Pertunjukan Indonesia*, **9**, pp. 177–98.

Kumar, A. (1987) 'Literary Approaches to Slavery and the Indies Enlightenment: Van Hogendorp's "Kraspoekoel"', *Indonesia*, **43**, pp. 43–65.

Kumar, A. (1989) 'A Swedish View of Batavia in 1783–4: Hornstedt's Letters,' *Archipel*, **37**, pp. 247–62.

Kurasawa, A. (1987) 'Propaganda Media on Java under the Japanese 1942–1945', *Indonesia*, **44**, pp. 59–83.

Kusno, A. (2000) *Behind the Postcolonial: Architecture, Urban Space, and Political Cultures in Indonesia*, Routledge, New York.

Laffan, M. F. (2003) *Islamic Nationhood and Colonial Indonesia: The Umma below the Winds*, RoutledgeCurzon, London and New York.

Lee, J. M. A. H. (1966) 'Minta Perhatian Buat Repertoire Drama', *Horison*, **1**, pp. 55.

Levinas, E. (1969). *Totality and Infinity: An Essay on Exteriority*, Duquesne University Press, Pittsburgh.

Levinas, E. (1981) *Otherwise than Being: or, Beyond Essence*, M. Nijhoff, Distributors for the US and Canada; Kluwer, Boston, MA, and the Hague.

Lewis, D. L. (2008) *God's Crucible: Islam and the Making of Europe, 570 to 1215*, W. W. Norton, New York.

Liem, E. (1966) 'Caligula Albert Camus di Bali Room H.I.', *Kompas* (1 July), Jakarta, p. 3.

Livy, Drakenborch, A. and Freinsheim, J. (1820) *Historiarum ab urbe condite libri, qui supersunt, omnes: Cum notis integris Laur. Vallae, M. Ant. Sabellici, Beati Rhenani, Sigism. Gelenii, Henr. Loriti Glareani, Car. Signonii, Fulvii Ursini, Franc. Sanctii, J. Fr. Gronovii, Tan. Fabri, Henr. Valesii, Jac. Perizonii, Jac. Gronovii; exerptis Petr. Nannii Justi Lipsii, Fr. Modii, Jani Gruteri; nec non ineditis Jani Gebhardi, Car. And. Dureri, et aliorum*, Stutgardiae.

Lombard, D. (1975) 'Une gazette en Français à Batavia: "la Lorgnette"', *Archipel* **9**, pp. 129–34.

Loomba, A. (1997) 'Shakespearean transformations', *Shakespeare and National Culture*, Ed. J. J. Joughin, Manchester University Press, Manchester. Distributed exclusively in the USA by St. Martin's Press, Manchester and New York, pp. 109–41.

Machdan, U. (2005) 'Nonton "HAMLET" nya Rendra', *Menonton Bengkel Teater Rendra*, Ed. E. Haryono, Kepel Press, Yogyakarta, pp. 557–9.

Maier, H. M. J. (2004) *We are Playing Relatives: A Survey of Malay Writing*, KITLV Press, Leiden.

Malna, A. and Usman, A. (2007) Personal interview conducted by E. D. Winet, Bandung, Jakarta.

Marre, J. de (1740) *Batavia, begrepen in zes boeken*, A. Wor en de Erve G. onder de Linden, Amsterdam.

Massardi, N. M. (2007) 'Bubarkan FTJ, Jadikan Kompetisi untuk Audisi', *Kompas* (7 January), Jakarta.

Maulana, S. F. (2004) 'Ketika Kata Kita Mati Dari Pentas Teater Payung Hitam', *Teater Payung Hitam: Perspektif teater modern Indonesia*, Ed. R. Sabur, Kelir, Bandung, Jawa Barat, Indonesia, pp. 263–8.

Meyer-Dinkgrèafe, D. (2001) *Approaches to Acting: Past and Present*, Continuum, London and New York.

Mihardja, A. K. (1954) *Polemik kebudajaan: Pokok pikiran St. Takdir Alisjahbana, Sanusi Pane, Dr. Purbatjaraka, Dr. Sutomo, Tjindarbumi, Adinegoro, Dr. M. Amir [dan] Ki Hadjar Dewantara*, Perpustakaan Perguruan, Djakarta.

Milone, P. D. (1967) 'Indische Culture and its Relationship to Urban Life', *Comparative Studies in Society and History*, **9**, pp. 407–26.

Milton, G. (1999) *Nathaniel's Nutmeg, or, The true and incredible adventures of the spice trader who changed the course of history*, Farrar, Straus & Giroux, New York.

Moeljanto, D. S. and Ismail, T. (1995) *Prahara budaya: Kilas-balik ofensif Lekra/PKI dkk: Kumpulan dokumen pergolakan sejarah*, Diterbitkan atas kerja sama Penerbit Mizan dan H. U. Republika, Bandung.

Mohamad, G. (1967) 'Existtensialisme & Kita', *Horison*, **1**, p. 318.

Mohamad, G. (1973) 'Pembelaan untuk Teater Indonesia Modern,' *Seks, Sastra, Kita*, Jakarta.

Mohamad, G. (1988) 'Camus dan Orang Indonesia', *Horison*, **23**, pp. 372–7.

Mohamad, G. (1991) *Modern Drama of Indonesia*, The Festival of Indonesia Foundation, New York.

Mohamad, G. (1993) 'Peristiwa "Manikebu": Kesusastraan Indonesia dan Politik di Tahun 1960-an', *Kesusastraan dan Kekuasaan*, Pustaka Firdaus, Jakarta, pp. 11–55.

Mohamad, G. (1997) 'Lirik, Laut, Lupa: Asrul Sani dan Lain-Lain, *Circa* 1950', *Asrul Sani 70 Tahun (Penghargaan dan Penghormatan)*, Ed. al., A. R. e., Pustaka Jaya, Jakarta, pp. 27–78.

Mohamad, G. (2002) 'Forgetting: Poetry and the nation, a motif in Indonesian literary modernism after 1945', *Clearing a Space: Postcolonial Readings of Modern Indonesian Literature*, Vol. 'Verhandelingen van het Koninklijk Instituut voor Taal-, Land- en Volkenkunde'; 202, Ed. K. Foulcher and T. Day, KITLV Press, Leiden, pp. 183–212.

Mohamad, G. and Lindsay, J. (1994) *Sidelines: Writings from Tempo*, Hyland House in association with Monash Asia Institute, Monash University, South Melbourne, Victoria.

Muhtarom, I. (2004) 'Tradisionalisasi Teater', Sinar Harapan Online (5 August).

Nadjib, E. A. (2004) 'Nation of the Laughing People', a lecture transcribed and translated by Ian Betts for inclusion in his forthcoming book, *The Lonely Pilgrimage of Emha Ainun Nadjib*.

Nadjib, E. A. (2006) *Kerajaan Indonesia*, Progress, Yogyakarta, Indonesia.

Nadjib, E. A. (2007) Personal interview conducted by E. D. Winet, Yogyakarta.

Nas, P. J. M. and Grijns, C. D. (2000) 'Introduction.' In *Jakarta-Batavia: Socio-Cultural Essays*, Ed. C. D. Grijns and P. J. M. Nas, KITLV, Leiden, pp. 1–23.

Nietzsche, F. W. (1887) *Zur Genealogie der Moral: Eine Streitschrift*, C. G. Naumann, Leipzig.

Nieuwenhuys, R. (1973) *Oost-Indische Spiegel: Wat Nederlandse schrijvers en dichters over Indonesië hebben geschreven, vanaf de eerste jaren der compagnie tot op heden*, Em. Querido, Amsterdam.

Noer, A. C. (1983) 'Teater Indonesia Masa Depan', *Bagi masa depan teater Indonesia*, Ed. S. WM, Y. Affendi, H. Dim and R. U. T., Granesia, Bandung, pp. 17–24.

Noer, A. C. (1987) 'Imam Kepada Fikiran: "Dasar" Sumur Tanpa Dasar', *Sumur Tanpa Dasar* program, Teater Ketjil Gedung Kesenian Jakarta, Jakarta, pp. 37–9.

Noer, A. C. (1989) *Sumur tanpa dasar*, Pustaka Utama Grafiti, Jakarta.

Noer, A. C. (1997) *Deklamasi: Sebuah pengantar*, Bengkel Deklamasi, Jakarta.

Noer, A. C. (2005) 'Indonesia: Teaternya dan Penontonnya', *Teater Tanpa Masa Silam: Sejumlah esai budaya*, Ed. A. R. Sarjono, Dewan Kesenian Jakarta, Jakarta, pp. 21–47.

Noer, A. C., Usman, K. and Panitia Pekan Semidrama DCI Djaja 1968 (1968) *Buku pekan seni drama DCI DJAJA 1968: Menjongsong HUT Djakarta ke-441. Ketua umum: K. Usman*, Panitia Pekan Semidrama DCI Djaja 1968, Djakarta.

Noerhadi, T. H. (1967) 'Existensialisme dalam Dimensi Realitas', *Horison* **1**, pp. 316–17.

Nurcahyoab, H. (1999) 'Teater Indonesia dalam Belenggu Teori Barat', *Sagang*, **4**, pp. 43–5.

O'Connor, R. (1995) 'Indigenous Urbanism: Class, City and Society in Southeast Asia', *Journal of Southeast Asian Studies*, **26**, pp. 30–45.

Oemarjati, B. S. (1971) *Bentuk Lakon Dalam Sastra Indonesia*, Gunung Agung, Jakarta.

Oltmans, J. F. and Stuvel, G. (1968) *De schaapherder. Een verhaal uit de Utrechtse oorlog '1481–1488,'* V. A. Kramers, Den Haag.

Ovid and Wheeler, A. L. (1924) *Ovid with an English translation: Tristia. Ex Ponto,* W. Heinemann; G. P. Putnam's Sons, London and New York.

Padmodarmaya, P. and Alisjahbana, P. (1994) *25 tahun TIM,* Yayasan Kesenian Jakarta, Jakarta.

Pane, A. (1953) 'Produksi film tjerita di Indonesia: Perkembangannja sebagai Alat Masjarakat', *Indonesia*, **4**, pp. 5–112.

Pausacker, H. (2004) 'Presidents as *Punakawan*: Portrayal of National Leaders as Clown-Servants in Central Javanese *Wayang*', *Journal of Southeast Asian Studies*, **35**, pp. 213–33.

Pemberton, J. (1994) *On the Subject of 'Java,'* Cornell University Press, Ithaca, NY.

Poerwa, A. (2004) 'Payung Hitam dan Semangat Utopia', *Teater Payung Hitam: Perspektif teater modern Indonesia*, Ed. R. Sabur, Kelir, Bandung, Jawa Barat, Indonesia, pp. 345–7.

Praamstra, O. (2003) *Een feministe in de Tropen: De Indische jaren van Mina Kruseman,* KITLV Uitgeverij, Leiden.

Prasetyo, H. (2005) 'Hamlet: Menonton Rendra dan Perjalanannya', *Menonton Bengkel Teater Rendra*, Ed. E. Haryono, Kepel Press, Yogyakarta, pp. 627–9.

Pusat Pembinaan dan Pengembangan Bahasa. (1993) *Citra manusia dalam drama Indonesia modern, 1920–1960,* Pusat Pembinaan dan Pengembangan Bahasa, Departemen Pendidikan dan Kebudayaan, Jakarta.

Quinn, M. (1990) 'Celebrity and the Semiotics of Acting', *New Theatre Quarterly*, **6**, pp. 154–61.

Raffel, B. (1967) *The Development of Modern Indonesian Poetry,* State University of New York Press, Albany, NY.

Rafferty, E. (Ed.) (1989) *Putu Wijaya in Performance,* University of Wisconsin-Madison Center for Southeast Asian Studies, Madison, WI.

Ramadhan, K. H. (1982) *Gelombang hidupku: Dewi Dja dari Dardanella,* Penerbit Sinar Harapan, Jakarta.

Rayner, A. (2006) *Ghosts: Death's Double and the Phenomena of Theatre,* University of Minnesota Press, Minneapolis.

Reid, A. (1994) *Early Southeast Asian categorizations of Europeans: Implicit understandings, observing, reporting, and reflecting on the encounters between Europeans and other peoples in the early modern era,* Ed. S. B. Schwartz, Cambridge University Press, Cambridge and New York, pp. 268–94.

Renan, E. (1990) 'What is a nation?', *Nation and Narration*, Ed. H. K. Bhabha, Routledge, London and New York, pp. 8–22.

Rendra, W. S. (1976) *Tentang Bermain Drama,* Pustaka Jaya, Jakarta Pusat.

Rendra, W. S. (1983a) 'From the mysteries of nature to structural analysis', *Prisma*, **29**, pp. 44–9.

Rendra, W. S. (1983b) 'Alternatif dari Parangtritis', *Mempertimbangkan tradisi: Kumpulan karangan*, Ed. P. Eneste, Gramedia, Jakarta, pp. 24–8.

Rendra, W. S. (1983c) 'Pidato Penerimaan Penghargaan dari Akademi Jakarta', *Mempertimbangkan tradisi: Kumpulan karangan*, Ed. P. Eneste, Gramedia, Jakarta, pp. 77–85.

Rendra, W. S. (1983d) 'Proses Kreatif Saya sebagai Penyair', *Mempertimbangkan tradisi: Kumpulan karangan*, Ed. P. Eneste, Gramedia, Jakarta, pp. 61–70.

Rendra, W. S. (1985) 'Komentar Terhadap Festival Teater Remaja X', *Gejolak teater remaja di Jakarta, 1973–1985*, Ed. S. M. Ardan and K. T. D. K. Jakarta, Dewan Kesenian Jakarta, Jakarta, pp. 74–8.

Riantiarno, N. (2007) Personal interview conducted by E. D. Winet, Bandung, Jakarta.

Ricklefs, M. C. (2001) *A History of Modern Indonesia since c.1200*, Stanford University Press, Stanford, CA.

Roach, J. R. (1996) *Cities of the Dead: Circum-Atlantic Performance*, Columbia University Press, New York.

Rosidi, A. and Sani, A. (1997) *Asrul Sani 70 tahun: Penghargaan dan penghormatan*, Pustaka Jaya, Jakarta.

S.J.S. and Medita, A. H. (2004) 'Wanita Hamil dan Pahlawan Kesaingan', *Teater Payung Hitam: Perspektif teater modern Indonesia*, Ed. R. Sabur, Kelir, Bandung, Jawa Barat, Indonesia, pp. 269–72.

Sabur, R. (2004) *Teater Payung Hitam: Perspektif teater modern Indonesia*, Kelir, Bandung, Jawa Barat, Indonesia.

Said, S. and Siagian, T. P. (1991) *Shadows on the Silver Screen: A Social History of Indonesian Film*, Lontar Foundation, Jakarta.

Saini, K. M. (1981) *Beberapa Gagasan Teater*, Nurcahaya, Bandung.

Saini, K. M. (2000) 'Teater Indonesia Sebuah Perjalanan dalam Multikulturalisme', *Interkulturalisme (dalam) teater*, Ed. N. Sahid, Yayasan Untuk Indonesia, Giwangan, Yogyakarta, pp. 30–47.

Saleh, M. and Ismail, U. (1967) *Seni sandiwara dalam dunia pendidikan: Dengen pangkal tolak sandiwara-sandiwara hasil karya Usmar Ismail*, Gunung Agung, Djakarta.

Salmon, C. (1981) *Literature in Malay by the Chinese of Indonesia: A Provisional Annotated Bibliography*, University Microfilms International, Ann Arbor, MI, and Éditions de la Maison des Sciences de l'Homme, Paris, France.

Samin, M. (1968) 'Kebinasaan Negeri Sendja', *Horison*, **3**, pp. 111–21.

Samson, L. (1994) 'The Banning of Pak Kanjeng', *Inside Indonesia*, **40**, pp. 28–30.

Sani, A. (1960) 'Tjatatan dari Penterdjemah', *Enam Peladjaran Pertama Bagi Tjalon Aktor*, Ed. R. Boleslavsky and A. t. Sani, PT Jaya Sakti, Jakarta, pp. 1–16.

Sani, A. (1997a) 'Badan Dana Yang Dibutuhkan', *Surat-Surat Kepercayaan*, Ed. A. Rosidi, Pustaka Jaya, Jakarta, pp. 207–10.

Sani, A. (1997b) 'Ibu Kami adalah Jakarta', *Surat-Surat Kepercayaan*, Ed. A. Rosidi, Pustaka Jaya, Jakarta, pp. 673–87.

Sani, A. (1997c) 'Medium yang Disia-siakan', *Surat-Surat Kepercayaan*, Ed. A. Rosidi, Pustaka Jaya, Jakarta, pp. 211–16.

Sani, A. (2007 [1987]) *Abang Thamrin dari Betawi*, Sanggar Pelakon, Jakarta.

Santa Maria, L. (1954) 'Significato e problematica dell'opera di Utuy Tatang Sontani', *Annali, Instituto Universitario Orientale di Napoli*, **15**, pp. 4–7.

Sarumpaet, R. (1997) *Marsinah: Nnyanyian dari bawah tanah*, Yayasan Bentang Budaya, Yogyakarta, Indonesia.

Sarumpaet, R. (1998) *Marsinah: A Song from the Underworld*, Aberrant Genotype Press, Australian Capital Territory.

Sarumpaet, R. (1999) *Marsinah Menggugat*, Network for Indonesian Democracy, Japan, Tokyo.

Sarumpaet, R. (2000) 'Marsinah Accuses', *Silenced Voices*, Ed. F. Stewart and J. H. McGlynn, University of Hawai'i Press, Honolulu, pp. 155–66.

Sarumpaet, R. (2003) *Alia: Luka Serambi Mekah*, Metafor, Jakarta, Indonesia.

Sarumpaet, R. (2004) *Anak-anak kegelapan: Naskah drama*, Satu Merah Panggung, Pustaka Pencerahan, Jakarta.

Sastrowardojo, S. and Hadian, S. (1956) 'Adakah Krisis Pentjiptaan Drama di Indonesia?', *Budaya*, **5**, pp. 87–109.

Schöffer, I. (1981) 'The Batavian myth during the sixteenth and seventeenth centuries', *Geschiedschrijving in Nederland: Studies over de historiografie van de nieuwe tijd*, Ed. P. A. M. Geurts and A. E. M. Janssen, Nijhoff, 's-Gravenhage, pp. 84–109.

Sears, L. J. (1996) *Shadows of Empire: Colonial Discourse and Javanese Tales*, Duke University Press, Durham, NC.

Setiyanto, A. (2006) *Bung Karno, maestro Monte Carlo: Kumpulan naskah drama Bung Karno selama masa pengasingan di Bengkulu*, Ombak, Yogyakarta.

Siegel, J. T. (1997) *Fetish, Recognition, Revolution*, Princeton University Press, Princeton, NJ.

Siegel, J. T. (1998a) 'Early Thoughts on the Violence of May 13 and 14, 1998, in Jakarta', *Indonesia*, **66**, pp. 75–108.

Siegel, J. T. (1998b) *A New Criminal Type in Jakarta: Counter-Revolution Today*, Duke University Press, Durham, NC.

Sihombing, W. (1980) '"Musuh Masyarakat" Karya Ibsen: Sebuah Studi Penafsiran', *Pertemuan Teater 80*, Ed. W. S. S. Sihombing, Ikraneagara, Dewan Kesenian Jakarta, Jakarta, pp. 36–71.

Silverman, K. (1996) *The Threshold of the Visible World*, Routledge, New York.

Slametmuljana, B. R. (1965) *Menudju puntjak kemegahan (sedjarah Keradjaan Madjapahit)*, Balai Pustaka, Djakarta.

Soedarsono, R. (Ed.) (1995) *Teater Tradisional Indonesia*, Yayasan Harapan Kita: BP3 Taman Mini Indonesia Indah, Jakarta.

Soekarno and Adams, C. H. (1965) *Sukarno: An Autobiography*, Bobbs-Merrill, Indianapolis.

Soekarno and McVey, R. T. (1970) *Nationalism, Islam, and Marxism*, Modern Indonesia Project, Southeast Asia Program, Dept. of Asian Studies, Cornell University, Ithaca, NY.

Soemanto, B. (2001) *Jagat Teater*, Media Presindo, Yogyakarta.

Soemanto, B. e. a. and Wijaya, P. (2000) 'Wawancara Putu Wijaya', *Kepingan riwayat teater kontemporer di Yogyakarta: Laporan penelitian existing documentation dalam perkembangan teater kontemporer di Yogyakarta, 1950–1990*, Ed. B. Soemanto, Diterbitkan atas kerjasama Kalangan Anak Zaman, the Ford Foundation [dan] Pustaka Pelajar, Yogyakarta, pp. i, 249.

Sontani, U. T. (1948) *Suling*, Balai Pustaka, Djakarta.

Sontani, U. T. (1951) 'Mengarang', *Orang-orang sial: Sekumpulan tjerita tahun 1948–1950.* Balai Pustaka, Djakarta, pp. 22–30.

Stockdale, J. J. (1911) *Sketches, civil and military, of the island of Java and its immediate dependencies: Comprising interesting details of Batavia, and authentic particulars of the celebrated poison-tree*, J. J. Stockdale, London.

Strehler (1833) *Bijzonderheden wegens Batavia en deszelfs omstreken: Uit het dagboek gedurende twee reizen, derwaarts in 1828–1830, van Dr. Strehler*, W. A. Loosjes, Haarlem.

Sugiyati and Gandara, E. (2007) Personal interview conducted by E. D. Winet, Bandung, Jakarta.

Suharno, F. (2007) Personal interview conducted by E. D. Winet, Bandung, Jakarta.

Sumardjo, J. (1992) *Perkembangan Teater Modern dan Sastra Drama Indonesia*, Citra Aditya Bakti, Bandung.

Sumardjo, T. (Ed.) (1950) *Special Issues 1:1–2 of 'Indonesia: Madjalah Kebyudajaan,' consisting of proceedings of the Kongres Kebudajaan Indonesia ke-2 (Magelang, 20–24 August 1948)*, Lembaga Kebudajaan Indonesia, Jakarta.

Suryadinata, L. (1996) *Sastra peranakan Tionghoa Indonesia*, Gramedia Widiasarana Indonesia, Jakarta.

Suryadinata, L. (2004) *The Culture of the Chinese Minority in Indonesia*, Marshall Cavendish Academic, Singapore.

Suryadinata, L. and Suryadinata, L. (1995) *Prominent Indonesian Chinese: Biographical Sketches*, Institute of Southeast Asian Studies, Singapore.

Sutton, R. A. (2001) '"Seni Reformasi?" Performanc Live and Mediated in Post-Suharto Indonesia', University of Wisconsin, School of Journalism website, Madison.

Tacitus, C. and Benario, H. W. (2006) *Agricola, Germany, and Dialogue on Orators*, Hackett Pub., Indianapolis.

Tajudin, Y. A. (2004) 'Kota dan Estetika dalam Journal of Moment Arts 2003', *LèBur Theater Quarterly*, **1**, pp. 10–62.

Tajudin, Y. A., Camus, A. and Sani, A. (1995) *Meta Morfosa Pengantin: Sehuah KOLASE, Sebuah VERSI, Sebuah INTERPRETASI atas Caligula*, Teater Garasi archive, Yogyakarta, p. 20.

Taylor, J. G. (1983) *The Social World of Batavia: European and Eurasian in Dutch Asia*, University of Wisconsin Press, Madison, WI.

Taylor, J. G. (1996) '*Nyai Dasima*: Portrait of a Mistress in Literature and Film', *Fantasizing the Feminine in Indonesia*, Ed. L. J. Sears, Duke University Press, Durham, NC, pp. 225–48.

Taylor, J. G. (2003) *Indonesia: Peoples and Histories*, Yale University Press, New Haven.

Teeuw, A. (1967) *Modern Indonesian Literature*, Martinus Nijhoff, The Hague.

Thomas, K. S. K. (1994) *Tradition and Modern Indonesian Theatre*, doctoral dissertation, Department of Southeast Asian Studies, University of California, Berkeley.

Thorn, W. (2004) *The Conquest of Java*, Periplus, Singapore.

Tiwon, S. (1996) 'Models and Maniacs: Articulating the Female in Indonesia', *Fantasizing the Feminine in Indonesia*, Ed. L. J. Sears, Duke University Press, Durham, NC, pp. 47–70.

Toda, D. N. (1984) 'Teater Baru Indonesia', *Hamba Hamba Kebudayaan*, PT Sinar Agape Press, Jakarta, pp. 34–40.

Tollens, H. and (trans.), C. C. F. (1845) 'Jan van Schaffelaar', *The Poets and Poetry of Europe: With Introductions and Biographical Notices*, Ed. H. W. Longfellow, C. C. Felton and Harris Collection of American Poetry and Plays (Brown University. Collections and Anthologies.) Carey and Hart. Stereotyped and printed by Metcalf, Philadelphia and Cambridge, pp. 397–8.

Valentijn, F. c. and Pre-1801 Imprint Collection (Library of Congress) (1724) *Oud en nieuw Oost-Indièen*, J. van Braam, Dordrecht.

Van den Berg, N. P. (1904) 'Het Tooneel te Batavia in Vroegeren Tijd', *Uit de Dagen der Compagnie*, H. D. Tjeenk Willink & Zoon, Haarlem, pp. 97–191.

Van den Berg, P. (2000) 'Unhealthy Batavia and the decline of the VOC in the eighteenth century', *Jakarta-Batavia: Socio-Cultural Essays*, Ed. C. D. Grijns and P. J. M. Nas, KITLV, Leiden, pp. 43–74.

Van der Veur, P. W. (1955) *Introduction to a Socio-Political Study of the Eurasians of Indonesia*, Cornell University Press, Ithaca, NY.

Van der Veur, P. W. (1968) 'The Eurasians of Indonesia: A Problem and Challenge in Colonial History', *Journal of Southeast Asian History*, **9**, pp. 191–207.

Van der Veur, P. W. (2006) *The Lion and the Gadfly: Dutch Colonialism and the Spirit of E. F. E. Douwes Dekker*, KITLV Press, Leiden.

van Erven, E. (1992) *The Playful Revolution: Theatre and Liberation in Asia*, Indiana University Press, Bloomington.

Veth, P. J. (1896) *Java, geographisch, ethnologisch, historisch, door*, De Erven F. Bohn, Haarlem.

Waldenfels, B. (2002) 'Levinas and the face of the other', *The Cambridge Companion to Levinas*, Ed. S. Critchley and R. Bernasconi, Cambridge University Press, Cambridge, pp. xxx, 292.

Weix, G. G. (1995) 'Gapit Theatre: New Javanese Plays on Tradition', *Indonesia*, **60**, pp. 17–36.

Wijaya, P. (1991) 'Lakon Diskusi Suami dan Istri', *Tempo* (21 September 21), p. 110.

Wijaya, P. (1997) 'Tubuh imajiner', *Ngeh: Kumpulan esai*, Pustaka Firdaus, Jakarta, pp. 92–5.

Wijaya, P. (2000) 'Tradisi Baru', *Interkulturalisme (dalam) teater*, Ed. N. Sahid, Yayasan Untuk Indonesia, Giwangan, Yogyakarta, pp. 56–64.

Wijaya, P. (2007) Personal interview conducted by E. D. Winet, Bandung, Jakarta.

Winet, E. D. (2005) 'The Critical Absence of Indonesia in W.S. Rendra's Naga Village', *Theatre and Nationalism*, Ed. K. Gounaridou, McFarland, Jefferson, NC, pp. 141–66.

Wirawan (2004) 'Kesaksian Teater Payung Hitam', *Teater Payung Hitam: Perspektif teater modern Indonesia*, Ed R. Sabur, Kelir, Bandung, Jawa Barat, Indonesia, pp. 297–300.

Worp, J. A. (1903) *Geschiedenis van het drama en van het tooneel in Nederland*, Langerveld, Rotterdam.

Yamin, M. (1945) *Gajah Mada: Pahlawan persatuan Nusantara*, Balai Pustaka, Jakarta.

Yamin, M. (1951) *Ken Arok dan Ken Dedes: Tjeritera sandiwara jang kedjadian dalam sedjarah Tumapel-Singasari pada tahun 1227 A.D.*, Balai Pustaka, Djakarta.

Yamin, M. and Abbas, A. A. A. (1935) *Kunst, tooneel en journalistiek*, Persbureau Malacca, Fort de Kock.

Young, R. (1995) *Colonial Desire: Hybridity in Theory, Culture, and Race*, Routledge, London and New York.

Zarrilli, P. B. and Williams, G. J. (2006) *Theatre Histories: An Introduction*, Routledge, New York and London.

Žižek, S. (1993) *Tarrying with the Negative: Kant, Hegel, and the Critique of Ideology*, Duke University Press, Durham, NC.

Zurbuchen, M. (1989). 'The "Cockroach Opera": Image of Culture and National Development in Indonesia,' *Tenggara*, **23**, pp. 123–50.

Index